The **Rough Guide** to

Rio de Janeiro

written and researched by

Robert Coates and Oliver Marshall

ROUGH
GUIDES

www.roughguides.com

Contents

Botecos colour section following p.80

Beach life colour section following p.176

BOTAFOGO
Corcovado

Colour maps following p.296

◄◄ Arcos da Lapa ◄ Museu de Arte Contemporânea, Niterói

Introduction to
Rio de Janeiro

Rio de Janeiro is undoubtedly one of the world's greatest cities. A magnificent natural landscape of beaches, lakes and mountains complements a series of bustling city districts, each one alert to the gaze of the iconic statue of Christ the Redeemer high overhead. Rio's flamboyant Carnaval and pulsating samba scene need no introduction as some of the most creative and exciting celebrations in existence, while the glitzy beaches of Copacabana and Ipanema provide kilometres of golden sand for its spirited residents – Cariocas – to play, parade and mingle amidst a jubilant, seductive atmosphere. Visitors leave Rio with little doubt of the validity of its synonym, the Cidade Maravilhosa ("marvellous city").

The city's appeal goes much deeper than music, costumes and beaches, however. As the capital of Brazil from 1763 until 1960 (when the administration moved to Brasília), Rio boasts a remarkable architectural heritage spanning over three centuries and showcasing innovative traditional and modernist styles. It also offers some of the country's best museums, galleries and cultural centres, as well as superb restaurants featuring Brazilian and international cuisine. Rio could well be seen as the centre of world **football**, too – something due as much to Brazil's success on the international soccer stage as to its gigantic stadium, the **Maracanã** – given a significant boost by its successful bid to host the 2014 World Cup final. For *Cariocas* it represents far more than just a game, having gone a long way to bring together a city founded by different races and classes. Week by week you can enjoy

4

the exuberant mood and passion that surrounds matches played between Rio's big four teams.

There is no other city worldwide that can compete with Rio's combination of urban sprawl and rainforest-clad mountains, wealth merged uneasily with poverty, a still-expanding population continually pushed upwards on the mountainsides and outwards along the coast. The conspicuous buying power of many of its residents contrasts sharply with the eight hundred-odd separate *favela* (shanty town) communities within the city boundaries. The rural poor flocked to Rio throughout the twentieth century to escape drought and poverty, an influx city authorities have failed to manage. The largest *favela*, **Rocinha**, is home to as many as 200,000 people and has living standards on a par with Sri Lanka, while its wealthy adjoining district, **Gávea**, has a standard of living similar to Norway's. Since the mid-1990s a new wave of dynamic Rio film-makers has gained international acclaim by documenting the experiences of those caught in a perpetual cycle of poverty and crime, made worse by a flood of cocaine into the hands of armed gangs. While sometimes tending to stereotype or even glamorize Rio's complicated social structures, the movies also illustrate rising social consciousness in the city's mainstream, which has led to some improvements for poor residents – most of whom are law-abiding citizens. The flip-side of a two-tier city is that *favelas* are also one of Rio's main cultural drivers,

Rio's international renown is bolstered by a series of incredible landmarks

where first samba and now *baile funk* music forms were born, and from where the second religions of football and Carnaval draw much of their core heartbeat. Most tourists who choose to visit (or even stay in) a *favela* experience an unexpected level of calm and normality as people go about their daily lives.

Despite inequality and its accompanying frenetic, multilayered street life, Rio simultaneously manages to maintain a cool and laid-back atmosphere. **Carnaval** is its most buoyant outward expression, where poor people

Defining Cariocas

Rio de Janeiro's inhabitants – **Cariocas** – have a reputation throughout Brazil as being the country's most direct, confident and egotistical residents. While the former points are undoubtedly true, the latter remark may well reflect jealousy for a city soaked in enthusiasm for its own way of life. Few *Cariocas* – while accepting the negatives of high crime – have any doubt that they are living in the most vibrant, creative and beautiful place on Earth, partly because countless tourists over the past hundred years have told them so. While you can easily meet people from São Paulo (*Paulistas*) and from Brazil's Northeast (*Nordestinos*) living all over the country – it is genuinely hard to find a *Carioca* anywhere outside Rio. With 7 million inhabitants (and 13m in its wider metropolitan area), Rio is the country's second largest city, leading to intense rivalry with São Paulo just a few hours' drive down the coast. *Cariocas* see their neighbour as an ugly and beachless urban nightmare, obsessed with unfettered work and moneymaking, while *Paulistas* stereotype *Cariocas* as lazy bandits with Lisbon accents who are too busy cavorting on the beach and dancing samba to earn a living. There's undoubtedly a touch of envy for Rio's perceived exotic, erotic social life, too.

While it's easy to make generalisations about *Cariocas'* temperaments, it's harder to identify their **origins**. Officially, Rio is classified as around 50 percent white (of mainly Portuguese, Italian, Spanish and Lebanese origins), 35 percent mixed race, 14 percent black (the descendants of slaves from mainly present-day Angola, Benin and Mozambique), and less than 1 percent indigenous Amerindian. In reality, however, recent studies have shown that Amerindian, African and European genes run to varying proportions through virtually Brazil's entire population, and in Rio especially, the distinction between who is white, black or mixed race is no easy matter to discern.

joyfully masquerade as kings and queens and rich people accompany them in fantastic glittering costumes with implausibly fast samba moves. However large it grows, the Carnaval party will always mean immeasurably more to *Cariocas* than to the thousands of excited visitors who swell their ranks each year. Day to day, too, Rio's residents come together to play sport and relax on its beaches, with the grand sweeps of **Copacabana** and **Ipanema** probably the most famous lengths of sand on the planet.

The aerial views over Rio are breathtaking, and even the concrete skyscrapers that dominate the skyline add to the appeal, moulded between an azure blue sea and the mountain range that provides a dramatic backdrop. Rio's international renown is bolstered by a series of incredible landmarks that rank as some of the most familiar symbols in the world, from the **Corcovado** ("hunchback") mountain supporting the **Christ statue**, to the rounded incline of the **Sugar Loaf mountain** standing at the entrance to Guanabara Bay, and the iconic sweep of Copacabana which recalls the golden age of **Carmen Miranda** and *Flying Down to Rio* (see p.100).

But aside from the natural sites, Rio is a bold and dynamic city with absorbing attractions to take in all year round. The energy and creativity of its inhabitants are on parade for the world to see, whether through elaborate Carnaval designs or remarkable modern architecture, engaging exhibitions or a distinctive theatre and film industry. Coupled with an exceptionally vibrant nightlife it is hard to imagine a more enthralling city destination.

What to see

With so much to see and do within and beyond the city, Rio can easily occupy a couple of weeks, and you may well find it difficult to drag yourself away. For starters, from the western shores of Rio's near-landlocked **Guanabara Bay** to the paradisiacal Bay of Sepetiba to the west, there are approximately 90km of sandy beaches. The two most famous – Copacabana and Ipanema – can occupy a few days in themselves if you like sunbathing, people watching and beach sports. The mix of urban and semi-rural landscapes in the city's **Zona Oeste** also offers beaches like **Prainha** and **Grumari** – perfect locations for both surfing and stress-free relaxation.

Rio's downtown area, **Centro**, combines modern offices with buildings of great historical significance. The **Paço Imperial** was the first residence of the Portuguese royal family in Brazil, while the audacious style of the Neoclassical period is on show in numerous buildings including the **Theatro Municipal** and **Igreja de Nossa Senhora da Candelária**. Colonial

▼ Centro skyline

remnants are found, too, such as the ornate gold-plated **Igreja de São Bento** or the narrow passageways of the **Arco de Teles**. Modern constructions primarily demonstrate a penchant for functionality over aesthetics – though fans of modernism will delight in the design of the Museu de Arte Moderna and Palácio Gustava Capanema. The **Museu Histórico Nacional** reveals fascinating insights into Brazil's turbulent history, something further illustrated by the **Museu Naval**. Innumerable *botecos* can be found across Centro and the wider city – informal bars every *Carioca* frequents for food, drink and friendly conversation.

Adjoining Centro, **Lapa** and **Santa Teresa** are excellent destinations for anyone interested in Rio's arts and **samba** scenes, the latter *bairro* dramatically clinging to the hillside and exhibiting nineteenth-century residential architecture where each resident tried to outdo the next in original design. Lapa comes alive at night with exceptional street parties drawing thousands and a series of excellent samba clubs.

The **Zona Sul**, the name used to cover just about everything south of Centro, though generally taken to mean just the *bairros* (districts) shouldering the coastline, has the most to attract visitors, mainly in terms of bars and beaches, though the sumptuous **Palácio do Catete** is open to the public and well worth seeing as the last presidential residence in Rio. Further into the Zona Sul, **Botafogo** is a commercial and residential district with a great street and bar life, while **Copacabana** is a bustling, often chaotic neighbourhood with a grand beach and a

> **Favelas are one of Rio's main cultural drivers**

long tradition as the global resort of choice for the rich and famous, most obviously illustrated by the iconic **Copacabana Palace Hotel**, city residence of countless stars including Marlene Dietrich, Janis Joplin and Robert de Niro. **Ipanema** and **Leblon** are nonetheless the new areas for the affluent, tucked between the most fashionable stretch of beach and the attractive inland lake **Lagoa Rodrigo de Freitas**. With table-front cafés, exclusive restaurants and a range of nightlife, many visitors fail to make it much further – except of course to visit the dramatic **Corcovado Christ statue** or **Sugar Loaf mountain**.

Close to the Lagoa, the ornate statues and historical gardens of the **Jardim Botânico** (botanical gardens) are a well-preserved oasis of calm, and nearby Rio's **Jockey Club** racecourse must have the most dramatic setting of any in the world. A hiker's and waterfall-lover's paradise stretches off into the green mountains beyond in the form of the **Parque Nacional da Tijuca**, a large rainforest with urban areas on all sides, accessible by tour or public transport.

Further west, the Auto-Estrada Lagoa-Barra leads into **São Conrado** and its western neighbour, **Barra da Tijuca**, the new ghetto of Rio's middle classes. Overlooking the prosperous residences and elegant Gávea Golf Club at São Conrado is *favela* Rocinha, a vast mountainside shantytown still expanding forestwards.

The northern part of Rio, **Zona Norte**, contains the city's industrial areas, with large expanses of *favelas* and other working-class residential *bairros* with little in the way of natural beauty. However, the **Museu Nacional** in the park **Quinta da Boa Vista** is a splendid collection well worth making time for. The **Feira Nordestina**, a fantastic market and performance space, and the **Maracanã Stadium**, Brazil's football Mecca, are further highlights to seek out. At night, Rio's top samba schools host rehearsals and parties at their *quadras* (community buildings) for a large chunk of the year. Across the bay in the neighbouring city of Niterói, the **Museu de Arte Contemporânea** – a striking modernist construction designed by Brazil's seminal architect Oscar Niemeyer – has more wonderful views of the Cidade Maravilhosa.

Outside of the city, Rio de Janeiro state is both beautiful and accessible, with easy and tempting trips either east along the **Costa do Sol** or west along the **Costa Verde**, taking in unspoilt beaches, washed by a relatively unpolluted ocean. **Ilha Grande** is a forested island paradise, while **Paraty**, a beautiful and historic colonial town by the sea. Inland routes make a welcome change from the sands, especially the trip to **Petrópolis**, a nineteenth-century mountain retreat for Rio's affluent.

When to go

▼ Street art in Santa Teresa

High season in Rio is between **Christmas** and the end of **Carnaval**, in February or early March depending on the calendar. This is also the **summer** season when tropical heat and

humidity can be intense day or night – though in recent years the weather has been annoyingly unpredictable. Other busy periods are the winter months of July and August, when it's a little cold at night but many days are generally warm enough for the beach, and the Easter holiday, especially popular with visiting Brazilians. The months of October and November have higher rainfall and it can get fairly cold at night – though unpredictability means you could also easily end up with a week or two's warm sunshine during this period.

The celebrations of **Reveillon** (New Year's Eve) and Carnaval bring tens of thousands of people into an already lively city, and you'll need to book ahead as early as November to be assured of reasonable accommodation. Room prices tend to triple for three days at New Year and for a week at Carnaval – and even meal prices go up in some establishments. Nonetheless, throughout January and February is easily the most exciting and energetic time to visit Rio. If you'd prefer to visit at a slightly calmer time of year, consider going between March and June when humidity is lower, temperatures remain mostly good, and the adrenaline of Carnaval is still fresh in people's' minds.

Average temperatures

	Jan	Feb	Mar	Apr	May	Jun	Jul	Aug	Sep	Oct	Nov	Dec
Max temp	30	30	28	29	26	25	25	25	25	26	28	28
Min temp	23	23	23	21	20	18	17	17	19	20	20	22
Rainy days	13	11	9	9	6	5	5	4	6	11	10	12

20

things not to miss

It's not possible to see everything that Rio de Janeiro has to offer in one trip – and we don't suggest you try. What follows is a selection of the city's highlights: spectacular beaches, mountains and forest, a nightlife second to none, and impressive, diverse architecture and museums. They're arranged in five colour-coded categories, to help you find the very best things to see and experience. All highlights have a page reference to take you straight into the Guide where you can find out more.

01 **Futebol** Page **240** • Experience the raw passion and vivid spectacle of a match at the Maracanã, the ultimate temple to football, Rio's second religion.

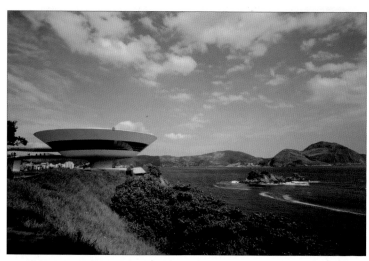

02 **Museu de Arte Contemporânea** Page **146** ● Located across Guanabara Bay in Niterói, this space-ship like building is one of the most impressive creations of Oscar Niemeyer, Brazil's foremost modernist architect.

04 **Sítio Burle Marx** Page **135** ● The former home of Brazil's seminal landscape designer offers guided visits around his vivid and beautiful gardens.

05 **Samba** Page **199** ● Feel the heartbeat of Rio de Janeiro in Lapa, the hub of city nightlife, or in one of many pulsating samba schools.

03 **Favelas** Page **120** ● Home to a third of the city's inhabitants, Rio's notorious yet culturally vibrant shantytowns are extraordinary hillside constructions. Staying in or visiting one is an enlightening experience.

07 Paraty Page **153** • Simple colonial-era houses and churches, cobbled streets, a relaxed atmosphere and undeveloped beaches combine to make this historic town a perfect place to escape the frenzy of the big city.

06 Carnaval Page **213** • The spectacular parades at the Sambódromo are unmissable – but there's enough year-round Carnaval activity for all visitors to experience a flavour of these unparalleled celebrations.

08 Christ the Redeemer Page **80** • Surveying the city far below, this iconic statue represents Rio to the outside world and in good weather can't fail to impress.

09 **Parque Nacional da Tijuca** Page **122** • Hike the trails or climb a choice of stunning peaks in one of the largest urban forests in the world, covering an area of 3953 hectares. A remnant of Brazil's depleted second tropical forest, the Mata Atlântica.

10 **Hang gliding** Page **238** • Take a tandem flight from high above the skyscrapers over forest-covered mountains, landing dramatically on the beach at São Conrado.

12 **Confeitaria Colombo** Page **48** • Stop by for tea and cakes at this palatial tearoom which retains the atmosphere of the Belle Époque.

11 **Santa Teresa** Page **74** • Taking a *bonde* (tram) to the cobbled streets and restaurants in this artistic neighbourhood is the perfect break from the beach.

13 **Museu da República** Page **86** • The last Rio residence of the president is located in the Palácio do Catete, notable for its interior splendour.

15 **Carnaval blocos** Page **218** • Away from the Sambódromo, Rio's masses dress up and hit the streets for huge raucous parties.

14 **Igreja de São Bento** Page **59** • Built during the era of seventeenth-century gold exploration, the interior of this ostentatious church is truly staggering.

16 **Ipanema Beach** Page **108** • Among tens of kilometres of sand and surf, fashionable Ipanema is the ultimate place to relax and watch the endless parade of the beautiful people.

17 Sugar Loaf mountain Page **96** • In a city of phenomenal views, the panorama from the pointed peak of the Sugar Loaf mountain is unbeatable.

18 Palácio Imperial Page **160** • Visit Petrópolis, Brazil's former summer capital in the mountains near Rio, where Emperor Dom Pedro II lived in regal splendour until 1889.

19 Botecos See *Botecos* **colour section** • No visit to Rio would be complete without at least a few hours spent drinking and eating at these atmospheric neighbourhood bars.

20 Ilha Grande Page **150** • Visit this natural paradise, a dazzlingly unspoilt island of quiet coves, long sandy beaches and rainforest. Enjoy boat trips and swimming in crystal-clear waters.

Basics

Basics

Getting there

Rio de Janeiro is second only to São Paulo as Brazil's most significant transport hub. There are an increasing number of direct flights from Europe and North America to Rio, though it's still common to have to fly via São Paulo.

If you're travelling to Rio from elsewhere in Brazil or South America, your options are either to fly or, from the southern part of the continent, go by bus. Airfares depend on the season: high season is generally July and August, and mid-December to 25 December; low season is at any other time, but specific dates vary between airlines. Airline competition tends to be fierce, however, and special offers outside peak periods are often available. Fares don't normally rise over Carnaval (in Feb or early March), but getting a seat can be difficult.

The web is rapidly making specialist travel agents less of an essential first stop, but you may want to use one if you prefer to book your first few days in a hotel before you arrive or you're looking for a tailor-made package. Apart from tickets available via the internet or specialist travel agents, it's worth checking fares directly with the airlines that fly to Brazil.

Flights from the US and Canada

There are numerous North American airline gateways to Brazil with flights leaving from Atlanta, Charlotte, Chicago, Dallas, Houston, Los Angeles, Miami, Newark, New York, Orlando, Washington and Toronto. Most of these flights arrive into São Paulo's congested and inefficient Guarulhos airport; non-stop flights to Rio are with American Airlines and TAM from Miami, United from Washington-Dulles, US Airways from Charlotte, Continental from Houston and Delta from Atlanta. **TAM** is the only Brazilian carrier serving the US, while the North American airlines are American, Air Canada (to São Paulo only), Continental, Delta and United; Japan Airlines and Korean Air also carry passengers between the US and São Paulo.

Ticket prices vary depending on your length of stay in Brazil, but fares are typically around $1000 out of New York, $900 out of Miami. For unrestricted fares, add at least $400.

Flights from the UK and Ireland

There are plenty of choices of carriers to Brazil **from the UK**, with São Paulo and Rio being the usual points of arrival. Two airlines operate **direct flights** to Rio from the UK: British Airways and TAM. Despite British Airways having a much higher level of service, the official fares to Rio of the two airlines are usually very similar, currently starting at around £650 return in low season, £900 high season (July, Aug & Dec 14–25). However, you may be able to get the same tickets through websites and specialist travel agencies at reduced prices.

There are usually good deals available from **travel agencies** specializing in Latin America as well as from general discount travel agencies; fares are sometimes as low as £500 in low season, rising to around £800 for high-season departures. The **cheapest Rio fares**, however, are often offered on **routes via Europe** – with Air France via Paris, TAP via Lisbon, Iberia via Madrid or Lufthansa via Frankfurt. Other inexpensive options, but to São Paulo only, include Alitalia via Milan, KLM via Amsterdam and Swiss via Zurich. Prices tend to be the same whether you begin your journey in London or at one of the UK's **regional airports**; you may find it better value and more convenient to use one of these airlines rather than flying out of Heathrow with British Airways or TAM.

There are no direct flights **from Ireland** to Brazil: connect via London or other European capitals. The best deals are available from budget or student travel agents in Ireland,

Six steps to a better kind of travel

At Rough Guides we are passionately committed to travel. We feel strongly that only through travelling do we truly come to understand the world we live in and the people we share it with – plus tourism has brought a great deal of **benefit** to developing economies around the world over the last few decades. But the extraordinary growth in tourism has also damaged some places irreparably, and of course **climate change** is exacerbated by most forms of transport, especially flying. This means that now more than ever it's important to **travel thoughtfully** and **responsibly**, with respect for the cultures you're visiting – not only to derive the most benefit from your trip but also to preserve the best bits of the planet for everyone to enjoy. At Rough Guides we feel there are six main areas in which you can make a difference:

- Consider what you're contributing to the **local economy**, and how much the services you use do the same, whether it's through employing local workers and guides or sourcing locally grown produce and local services.
- Consider the **environment** on holiday as well as at home. Water is scarce in many developing destinations, and the biodiversity of local flora and fauna can be adversely affected by tourism. Try to patronize businesses that take account of this.
- Travel with a purpose, not just to tick off experiences. Consider **spending longer** in a place, and getting to know it and its people.
- Give thought to how often you **fly**. Try to avoid short hops by air and more harmful night flights.
- Consider **alternatives to flying**, travelling instead by bus, train, boat and even by bike or on foot where possible.
- Make your trips "**climate neutral**" via a reputable carbon-offset scheme. All Rough Guide flights are offset, and every year we donate money to a variety of charities devoted to combating the effects of climate change.

but it's also worth contacting specialist agents in England for cheap fares, an unusual route or a package.

Flights from Australia, New Zealand and South Africa

The best deals and fastest routing to Brazil **from Australasia** are offered by Aerolíneas Argentinas and LanChile. There are fewer options flying via the US; fares are more expensive and flights take much more time. Round-the-world fares that include South America tend to cost more than other RTW options, but can be worthwhile if you have the time to make the most of a few stopovers.

From Australia, flights to South America leave from Sydney. The most direct route is with Aerolíneas Argentinas, which flies via Auckland to Buenos Aires, from where there are good connections direct to Rio. LanChile has a weekly direct flight via Auckland to

Santiago, with onward connections to Rio. On the **more direct routes** with Aerolíneas Argentinas you should be able to get a return fare for A$2400/NZ$2600. Flying via Santiago with LanChile you can expect to pay around A$3100/NZ$3300.

Rio can be reached from Johannesburg with South African Airlines daily flights to São Paulo followed by an internal flight. Alternatively, South African Airlines flies twice a week from Johannesburg to Buenos Aires. Malaysian Airlines will also take you from Johannesburg and Cape Town will take you to Buenos Aires where you can connect to a direct flight to Rio. Also worth investigating are daily flights with TAAG Angolan Airlines from Johannesburg to Rio via Luanda.

Airlines

Aerolíneas Argentinas UK, Australia ☎ 02/9252-5150, New Zealand ☎ 09/379-3675; ⊛ www .aerolineas.com.

Air Canada ☎1-888/247-2262, 🖳www
.aircanada.com.
Air France UK ☎0845/084-5111, 🖳www
.airfrance.co.uk. Republic of Ireland ☎01/844-
5633; 🖳www.airfrance.ie.
Alitalia UK ☎0870/544-8259, 🖳www.alitalia
.co.uk. Republic of Ireland ☎01/677-5171;
🖳www.alitalia.ie.
American Airlines US & Canada ☎1-800/433-
7300, UK ☎0/7365-0777 or 0845/7789-789,
Republic of Ireland ☎01/602-0550; 🖳www.aa.com.
British Airways UK ☎0870/850-9850, Republic
of Ireland ☎1800/626-747; 🖳www.britishairways
.com.
Continental Airlines US & Canada ☎1-800/523-
3273, UK ☎0845/607-6760, Republic of Ireland
☎1890/925-252, Australia ☎2/9244-2242,
New Zealand ☎9/308-3350, International
☎1-800/231-0856; 🖳www.continental.com.
Delta US & Canada ☎1-800/221-1212,
UK ☎0845/600-0950, Republic of Ireland
☎1850/882-031 or 01/407-3165, Australia
☎1-300/302-849, New Zealand ☎09/379-3370;
🖳www.delta.com.
Iberia UK ☎020/7830-0011, Republic of Ireland
☎01/677-9846; 🖳www.iberia.com.
JAL (Japan Air Lines) US & Canada
☎1-800/525-3663, 🖳www.jal.com.
KLM (Royal Dutch Airlines) UK ☎0870/507-
4074, Republic of Ireland ☎0870/507-4074;
🖳www.klm.com.
Korean Air US & Canada ☎1-800/438-5000,
🖳www.koreanair.com.
LanChile US & Canada ☎1-866/435-9526,
UK ☎0800/917-0572, Australia ☎1-300/361-400
or 02/9244-2333, New Zealand ☎09/977-2233;
🖳www.lan.com.
Lufthansa UK ☎0845/773-7747 or 0845/773-
7747, Republic of Ireland ☎01/844-5544;
🖳www.lufthansa.com.
Malaysia Airlines South Africa ☎021/419-8010
or 27-11-880-9614, 🖳www.malaysiaairlines.com.
South African Airways South Africa ☎0861-
359722, 🖳www.flysaa.com.

Swiss UK ☎0845/601-0956, 🖳www.swiss.com.
TAM UK ☎020/8903-4003, 🖳www.tam.com.br.
TAP (Air Portugal) UK ☎0845/601-0932,
🖳www.flytap.com.
United Airlines US & Canada ☎1-800/538-2929,
UK ☎0845/844-4777, Republic of Ireland
☎1-800/535-300, Australia ☎13 17 77;
🖳www.united.com.
US Airways US & Canada ☎1-800/428-4322,
UK ☎0845/0845-600-3300, Republic of Ireland
☎1-890-925065; 🖳www.usairways.com.

Specialist agents and operators

Brazil Nuts US ☎1-800/553-9959, 🖳www
.brazilnuts.com. Tours that promise to take you off
the beaten track to experience Brazil's cities, the
Amazon basin and the Pantanal.
Brazil Tours UK ☎0870/442-4241, 🖳www
.braziltours.co.uk. Flight agents and tour operators to
Brazil, including Rio.
Journey Latin America UK ☎020/8747-3108
🖳www.journeylatinamerica.co.uk. Flight agents and
tour operators offering taylor-made packages,
including the city and state of Rio.
South American Experience UK ☎0845/277-
3366, 🖳www.southamericanexperience.co.uk. One
of the more experienced British South American travel
specialists offering flights, tours and tailor-made
packages.
Solar Tours US ☎202/861-5864, 🖳www
.solartours.com. A big operator throughout Latin
America, including Rio and Carnaval specials.
South America Travel Centre Australia
☎1800/655-051 or 03/9642-5353, 🖳www
.satc.com.au. Specializes in tailor-made trips to
Brazil.
Steamond Travel UK ☎020/7730-8646, 🖳www
.easyticket.com. Flight agents and tour operators for
Brazil and Latin America.
Veloso Tours UK ☎020/8762-0616 🖳www
.veloso.com. Latin American flight specialist and tour
operator with a good range of Brazilian options
including Rio, Paraty, Ilha Grande and Búzios.

Red tape and visas

Citizens of most EU countries, New Zealand and South Africa only need a valid passport and either a return or onward ticket – or evidence of funds to pay for one – to enter Brazil.

You fill in an entry form on arrival and get a tourist visa for ninety days. Australian, US and Canadian citizens need visas in advance, available from Brazilian consulates abroad; a return or onward ticket is a requirement. You'll need to submit a passport photo with your visa application and pay a processing fee (consulates in the US only accept postal money orders, while consulates in other countries may accept bank or personal cheques). Fees vary according to nationality: US citizens currently pay US$130, Canadians CDN$117 and Australians AUS$63.

Try not to lose the **carbon copy of the entry form** the police hand back to you at passport control when entering Brazil. You'll be fined as you leave the country if you overstay your tourist permit or visa. For a fee of R$120, visitors can usually extend a tourist permit for an additional ninety days, but it will only be extended once; to stay longer you'll have to leave the country and re-enter. The Polícia Federal handle tourist permit and visa extensions at their centre in Terminal 1 at **Galeão** airport (☎21/2203-4000, ⊛www .dpf.gov.br; Mon–Fri 8am–4pm). You'll need to take two passport-sized photos. For details of the application process, you are advised to phone the Polícia Federal.

Brazilian embassies and consulates abroad

Australia Embassy and consulate: 19 Forster Crescent, Yarralumla, Canberra, ACT 2600 ☎02/6273-2372, ⊛www.brazil.org.au; Consulate: 31 Market St, Sydney ☎02/9267-4414, ⊛www.brazilsydney.org.
Canada Embassy and consulate: 450 Wilbroad St, Ottawa, ON K1V 6M8 ☎613/237-1090 ⊛www .brasembottawa.org; consulates also in Montréal ☎514/499-0968, ⊛www.consbrasmontreal.org; and Toronto ☎416/922-2503, ⊛www.consbrastoronto .org; and Vancouver ☎604/696-5311, ⊛www .consbrasvancouver.org.

Ireland Embassy and consulate: HSBC House, 41–54 Harcourt Centre, Harcourt St, Dublin 2 ☎01/475-6000, ⊛www.brazil.ie.
New Zealand Embassy and consulate: 10 Brandon St – Level 9, P.O. Box 5032, Wellington ☎04/473-3516, ⊛www.brazil.org.nz.
South Africa Embassy and consulate: Block C, 1st Floor, Hatfield Office Park, 1267 Pretorius St, Hatfield, Pretoria ☎012/426-9400, ⊛www .brazilianembassy.org.za; also consulate in Cape Town ☎021/421-4040.
UK Embassy: 32 Green St, London W1Y 4AT ☎020/7499-0877; Consulate: 6 St Alban's St, London SW1Y 4SQ ☎020/7930-9055, ⊛www.brazil.org.uk.
US Embassy: 3006 Massachusetts Ave NW, Washington DC 20008 ☎202/238-2700, ⊛www .brasilemb.org; consulates in Atlanta ☎1-404/949-2400; Boston ☎617/542-4000; Chicago ☎312/464-0244; Houston ☎713/961-3063; Los Angeles ☎323/651-2664; Miami ☎305/285-6200; New York ☎917/777-7777; San Francisco ☎415/981-8170; and Washington ☎202/238-2828.

Foreign consulates in Rio de Janeiro

Most countries have consular representation in Rio, though for some the nearest office is located in São Paulo or Brasília.
Argentina Praia de Botafogo 228, Botafogo ☎21/2553-1646.
Australia Av. Presidente Wilson 231, 23rd floor, Centro ☎21/3824-4624.
Canada Av. Atlântica 1130, 5th floor, Copacabana ☎21/2543-3004.
Ireland Contact consulate in Brasília: ☎61/3248-8800.
New Zealand Contact consulate in São Paulo: ☎11/3148-0870.
South Africa Contact consulate in São Paulo: ☎11/3265-0449.
UK Praia do Flamengo 284, 2nd floor, Flamengo ☎21/2555-9600.
US Av. Presidente Wilson 147, Centro ☎21/3823-2000.
Uruguay Av. Praia de Botafogo 242, Botafogo ☎21/2552-6699.

Arrival

You're most likely to fly into Rio or arrive by bus. There are two airports although the one in the city centre only serves São Paulo and a few short-local destinations. Most international and national long-distance buses arrive at the Rodoviária Novo Rio.

By air

Rio de Janeiro is served by two airports. The **Tom Jobim international airport** (℡21/3398-4526) – usually referred to by its old name, **Galeão** – lies 20km north of the city. Apart from international flights, this airport also serves destinations throughout Brazil. On arrival, make sure that your passport is stamped and that you retain your immigration form, as failure to do so can cause problems on departure. In the arrivals hall you'll find **tourist information** desks – Riotur or TurisRio – which supply very basic information about the city and state. **Changing money** is not a problem as there are bank branches and ATMs in the arrivals hall and on the airport's third floor

To reach a hotel in **Centro**, the cheapest option is to take an air-conditioned **executivo bus** (R$4 one way) **to Santos Dumont airport**. If you're heading to **Zona Sul**, there's an executivo bus service (R$6.50 one way) along the coast to Flamengo, Copacabana, Ipanema and Leblon. Both services run roughly every 45 minutes between 5.20am and 11pm. Outside these hours, a **taxi** ride is the only alternative. Buy a ticket at the taxi desks, near the arrivals gate, and give it to the driver at the taxi rank; a ticket to Centro or Flamengo costs R$60 and to Botafogo, Copacabana or Ipanema R$80. Unless you're familiar with the city, it's best not to take the ordinary taxis – the driver may not know where your hotel is and you're likely to end up being overcharged. Above all, don't risk accepting a lift from one of the unofficial drivers hanging about in the airport. Unless you hit rush hour, the ride takes about fifteen minutes into the centre or approximately half an hour to Zona Sul.

Heading out to the international airport, ask your hotel to arrange for a **fixed-fare taxi** to pick you up, or take the **executivo bus** – allow at least an hour from the beaches.

Inside Galeão, departure desks are split into three sections: internal Brazilian flights from Sector A; Sectors B and C for international flights. Duty-free shops only accept US currency or credit cards – not Brazilian *reís*.

Santos Dumont airport (℡21/3814-7070) at the north end of the Parque de Flamengo in the city centre mainly handles the shuttle services to and from São Paulo. If you're flying to Rio but changing planes in São Paulo you will almost certainly arrive at Galeão and not Santos Dumont. **Ordinary taxis** (yellow with a blue stripe) are readily available from outside the terminal but you risk being overcharged by drivers not willing to activate the meter if you're obviously new to town – the fare should cost around R$35 to Copacabana. A less stressful option is to purchase a voucher from one of the radio-taxi stands within the terminal. You'll be directed to your cab and will be charged a flat rate of R$45 to Copacabana or R$55 to Ipanema. Alternatively, cross the road and catch an ordinary bus from Avenida Marechal Câmara, which you can reach by taking the pedestrian walkway in front of the airport terminal: #438 to Ipanema and Leblon via Botafogo; #442 to Urca; #472 to Leme. For Copacabana, #484 goes from Avenida General Justo, over which the walkway also crosses.

By bus

All major inter-city bus services arrive at the **Rodoviária Novo Rio** (℡21/3213-1800), 3km north of Centro in the São Cristovão *bairro*, close to the city's dockside at the corner of Avenida Rodrigues Alves and Avenida Francisco Bicalho. **International buses** from Santiago, Buenos Aires,

Montevideo and Asunción, among others, use this terminus, too. The *rodoviária* has two sides, one for departures, the other for arrivals: once through the gate at arrivals, either purchase a voucher for a taxi (about R$15 to Centro, R$30 to Copacabana or R$35 to Ipanema), catch an *executivo* air-conditioned bus along the coast towards Copacabana, Ipanema and Leblon (R$4; every half-hour from directly outside the arrivals side of the station), or cross the road to the ordinary bus terminal in Praça Hermes. Alternatively, go to platform 60 where you can catch the *Itegração Expressa* bus (#406A; R$3.50) to Largo do Machado

metrô station from where you can transfer to a train towards Copacabana.

Leaving Rio by bus at weekends and peak times such as around Carnaval and Easter, it's best to book two days in advance to popular in-state destinations, such as Búzios or Paraty. Most **tickets** can be bought from travel agents all over the city, while inside the main *rodoviária*, on both sides, upstairs and down, you'll find the ticket offices of the various bus companies. You can reach the *rodoviária* on bus #104 from Centro, #127 or #128 from Copacabana, and #456, #171 or #172 from Flamengo.

City transport

Rio's public transport system is fairly inexpensive and efficient: most places can be easily reached by metrô, bus or taxi, or a combination of these. Bus services for getting around the state are excellent but for greater freedom you might want to rent a car – though driving in the city itself is not recommended unless you have nerves of steel.

The metrô

The most comfortable way to travel is by using Rio's **metrô** system, in operation since 1979. It's limited to just two lines, which run from Monday to Saturday, 5am to midnight and Sunday and holidays 7am to 11pm: **Linha 1** runs from central Copacabana (Cantagalo station – though the line's extension to Praça General Osório station in Ipanema is expected to be completed during 2010) north through Centro and then out to the Sãens Pena station in the *bairro* of Tijuca in Zona Norte; **Linha 2** comes in from Maria de Graça, to the north of the city, via the Maracanã stadium, and meets Linha 1 at Estácio station, two stops southwest of Dom Pedro II train station ("Central"). The system is well designed and efficient, the stations bright, cool, clean and secure, and the trains gently air-conditioned, which is a relief if you've just descended from the scorching world above.

A single ticket (*unitário*) costs R$2.60. Until the much-delayed Linha 1 extension is completed, you can also buy a combined bus/*metrô* ticket (*integrado* or *superfície*) onwards to Ipanema and Leblon for the same price. *Metrô* buses currently connect with Copacabana's Siqueira Campos station. Other combined bus/*metrô* tickets are available to Barra (the Alvorada terminus near to giant mall Barra Shopping) for R$3.50 (buses also leave from Siqueira Campos) and to Jardim Botânico from Botafogo station.

Buses

While some people avoid using the **city buses** because they're badly driven and prone to petty theft, it's well worth mastering the extensive system. With hundreds of routes and many thousands of buses, you never have to wait more than a few moments, and most run till midnight,

Rio: useful bus routes

If you need to find out which bus to take and you know the origin and destination street names – or you want to find out where a particular bus passes – use the very helpful Guia de Itinerários at ⓦ www.rioonibus.com.

From Avenida Rio Branco: #119, #121, #123, #127, #173 and #177 to Copacabana; #128 (via Copacabana), #132 (via Flamengo) and #172 (via "Jóquei Clube") to Leblon.

From Praça XV de Novembro: #119, #154, #413, #415 to Copacabana; #154 and #474 to Ipanema.

From Avenida Beira Mar, in Lapa, near the Praça Deodoro: #158 (via "Jóquei Clube"), #170, #172 (via Jardim Botânico), #174 (via Praia do Botafogo), #438, #464, #571 and #572 to Leblon; #472 to Leme; #104 to Jardim Botânico.

From Copacabana: #455 to Centro; #464 to Maracanã.

From Urca: #511 (via "Jóquei Clube") and #512 (via Copacabana) to Leblon.

From the Menezes Cortes terminal, adjacent to Praça XV de Novembro: air-conditioned buses along the coast to Barra de Guaratiba, south of Rio; on the return journey, these buses are marked "Castelo", the name of the area near Praça XV.

From Rodoviária Novo Rio: #104 from Centro, #127 or #128 to Copacabana, and #456, #171 or #172 to Flamengo.

Parque do Flamengo: any bus marked "via Aterro" passes along the length of the Parque do Flamengo without stopping.

Between Centro and the Zona Sul, most buses run along the coast as far as Botafogo; those for Copacabana continue around the bay, past the Rio Sul shopping centre, and through the Pasmado Tunnel; those for Leblon, via the "Jóquei Clube", turn right at Botafogo and travel along Avenida São Clemente.

---

with some routes running throughout the night.

Numbers and destinations are clearly marked on the front of buses, making it difficult to get lost, and there are also plaques at the front and by the entrance detailing the particular route. You get on at the front, pay the seated conductor (the price, in most cases around R$2.50, is on a card behind his head) and then push through the turnstile and find yourself a seat. Buses are jam-packed at rush hour (around 7–9am and 5–7pm), so if your journey is short, start working your way to the back of the bus as soon as you're through the turnstile; you alight at the back (or, in some cases, middle). If the bus reaches the stop before you reach the back, haul on the bell and the driver will wait. In the beach areas of the Zona Sul, especially along the coast, bus stops are not always marked. Stick your arm out to flag the bus down, or look for groups of people by the roadside facing the oncoming traffic, as this indicates a bus stop.

As a precaution against being robbed on the bus, don't leave wallets or money in easily accessible pockets and don't flash cameras around. If there's a crush, carry any bags close to your chest. Have your fare ready so that you can pass through the turnstile immediately – pickpockets operate at the front and rear of the bus, where they can make a quick escape – and make sure that you carry any items in front of you as you pass through the turnstile. Special care should be taken on buses known to carry mostly tourists (such as those to Pão de Açúcar – Sugar Loaf mountain) and that are consequently consid-ered easy targets by thieves.

Taxis

Taxis in Rio come in two varieties: yellow ones with a blue stripe that cruise the streets and the larger, newer, air-conditioned radio cabs, which are white with a red-and-yellow stripe and are ordered by phone. Both have meters and, unless you have pre-paid at the airport, you should insist that it is activated. The flag, or *bandeira*, over the meter denotes

Tours

Pretty-well every hotel in Rio will happily arrange a tour taking in the Corcovado, Sugar Loaf mountain and the city's other main sights, while most youth hostels organise groups to sample the city's nightlife, with Lapa (p.69) as the main destination. There are, however, a steadily growing number of **specialist tour operators** that specialize in either the natural environment or *favelas*. Rio Hiking (Ⓦwww.riohiking.com.br) are the pioneers of **urban ecotourism**, taking small groups to the Parque Nacional da Tijuca, up Pedra da Gávea and to destinations around the state. There are now several other reliable companies leading similar tours of the Floresta da Tijuca (see p.124). Also worth taking is a **favela tour**. While wandering into a *favela* unaccompanied by a local would be foolish, tour groups are looked after and tours will be cancelled if the organisers hear of particular gang or police action in the community being visited (see p.120). Marcelo Armstrong's Favela Tour (Ⓦwww.favelatour.com.br, see p.120) is the most reliable and insightful of these.

the tariff. Normally this will read "1", but after 10pm, and on Sundays and holidays, you have to pay twenty percent more; then the *bandeira* will read "2".

Generally speaking, Rio's taxi services are reasonably priced (Centro to Ipanema costs around R$25, Botafogo to Copacabana R$10-20) and it is not in the cabbies' interest to alienate tourists by ripping them off; the only time to avoid ordinary (yellow and blue) taxis is when you're coming into town from an airport – unless you've paid your fare at the airport taxi booth in advance and are directed into one. However, late at night, drivers often quote a fixed price that can be up to three times the normal fare. Radio cabs are thirty percent more expensive than the regular taxis, but they are reliable; recommended companies include Coopertramo (Ⓣ21/2560-2022) and Transcoopass (Ⓣ21/2560-6891).

Ferries and hydrofoils

From Praça XV de Novembro **ferries** transport passengers across Guanabara Bay to the city of Niterói and to the Ilha de Paquetá, a popular day-trip destination to the north of Guanabara Bay (see p.58). The ferries are cheap and the view of Rio they afford, especially at sunset, makes this an ideal excursion. There's also a regular **hydrofoil** service to Niterói (see p.145).

Trams

Rio's iconic *bondes* (pronounced "bonjis"), the city's last remaining **trams**, climb from

near Largo Carioca, across the eighteenth-century Aqueduto da Carioca, to the inner suburb of Santa Teresa and on to Dois Irmãos. The tram station is downtown, behind the monumentally ugly Petrobrás building and adjacent to the Nova Catedral. The fifteen-minute trip affords wonderful views of Centro, while the breakneck speed that the rickety, century-old *bondes* travel at is almost as exhilarating as a fairground ride.

Car rental

Ensure that you understand what you're letting yourself in for before deciding to rent a car in Rio. The city's road system is characterized by a confusion of one-way streets, tunnels, access roads and flyovers, and **parking** is either difficult or impossible. **Lane markings**, apart from lending a little colouring to the asphalt, serve no apparent practical purpose, **overtaking** on the right appears to be mandatory and, between 10pm and 6am, to avoid an armed hold-up, you merely have to slow down as you approach a red **traffic light**.

If you do rent a car, you're well advised to use it only to venture out of the city where, as long as you avoid the **Via Dutra highway**, linking Rio and São Paulo, driving is fairly relaxed. That said, if at all possible, avoid driving at night: because of lack of lighting, potholes and *lombadas* (speed bumps) may not be obvious, and breaking down after dark in a strange place could be dangerous.

Electronic speed traps are widely used everywhere, and if you get caught by one in a rental car, the fine will simply be added to your credit card. Since 2008 a zero tolerance law has been enforced making it strictly illegal to drive after consuming any amount of alcohol, a response to the enormous death toll caused by drunk drivers. Offenders risk severe punishments if tests detect any amount of alcohol in their blood – expect at least a hefty fine and the threat of imprisonment.

An **international driving licence** is useful: although foreign licences are accepted for visits of up to six months, you may have a hard time convincing a police officer of this. Your car may be stopped by police at some point during your travels, but when they realize you are a foreigner they are likely to leave you alone, unless there is something obviously amiss with your car. Occasionally they can be quite intimidating as they point to trumped up contraventions (for example, that your driving licence isn't valid, that the car's licence plates are somehow irregular). What the police are probably angling for is a bribe and an on-the-spot *multa*, or fine, may be suggested. It's a personal judgement whether to stand one's ground (which may take up a long time) or just pay up. Whatever you do, no matter how certain you are of the righteousness of your position, try and stay calm and bend over backwards to appear polite.

Service stations sell both petrol (*gasolina*) and ethanol (*álcool*), with rental cars usually capable of running on either fuel. *Álcool* is considerably cheaper than *gasolina* and there's no longer a noticeable difference in terms of performance.

To avoid experiencing the worst of city diving, consider collecting a car on a Sunday morning when traffic is at its lightest. Better still, arrange to collect the car at one of the airports: if you're headed towards Búzios and the Costa do Sol, collect the car at Santos Dumont airport, located near to Rio-Niterói bridge; if you're going to either the mountains or Paraty and the Costa Verde, arrange to pick up the car at Galeão airport.

Car rental companies

Rates start from around R$120 a day for a basic car (a Fiat Punto or similar) without air-conditioning including unlimited mileage; a basic air-conditioned model will start at around R$140, also including unlimited mileage. Prices don't always include **insurance** – a comprehensive policy will be an additional R$25 per day or so with a deductible of R$500. If you have a US credit card, you may find that it can be used to cover the additional liability – check before leaving home. In any case, a credit card is essential for making a deposit when renting a car. It's not a bad idea to reserve a car before you arrive in Brazil, as you can be sure to get the best available rate.

Most companies are represented at the international airport and, in Centro, at Santos Dumont airport. In Zona Sul, most have an office in Copacabana, usually on Avenida Princesa Isabel.

Avis US ☎1-800/331-1084, Canada ☎1-800/272-5871, UK ☎0870/606-0100, Northern Ireland ☎028/9024-0404, Republic of Ireland ☎01/605-7500, Australia ☎13 63 33 or 02/9353-9000, New Zealand ☎09/526-2847 or 0800/655-111; ⊛www.avis.com.

Budget US ☎1-800/527-0700, Canada ☎1-800/268-8900, UK ☎0800/181-181, Republic of Ireland ☎09066/27711, Australia ☎1300/362-848, New Zealand ☎09/976-2222; ⊛www.budget.com.

Dollar US & Canada US ☎1-800/800-3665, UK ☎0808/234-7524, Republic of Ireland ☎1-800/515-800; ⊛www.dollar.com.

Hertz US ☎1-800/654-3001, Canada ☎1-800/263-0600, UK ☎0870/844-8844, Republic of Ireland ☎01/676-7476, Australia ☎13 30 39 or 03/9698-2555, New Zealand ☎0800/654-321; ⊛www.hertz.com.

Interlocadora Brazil ☎0800/138-000, ⊛www.interlocadora.com.br.

Localiza Brazil ☎0800/992-000, ⊛www.localiza.com.br.

Unidas Brazil ☎0800/121 121, ⊛www.unidas.com.br.

Costs, money and banks

For visitors, Rio is the most expensive city in Brazil, largely because of the relatively high cost of hotel accommodation. North Americans and Europeans are likely to find prices broadly comparable with home.

Average costs

Food (including eating out) and transport are reasonably priced, but hotels, sunblock, good quality clothing, cameras, computers and computer accessories are relatively expensive. Overall, Rio is a viable destination for the budget traveller. The cheapness of food and the availability of hostels and budget hotels – and the fact that the best attractions, like the beaches and scenery, are free – still make it possible to have an enjoyable time for under R$125 a day if staying in a hostel or R$175 a day if staying in a modest hotel. Staying in good hotels, eating at more refined restaurants and not scrimping on the extras soon causes costs to escalate and is likely to cost you around R$400 a day.

Currency and cash

The currency of Brazil is the *real* (pronounced "hey-al"); its plural is *reais* (pronounced "hey-ice"), written R$. The *real* is made up of one hundred *centavos*, written ¢. Notes come in 2, 5, 10, 20, 50 and 100 real denominations; coins are 1, 5, 10, 25, 50 *centavos* and 1 *real*. You will very occasionally see a tattered one *real* note but these are being phased out, although they are legal tender. Throughout the Guide all prices are given in Brazilian *reais* unless otherwise noted.

Banks, ATMs and exchanging money

In the years immediately preceding the financial crisis of 2008, the *real* was strong against the US dollar, sterling and the euro. However, the *real* has now weakened greatly with **exchange rates** making Brazil a cheaper destination for North Americans and Europeans. At the time of writing US$1=R$2.02, £1=R$3.20 and €1=R$2.80;

you can check the current exchange rates at Ⓦ www.xe.net/ucc.

Changing money in Brazil is simple; just take your bank or credit card with PIN (Personal Identification Number, which you must set up with your bank before your trip), and use **ATMs** – they are now ubiquitous in Brazil, to be found in most supermarkets, many pharmacies and all airports, as well as banks. Not all ATMs accept foreign-issued cards, but those that do are clearly marked with multilingual instructions given. Only Visa cards can be used to withdraw cash advances at the ATMs of Banco do Brasil; only Mastercard at Itaú and Banco Mercantil. Increasing numbers of Brazilian banks are linking their cash dispensers to the Cirrus and Maestro networks; Banco Bradesco, Banco 24 Horas network and HSBC accept all of the above cards. One important thing to note is that for security reasons most bank ATMs stop dispensing cash after 8pm or 10pm, although Banco 24 Horas in large supermarkets will dispense until 10pm. Airport ATMs (or private ATMs requiring a withdrawal fee in petrol stations such as in Leblon) are the only ones which dispense cash all hours.

Credit/debit cards and traveller's cheques

The main **credit cards** are widely accepted by shops, hotels and restaurants. Mastercard and Visa are the most prevalent, with Diners Club and American Express also widespread. It's a good idea to inform your credit or debit card issuer about your trip before you leave so that the card isn't stopped for uncharacteristic use.

Given the ease of using plastic, **traveller's cheques** are not recommended, unless you want a small emergency reserve. Only the head offices of major banks (Banco do Brasil, HSBC, Banco Itaú, Banespa) will have an exchange department (ask for *câmbio*); whether changing cash or traveller's cheques you'll need your passport. You can also change cash and traveller's cheques in smart hotels (usually at poor rates) and in some large travel agencies. Exchange departments of banks often close early, sometimes at 1pm, although more often at 2pm or 3pm. Airport banks are open seven days a week, others only Monday to Friday.

Crime and personal safety

Although it sometimes seems that one half of Rio is constantly being robbed by the other, don't let paranoia ruin your stay. It's true that there is quite a lot of petty theft in Rio: pockets are picked and bags and cameras swiped. But use a little common sense and you're unlikely to encounter problems. Most of the serious violence affecting Rio is drug related and concentrated in the *favelas*. In addition, there are certain areas that should be avoided.

In **Centro**, contrary to popular belief, Sunday is not the best time to stroll around – the streets are usually empty, which means you can be more easily identified, stalked and robbed. The area around **Praça Mauá**, just to the north of Centro, should be avoided after nightfall, and even during the day care should be taken. In the Zona Sul's **Parque do Flamengo** it's also inadvisable to wander unaccompanied after nightfall. Similarly, tourists who choose to walk between **Cosme Velho** and the **Corcovado** have been subject to **assaltos** (hold-ups); risky situations are best avoided by taking the train or walking in a group. **Copacabana**'s record has improved since the authorities started to floodlight the beach at night, but it's still not a good idea to remain on the sand after sunset. Outside of the city, in tourist destinations such as Paraty, Búzios and Petrópolis, **assaltos are extremely rare**.

Robberies, hold-ups and thefts

Criminals know that any injury to a foreign tourist is going to mean a heavy clampdown, which in turn means no pickings for a while. So unless you resist during an incident, nothing is likely to happen to you. That said, having a knife or a gun held on you is a huge shock: it's very difficult to think rationally. But if you are unlucky enough to be the victim of an **assalto** try to remember that it's your possessions rather than you that's the target. Your money and anything you're carrying will be snatched, your watch will get pulled off your wrist, but within a couple of seconds it will be over. On no account resist or chase after the offender: it isn't worth the risk.

Taking precautions

Most *assaltos* take place at night, in back streets with few people around, so stick to busy, well-lit streets; it's always a lot safer to take a taxi than walk. Also, prepare for the worst by locking your money and passport in the hotel safe (*caixa*) – the one in your room is more secure than the one at reception. If you must carry them, make sure they're in a **moneybelt** or a **concealed internal pocket**. Do not carry your valuables in a pouch hanging from your neck. Only take along as much money as you'll need for the day, but do take at least some money, as the average *assaltante* won't believe a *gringo* could be out of money, and might get rough. If you have more than one credit card, don't carry both with you. Don't wear an expensive watch or jewellery. And keep wallets and purses out of sight – pockets with buttons or zips are best.

Drugs

The notorious drug wars in the *favelas* are unlikely to have any impact on foreign tourists. But you should be extremely careful about using **drugs in Brazil**. **Marijuana** – *maconha* – is common, but you are in trouble if the police find any on you. If quick off the mark, you'll be able to bribe your way out of it, but it'll cost you dearly. Foreigners – usually single young men – occasionally get targeted for a shakedown and have drugs planted on them. The idea isn't to lock you up but to get a bribe out of you, so play it by ear. If the bite isn't too outrageous it might be worth paying to save the hassle, but the best way to put a stop to it would be to deny everything, refuse to pay and insist on seeing a superior officer and telephoning the nearest consulate – this approach is only for the patient.

Cocaine is not as common as you might think; most of it simply passes through Brazil from Bolivia or Colombia bound for Europe – and visitors to the city are unlikely to come across it. Nevertheless, the local Rio market has grown in recent years,

controlled by young and vicious gang leaders from the *favelas*.

Police

If you are robbed or held up, and need a police report for insurance purposes, report to the **Polícia de Turismo**, or tourist police, at Avenida Afrânio de Melo Franco (opposite the Teatro Casa Grande) in Leblon (℡21/3399-7170; open 24 hours a day, 7 days a week); they are helpful, speak English and efficiently process reports of theft or other incidents. The city's beach areas have police posts located at regular intervals; although the officers are usually friendly enough, they're highly unlikely to speak any English. The emergency phone number is ℡190, but you'll need someone to speak in Portuguese.

Women

Women planning on travelling alone in Rio de Janeiro can do so with confidence. Few people will find it strange that you are travelling unaccompanied, and in contrast with cities in many other Latin American countries, you're unlikely to be the target of comments in the street any more frequently than you might be at home.

Health

There are no compulsory vaccinations required to enter Brazil from Europe or North America. Taking out travel insurance is vital (see p.35), but if you are unfortunate enough to develop a health problem while in Rio, you'll find good medical care is available.

Health facilities

Pharmacies – *farmácias* – in Rio are plentiful, well stocked and can be a useful first port of call for help with minor medical problems: prescriptions are not necessary. A pharmacy will also give injections (you need a series of rabies jabs if you get bitten by a dog). Medicines are relatively inexpensive.

If you are unlucky enough to need more complex **medical treatment** in Rio, unless faced with an emergency, forget about the public hospitals as they're extremely crowded and the level of treatment may be poor. You can, however, get good medical and dental care privately: hotels will have lists of English-speaking **doctors** (ask for a *médico*) or contact your consulate for advice. Private hospitals with excellent reputations include Hospital Samaritano (Rua Bambina 98, Botafogo; ☎21/2537-9722, ⓦwww.hsamaritano.com.br) and Hospital Copa D'Or (Rua Figueiredo de Magalhães 875, Copacabana; ☎21/2545-3600, ⓦwww.redelabsdor.com.br).

Health hazards

By being aware of basic health issues relating to food and water and medical conditions such as HIV and dengue fever – you're unlikely to have any serious problems during your stay.

Food and drink

Many diseases are directly or indirectly related to impure **water** and contaminated **food**, and care should be taken in choosing what to eat and drink. Tap water in Rio is supposedly safe to drink but in practice you'd be well advised to only drink filtered or bottled water: **mineral water** (*água mineral*), either sparkling (*com gás*) or still (*sem gás*), is easily available and cheap. In Rio, ice is usually made with filtered water, even at fairly modest cafés and restaurants.

With food, as anywhere else with a hot climate you should take particular care with seafood, especially **shellfish** – don't eat anything that's at all suspicious. To enjoy your stay to the full, there's no sense in being too paranoid and so it's best to assume that fruit and salad ingredients are washed in filtered water (or that the claim that Rio tap water is safe).

Even if you're careful with food and water, **diarrhoea** is something that you may well get at some stage. If you are affected, there's little to be done except drink a lot (but not alcohol) and bide your time. You should also replace salts either by taking oral rehydration salts or by mixing a teaspoon of salt and eight of sugar in a litre of purified water. In the unlikely event that your diarrhoea contains blood or mucus, the cause may be **dysentery** and you should seek medical advice.

Dengue fever

Rio is not in a malaria-infected area, but a significant health problem in the city has been outbreaks of **dengue fever**, a viral disease transmitted by mosquito bites. Once you arrive in Rio, you're likely to be aware of the disease as it has become the focus of much educational and preventive work by the Brazilian and city governments, with posters warning of the risk of stagnant water and suggesting that you apply mosquito repellent. The illness is highly seasonal, peaking in the summer months, from December through March. The symptoms are debilitating rather than dangerous: light but persistent fever, tiredness, muscle and joint pains, especially in the fingers, and nausea and vomiting. It is easily treatable, but you will feel dreadful for a week or so. It is much more widespread than any other disease in urban areas, and is currently the focus of much educational and preventive work by the Brazilian government.

HIV and AIDS

Brazil has a relatively high incidence of people with **AIDS and HIV**, and a significant number of those affected live in Rio. There are many reasons for this: a scandalous lack of screening of blood supplies in the 1980s; the level of gay sex between Brazilian men, amongst whom bisexuality is common; the popularity of anal sex, not least amongst heterosexual couples; and the sharing of needles, both amongst drug users in large cities and, in the past, when injections were given for medical purposes, even in hospitals. Since the 1990s, however, Brazil has been a world leader in dealing with the epidemic and today all HIV-positive Brazilians now receive free anti-retroviral medicines in a programme that has become a model for developing countries, while safe-sex campaigns are aggressive and imaginative.

If you do think that you might have sex with someone you meet, be sure to carry with you – and use – a **condom**. They are widely available in pharmacies, where you should ask for a *camisinha*. If you require hospital treatment requiring a transfusion, you'll be quite safe in Rio as blood products are now always carefully screened for infections.

The media

As in the US, Brazil has a regional press rather than a national one. Even the best Rio newspapers are a little parochial but are always valuable for listings of local events. Brazil also boasts a lurid but enjoyable yellow press, specializing in gruesome murders, political scandals and football.

Newspapers and magazines

The most respected Rio-based **newspapers** are the right-of-centre *O Globo* (ⓦwww .oglobo.globo.com) and the slightly left of centre *Jornal do Brasil* (ⓦwww .jbonline.terra.br). Both are independent and have extensive international news, cultural coverage and entertainment listings, but are respectable rather than exciting. Of Rio's tabloids, dip into the celebrity and lurid crime stories of *O Dia* (ⓦwww.odia.terra.br) and its competitor *Extra* (ⓦextra.globo.com/). The most enjoyable of yellow press is Rio's *Última Horai*; its simplistic articles and picture-heavy content make it especially good for beginners in Portuguese.

Of the weekly current affairs **magazines**, the most useful for visitors is *Veja*; although published in São Paulo, the edition that's sold in Rio includes a glossy Rio supplement (*Veja Rio*) featuring articles, reviews and listings relating to local cultural events. You will find Brazilian editions (usually published in São Paulo) of most major fashion and women's magazines. In particular, *Vogue Brasil* is a quality magazine offering great insight into the style of the Brazilian elite, while *Plástica* is a glossy monthly magazine that offers insights into Brazil's apparent obsession with plastic surgery. The weekly *Placar* is essential for anyone wanting to get to serious grips with Brazilian football.

There are no English-language newspapers published in Brazil, but in Rio you can find foreign-language newspapers and magazines in kiosks at junctions along Av. N.S. de Copacabana, Copacabana, on Rua Visconde de Pirajá in Ipanema, and along Av. Rio Branco in Centro. The *Herald Tribune* and the *Financial Times* are the most commonly available English-language newspapers, and *Time*, *Newsweek* and the *Economist* are also easy to find.

Radio

FM stations abound everywhere playing a mixture of commercial local and foreign popular music. Shortwave reception for the BBC World Service is good in Brazil.

Television

Even if you don't understand a word of Portuguese, do take a look at Brazilian TV – you're likely to find the programmes simultaneously both gripping and appalling. There are several national channels, of which the most dominant is TV Globo, the centrepiece of the Globo empire, Latin America's largest media conglomerate. The empire was built up by Brazil's answer to Rupert Murdoch, Roberto Marinho, who died in 2003. One of the most powerful men in Brazil, Marinho was very cosy with the military regime and prone to use his papers and TV channels as platforms for his ultra-conservative views. The other major national channels are Manchete, Bandeirantes, Record, SBT and TVE.

With the exception of the Ministry of Education's TVE, the channels are dominated by **telenovelas**, glossy serials that appear for a season, their episodes spread across a few months, which have massive audiences in the early evenings with the most talked-about *telenovelas* broadcast on TV Globo. **Football coverage** is also worth paying attention to, a gabbling and incomprehensible stream of commentary, punctuated by remarkably elongated shouts of "Gooooool" whenever anyone scores – which is often, Brazilian defences being what they are.

Culture and etiquette

European and North American visitors to Rio will find the culture remarkably familiar and, thanks to the generally relaxed nature of Cariocas, welcoming. Apart from language, the main difference is that of time-keeping, something that can be especially frustrating for business visitors.

Clothes

Rio's climate during most of the year is hot and the prevailing style of dress is casual, but neat. Business attire is very relaxed with suits and ties far less common than in North America, Europe or even São Paulo. In the evenings men hardly ever wear ties, and the dress code of even the most expensive restaurants is smart-casual. Clubs, too, have a refreshing lack of dress requirements – though a rather conservative form of a casual look predominates.

Drinking

Brazilian attitudes to drinking tend to be similar to those in southern Europe: alcohol is fine in moderation, and usually taken with food, even if only *petiscos* (snacks). Public drunkenness is quite rare. Wine is rarely consumed in bars, while in restaurants it's usually expensive and often not very good. Instead, the alcoholic drinks of choice for most people are *chopp* (draught beer), always served ice-cold or *caipirinha*, a simple cocktail made with *cachaça*, lime, sugar and ice. Soft drinks are hugely popular: even in Rio's finest restaurants it's not uncommon to see people being served Coca Cola or Guaraná to accompany a meal.

Greetings

Brazilians tend to be very tactile, something that is especially apparent when greeting people or saying goodbye. It's customary for women to be kissed on both cheeks, a simple handshake alone seeming quite odd. Men who know each other are likely to hug, emphasizing their masculinity by slapping each other on the back, often surprisingly forcefully. For men who don't know each other well, a strong handshake is typical.

Language

The majority of people working directly with tourists and business visitors in Rio speak some English. Most Brazilians, however, do not speak English and it's well worth learning some key phrases. Typically, though, people will bend over backwards to try to communicate. Acquiring a basic knowledge of Portuguese is, of course, useful and polite, but people will not take offence if you resort to Spanish, a language that most Brazilians can understand if spoken slowly.

Timekeeping and punctuality

To Brazilians punctuality can sometimes seem like an alien concept. Be prepared to have to wait for either a business or social engagement and for plans to be changed almost at the last moment. Arriving on time is not, however, considered pushy or impolite – just a little odd, though expected of foreigners. On the other hand, you can count on shops and banks to always open and close on time, and films to start on schedule. While any times that may be listed on urban bus timetables are merely approximate or decorative, interurban buses almost always depart on time.

Tipping

Bills usually come with ten percent *taxa de serviço* included, in which case you don't have to tip – otherwise add ten percent. You don't have to tip taxi drivers but most people round up the fare to the nearest *real*. Otherwise you are expected to tip barbers, hairdressers, porters, and you should also leave a tip in your hotel room for the maid.

Travel essentials

Electricity

Voltage in Rio is 110V/60 cycles, though some hotels take 220V to cater to European travellers. Most sockets accept both North American-style flat two-pin plugs and continental European-style round two-pin plugs.

Insurance

Prior to travelling, you should take out an insurance policy to cover against theft, loss and illness or injury. Before paying for a new policy, however, it's worth checking whether you already have some degree of coverage. Credit-card companies, home-insurance policies and private medical plans sometimes cover you and your belongings when you're abroad. Most travel agents, tour operators, banks and insurance brokers will be able to help you, or you could consider the travel insurance offered by Rough Guides. Remember that when securing baggage insurance, make sure that the per-article limit – typically under £500 equivalent – will cover your most valuable possession.

Internet

Brazil has the highest number of computers with web access per head of the population in South America, and all things related to the internet are well developed. In Rio, you'll find internet cafés on almost every corner – expect to pay anything from R$2 to R$15 for an hour's usage. All hotels and hostels will have internet access, usually – but not always – for a fee, and wi-fi is now very common.

Laundry

All hotels have laundry services available to wash and iron your clothes but these are usually expensive. Most hostels have facilities to allow you to do your own laundry. Fairly common are *lavandarías*, which operate a very useful *por peso* system of service washes – the clothes are weighed at the entrance, you pay per kilo, and pick

them up washed and folded the next day. Ironing – *passar* – costs a little more. You shouldn't have much trouble finding a *lavandaría* near to where you're staying, but good prices for service washes and dry cleaning are offered by Lavanderia Ipanema, Rua Farme de Amoedo 55, Ipanema (Mon–Sat 7.30am–9pm) and Lavakilo, Rua Almirante Gonçalves 50, Copacabana (Mon–Fri 7.30am–7.30pm & Sat 8am–5pm).

Living and working in Rio de Janeiro

It's easy to be seduced by Rio, and plenty of foreigners choose to live there long term. Should you choose to do this, remember that if you enter as a tourist you will be permitted to stay in Brazil for ninety days, which can be extended by a further ninety days (see p.22). Many medium-term residents then leave Brazil to get a new entry stamp but this approach can create suspicion and you cannot be sure that you will in fact be allowed back in the country.

Without good contacts, long-term accommodation can be difficult to find and to rent an apartment you're likely to need a local as a guarantor. Until you find your feet – and if your budget permits – the easiest way is to approach an agency that rents apartments to tourists or business travellers, or at one of the many apartment hotels – prices vary considerably according to size, location, season and length of stay. Recommended is Rio Apartments (☎21/2247-6221, ⓦwww.rioapartments.com), which manages studio and one-bedroom apartments in Copacabana and Ipanema. In Copacabana, Edifício Jucati at Rua Tenente Marones de Gusmão 85 (☎21/2547-5422, ⓦwww.edificiojucati.com.br) also offers studio and one-bedroom apartments. Otherwise, accommodation of various kinds is often offered on the noticeboards at the Pontifícia Universidade Catolica's languages department at Rua Marquês de São Vicente 225, casa XV, Gávea.

If you're hoping to support yourself by working, remember that there are almost always plenty of Brazilians available for the jobs going. English-speaking foreigners sometimes support themselves by teaching English, but reputable language schools are unlikely to employ someone without a work permit, something that's very difficult to obtain. You may, however, be able to build up a roster of students via word of mouth and ads placed on notice boards. Working in tourism is another possibility – a substantial proportion of the *pousadas* in Búzios and Paraty are owned and run by foreigners who are often prepared to turn a blind eye to the lack of the correct documentation.

Mail

A **post office** is called a *correio*, identifiable by their bright yellow postboxes and signs. You'll find offices and kiosks scattered throughout Rio, open Mon–Fri 8am–6pm, Sat 8am–noon. Main post offices in Rio are at Rua Primeiro do Março (corner of Rosário) in Centro; Av. N.S. de Copacabana 540 in Copacabana; Rua Visconde de Pirajá 452 in Ipanema; and Av. Ataúlfo de Paiva 822 in Leblon. **Stamps** (*selos*) are most commonly available in two varieties – either for mailing within Brazil or abroad. A foreign postage stamp costs around R$1.70 for either a postcard or a letter up to 10 grams. It is expensive to send parcels abroad.

Airmail letters to Europe and North America usually take about a week, or sometimes even less, to arrive at their destination. **Surface mail** takes about a month to North America, and two to Europe. Although the postal system is generally very reliable, it is not advisable to send valuables through the mail.

Maps

The maps in this guide should be more than adequate for most purposes. If, however, you're staying in Rio for a while, you may find it worthwhile to purchase, for around R$30, a *Guia de Ruas – Rio de Janeiro* (a street compendium) published by Guias Quatro Rodas. If you're planning on travelling outside of the city by car, then you'll find a good map to be essential: Quatro Rodas also publish a very clear 1:950,000 map of the state of Rio de Janeiro for around R$10. These maps and street guides are sold in most local bookstores and newspaper kiosks.

Opening hours and public holidays

Office business hours are generally weekdays 9am to 6pm. Shops are usually open from 9am to 7pm on weekdays while on Saturdays many close at 1pm, though they are increasingly remaining open until the late afternoon. Most shopping centres are open Monday to Saturday 10am to 10pm and on Sunday 3pm to 9pm. Banks open on weekdays from 10am and close at 4pm, except at the airports.

There are plenty of public holidays, but on the national holidays given in the box below just about all shops and offices in Rio will be closed.

Phones

Phones are operated by **phonecards** (*cartão telefônico*), which are on sale everywhere – from newspaper stands, street sellers' trays and most cafés. For local calls a 5-*real* card will last for several conversations; for long-distance or international calls, higher-value phonecards come in 10, 20, 50 or 100 *real* denominations. Calls to the US

Public holidays

January 1 New Year's Day

February/March (varies) Carnaval – the four days leading up to Ash Wednesday

March/April (varies) Good Friday

April 21 Tiradentes Day

April 23 St George's Day

May 1 Labour Day

June (varies) Corpus Christi

September 7 Independence Day

October 12 Nossa Senhora Aparecida – Children's Day

November 2 Dia dos Finados (the Day of the Dead – All Soul's Day)

November 15 Proclamation of the Republic

December 25 Christmas Day

or Europe cost about R$4 per minute. Before dialling direct, lift the phone from the hook, insert the phonecard and listen for a dialling tone. Note that long-distance calls are cheaper after 8pm.

In theory, visitors with UK, European, Australian and New Zealand mobiles should be able to use their GSN phones in Rio. Calls, though, will be extremely expensive, especially if making a call within Brazil. Your phone will be able to work more affordably with a local SIM card (a chip) which you can purchase for about R$15 at any one of the many mobile (*celular*) phone stores where you can also add credit. Be sure that your phone is unlocked. US and Canadian phones use a different system and unless you have a tri-band phone it is unlikely to be usable in Rio.

International phone codes

Note that the initial zero is omitted from the area code when dialling the UK, Ireland, Australia and New Zealand from abroad. Ask your hotel for the international access code – it will depend on the telephone company that they use.

Australia international access code + 61 + city code.
New Zealand international access code + 64 + city code.
Republic of Ireland international access code + 353 + city code.
South Africa international access code + 27 + city code.
UK international access code + 44 + city code.
US & Canada international access code + 1 + area code.

Calling Rio de Janeiro from abroad

To call the city of Rio de Janeiro from abroad, dial your country's international Direct Dialling prefix, then:
+ 55 (Brazil's country code)
+ 21 (Rio de Janeiro local code)
+ destination number

Note that local codes for towns elsewhere in the state of Rio vary but include +24 for Paraty, Angra dos Reis, Ilha Grande and Petrópolis; and +22 for Búzios and Cabo Frio.

Portuguese-language classes

The most well-recognised course is offered by the **IBEU** (Instituto Brasil-Estados Unidos) at their Copacabana branch: Av. N. Sra. De Copacabana, 690/5° Andar, ☎21/2548-8430, ⊛www.ibeu.org.br. Each course offers two hours of small group tuition per day Monday to Thursday for a total of 36 hours, and start all year round.

If you can't stay a full month then **Lingua Solta** at Rua Candelária 106, Centro ☎21/2253-2499, ⊛www.linguasolta.com.br offers reasonably-priced courses with accommodation packages.

If you are fine with less intensive courses and plan to be in Rio between March and June, consider the evening classes offered by the **Departmento de Letras** PUC (Pontifícia Universidade Catolica) at Rua Marquês de São Vicente 225, casa XV, Gávea ☎0800-970-9556, ⊛www.cce.puc-rio.br/letras/portuguesingles.htm.

Finally, informal (and cheaper) tuition can be arranged with **Mais Brasil**, based in the Catete area close to hostels and hotels, ☎21/8502-0934. If booking a course and accommodation through a Centro-based school, make sure your accommodation is arranged within easy reach of your classes. If you're housed anywhere other than on the *metrô* this can mean an hour's commute twice per day through heavy traffic.

Time

Rio de Janeiro is usually three hours behind GMT, which changes to four hours behind during the northern hemisphere summer. To confuse things further, Brazil has daylight saving during its summer which means that clocks go forward an hour in late November and go back again in late February. During this period Rio is just two hours behind GMT.

Tourist information

There are two official **tourist agencies** in the city of Rio, neither of them particularly useful. Information about the city is from Riotur (⊛www.rio.rj.gov.br/riotur/en/), which distributes maps and brochures and has an English-speaking telephone informa-tion service, Alô Rio (Mon–Fri 9am–6pm;

⊕0800/285-0555 or 21/2542-8080). There are information offices or booths at the following locations:

Galeão international airport
International and domestic arrivals halls (daily 6am–midnight)
Novo Rio Rodoviária
Arrivals area (daily 8am–8pm)
RioTur Information Centre
Av. Princesa Isabel 183, Copacabana (Mon–Fri 9am–6pm)

Basic information about other parts of the state of Rio is available from **TurisRio** (ⓦwww.turisrio.rj.gov.br; ⊕0800/282-2007 & 21/2544-7992), with its office located at Rua da Ajuda 5 in Centro (Mon–Fri 9am–6pm, ⊕0800/282-2007). Most towns around the state of Rio have their own tourist information offices which can be good sources of local advice. Details of these tourist offices are found in the "Out of the city" chapter of this guide.

Travellers with disabilities

Travelling in Rio for people with disabilities who require special facilities can be challenging. For example, access even to recently constructed buildings may be impossible, as lifts are often too narrow to accommodate wheelchairs or there may be no lift at all. Luxury hotels, though, have facilities that travellers with disabilities have come to expect in Europe and North America. You'll also find that people are very helpful and will try to compensate for any deficiencies in access and facilities.

Wheelchair ramps to access the city's pavements are increasingly common; especially in Centro and in the Zona Sul of the city. However, in Búzios and, especially, Paraty, the cobblestone streets are extremely difficult for wheelchair users. Access to buses in Rio is only really possible for the agile, while once on buses passengers have to expect to be thrown about as seating is limited and drivers tend to break suddenly and take corners at terrifying speeds.

Taxis, however, are plentiful. Inter-city buses are generally quite comfortable, with most offering reclining seats. Wheelchairs are available at both of Rio's airports.

The City

The City

Centro

Towering office blocks intermingled with elegant colonial and Neo-classical buildings dominate **Centro** – the commercial and historic centre of Rio. The influences that have shaped the city's architecture through its five centuries of existence – the austerity of the city's European founders, divisive colonial rule and the grandiose design of the Enlightenment – can all be found within its busy streets. The surviving historic squares and churches, and numerous museums and galleries make an excellent day or two's sightseeing. Centro's heavy traffic and confusing layout often causes visitors to overlook it in favour of the Zona Sul beaches and the heights of the Sugar Loaf mountain and Corcovado. Nonetheless, the area has rich historical appeal and an amazing mix of people; residents of the city's diverse *bairros* come together here in a cacophony of commerce and **street life**. Additionally, Centro contains a staggering number of **art exhibition** spaces, partly due to government policy requiring corporations to invest in cultural development.

The administration of engineer and mayor **Francisco Pereira Passos** in the first decade of the twentieth century left the greatest mark on Centro. Rio went through a period of **urban reconstruction** under Passos's direction that all but destroyed the last vestiges of its colonial design; the city was torn apart by frenzied demolition and reconstructed in a style of monumental splendour modelled on the *Belle Époque* of Paris. Public buildings, grand avenues, libraries and parks were built to embellish the city, lending it the dignity perceived as characteristic of the great capital cities of the Old World. **Praça Floriano** in Centro's southern **Cinelândia** district is the best example of Passos-era Parisian extravagance, its Neoclassical **Biblioteca Nacional** and **Theatro Municipal** the clear highlights. The narrow colonial streets of nineteenth-century Rio, though limited to tiny districts, can still be found too, most notably around **Rua do Ouvidor** close to **Praça XV de Novembro** at Centro's eastern seaboard. Near here is also the gateway for boat trips to **Ilha de Paquetá** in Guanabara Bay – a great day out.

Many other historical squares, streets and buildings disappeared from the 1940s onwards as industrial modernisation took hold and the motor car began to dictate urban development. Functional office buildings and multi-lane thoroughfares were erected aplenty, decimating most of the grand buildings of Passos's showpiece north-south artery, now called **Avenida Rio Branco**, in favour of faceless (and often fading) skyscrapers. Old colonial streets to the north of Centro also bore the brunt of the overzealous modernisers in the shape of giant **Avenida Presidente Vargas**, a full twelve lanes of traffic running at right angles to Rio Branco from the grand Neoclassical **Candelária** church to **Central do Brasil train station** and on to the **Sambódromo**, the venue for the five nights of Carnaval processions each year. This later twentieth-century

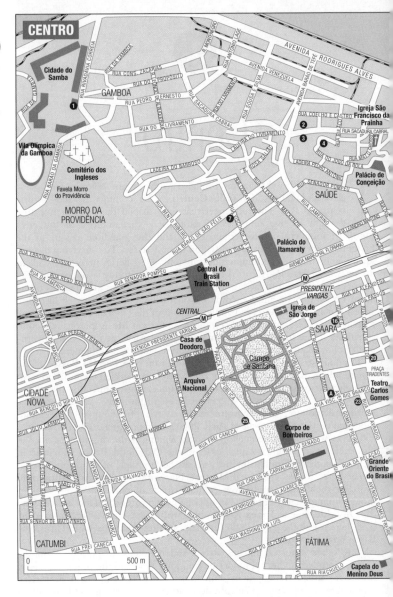

development, broken only by the odd piece of interesting **modern architecture** and intermittent reminders of the glorious past, lends parts of Centro an Eastern European communist-like feel, a sentiment better understood by considering Brazil's decades of twentieth-century dictatorship.

Centro undoubtedly went through a period of decline as Rio lost its capital city status to Brasília in the 1960s and its standing as the country's premier

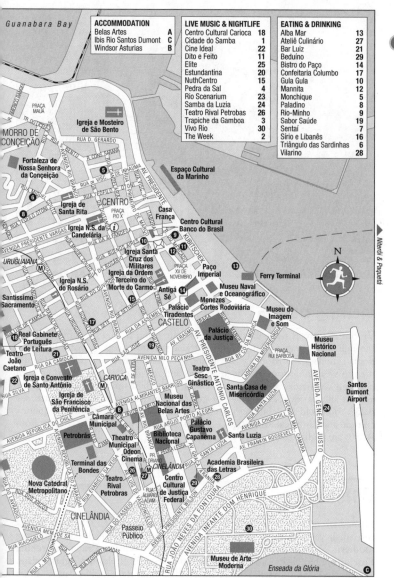

ACCOMMODATION

Belas Artes	A
Ibis Rio Santos Dumont	C
Windsor Asturias	B

LIVE MUSIC & NIGHTLIFE

Centro Cultural Carioca	18
Cidade do Samba	1
Cine Ideal	22
Dito e Feito	11
Elite	25
Estundantina	20
NuthCentro	15
Pedra da Sal	4
Rio Scenarium	23
Samba da Luzia	24
Teatro Rival Petrobas	26
Trapiche da Gamboa	3
Vivo Rio	30
The Week	2

EATING & DRINKING

Alba Mar	13
Ateliê Culinário	27
Bar Luiz	21
Beduíno	29
Bistro do Paço	14
Confeitaria Columbo	17
Gula Gula	10
Mannita	12
Monchique	5
Paladino	8
Rio-Minho	9
Sabor Saúde	19
Sentaí	7
Sírio e Libanês	16
Triângulo das Sardinhas	6
Vilarino	28

commercial centre to São Paulo in the 1970s and 1980s. Nevertheless, with the recent renovation of business areas like **Cidade Nova** and the construction of the remarkable **Cidade do Samba** in the much-maligned port area of **Gamboa** – not to mention the conversion of many former business and government buildings into cultural centres and galleries – Rio's centre is again finding its feet as a cultural capital for the twenty-first century.

▲ Centro skyline

Visiting Centro

Visiting Centro is fairly easy on foot, despite often having to fight your way through heavy traffic. Many Centro attractions are closed on Saturday afternoons, Sundays and Mondays. Be aware, also, that many civic buildings require men to wear long trousers. The area's bars and restaurants come into their own between Wednesday and Friday after 4pm – the best time to get a feel of the vibrant after-work social scene. For good urban walking routes in Centro, see p.239. You could also consider taking a guided walking **tour**: Carlos Roquette's cultural and historical tours (☎21/3322-4872, ⓦ www.culturalrio.com.br; from R$50) are highly rated.

Cinelândia

Named after (mostly) long-gone movie houses built in the 1930s, **Cinelândia** is a small yet striking area bordering Lapa (see p.69), which surrounds the southern end of Avenida Rio Branco and the square **Praça Marechal Floriano**. Though Praça XV de Novembro (see p.52) holds the rightful claim as the city's (and Brazil's) most historically important public space, Praça Floriano boasts the most impressive architecture and has an easy *metrô* link, effectively making it – for the Zona Sul population at least – the main square of downtown Rio.

At the head of the square stands the grand **Theatro Municipal**, while on the eastern side busy **Avenida Rio Branco** is lined with Neoclassical buildings, including the **Museu Nacional das Belas Artes** and the **Biblioteca Nacional**. Originally named Avenida Central, Rio Branco was at one time Latin America's most impressive urban thoroughfare, its entire length bordered by three-storey Neoclassical buildings, tree-lined pavements and a promenade running right down the centre. Nowadays, however, beyond Cinelândia it is marred by ugly office buildings and traffic pollution.

On the western side of Praça Floriano is Rio's council chamber the **Câmara Municipal** (Mon–Fri 9am–5pm; ⓦ www.camara.rj.gov.br) – officially called the Palácio Pedro Ernesto. Chiefly of interest to fans of eclectic 1920s architecture – and those wishing to get more acquainted with Rio's shady city politics, – it occasionally draws large demonstrations and political campaigners to the square. The impressive debating chamber has an open public gallery with some interesting artwork, including a large 1920s mural tracing the history of Rio. Several neighbouring sidewalk bars and restaurants serve as popular central meeting points in the evening, when the surrounding buildings are illuminated and at their most elegant – an ideal place to enjoy a cool drink. At **Carnaval**, Rio's largest *bloco* (see p.218), the *Bola Preta*, is also held around the whole district, drawing crowds in excess of 200,000. In the centre of the praça is a bust of **Getúlio Vargas** (see p.251), still anonymously decorated with flowers on the anniversary of the ex-dictator's birthday, March 19.

At the southern end of the square is the Art Nouveau **Odeon Cinema**, the last remaining in Cinelândia, which maintains lively programming including all-night film marathons (with bar) every other week and a *cachaça* film club (see p.207). Just west of the praça on Rua Alvaro Alvim is the excellent **Teatro Rival Petrobras** (see p.197), a cabaret-style venue hosting nights of both traditional and popular Brazilian music.

A short walk east of Praça Floriano the grandly-named **Palácio Gustavo Capanema** contains a government ministry, though is in fact a temple of modern architecture. Lying a short walk away at the northern end of the Parque do Flamengo – but most easily accessed from Cinelândia – is another modernist structure, the Museu de Arte Moderna, Rio's largest gallery of modern painting and other art.

The Theatro Municipal

Extensively refurbished for its centenary in 2009, Rio's Neoclassical **Theatro Municipal** (Mon–Fri 1–4pm; guided tours in English 1pm Tues & Thurs, phone ⓣ 21/2299 1667 or 21/2299 1711 or enquire at the box office at the back of the building; free; ⓦ www.theatromunicipal.rj.gov.br), the city's most prestigious artistic venue, was commissioned by Mayor Passos and opened in 1909 with the explicit aim of putting Brazil on the world arts map. It was modelled on the Paris Opéra – all granite, marble and bronze, with a spectacular front-of-house decorated in the white and gold characteristic of Louis XV style. Foot-wide green onyx handrails with white marble supports guide you up the foyer stairs, where crystal mirrors, antique furniture, and stained-glass windows illustrating period tragi-comedies greet you at the top. Even the building's precise position, with the Corcovado, Sugar Loaf mountain and Arcos da Lapa all visible, was carefully considered.

The auditorium seats just under two thousand people, with a fifteen-hundred-kilo chandelier dazzling overhead which illuminates an ambitious painting by celebrated Italian-Brazilian painter **Eliseu Visconti**. Reportedly the fourth biggest in the world, the stage hosts orchestras, ballets and opera, and is home to the city's ballet troupe, opera company and the Orquestra Sinfônica Brasileira. The **Café do Theatro** (Mon–Fri 11am–4pm), a large restaurant located in the basement and richly adorned with Assyrian-inspired mosaics, is certainly worth a look around even if you decide not to eat.

Museu Nacional das Belas Artes

Facing the Theatro Municipal, on the opposite side of Rio Branco, is the **Museu Nacional das Belas Artes** (Tues–Fri 10am–6pm, Sat, Sun & public holidays noon–5pm; R$5; ☎21/2240-0068, ⓦwww.mnba.gov.br), a grandiose Neoclassical pile built in 1908 as a school of art; the museum was created in 1937. The modest European collection includes works by Boudin, Tournay and Franz Post, but the more modern **Brazilian collection** is the main attraction. Organised in chronological order, each room shows various stages in the development of Brazilian painting and highlights influences imported from Europe: the years of diversification (1919–28) includes a number of pieces by Eliseu Visconti; the movement into modernism (1921–49); and the consolidation of modern forms between 1928 and 1967, especially in the works of Cândido Portinari, Djanira and master illustrator Oswaldo Goeldi. Amongst the most striking works are Portinari's *Café* (1935), an imaginative scene featuring a coffee *fazenda*, and great Brazilian modern artist Emiliano di Cavalcanti's nine-metre mural *Navio Negrero*, a thought-provoking forest encounter of Brazil's different racial groups in the 1930s.

Aside from paintings there are two halls of space-filling **sculptures** – mostly badly damaged reproductions from the Louvre – which are best bypassed in favour of a few excellent Brazilian sculptures on the second floor. The third floor is dedicated almost exclusively to (abstract) plastic arts, with a couple of notable pieces by Regina Vater contemplating the realities of contemporary Brazilian womanhood.

Biblioteca Nacional

In the centre of Praça Floriano on Avenida Rio Branco is the **Biblioteca Nacional** (Mon–Fri 9am–8pm, Sat 9am–3pm; free; guided tours in English 1pm Mon–Fri; R$2; ☎21/2220-9484, ⓦwww.bn.br;), Rio's ornate reference library, completed in 1910 and restored in 1995. Its architect, the Baianan Francisco Sousa Aguiar, became Rio's mayor, following Passos, in 1909. The elaborate reading rooms feature Art Nouveau ceilings, one a beautiful multi-domed design using stained glass, and the stairway was decoratively painted by some of the most important Brazilian artists of the nineteenth century – Modesto Brocas, Eliseu Visconti, Rodolfo Amoedo and Henrique Bernadelli. Many of the materials used in the library's construction were imported from Europe; British bronze, German metalwork and Italian marble statues all feature in the interior.

The library's **collection** started to be compiled in 1810 and, with more than eight million volumes, is now the largest in Latin America. Among its older items are newspapers from 1808, Portuguese scripts dating back to the eleventh century, maps and documents relating to slave trading and colonial commerce from 1500, as well as books and photos on the Brazilian royal couple, **Dom Pedro** and **Teresa Christina** (see p.249).

Centro Cultural Justiça Federal

The **Centro Cultural Justiça Federal** (Tues–Sun noon–7pm; ⓦwww.ccjf .trf2.gov.br) is the last building of note on the Praça Floriano and another example of the area's architectural eclecticism. The southern neighbour of the Biblioteca, the building dates from 1905 and served as the Brazilian Supreme Court from 1909 to 1960 before the capital moved to Brasília. The facade is in classical French style, and the interior features an Art Nouveau wrought iron staircase and Gothic and Renaissance designs on walls, doorways and ceilings. The cultural centre contains gallery space for visual art **exhibitions** including photography and film, and also functions as a venue for **classical music** concerts and courses on topics as diverse as origami and Nietzsche.

Museu de Arte Moderna

Inaugurated in 1958, the hangar-like glass and concrete **Museu de Arte Moderna** (**MAM**; Tues–Fri noon–6pm, Sat & Sun noon–7pm; R$5; ☎21/2240-4944, ⓦwww.mamrio.com.br) was designed by the Brazilian architect and urbanist **Affonso Reidy** – a modernist who, like others before him (see below), saw fit to raise his building off the ground. Located south of Praça Floriano at the northern end of the Parque do Flamengo (cross busy Av. Presidente Wilson and traverse the footbridge from Rua João Neves da Fontoura), the museum adjoins the large music venue, **Vivo Rio** (see p.197), with surrounding gardens landscaped by **Roberto Burle Marx**, who also worked on the entire Parque do Flamengo (see p.88).

The museum's collection was unfortunately devastated by a fire in 1978, but since reopening in 1990 MAM has gradually regained its status and now boasts works by some of the great names of twentieth-century Brazilian art, as well as hosting visiting exhibitions from across Latin America. It makes sense to start on the upper floor where you'll find sculptures and paintings from the 1920s and 1930s – Cavalcanti, Monteiro, Portinari and Segall are all represented – before progressing downstairs to the 1960s and beyond (the ink drawings by Roberto Magalhães are a highlight).

North to the Palácio Gustavo Capanema

Heading north again back into Centro-proper, at Avenida President Wilson 203 is the *Petit Trianon* at the **Academia Brasileira das Letras** (☎21/3974-2500, ⓦwww.academia.org.br), another majestic Neoclassical edifice with an exhibition and cultural centre hosting lectures, theatre and cinema, exclusively in Portuguese. Northwards on Avenida Graça Aranha you'll pass the **Teatro Sesc Ginástico** (ⓦwww.sescrio.com.br; see p.206), a venue for music concerts and theatre productions, and a block further (before **Rua Araújo Porte Alegre**), fans of modern architecture will delight in the **Palácio Gustavo Capanema** – more of a high-rise office building than a palace, and now the seat of the Brazilian Ministries of Education and Health. The building project was led by Swiss architect Le Corbusier with an outstanding – and young – Brazilian team comprising Lucio Costa, Oscar Niemeyer and landscaper Roberto Burle Marx – who all went on to design the new capital, Brasília. Extremely radical for its time, it took nearly ten years to complete and was finally inaugurated in 1945.

The building is supported by rows of giant pillars which span its entire height, creating an open square beneath now surrounded by tall palms and containing a granite sculpture, the *Monumento a Juventude*, that somehow captures the youthfulness of Brazil. If you have photographic identification with you (men also need long trousers), there is a permanent exhibition on the building's construction located on the second floor. Here, too, is a noteworthy mural by **Candido Portinari** (see p.69), which covers three sides of a room and depicts the construction of Brazil. Portinari was also responsible for some of the building's external tiling and artistic work.

Largo da Carioca and around

A couple of blocks north of Cinelândia and the Praça Floriano is the **Largo da Carioca**, a rather faceless square which has undergone considerable transformation since the city's foundation. Unbelievably there was a lake here until 1679, when the early Franciscans at the neighbouring convent insisted it be filled in. The eighteenth-century buildings which followed were all demolished in the twentieth century to allow widening of the square and the improvement of nearby roads; and in the 1960s the towering office block and electronics shopping centre **Edifício Avenida Central** was constructed to add to the hustle and bustle. Today, street traders selling leather goods dominate the centre of the square, while a couple of places of interest remain, most notably the oldest church in Rio, the **Igreja e Convento de Santo Antônio**, and its stunning adjoining church, the **Igreja de São Francisco da Penitência**. From here you'll notice the startling modern architecture of the headquarters of state oil company Petrobras to the southwest, while just beyond it is the equally astonishing conical **Nova Catedral Metropolitana**. Directly behind the Petrobras building, accessed from Rua Lélio Gama, is the **tram terminal** for *bondes* to Santa Teresa across the Arcos da Lapa (see p.76).

The streets north of Largo da Carioca are a maze of shops, markets and historical squares beginning with **Rua Uruguaiana** (pedestrianized most of the way north to Avenida President Vargas). If you're looking for a cool beer near Carioca, Rio's oldest *cervejaria*, the bustling *Bar Luiz* (Mon–Thurs 11am–10pm; Sat 11am–midnight; see p.180) is at no. 39 Rua da Carioca. It's been here since 1887, changing its original name – the *Bar Adolfo* – following World War II, for obvious reasons. Also nearby, a block north of Carioca at Rua Gonçalves Dias 32, is the wonderful Art Nouveau *Confeitaria Colombo* (see p.179), a great bet for European-style **tea and cakes** in the afternoon, or even a grand Brazilian buffet breakfast or à la carte lunch in its upstairs dining room. Founded in 1894, the *Colombo* recalls Rio's Belle Époque, with its ornate interior and air of tradition (Mon–Fri 9am–8pm, Sat 9am–4pm).

Igreja e Convento de Santo Antônio and Igreja de São Francisco da Penitência

Rio's oldest church, the **Igreja e Convento de Santo Antônio** (Mon–Fri 8am–7pm, Sat 8–11am & 4–6pm, Sun 9–11am), within which the **Igreja de São Francisco da Penitência** is also located, stands above the Largo da Carioca, and is known as St Anthony of the Rich (to differentiate it from St Anthony of the Poor, which is located four blocks west of here). A tranquil, cloistered refuge amidst the heart of commercial Rio, it is accessed by means of a pedestrian tunnel on the western side of the Largo, close to the *metrô* (an elevator hauls you up into the complex). The convent was built between 1608 and 1620 and founded by Franciscan monks who arrived in Brazil in 1592. A popular saint in Brazil, St Anthony's help was sought as the army's protector during the French invasion of 1710: his image was then made captain in the Brazilian army, but in a startling lack of progress through the ranks it was 1814 before he was promoted to lieutenant-colonel, retiring from service in 1914. The Convento's crypt is also home to the tomb of the intriguing **Wild Jock of Skelater** – a Scottish mercenary who entered the service of the Portuguese Crown during the Napoleonic Wars, he was later appointed commander-in-chief of the Portuguese army in Brazil.

The interior of the **main church** boasts a beautiful sacristy, constructed from Portuguese marble and decorated in *azulejos* depicting the miracles performed by St Anthony. There is rich wooden ornamentation throughout, carved from jacaranda, including the great chest in the sacristy.

The undoubtedly more striking Baroque **Igreja de São Francisco da Penitência**, dating from 1772, is situated next to the Igreja de Santo Antônio. Though smaller than its neighbour, it contains remarkable and extensive gold-coated sculpture as well as silver ornamentation. Infuriatingly its opening times are different to the Convento as a whole: 1–4pm, Tues–Fri.

Edificio Sede da Petrobras

Southwest of the Largo da Carioca and visible throughout Centro and Santa Teresa is the **Edificio Marechal de Queiroz** (commonly called 'Edise' – the Edificio Sede da Petrobras), the glass, steel and concrete hulk that is the headquarters of the state oil company. No other building in Rio causes quite such a stir: some find it an extreme modernist monstrosity while others consider it an arresting site amidst an otherwise anonymous mix of mid-twentieth-century offices. Whilst it's not likely to win awards for aesthetic beauty, it is impossible not to marvel at the audacity of it; architect Roberto Gandolfi was the man responsible for its 1974 completion, while Burle Marx contributed to the 'hanging' gardens visible on each floor.

Nova Catedral Metropolitana

The unmistakeable shape of the **Nova Catedral Metropolitana** (Av. República do Chile, ⓦ www.catedral.com.br; daily 7.30am–6pm) rises up like some futuristic teepee, just to the west of the Edificio Sede da Petrobras. Built between 1964 and 1976 and designed by a Catholic University of Rio (PUC) professor and architect, **Edgar Fonseca**, it's an impressive piece of modern architecture

▲ Nova Catedral Metropolitana

and a considerable engineering feat. The **Morro de Santo Antônio**, a hill which extended across this whole area from the Convento de Santo Antônio, was levelled to make way for the cathedral, and the thousands of tons of reclaimed soil were used to construct the Parque do Flamengo (see p.88). The cathedral is 75m high with a diameter of 106m and has a capacity of 20,000. Inside, it is vast, and the remarkable sense of space is enhanced by the absence of supporting columns. Filtering the sunlight, four huge stained-glass windows dominate, each measuring 20m by 60m and corresponding to a symbolic colour scheme – ecclesiastical green, saintly red, Catholic blue and apostolic yellow. Fonseca's inspiration for the project was the Maya pyramids of the Mexican Yucatán peninsula, though he favoured a conical shape to symbolize the equi-distance of God from all mortals below.

A well-hidden and barely-open museum, the **Museu de Arte Sacra** (Wed, Sat & Sun 9am–noon) is located underneath the structure, with a collection of sculpture, religious oddments, colonial-era paintings, books and commemorations of Pope John Paul II's two visits in 1980 and 1997.

Castelo and Praça XV de Novembro

Heading three to four blocks east from Largo da Carioca and Avenida Rio Branco, the areas of Castelo and **Praça XV de Novembro** (known simply as 'Praça Quinze') hold several interesting historical sights and museums. Bear in mind that much of this area is deserted from Saturday lunchtime to Monday morning: certainly not the best times to explore.

While Castelo is a busy bus terminus, the "castle" itself – and the hill it was constructed on four hundred years ago to defend the new city – disappeared during a 1920s urban development plan designed to reduce health risks. Additionally, the resultant rock and earth provided for an ambitious land reclamation project which became the neighbouring Aeroporto Santos Dumont. In the *castelo*'s place is a series of mostly ugly office buildings, the exception being the extravagant and imposing **Fazenda Federal**, the Federal Treasury building impossible not to notice on Avenida Presidente Antônio Carlos. Despite the untidy urban din, two of Rio's best museums are located here, the **Museu Historical Nacional** and the **Museu Naval**, both offering great insights into Brazil's fascinating history.

As the country's most important historical square, Praça XV itself is surrounded by interesting sights, among them the old royal palace, Paço Imperial, the Neoclassical state legislature, Palácio Tiradentes, and the Arco de Teles – the most well-preserved remaining area of narrow colonial passageways in the city – which remains characterized by noisy street life. The beautiful **Centro Cultural Banco do Brasil**, one of Rio's foremost arts centres, is also located just north of here.

Around Santa Casa de Misericórdia and the Museu do Imagem e Som

The one remaining sign there was ever a hill at Castelo at all is the rundown (and tiny) sixteenth-century incline **Ladeira da Misericórdia**, an old cobbled street off Rua da Misericórdia, at the back of the Igreja de Nossa Senhora de Bonsucesso, which forms a part of the Misericórdia complex (see below). Right opposite, with its entrance on Praça Rui Barbosa, is the **Museu do Imagem e Som** (Mon–Fri noon–5pm ☎21/2220-3481, ⓦwww.mis.rj.gov.br), which explains Rio's social history using records, tape recordings, books and film. There's also a fascinating photographic collection documenting the city's cultural life from the turn of the nineteenth century until the 1940s (there are plans afoot to relocate this museum to Copacabana in 2010).

Heading around the corner onto Rua Santa Luzia is the entrance to the **Santa Casa de Misericórdia**, a sprawling colonial structure dating from 1582 and built by the Sisterhood of Misericórdia, a nursing order dedicated to caring for the sick and providing asylum to orphans and invalids. It was here in 1849 that, for the first time in Rio, a case of yellow fever was diagnosed, and from 1856 to 1916 the building was used as Rio's Faculty of Medicine. The Santa Casa is not open to the public, but you can visit the tiny **Museu da Farmácia** (Mon–Fri 8am–noon & 1–5pm) to see its collection of pharmacological implements and the attached **Igreja de Nossa Senhora de Bonsucesso** (Mon–Fri 9am–noon), which contains finely detailed altars, a collection of Bohemian crystal and an eighteenth-century organ.

On Avenida Presidente Antônio Carlos, close to the Fazenda Federal (see opposite) is the **Igreja de Santa Luzia**, a somewhat kitsch eighteenth-century church whose predecessor stood on the seashore – hard to believe now the site is overwhelmed by surrounding office buildings. On December 13 each year devotees enter its "room of miracles" and bathe their eyes in water from the white marble font – reputedly a miraculous cure for eye defects.

Museu Histórico Nacional

The building which houses the **Museu Histórico Nacional** (Tues–Fri 10am–5.30pm, Sat, Sun & public holidays 2–6pm; R$6; ☎21/2550-9255, ⓦwww.museuhistoriconacional.com.br) was built in 1762 as an arsenal, later serving as a military prison where escaped slaves were detained. In 1922 it was converted into an exhibition centre for the centenary celebrations of Brazil's independence and has remained a museum, now one of Brazil's most important, ever since. The museum is located at the eastern end of Castelo sitting uncomfortably in the shadow of the Presidente Kubitschek "Perimetral" flyover that runs into the Parque do Flamengo.

The large **collection** contains some valuable pieces – from furniture to nineteenth-century firearms and locomotives. The second floor displays attempt a detailed documentation of Brazilian **history** – and in part succeed, with clear thought given to indigenous societies. Nonetheless, the monarchy claims disproportionate weight, and the reality of four hundred years under Portuguese control isn't particularly well confronted, with scant acknowledgment of either the fate of the majority of Amerindians or the experiences of Brazil's tens of millions of Africans. What *is* here is often fascinating, however, with artefacts and charts tracing the country's development from European discovery to the proclamation of the Republic.

Clearly demonstrated, for example, is the structure of sixteenth-century Brazilian high society, including the system of hereditary *sesmarias*, or enormous royal land grants, which provided the basis for the highly unequal system of **land tenure** that endures today. Scale models and artefacts explain the agrarian and cyclical nature of Brazil's **economic history**, organized around a plantation and mining slave system that produced – at different times – sugar cane, cattle, cotton, rubber, coffee and gold, for European markets. The impact of Britain's Industrial Revolution and the spread of new ideas following the

French Revolution are also considered – the story of independence advocate Tiradentes, who was hung, drawn and quartered and his body parts displayed along the road to rebellious Ouro Preto, illustrates the nervousness of the monarchy. Later immigration is briefly examined, too, including the arrival of 800,000 Italians after 1888 to work on coffee farms.

Also of interest are numerous paintings, including a remarkable 1987 mural by Peredo illustrating Brazil's story through flags, emblems and faces (Pele is at the centre), and a series of eighteenth-century canvases of Rio de Janeiro, some featuring the Arcos da Lapa. More recent twentieth-century developments are taken up by the **Museu da República** in Catete (see p.86).

The Museu Naval e Oceanográfico

Just north of Castelo close to Praça XV de Novembro is the excellent **Museu Naval e Oceanográfico** (Tues–Sun noon–4pm; free; English translations throughout; Rua Dom Manuel 15) which demonstrates far more than the military experience. Its collection examines Brazil's naval history and includes sixteenth-century nautical charts, scale replicas of European galleons, paintings depicting scenes from the Brazil–Paraguay War and exhibits of twentieth-century naval hardware. Above all, it provides an insight into the colonization of Brazil and fills in some of the gaps left by the Museu Histórico National. The exhibits show that Brazilian naval engagements were determined by the interests of the Portuguese Empire until the nineteenth century; as a primarily slave-based plantation economy until 1888, Brazil's military hardware came from the foundries of industrialized Europe. The most impressive items on display are the handcrafted replicas of sixteenth-century galleons – the *São Felipe* complete with its 98 cannons – and the first map of the New World, drawn by Pedro Alvares Cabral between 1492 and 1500. Alongside many model ships, a variety of other child-friendly exhibits including cannons and interactive maps are on display.

Praça XV de Novembro

Once the hub of Rio's social and political life, **Praça XV de Novembro** ('Praça Quinze') takes its name from the day (Nov 15) in 1889 when **Marechal Deodoro de Fonseca**, the first president, proclaimed the Republic of Brazil (see p.251). Known first as the Largo do Carmo, then as the Largo do Paço, the latter name survives only in the imposing **Paço Imperial**, built in 1743 to serve as the palace of Portugal's colonial governors in Rio and later as the court of the Portuguese monarch, Dom João VI. Following the departure of the monarch to Portugal, his son, Dom Pedro, was crowned the first Emperor of Brazil here in 1822.

These days the praça has lost much of its former grandeur, partly due to its location on Centro's fringe away from the *metrô*, but also as a result of the city's poor planning decisions; in the 1950s the Avenida Presidente Kubitschek overpass was constructed to the east of the square, joined in the 1990s by a noisy underpass crammed with buses. Unfortunately this gives the square a slightly transient and dejected feel. Nevertheless, political demonstrations and striking Rio state workers can still be found outside the grand state legislature, **Palácio Tiradentes**, and at night rock and *MPB* music concerts occasionally take place. If you can, visit on a Thursday or Friday morning when Praça XV hosts one of Rio's oldest **markets** – stalls are packed with typical foods, handicrafts, ceramics and paintings – and there's a brisk trade in stamps and coins, too.

Adjoining Praça XV is the **Praça Mercado Municipal**, reclaimed from the ocean in the 1960s along with the Parque do Flamengo (see p.88). At the point where the two squares meet, you'll notice a small pyramid-like tower regrettably half-hidden by the entrance to the road underpass. Known as the **Chafariz do Mestre Valentim** after prominent sculptor and architect Valentim de Fonseca e Silva (who also designed the Passeio Público park in Lapa, see p.73), it was completed in 1789 and designed as an entrance to the city for boats moored below, but became better known as a major work by an accepted non-white designer, primarily due to the artist's talent – though at the time blacks and mulattos were barred from (officially at least) earning money from their trade. It includes sections in granite and white marble.

Beyond, at the far side of the square, is the gateway for ferries and **boat trips** to Niterói (see p.145) and around Guanabara Bay (see p.58).

The Paço Imperial

Constructed between 1743 and 1791, the sprawling **Paço Imperial** (Tues–Sun noon–6pm; free; ☏21/2533-4407, ⊛www.pacoimperial.com.br), although not visually appealing, compensates for this with its fascinating history. In 1808, Portuguese monarch Dom João VI established his Brazilian court here before choosing to move to the Palácio da Quinta da Boa Vista, now the Museu Nacional, in São Cristóvão (see p.138). Known as the Paço Real, it was only in 1822 following Dom Pedro's proclamation of independence that the building took on the 'Imperial' moniker. It continued to be used for royal receptions and special occasions, including Princess Isabel's proclamation of the end of slavery on May 13, 1888, before later serving as a government department.

Today, the Paço Imperial has a number of separate **exhibition spaces** with entrances from both ends of the building – installations are usually themed around modern art and architecture, often with large murals and interactive displays. Inside the Rua Primeiro de Março entrance, there's a courtyard holding the excellent **Bistro do Paço** (see p.180) and a small exhibition (in Portuguese) on the building's history.

Palácio Tiradentes

Next door, bold, Neoclassical **Palácio Tiradentes** (Mon–Fri 11am–5pm; free; ☏21/2588 1251, ⊛www.alerj.rj.gov.br) has served as the Rio de Janeiro State Parliament since 1975, although it was originally built to be the Brazilian federal legislature. Completed in 1926, democratic debate survived only a few years here until dictator Getúlio Vargas overthrew the government and converted the building into his Ministry of Propaganda. Though the **permanent exhibition** on the struggle for democracy is entirely in Portuguese, guided tours are available in English by calling in advance, and there are computers with English translations of the building's history. Additionally, both the Grand Salon and the Assembly chamber are impressive halls; at the latter you can sit in the **public gallery** and hear political hot air of an especially Brazilian kind (long trousers essential for men, no restriction for women).

Arco de Teles and Rua do Ouvidor

On the northern side of the square, the **Arco de Teles** was named after the judge and landowner Francisco Teles de Meneza, who ordered its construction upon the site of the old *pelourinho* (pillory) around 1755. The *arco* links Praça XV to the

Rio's colonial remnants

Architecture is the most significant cultural legacy of Rio's colonial period. From the city's foundation in 1565 to the arrival of the Portuguese royal family in 1808, Rio was a densely populated garrison settlement, with houses so closely constructed that their walls touched. The squares and parks that emerged did not arise from any deliberate planning – they were simply open spaces that were overlooked during this time of extensive building. Political and social conditions in the city were generally static, and the striking lack of change in basic design and construction techniques mirrored this. **Mannerist**, **Baroque**, **Pombaline** and **Rococo** architectural influences did reach the colony where, to a degree, they were adapted to local conditions, however, construction sometimes took so long that completed buildings were a patchwork of styles.

Colonial buildings were either military, civilian or religious. Military constructions were utilitarian – designed to defend the port and settlement. A few, including the eighteenth-century **Forte de Leme** (see p.102) and the seventeenth-century **Fortaleza de Santa Cruz** – across Guanabara Bay in Niterói (see p.145), have survived the ravages of time; their presence a visible testament to Rio's past strategic significance. Civilian architecture, restrained by economic factors, was also plain and practical. Few traces of civilian buildings from the period remain; amongst the only surviving structures are the **Paço Imperial** (see p.53), built in 1743 as the residence of governors of the colony, and the **Arco de Teles** (see p.53) – an eighteenth-century stone gateway to what was once the home of a wealthy merchant.

In Rio, as elsewhere in Portugal's vast empire, religious architecture was an instrument of spiritual comfort and social status, with churches constructed for different sectors of society – from slaves to the wealthy elite. Prior to the early eighteenth century, the most important religious structures were convent churches, located on hilltops as symbolic landmarks visible throughout the city. From the early 1700s, churches were established all over Rio; while their exteriors were remarkably simple in appearance, their interiors reflected colonial tastes for lavish ornamentation and embellishment. The **Igreja de Nossa Senhora de Glória do Outeiro** (see p.85), perhaps the prettiest colonial building in Rio, displays the classical, geometric whitewash exterior pattern of Mannerism and, in its interior, the dynamism of the Baroque. On a grander scale, the contrast between the sober facade of the **Igreja e Mosteiro de São Bento** (see p.59) and its elaborately gilded interior is quite striking. Rio's beautiful churches largely survived the developers, and it retains the largest number of colonial religious buildings in Brazil – though they are often overlooked and unappreciated, scattered amidst a fast-changing city.

Rua do Ouvidor, and originally contained three houses; one of these was home to the Menezes family, but all were severely damaged by fire in 1790. The social history of the Arco de Teles and its immediate vicinity is more engaging than the building itself. Families belonging to Rio's wealthy classes lived in the luxurious apartments above street level, while the street below was traditionally a refuge for "beggars and rogues of the worst type; lepers, thieves, murderers, prostitutes and hoodlums" – according to Brasil Gerson in his 1954 book *História das Ruas do Rio de Janeiro*. In the late eighteenth and early nineteenth centuries, one of the leprous local inhabitants – Bárbara dos Prazeres – achieved notoriety as a folk devil: it was a common belief that the blood of a dead dog or cat applied to the body provided a cure for leprosy, and Bárbara is said to have earned her reputation around the Arco de Teles by attempting to enhance the efficacy of this cure by stealing newborn babies and sucking their blood.

Behind the Arco de Teles is the Beco de Teles, a narrow cobblestone alley which runs immediately into the **Travessa do Commercio**, each with some charming nineteenth-century buildings. For two blocks beyond here, around **Rua do Ouvidor** and **Rua do Rosário**, you'll find the best-preserved Portuguese colonial streets in Rio, almost every house has been transformed into a restaurant, *boteco*, or old bookshop – the best of which, the Livraria Folha Seca (Rua do Ouvidor 37) is a specialist on old Rio, samba music and macumba spirituality. Rua do Ouvidor, especially, gets busy after work – it's a good place to cool off after a day's sightseeing – and hosts the excellent 🎷 **Samba do Ouvidor** on alternate Saturdays from 2pm. One of the best known *Rodas de Samba* in Rio, the surrounding streets become packed with weekend partiers.

Igreja de Nossa Senhora do Carmo da Antigá Sé

At the corner of Praça XV de Novembro on Rua Primeiro de Março, you'll find the **Igreja de Nossa Senhora do Carmo da Antigá Sé** (Mon–Fri 9am–5pm), which served, until 1980, as Rio's cathedral. Construction started in 1749 and, to all intents and purposes, continued right into the twentieth century as structural collapse and financial difficulties prompted several restorations and delays: the present tower was built in 1905 by the Italian architect **Rebecchi**. Inside, the high altar is detailed in silver and boasts a beautiful painting by Antônio Parreires, which represents Nossa Senhora do Carmo seated amongst the clouds and surrounded by the sainted founders of the Carmelite Order. Below, in the **crypt**, are the supposed mortal remains of **Pedro Alvares Cabral**, Portuguese discoverer of Brazil, though this seems unlikely as he was almost certainly laid to rest in Santarém in Portugal. A small **archeological museum** is open for guided visits only (Tues–Fri noon–3pm; free).

The attached early seventeenth-century **Convento do Carmo** (Mon–Fri 10am–5pm) was the first Carmelite convent to be built in Rio. Later used as a royal residence (after 1808 the Dowager Queen, Dona Maria I, lived here), the building has since been altered several times, and now houses part of the Universidade Cândido Mendes.

Igreja de Ordem Terceira do Monte do Carmo

The late eighteenth-century **Igreja de Ordem Terceira do Monte do Carmo** (Mon–Fri 8am–4pm, Sat 8am–noon), located next to the Igreja de Nossa Senhora do Carmo da Antigá Sé, contains seven altars – each bearing an image symbolizing a moment from the Passion of Christ, from Calvary to the Crucifixion, sculpted by Pedro Luiz da Cunha. The high altar, beautifully worked in silver, is particularly striking. The church and adjacent convent are linked by a small public chapel, dedicated to Our Lady of the Cape of Good Hope, and decorated in *azulejos* tiling.

Igreja Santa Cruz dos Militares

Between Ruas do Ouvidor and do Rosario on Rua Primeiro de Março is the museum and church of **Santa Cruz dos Militares** (Mon–Fri 10am–3pm). Its name hints at its curious history; in 1628, a number of army officers organized the construction of the first church here on the site of an early fort. It was used for the funerals of serving officers until, in 1703, the Catholic Church attempted to take over control of the building. The proposal met stiff resistance and it was only in 1716 that the Fathers of the Church of São Sebastião, which had become severely dilapidated, succeeded in installing themselves in Santa Cruz. Sadly, they were no more successful in maintaining control of the church, and by 1760 it had been reduced to a state of ruin – only reversed when army officers again took control of reconstruction in 1780, completing the granite and marble building that survives today. The nave, with its stuccoed ceiling, has been skilfully decorated with plaster relief images from Portugal's imperial past. The two owners since reconciled, there's a small **museum** on the ground floor with a collection of military and religious relics.

Centro Cultural de Correios

The **Centro Cultural de Correios** (Tues–Sun noon–7pm; free; ℡21/2253 1580, ⓦwww.correios.com.br/institucional – follow links to 'ações culturais') is located a block north of (and behind) the Igreja Santa Cruz at no. 20 Rua Visconde de Itaborai. An excellent exhibition space on three floors with a theatre attached, variety is key here with past exhibitions covering cartoons, iron sculpture and Tennessee Williams.

Centro Cultural Banco do Brasil

A block northwards again as you approach the Candelària church is the large Centro Cultural Banco do Brasil (Tues–Sun 10am–9pm; ℡21/3808-2020, ⓦwww.bb.com.br/cultura), one of Rio's most dynamic arts centres (see p.205). It puts on a varied, and often free, programme of exhibitions, as well as films, music and plays – abstract art, a human rights film festival and classical recitals have all featured. Situated in the impressive former headquarters of the Banco do Brasil and built in 1880, the building has a round domed hall with several exhibition rooms, a cinema, two theatres, a ground floor restaurant and third floor tearoom – the latter is perfect to wind down away from the noisy urban sprawl.

Casa França Brasil

Formerly the **Alfândega Antiga** (old Customs House), this splendid building was constructed in 1820 in Neoclassical style by the French architect Grandjean de Montigny, but now serves as the Casa França Brasil (℡21/2253-5366, ⓦwww .fcfb.rj.gov.br), a cultural centre aimed at extending links between the two nations, and which contains exhibition spaces and a restaurant occupying part of the rear of the building (under renovation and closed at the time of writing). It's been home to a bizarre array of organizations in the past: the English merchants who arrived after the opening of the port to free trade in 1808; the Mauá Gas Company; the Brazilian Society for the Protection of Animals; and the Socialist organizers of Rio's 1918 general strike. The centre's situated next to the Centro Cultural Banco do Brasil across Rua Visconde de Itaborai.

Espaço Cultural da Marinha and Ilha Fiscal

A long dockside building once used as the port's main customs point, the **Espaço Cultural da Marinha** (Tues–Sun noon–5pm; free; ℡21/2101-0886, ⓦwww.sdm.mar.mil.br;) today houses an exhibition hall aimed primarily at naval enthusiasts, including numerous small models of boats and one life-size reconstruction. Of greater interest is a Brazilian naval submarine docked here – you can walk right through it and really get a feel of life onboard. Located

▲ Ilha Fiscal

on the seashore directly across from the Casa França Brasil (though crossing roads here can prove problematic), the **Espaço Cultural** is also reached from Praça XV by walking along the bayside Avenida Alfredo Agache. Two boat excursions are available from here, both taking in Ilha Fiscal (see box, p.58).

Candelária and north to São Bento

Standing imposing at the eastern end of Avenida Presidente Vargas is the **Igreja de Nossa Senhora da Candelária**, the largest of Rio's older places of worship. Hemmed in by buildings until 1943, it was appointed its own space when the giant road was constructed, opening up new vistas to the west of the city. Avenida Rio Branco traverses Presidente Vargas here, as well as Rua Uruguaiana a block further west. North towards Praça Mauá and the port area of Gamboa (see p.65), the hilltop **Igreja e Mosteiro de São Bento** is Rio's most opulently decorated church and a must-see. Even better views of the city are to be had from another small hill, however – the **Morro de Conceiçao** on the western side of Avenida Rio Branco in the historic *bairro* of **Saúde**. At the hill's southern base by the quaint church and square of Santa Rita, a couple of eating and drinking options make good early evening spots for relaxing and people-watching.

Igreja de Nossa Senhora da Candelária

The **Igreja de Nossa Senhora da Candelária** (Mon–Fri 7.30am–4pm, Sat 8am–noon & Sun 9am–1pm), located on Praça Pio X, resembles a traditional European cathedral. A closer look, however, reveals an interesting combination of Baroque and Renaissance features – variations resulting from financial

Boat trips from Centro

Boat trips are available from the docks by the Espaço Cultural da Marinha on recon-structed **old colonial vessels**, and **ferries** to the Ilha da Paquetá operate from the ferry terminal by Praça XV.

Ilha Fiscal

Connected by a series of lengthy causeways that lead from the mainland and the Ilha das Cobras, tiny **Ilha Fiscal** (Thurs–Sun noon–5.30pm) has as its sole occupant a wonderful green-coloured castle-like structure, built in an ornate Gothic-Moorish style and surrounded by swaying palm trees. It was the venue for the last grand Imperial ball, just days before the collapse of the monarchy in November 1889. Inside, there is a brief history of the island, an unremarkable naval exhibition and a bizarre display on the Brazilian Antarctic station, complete with synthetic snow machine.

The boat is the easiest way to get there (Thurs–Sun 1pm, 2.30pm and 4pm; R$8; 15min); to ensure a place, arrive at the **Espaço Cultural da Marinha** (see p.56) at least an hour in advance. Given that the best thing about Ilha Fiscal is the view of the castle, you may choose to take the second boat cruise from the same location (departs Thurs-Sun 1pm and 3pm; R$12), which sails around the mouth of the bay without mooring.

Ilha de Paquetá

Ilha de Paquetá is an island of one square kilometre in the north of Guanabara Bay, an easy and pleasant day-trip that is very popular with *Cariocas* at weekends. It was first occupied by the Portuguese in 1565 and later became a favourite resort of Dom João VI, who had the São Roque chapel built here in 1810. About 2000 people live here, although the island is almost entirely dediacted to tourism and at weekends that number is significantly multiplied by visitors from the city. They come for the tranquil-lity – the only motor vehicle allowed is an ambulance – and for the beaches, which, sadly, are now heavily polluted. Still, its colonial-style buildings retain a certain shabby charm – and the trip is an attraction in itself, given the views of the bay: if possible, time your return to catch the sunset over the city as you sail back. Weekdays are best if you want to avoid the crowds, or come in August for the wildly celebrated **Festival de São Roque**.

The best way to get around Ilha de Paquetá is by bike, hundreds of which are available to rent very cheaply (R$15 per day) from alongside the ferry terminal; there are also horse-drawn carts (*charrete*). When you disembark, head along the road past the Yacht Club and you'll soon reach the first beaches: Praia da Ribeira and Praia dos Frades. Praia da Guarda, a little further, has the added attraction of the *Lido* restau-rant and the **Parque Duque de Mattos**, with panoramic views from the top of the Morro da Cruz.

Regular ferries for Paquetá leave from near Centro's Praça XV de Novembro, adjacent to the Niterói boat (R$5 on weekdays, R$7 at weekends; 70min). Organized **day boat tours** are a more enjoyable and atmospheric option (10am; alternate Sundays). Most have a bar and live *chorinho* or samba music on board, and you're allowed two to three hours on the island. If you want to stay over, there are a few pleasant small hotels, the cheapest being the *Pousada Sao Roque* (☏21/3397-0317). More expensive, but with air-conditioning, are the *Lido*, Praia José Bonifácio 59 (☏21/3397-0377) and the large *Hotel Palace de Paquetá* (☏21/3397-0464). There's a tourist information office close to the ferry landing.

difficulties that delayed the completion of the building for more than a century after its foundation in 1775. Inside, the altars, walls and supporting columns are sculpted from variously coloured marble, while the eight pictures in the dome represent the three theological virtues (Faith, Hope and Charity), the cardinal virtues (Prudence, Justice, Strength and Temperance) and the Virgin Mary – all the late nineteenth-century work of the Brazilian artist João Zeferino da Costa. There's more grand decoration in the two pulpits, luxuriously worked in bronze and supported by large white angels sculpted in marble.

Just outside the church's main entrance you'll find the outlines of eight figures on the ground – all different – together with a wooden cross with eight names. These were the street children killed outside the Candelária by scores of off-duty Rio policemen on July 23 1993 – an event which focused international attention on Rio's police force and social injustice in Brazil. Many other children witnessed the attack or were injured; one survivor, Sandro Rosa do Nascimento, later became infamous as the hostage-taker on a city bus in Jardim Botânico in 2000, dramatized in the award-winning documentary film, *Ônibus 174* (see p.264). The Candelária continues to provide food and medical attention for street chidren in Rio.

Igreja e Mosteiro de São Bento

Heading north from the Candelária, on Rua Primeiro de Março, the extravagant **Igreja e Mosteiro de São Bento** (daily 7am–6pm; guided visits by university students 9am–4pm; also open for Mass with Gregorian chant Sun 10am) is accessed by means of the Ladeira de São Bento steps or by a narrow road from Rua Dom Gerardo. Within the *bairro* of Saúde, the monastery commands an impressive position amidst modern urban Rio, overlooking the Ilha das Cobras. It was founded by Benedictine monks who arrived in Rio in 1586 by way of Bahia; building started in 1633 and was completed nine years later. The facade displays a pleasing architectural simplicity, its twin towers culminating in pyramid-shaped spires, while the interior is richly adorned in gold. Images of saints decorate the altars, and there are statues representing various popes and bishops, work executed by the deft hand of Mestre Valentim (see p.73). Panels and paintings from the late seventeenth century, valuable examples of colonial art, are also worth looking out for.

▲ Igreja e Mosteiro de São Bento

Largo de Santa Rita

West along Rua Dom Gerardo from the monastery leads you to the northern end of Avenida Rio Branco, on the west side of which (off Rua Marechal Floriano) is **Largo de Santa Rita** and its church, the **Igreja da Santa Rita** (Mon–Sun 8–11.30am & 2.30–5pm). Built on land previously used as a burial ground for slaves, the structure dates from 1721 – its bell tower tucked to one side gives it a lopsided look. It's not one of Rio's more attractive churches, but the interior stonework is a fine example of Rococo style and is magnificently decorated with a series of painted panels, three on the high altar and eight on the ceiling, which depict scenes from the life of Santa Rita.

Opposite the church at Rua Miguel Couto, refreshments are to be found at the **Triângulo de Sardinhas** (Sardines Triangle), a group of bars with outside tables that have been serving beer and breaded, fried sardines to hundreds of after-work customers for decades. If you can, visit on Thursday or Friday afternoons from 4pm when there's a great atmosphere.

Morro de Conceição

At the top of Rua Miguel Couto off Rua Acre, an interesting diversion on foot is up a small hill, the **Morro de Conceição**. The hill's main claim to fame is its occupation by five thousand French troops led by Duguay-Trouin in the French invasion of Rio in 1711. The French were really more interested in the lucrative gold trade from Minas Gerais than in the city, however, and to avoid further pillaging a ransom was provided to ensure their swift departure.

Today, a ten-minute stroll to Praça Major Valo at the hill's summit reveals great views of the city, as well as the **Fortaleza de Nossa Senhora da Conceição**; constructed immediately after the French invasion in order to deter future pretenders, it remains Brazilian army property. The hill was a residential area from 1560, around the time of the city's foundation and long before the French disturbance. A shrine to Nossa Senhora da Conceição was in place from 1590, and the hill took its name at that point. Later, the area became known for its samba music on account of resident sambistas Donga and João de Prazeres – a lively street samba is still held on Monday evenings at Pedra da Sal on the Gamboa side of the hill (see p.66). Still predominantly residential, a right turn at the praça brings you down Ladeira João Homem, full of beautiful if slightly dilapidated old colonial houses and children playing in the street. The area is reasonably secure on account of the army's presence, but the usual precautions still apply.

Uruguaiana to Saara and Praça Tiradentes

A lively shopping street with plenty of street trading, Rua Uruguaiana crosses Avenida Presidente Vargas and runs south to the Largo da Carioca (see p.48). There are a number of interesting sights here and throughout the streets westwards; the **Igreja Nossa Senhora de Rosário e São Benedito** has a small museum relating to slavery and Afro-Brasilian religion, the **Museu do Negro**, while the nearby **Igreja de São Francisco de Paula** (located on the largo of the same name) has hosted several significant moments in Brazil's history and is decorated lavishly. The wonderful historic library **Real Gabinete Português de Leitura** is a highlight among Rio's buildings due to its incredibly ornate interior, and bordering the *bairro* of Lapa to the south, **Praça Tiradentes** is another of the main city squares, holding two of the city's theatres. The bustling market area of **Saara** lies in the streets north of Praça Tiradentes – easily the best place in Rio for shopping bargains and Carnaval fancy dress.

Igreja de Nossa Senhora do Rosário e São Benedito dos Homens Pretos

At Rua Uruguaiana 77, at the junction with Rua Rosário, is the **Igreja de Nossa Senhora do Rosário e São Benedito dos Homens Pretos**. Though there was a religious structure here from 1640, the present church dates from the 1730s and was built by slaves as a place of worship and burial chamber (it was partially rebuilt after a fire in 1967). Though clearly in need of refurbishment, the church's simplicity stands in stark contrast to the city's other Catholic churches and is the best place to see Mass – for the working masses. At the northwestern side of the building is the entrance to the **Museu do Negro** (9am–noon and 1–4pm Mon–Fri; donation). If you're expecting a comprehensive coverage of slavery and the Afro-Brazilian experience then you'll be sorely disappointed, but amidst its sparse and clearly underfunded collection it does have one or two interesting items relating to the church's role in ending slavery, and Afro-Brazilian cults that have been incorporated into Catholic worship. The story of **Zumbi dos Palmares** – an eighteenth-century rebel slave turned 'slave to the world' who battled for emancipation – is briefly covered here. His name is given to a national holiday on November 20 when day-long masses and skits are held in the church below (there's a monument to Zumbi close to the Sambódromo). There is also a cult wall in homage to **Princesa Anastácia**, a legendary slave depicted with a manacle and gag to whom messages are offered to appeal for freedom from life's constraints.

Igreja de São Francisco de Paula

Just west of Uruguaiana and two blocks north of Rua da Carioca you'll find the **Largo de São Francisco de Paula**, whose church, the **Igreja de São Francisco de Paula** (Mon–Fri 9am–1pm), has played a significant role in Brazilian history. Behind the monumental carved wooden entrance door, the *Tê Deum* was sung in 1816 to celebrate the country's promotion from colony to kingdom, and in 1831, the Mass celebrating the "swearing-in" of the Brazilian Constitution was performed here. More tangibly, the chapel of **Nossa Senhora da Vitória**, on the right as you enter, was dedicated by Pope Pius X to the victory of the Christian forces over the Turkish in the naval battle of Lepanto in 1571. The meticulous decoration is attributed to Mestre Valentim (see p.73), who spent thirty years working on the chapel, while the paintings on the walls were created by a slave who called himself Manoel da Cunha. With the consent of his owner, Manoel travelled to Europe as assistant to the artist João de Souza, and returned to buy his freedom with money earned from the sale of his artwork.

Real Gabinete Português de Leitura

Two blocks from the Largo de São Francisco de Paula and just around the corner from Praça Tiradentes is the astonishing royal reading room **Real Gabinete Português de Leitura** (Mon–Fri 9am–6pm; ☏21/2221-3138,

Ⓦ www.realgabinete.com.br), a library dedicated to Portugal and Portuguese literature and one of the most beautiful buildings in Rio. It was completed in 1887 and has a magnificently ornate facade, styled after fifteenth-century Portuguese architecture. The intricate interior is lit by a red, white and blue stained-glass skylight and contains many of the library's 350,000 mostly leather-bound volumes. Amongst the rarest is the 1572 first edition of *Os Lusíados*, the Portuguese national epic poem by Luis de Camões based on Vasco da Gama's voyage of exploration – which is occasionally on view. Many of the other texts relate to the independence years, when the new library encouraged the spread of knowledge amongst young people in the new Brazil.

Praça Tiradentes and around

Three blocks west of Largo da Carioca and just north of Lapa is **Praça Tiradentes**, named after Joaquim da Silva Xavier, known as Tiradentes ("pull-teeth"), a dentist. Silva Xavier was also leader of the so-called **Minas Conspiracy** of 1789, a plot hatched in the state of Minas Gerais to overthrow the Portuguese regime (see p.52). Regardless of Tiradentes's significance, however, it is Dom Pedro I who takes centre stage at the square, on horseback with Amerindian statues in awe. The Art Deco **Teatro Carlos Gomes** (see p.205) at the southern end of the square puts on popular plays, while the **Teatro João Caetano** (see p.205), named after actor João Caetano dos Santos who based his drama company in the theatre from 1840, is situated on its northern side. Caetano also notches up a bust that stands in the square, a reward for producing shows starring such theatrical luminaries as Sarah Bernhardt. In the second-floor hall of the theatre hang two large panels painted in 1930 by Cavalcanti, which explore the themes of Carnaval and popular religion in the strong tropical colours typical of his work. The original theatre on this site, the Teatro Real, erected in 1813, had a much more political history: it was here in 1821 that Dom João VI swore obedience to the Constitution promulgated in Lisbon after the Porto Revolution. Three years later, at the end of the ceremony proclaiming Dom Pedro I Emperor of Brazil, a fire razed the building to the ground.

Between the **Teatro João Caetano** and **Real Gabinete** library is the **Centro Cultural Carioca** (or CCC; see p.196), a daytime (and fairly average) restaurant which transforms into a superb venue for dancing and live music at night. The historic building was Rio's most exclusive women's clothes store in 1900, and was the first in Brazil to introduce mannequins – causing quite a stir amongst passing pedestrians.

Saara market

The streets running from Praça Tiradentes all the way up to Avenida Presidente Vargas, the Campo de Santana and eastwards towards Uruguaiana are known as **Saara**, and contain the most interesting concentration of shops in Rio. Traditionally the cheapest shopping area, it was peopled by Jewish and Arab merchants who moved here after a ban prohibiting their residence within the city limits was lifted in the eighteenth century. A new wave of Arab business owners – along with, most recently, Chinese and Koreans – has now moved in. The narrow streets are lined with stores selling anything from trinkets to basic beachware, handicraft items and expensive jewellery; the throngs of traders and folk musicians always make it a lively place to visit. Particularly good buys include sports equipment, musical instruments and CDs. A number of food-stalls selling some of the best Lebanese *kibe* and *esfihas* (lamb or vegetable-based savoury snacks) in town can be found along Rua Senhor.

Campo de Santana and around

Until the beginning of the eighteenth century the western end of Centro was outside the city limits, which extended only as far as Rua Uruguaiana. Its sandy and swampy soils made it unsuitable for cultivation, and the only building here was the chapel of St Domingo, situated in the area now covered by the Presidente Vargas asphalt and used by the Fraternity of St Anne to celebrate the festivals of their patron saint – hence the name, Campo de Santana ("field of St Anne").

By the end of the eighteenth century the city had spread to surround the Campo de Santana, and in 1811 a barracks was built to house the Second Regiment of the Line, who used the square as a parade ground. It was here that Dom Pedro I proclaimed Brazil's independence from the Portuguese Crown in 1822, and from 1889 the lower half of the square became known as **Praça da República**. At the start of the twentieth century, the square was landscaped in the English garden style, and today it's a pleasant place for a walk, with lots of trees and small lakes ruled by swans. Peacocks can often be seen strutting around, and allegedly, monkeys have been spotted in the trees. In the late afternoon, other small, furry rodents emerge to scuttle about in the gloom – agoutis, happily, not rats. The **Parque Júlio Furtado** lies in the centre of the Campo, surrounding a statue of Benjamin Constant, the military man credited with having overthrown the monarchy in 1889.

On the southern side of the Campo de Santana is the striking bright-red facade of the **Corpo de Bombeiros** (fire station), completed in 1903 by architect **Souza Aguiar**. Radical for its time, it made use of the abundance of new metals mined in Brazil, like tin and iron, to build two front turrets – diverging from traditional Neoclassical style. You can normally have a quick look at the huge courtyard behind – it's as red as it is impressive, and pleasing to see an effective building still in good use.

On the eastern side of the Campo at the edge of the Saara bazaar, is the attractive early nineteenth-century **Igreja de São Jorge**. If you're lucky enough to be in town on Saint George's day (April 23), now a Rio state holiday, huge masses and processions take place here from 5am and run throughout the day. Saint George has many followers in Rio, particularly as he is linked in Afro-Brazilian *Candomblé* worship to *Ogum*, the orisha (deity) from Yoruban areas of the Niger delta in West Africa, also represented by the colour red, of iron.

The first president of the new republic, **Deodoro de Fonseca**, lived at no. 197 Praça da República, a house now rudely neighboured by Avenida Presidente Vargas at the Campo's western edge. Despite the polluted and harried location, it has nonetheless been made into a small **museum** (Tues–Fri, 10am–5pm; free), containing little more than a bust of the man himself, his medals and a couple of period paintings. The only exhibit really of interest is an original newspaper from November 16, 1889, with the headline in outdated Portuguese, "Deodoro da Fonseca proclamos hontem a República!" accompanied by an artist's impression of scenes of street jubilation.

Next door the late nineteenth-century Neoclassical **Arquivo Nacional** (Mon–Fri 8.30am–6pm; ⓦ www.arquivonacional.gov.br) was originally built as the central bank of Brazil, but now holds millions of documents, photos, maps and discs, mostly available on microfiche. Among documents of particular importance are the archives brought from Portugal by Dom João in 1808, and the original Brazilian Constitution manuscript from 1824. The building also hosts interesting cultural **exhibitions** – from Brazilian football to academic topics.

Avenida Presidente Vargas

The giant scar running through Centro and dominating western Rio, **Avenida Presidente Vargas** began construction in 1941 with understandable opposition from the owners of the houses and businesses that were demolished in its path – not to mention clerical dissent at the destruction of a number of churches. It also carved through the northern section of the Campo de Santana, effectively halving Centro's largest park. The avenue was inaugurated with a military parade in 1944, watched by Vargas himself in the year before he was deposed by a quiet coup. The rapid expansion of *favelas* close to Centro followed – communities such as **Providência**, in clear view on the hill to the north (see p.66) – as large numbers of working people were forced from their homes in the centre of the city. Today it's Rio's broadest avenue, running east to west for almost three kilometres and comprising at its widest fourteen lanes of traffic.

Around Central do Brasil

The **Dom Pedro II train station** – known more commonly as Central do Brasil and made famous by Walter Salles' 1997 film *Central Station* – is an unmistakeable landmark, its tower rising 110m into the sky and supporting clock faces measuring 7.5m by 5.5m, all linked to a central winding mechanism. It's worth popping in to have a quick look around the station's mostly Art Deco interior – and if you're in town on December 4, trains loaded with samba musicians and revellers leave for the suburbs (see p.222). In front of the station is the Praça Duque de Caxias and the **Panteão Nacional**, on top of which stands the equestrian statue of the Duque de Caxias, military patron and general in the Paraguayan War – his remains lie below in the Pantheon.

The area **behind Central** is made up of seedy hotels and cheap market stores where the city's tradesmen purchase their wares. While many of the streets are constructed of interesting (and crumbling) old colonial houses, this is an unpredictable area and should be avoided unless you're accompanied by a local. The one exception is to join the very loyal clientele of strangely fashionable *Sentaí* Portuguese seafood restaurant for lunch (see p.180) – though you'll probably want to take a taxi. Under no circumstances walk along Rua Bento Ribeiro, passing through the tunnel under Providência *favela* from Central do Brasil to reach the Cidade do Samba and Gamboa (see p.65).

Palácio do Itamaraty and the Museu Histórico e Diplomático do Itamaraty

A block east of the station, at Av. Marechal Floriano 196, the **Palácio do Itamaraty** (Mon, Wed & Fri; guided visits only 2pm, 3pm & 4pm; free; long trousers needed for men) is one of Rio's best examples of Neoclassical architecture. Completed in 1853 as the pied-à-terre of the great landowner Baron of Itamaraty, it was purchased by the government and became home to a number of the republic's presidents before becoming the seat of the Ministry of Foreign Relations. Although the ministry was moved to Brasilia in 1970, Brazil's foreign service is still known as Itamaraty. A large section of the building has been painstakingly restored with period furnishings and paintings to show how the upper classes lived in the nineteenth century, and the tour, though in Portuguese only, provides a real sense of the lifestyles of Brazil's nobility. Amazingly, you're accompanied by a hard-hat-wearing security guard throughout the visit.

The *palácio* now also houses the **Museu Histórico e Diplomático do Itamaraty**, which contains a permanent exhibition (Portuguese only) on Brazilian diplomacy, with a much more detailed take than either the Museu Histórico Nacional or the Museu Naval. Exhibits cover the devastating Paraguayan War of the 1860s, and the standoff between Brazil and Great Britain in 1845 after Britain permitted the imprisonment of foreign slave traders. Documents, books and maps are primarily of interest to serious researchers (archives open by appointment Mon–Fri 1–5pm; ☎21/2253-7691).

Cidade Nova and the Sambódromo

Four blocks west from Central do Brasil is the **Monumento a Zumbi Dos Palmares**, an ornate bronze sculpture in the style of West African kingdoms, commemorating the rebel slave whose name is given to a national holiday on November 20 (see p.61).

The **Sambódromo**, or to give it its full name, the Sambódromo da Marquês de Sapucaí, lies directly south of the monument, rightly famous for its role during the five festive nights of Rio's **Carnaval** each February. Designed by famous Brazilian architect **Oscar Neimeyer** and inaugurated in 1984, it is 700 metres in length with a capacity of 88,000 people. For most of the year, this concrete monument to theatre and fantasy is redundant, but in the run-up to the main event samba schools practise here at *ensaios*, always with a good crowd of spectators (see p.215).

The area of modern office buildings beyond the Sambódromo and around *metrô* station Praça Onze (named after a square long since decimated by Av. Presidente Vargas) is called **Cidade Nova**. A predominantly poor housing area surrounding the city's administrative offices, it was a red-light district until the 1970s, but recent developments including massive office space, car parks and a few office-oriented lunch-spots, have changed its face for good. The one building of interest to those serious about modern architecture belongs to Petrobras, at Rua Ulysses Guimarães 565. Completed in 2007, it has already won awards for its green credentials. Recycled materials were used throughout its construction; rain accounts for forty percent of its water consumption; natural light is maximized by a central glass-covered square; and, most amazingly, natural air conditioning drives hot air currents up to the roof. Visits are allowed to the foyer only. Outside of office hours the area is deserted and visiting is not recommended.

Gamboa

Adjoining Centro to the north is **Gamboa**, traditionally a deprived port area, but also one of the oldest parts of Rio and home to its first *favela*, **Providência** (see p.66). Since the turn of the millennium the area has been

Providência: the first *favela*

High above Rio's port, Central do Brasil train station and the Cidade do Samba, the incredible views across the city to Corcovado are, for the moment at least, exclusive to the residents of the **Morro da Providência** – Brazil's first *favela*.

A few wealthy homes, slave dwellings and a chapel existed on the hill from as early as the seventeenth century; but it was the arrival of thousands of soldiers by boat in 1897 which first populated the community you see today. Fresh from the Canudos War in the state of Bahia (1896–7) – a vicious crushing of a 10,000-strong religious sect which had declared itself an independent republic – the soldiers camped here, directly above the Brazilian military headquarters, and waited in vain to be given land rights promised to them in return for their services in battle. They identified themselves as soldiers of the Morro da Favela – where their campground at Canudos had been located.

The veterans set up home at their Favela do Morro da Providência, and were joined in the early twentieth century by people forced from their homes during the housing clearances that made way for roads like Avenida Presidente Vargas. **Samba** was born in these circumstances, and the elderly of Providência still remember their community's significant role in the musical genre's early development.

Like many other *favelas* in Rio, Providência today lurches from manipulation by *traficantes* (drugs gangs), to politicians and police, with occasional all-out war flaring up. Ironically considering the history, in recent years the Brazilian army has been called in, raising the military game on both sides with many more innocents conse-quently killed by stray bullets. In 2008 one outrage made international news: the army's kidnapping and effective murder of four Providência boys when they gave them to rival *traficantes* in another *favela* – the results were predictably gruesome. Actions like these do nothing for residents' trust in the state, instead preferring churches, NGOs – and of course *traficantes* – for their advancement.

That said, the government's *favela bairro* project (see p.255) attempted to create a "living museum" in Providência in 2002, with tourist walking routes and visits to elderly sambistas – though they were soon abandoned due to violence. It is hoped that further revitalisation of the port (such as the Cidade do Samba) will aid the search for security – it just may not be any time soon. To understand more about Rio's *favelas*, watch the excellent documentary film (with English subtitles) **Notícias de Uma Guerra Particular** (*News from a Secret War*).

going through a period of revitalisation, and alongside the refurbished docking points for cruise ships, some of the huge quayside warehouses are now used as spaces for theatre productions and exhibitions. Leading the development is the enormous **Cidade do Samba**, an area – open to the public – for Rio's numerous samba schools to build their floats for Carnaval. Nearby, the old atmospheric **Cemitério dos Ingleses** points to Great Britain's significant role in the story of Brazil's development. Despite such regeneration, Gamboa still has a reputation for being dangerous – it's best to visit all the sights by taxi.

Closer to **Praça Mauá** (and officially in the Saúde *bairro*), seedy strip clubs are mostly the order of the day – though the area around Rua Sacadura Cabral is widely tipped to be the "new Lapa", with two exciting venues already open: a huge gay club, *The Week*, and *Trapiche de Gamboa*, a samba spot for the affluent artsy crowd (see p.197). A further event, and little known to anyone except *Carioca* samba fanatics, is the Monday evening street samba at **Pedra de Sal** at the northern foot of the Morro de Conceição (see p.60). Located just south of Rua Sacadura Cabral at the end of Rua da Prainha, it's a wonderful event in a small square used as a slave disembarkation point centuries ago.

Cidade do Samba

The most important project in Rio's cultural and touristic development in the past ten years has been the Cidade do Samba (Tues–Sat 10am–5pm; R$10; closed immediately after Carnaval for up to one month), located on Rua Rivadávia Correia. It's a vast complex where Rio's fourteen top samba schools practise and make their floats for Carnaval. The main pavilion was officially opened in 2006, and with schools gradually moving their construction operations, 2009 Carnaval was the first to see almost all floats manufactured here. The development's location next to Providência *favela* and within the city's rundown port area is telling, both due to the *favela's* important influence in samba's history and as a positive sign that authorities are genuinely interested in urban rejuvenation. New jobs have been created here, and it provides contact between samba schools from the diverse communities of Zona Norte where most of the bands' homes are (see p.215).

An hour's informal wander around here allows you to tour the giant central courtyard surrounded by each school's construction warehouse. Huge floats and characters from past Carnavals are scattered throughout, and you get the chance to see construction workers in action – busier and more intensive as Carnaval approaches. A long walkway around the complex is raised about forty feet off the ground, providing perspective on the vastness of some of the floats. There is also a souvenir shop, a bar/café, and a basic (for staff, though open to all) *por kilo* restaurant. On Thursday nights, a show is put on aimed at tourists unable to stay for Carnaval; which especially attracts visitors from cruise ships and large hotels (see p.196).

Cemitério dos Ingleses

Right alongside the Cidade do Samba and surrounded on three sides by Providência *favela* is the strangely beautiful and well-kept **Cemitério dos Ingleses**, or English Cemetery (Rua Barão da Gamboa 181, Mon–Fri 8am–4pm, Sat & Sun 8am–12.30pm), the oldest Protestant burial site in the country. In 1809 the British community was given permission to establish a cemetery and Anglican church in Rio – essential if English merchants were to be attracted to the newly independent Brazil. At least half the deceased were Scots (or of Scottish origin), with many gravestones bearing Celtic crosses. The inscriptions on many of the stones make poignant reading, recalling the days when early death was almost expected. Still in use today, the cemetery is dramatically set in a lower-hillside location with the *favela* towering around it – the contrast is astonishing. Given the setting, it is best to visit when the Cidade do Samba is open as taxis can be called from there.

Lapa, Santa Teresa and the Corcovado

Bohemian **Lapa** and artistic **Santa Teresa** share more than just their reputation as hotbeds of Brazilian music and art. The monumental Roman-style aquaduct, the **Arcos da Lapa**, which once chanelled water from the hills right into the heart of the city, now carries trams (known as *bondes*) up the hill to leafy Santa Teresa. Still towering overhead, the arches signify your arrival in this the liveliest night-district of Rio. An exciting inner-city red-light district, Lapa is certainly rough-around-the-edges, but comes to life with samba clubs, numerous bars and enormous street parties each and every weekend. Its past grandeur is still reflected in the faded elegance of its **Passeio Público** park, however, and it's worth having a look around the whole *bairro* in daylight.

Lapa's designation as the "Montmartre of the Tropics" extends to Santa Teresa on account of the latter's vibrant restaurants, museums, art shops and galleries, not to mention its beautiful and diverse nineteenth-century **architecture** – contrasting Art Deco, Art Nouveau, Neoclassical and Gothic styles are all visible on its streets. An excellent respite from the steamy hubbub of Rio's main thoroughfares, "Santa", as it's affectionately known, is Rio's most strikingly mixed neighbourhood, where *favelas* are intermingled with upper-class and middle-class homes. In both Lapa and Santa Teresa this cross-section of Rio's inhabitants is part of the area's charm, but its busy atmosphere can make visitors especially easy targets for opportunistic thieves. At night Lapa is a prime spot for pickpockets, and quieter streets in Santa Teresa are also vulnerable in the daytime.

Santa Teresa's cobbled streets wind their way upwards and southwest-wards to the **Corcovado**, whose statue of Christ needs no introduction as the city's most famous landmark – a visit to Rio without making this tourist pilgrimage is nigh-on unthinkable. Many people arrive at Corcovado by train from **Cosmo Velho**, a hillside residential area adjoining Laranjeiras and Flamengo, which is also home to the **Museum of Naïve Art**.

Lapa and around

One of Rio's oldest *bairros*, the story of Lapa has always been one of changing fortunes. It was traditionally known as an "area of 'cabarets' and bawdy houses, the haunt of scoundrels, of gamblers, swashbucklers and inverteds, and the 'trottoir' of poor, fallen women", as Brasil Gerson wrote in his *História das ruas do Rio de Janeiro* – evidently a place to rush to, or avoid, depending upon your taste in entertainment. Until the mid-seventeenth century Lapa was a beach, known as the "Spanish Sands", but land reclamation and development assisted its slide into shabby grandeur. These days, while Lapa undoubtedly retains much of its bohemian past, a generation of smarter samba clubs and other music venues have opened up – places like *Rio Scenarium* and *Carioca da Gema* have a distinctly chic, Zona Sul, feel to them, while the area attracts people from across Rio's Zona Norte, too. Lapa is one of the few places in the city where *Cariocas* (residents of Rio de Janeiro) in all their diversity get out on the street together.

The Lapa scene

In the first half of the twentieth century, Lapa came into its own as an exciting meeting point for artists and musicians. **Carmen Miranda** was raised on Rua Joaquim Silva from the age of 6, while famous *Paulista* artist **Portinari** made Rua Teatônio Regadas his home in the 1930s. During the same decade major *choro* and samba musicans like Jacob do Bandolim and Assis Valente developed these new genres in this inspiring *bairro*. And with its seedy nightspots and reputation for tolerance, transvestites and Carnavalistas found themselves amongst friends – renowned *capoeirista*, drag queen and general agitator **Madame Satá** (immortalized in the film of the same name) lived and worked in Lapa.

From the 1940s and 1950s, Lapa experienced a downturn as cabarets and casinos were prohibited and Copacabana rapidly became the heart of Rio's nightlife scene. Firmly an area of disrepute, it took until the 1990s for Lapa to regenerate, blossoming into Rio's most important area for **nightlife and live music** (see p.195). Santa Teresa had an impact on Lapa's musical reinvention as legendary 1990s samba sessions in restaurants like *Sobrenatural* (see p.182) attracted such large crowds that the residential neighbourhood could no longer support them – moving down the hill was a natural progression. Bars like *Semente* opened up in Lapa in the late 1990s, attracting a more affluent and artsy crowd and nurturing musical talent that now performs across Lapa, Brazil and even overseas – artists like Teresa Christina, Tira Poeira, Garrafieira and guitar genius Yamandu Costa shouldn't be missed if you see them billed.

In the twenty-first century Lapa has changed significantly. Smart venues like *Carioca da Gema*, *Estrela da Lapa* and *Rio Scenarium* – some located in converted furniture stores – give a more exclusive air to Avenida Mem da Sá and Rua do Lavradio, west of the **arches**. A lively *feira* (see p.73) at the latter street on the first Saturday of each month now draws thousands. East of the arches around the Largo da Lapa and Rua Joaquim da Silva is where you'll find the liveliest street party on Friday nights, and the area also has numerous smaller packed bars.

All kinds of Brazilian sounds and fusions can be heard in Lapa, from samba to *forró*, from rock to the new craze, *funk carioca* – and although tourists are attracted here in increasing numbers, the clubs and bars remain largely filled by locals of all ages. If you feel uncomfortable visiting alone – or simply want company – contact **Rio Hiking** (see p.238), which regularly takes small groups bar-hopping. For more information on what's happening around Lapa, check ⊛www.lanalapa.com.br.

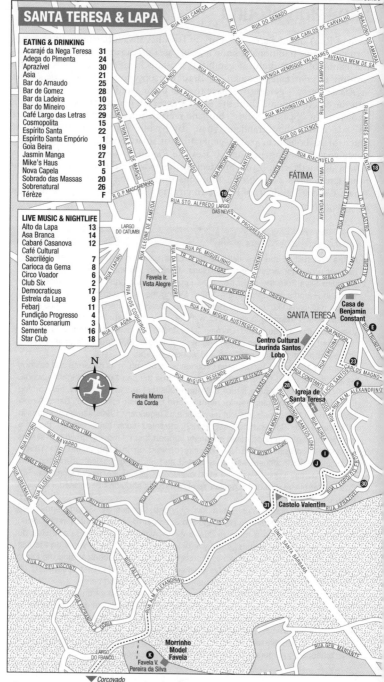

▼ Corcovado

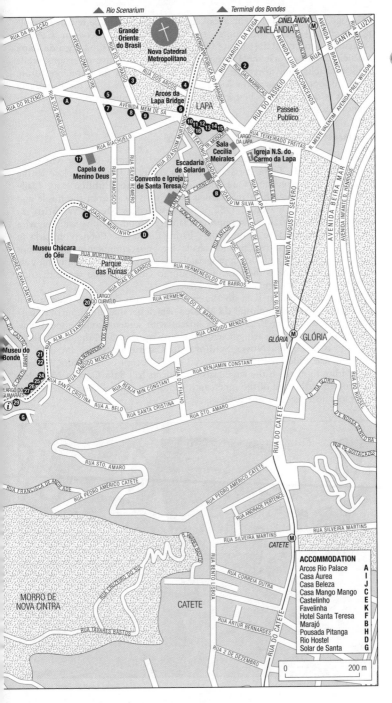

Rio Scenarium

Terminal dos Bondes

CINELÂNDIA

CINELÂNDIA

Grande Oriente do Brasil

Nova Catedral Metropolitano

Passeio Publico

Arcos da Lapa Bridge

LAPA

Sala Cecília Meirales

Igreja N.S. do Carmo da Lapa

Escadaria de Selarón

Convento e Igreja de Santa Teresa

Capela do Menino Deus

Museu Chácara do Céu

Parque das Ruínas

GLÓRIA

GLÓRIA

Museu do Bonde

CATETE

MORRO DE NOVA CINTRA

CATETE

ACCOMMODATION	
Arcos Rio Palace	A
Casa Áurea	I
Casa Beleza	J
Casa Mango Mango	C
Castelinho	E
Favelinha	K
Hotel Santa Teresa	F
Marajó	B
Pousada Pitanga	H
Rio Hostel	D
Solar de Santa	G

0   200 m

Though most visited at night, a look around Lapa in daytime reveals a couple of interesting sights and some striking architecture. Between Centro's Cinelândia district and the *bairro* of Glória just to the south, the **Largo da Lapa** and neighbouring park, the **Passeio Público**, are attractive diversions, while you'll probably want to see the giant arches, the **Arcos da Lapa**, both from below on foot and above on a *bonde* (tram). Close to the largo, the **Escadaria Selarón** is one of Lapa's best-known sights, an amazing work of mosaic art ascending a hillside stairway.

Around the Largo da Lapa

As it's dissected by four lanes of traffic, it's hard to know exactly where the historic **Largo da Lapa** starts and finishes. At its eastern edge, close to the Parque do Flamengo and Cinelândia, is the **Passeio Público** park (daily 7.30am–9pm), a beautifully maintained green oasis away from the hustle and bustle of the city. Opened in 1783, it was designed by **Mestre Valentim da Fonseca e Silva**, Brazil's most important late eighteenth-century sculptor, who here turned his hands to landscaping – basing the Passeio Público on parks in Paris and Lisbon. Its trees provide shade for busts commemorating famous figures from the city's history, appropriately including Mestre Valentim himself; a more recent fixture is the bust of Chiquinho Gonzaga, who wrote the first recorded samba for Carnaval – *Pelo Telefone*.

Opposite the park on Rua do Passeio you'll notice the grand Neoclassical facade of the **Escola Nacional da Música**, which became the home of Brazil's oldest music school in 1913 and still buzzes with students today; though it is not open to the public. Facing it across the busy main road on the other side of the largo is the **Igreja Nossa Senhora do Carmo da Lapa**, attractive yet unremarkable aside for its tower covered in nineteenth-century tiles. A block west within the largo is the large classical concert hall **Sala Cecília Meireles**, constructed at the end of the nineteenth century as a hotel and converted for use as a concert venue since 1965.

▲ Antiques stall, Feira Rio Antigo

Mestre Valentim da Fonseca e Silva

One of the most significant artists in colonial Rio was Valentim da Fonseca e Silva, better known as **Mestre Valentim**, who was responsible for some of the city's most impressive Baroque sculpture and design in the late eighteenth-century. Born to a Portuguese father and Afro-Brazilian mother, Mestre Valentim was one of few *mulattos* in the period who successfully navigated white prejudice – rising to be held in high esteem across Rio society. Working 100 years before the end of slavery in Brazil, *mulattos* at this time were not allowed to commission their own work and had to be directed by churches and government. Mestre Valentim's largest work was designing the **Passeio Público**, a park inspired by the courtyards of the European aristocracy. Elsewhere, his most famous pieces are to be found at the **Igreja de São Bento** (see p.59) and the **Igreja da Ordem Terceira de São Francisco** de Paula (see p.61), while his **Chafariz do Carmo** is a small structure located at the centre of Praça XV de Novembro (see p.53). Valentim is pictured in numerous period paintings – a key individual in Rio's slow move towards a less racially-divided society.

Walking one block uphill to the south from here leads you to Rua Joaquim Silva where a steep flight of steps officially called Rua Manuel Caneiro climbs upwards to Santa Teresa. This is where you'll find the **Escadaria Selarón** (Ⓦwww.selaron.net), a remarkable feat of art, vision and obsession by eccentric Chilean Selarón. The man himself can be found most days adding new tiles to his ascending mosaic in Brazilian colours, and he also has a small giftshop in his room halfway up – if you're lucky, he'll show you pictures of U2, Snoop Dog and a *Playboy* model posing nude (the latter, that is, not Snoop) on his steps.

The Arcos da Lapa and around

The Lapa arches – officially called the **Aqueduto da Carioca** and inaugurated in 1750 – are one of the trademark sights of Rio, given their longevity amidst all the surrounding development. Each Friday night, the area surrounding the arches hosts numerous musicians and makeshift bars as many thousands of people turn the surrounding streets into a giant party – the centre of the dynamic music scene across the *bairro*. But even in the daytime the arches are an imposing sight, illustrating the city's rich history. Access to fresh water had long been a problem for the city's eighteenth-century developers, and the solution, at vast expense, was to channel part of the Rio Carioca, via a new reservoir at the hill's summit, directly into the centre of the city. A by-product of the construction was the opening up of the new Santa Teresa hillside to residential development for the city's new elite. By the 1890s more advanced water engineering had made the aqueduct obsolete, and in 1896 it was converted to carry fashionable new trams up the hill; today the arches are all the more impressive when seen still supporting heavily laden trams.

At the arches northern end the cobbled Ladeira de Santa Teresa climbs upwards towards the Convento de Santa Teresa (see p.77), and in the daytime one or two private homes at the street's base sell paintings and henna tattoos from their front rooms, hoping to attract passing tourists. West of the arches, the main road Avenida Mem da Sá intersects with Rua do Lavradio, the location of the fantastic **Feira Rio Antigo** on the first Saturday of each month (10am–8pm), when it's closed to traffic and taken over by samba bands, antique-hunters and *Cariocas* out for a full day's party. Continuing along Rua do Lavradio you pass the Nova Catedral Metropolitano and eventually reach Praça Tiradentes, while Avenida Mem da Sá heads west out to the Sambódromo (see p.65).

▲ Street party, Arcos da Lapa

Fátima

Following Rua Riachuelo west from the Arcos da Lapa, the **bairro de Fátima** is a small and predominantly residential neighbourhood with a great street atmosphere from Thursday through to Sunday. Low-key bars, cafés and restaurants surround the few blocks around its central incline, Avenida Nossa Senhora de Fátima, which also plays host to a celebratory procession and festival in its namesake's honour each October 23 – worth the trip if you happen to be in town. A statue of Nossa Senhora is carried through the streets followed by hundreds of devotees, and left at a small shrine at the head of the Avenida. Fátima is named after a town in Portugal that was the lucky recipient of an apparition of the Virgin Mary in 1917.

Santa Teresa

Santa Teresa, a leafy *bairro* of labyrinthine, cobbled streets and steps (*ladeiras*), with stupendous vistas of the city and bay below, makes a refreshing contrast to the city centre. Clinging to the sides of two hills and stretching back from Lapa

2

Arte de Portas Abertas

Every July, around fifty Santa Teresa artists open their studios in an event called **Arte de Portas Abertas** (open door art), offering the public – over 25,000 people attended in 2008 – an opportunity to buy or simply look at their work, from painting to sculpture to house and furniture design. All the *bairro*'s main streets close in a carnivalesque atmosphere, with lots of live music, eating and drinking. As Santa Teresa has some of the city's most beautiful houses, visits can be an architecturally rewarding experience too. For details of participating artists, see ⓦ www.vivasanta .org.br, or pick up a flyer.

for 5km to Cosme Velho beneath the Christ statue, it's a slightly dishevelled residential area dominated by the early nineteenth-century mansions and walled gardens of a prosperous community that still enjoys something of a bohemian reputation. The cooler climate of the hills attracted the prosperous middle-and upper-classes, and became the meeting point for forward-thinking intellectuals, political activists, artists and musicians – the *bairro* remains an important artistic centre, with many artists choosing to live and work here.

Its attractions are enhanced by an absence of the kind of development that has turned parts of Rio into a cracked, concrete nightmare. In 1984, Santa Teresa was declared an area of "Protecão Ambiental", finally implementing the kind of preservative building restrictions that came far too late for some other parts of the city. Art Deco, Art Nouveau, Neoclassical and Gothic styles are preserved here in all their glory, a melting pot of architecture where each and every house is different. In the last ten years, foreigners have converted some of the properties into exclusive hotels, *pousadas* and restaurants, with property values soaring – a hotly debated topic in the bars of Santa Teresa.

The other striking feature of the *bairro* is its mix of social classes, with six significant *favelas* located within or surrounding the district. Some of the *favelas* originate from *quilombos*, communities of escaped slaves from the nineteenth century – but they've long since expanded through northeastern immigration to represent the full Brazilian racial brew. With drugs and violent crime on the increase – and new films highlighting Rio's reputation for social injustice – the late 1990s saw Santa Teresa start to instigate a more inclusive community approach, with more contact between the *favelas* and *asfalte* (city streets). *Favela* community leaders were for the first time invited to Santa Teresa's community meetings, and conversely, people from the *asfalte* began visiting and undertaking social projects in larger *favelas* like Morro das Prazeres.

Beyond the architecture and restaurants, Santa also has a few interesting sights, namely the art gallery **Museu Chácara do Céu** and its neighbouring **Parque das Ruínas**, atmospheric ruins with a breathtaking view. The **Museu do Bonde** (tram museum) is a good diversion, too, if you want to know more about the impact of trams on the city. There are also art shops dotted around the *bairro*, ideal places to buy original crafts. They're located both east and west of Largo do Guimarães, the best being **La Vereda** (open weekends and sporadically at other times). **Carnaval**, too, is a major draw; the biggest party is the *Bloco de Carmelites* at Largo das Neves (see p.219), named after the *bairro*'s founding convent order. Efforts to promote *favela* tourism here are still in their early days, but opportunities do exist to visit *favela* art project **Morrinho** (see p.79), and occasionally *favela* **Morro das Prazeres** (see p.79).

Getting to Santa Teresa

Most people take the tram to Santa Teresa, but regular **buses** exist too: #214 and #206 depart from the Central do Brasil train station and Castelo respectively, the latter passing through Largo da Carioca, and both travel through Rua Gomes Freire in Lapa (5am–10pm). A **combi van** service also runs from Largo do Machado via Laranjeiras to Santa's upper reaches, and at night there are combis from Lapa if you're staying there (all are around R$2). Alternatively, take the excellent **Santa Teresa Tour** (prices vary depending on group size; ℡2509 6875, ⓦwww.santateresatour.com.br) from Largo do Guimarães, which gives a good overview of the area's streets and history.

Taking the tram

Rio's last remaining electric trams, the **bondes** (pronounced "bonjis"), climb to Santa Teresa from Centro near Largo da Carioca (the terminal is behind the massive, modern and instantly recognizable Petrobrás building; either Carioca or Cinelândia *metrô* stations) – a bone-rattling trip that's highly recommended. Passing across the Arcos da Lapa, the trams haul their human load up and down the hill, past the Carmelite Convento de Santa Teresa to the area's de facto centre, **Largo do Guimarães**, and onwards to either Largo das Neves (labelled Paula Matos) or **Dois Irmãos**. Trams leave every thirty minutes between 6am and 9pm: the one for Dois Irmãos permits you to climb much higher and hence see more of Santa Teresa – though once in the *bairro* you can jump on and off them as you please.

The trams still serve their original purpose of transporting locals, and haven't yet, despite rumours of privatization, become a tourist service. The best times to ride are mid-morning and mid-afternoon when it's less crowded and, consequently, less chaotic. The views of Rio are excellent, but beware of thieves who occasionally jump aboard and attempt to relieve passengers of their possessions – if you're worried about safety, a special tram service, the **Bonde Turístico Especial**, runs for tourists on Saturdays at 10am (R$5), complete with tour guide – though you shouldn't generally have any problems. Waiting passengers stand in an impossibly long line for the size of tram, with many ending up standing up on the tram's sides; not the safest of positions when crossing the Lapa arches. The fare is just 60¢, which you pay at the station turnstile going up, and on board going down. When the tram reaches either terminus, you can choose to stay on (and pay again) to descend to any of Santa Teresa's excellent restaurants or bars.

Largo do Guimarães

Largo do Guimarães is the central "square" of Santa Teresa, a meeting of three roads and the point at which buses and trams all stop before continuing on their divergent routes either uphill 3km towards the Christ statue or on a level to Largo das Neves. The square is most animated at weekends and after-work, when neighbouring bars and restaurants often fill to bursting. The *Bar do Arnaudo* is a short walk east of the Largo, and the *Bar do Mineiro* the same distance west – both traditional meeting places of artists and intellectuals. In the centre of the square is Santa's small cinema (ⓦwww.cinesanta.com.br), which shows both commercial and arthouse films, and an information point. Just above the largo on the hill is the *Livraría e Café Largo das Letras* (Wed–Sat 2–10pm & Sun 2–8pm), a delightful community bookshop housed in an attractive mansion and a pleasant place for a coffee or cold drink.

On the other (northern) side of the square a short walk along Rua Carlos Brant, is the slightly dilapidated **Museu do Bonde** (daily 10am–4pm; free), worth a visit even if you're not especially interested in transport. The small and attractively displayed collection includes an old tram, photos and memorabilia documenting

the history of trams in Rio from their nineteenth-century introduction. Unt.
1894 and the introduction of electricity the *bondes* were all donkey-drawn. It's also
curious to see how they enabled the city to expand so rapidly along the coast
through Copacabana and Ipanema – still fishing villages at the time. Routes were
cut back in 1963, many trams finishing up with US collectors.

Rua Joaquim Murtinho and around

The main artery from Lapa into Santa Teresa carries trams and buses up to the
Largo do Guimarães and contains some of the *bairro's* most striking Gothic
architecture; all private houses whose nineteenth-century owners did their best
to out-do each other in expensive design. Closer to Largo do Guimarães, the
first official tram-stop at **Largo do Curvelo** offers a good view southwest to
Catete, while Rua Dias de Barros heads east to the tiny street Rua Murtinho
Nobre and an even better viewpoint at its **Parque das Ruínas**. Next to
the park is a beautiful art gallery, the **Museu Chácara do Céu**. Between Lapa and
Rua Dias de Barros, the cobbled road Ladeira de Santa Teresa holds the
impressively-located **Convento de Santa Teresa**.

Parque das Ruínas

The **Parque das Ruínas** (Wed–Fri & Sat 10am–10pm, Sun 10am–5pm; free;
Rua Murtinho Nobre) is an attractive public garden containing the ruins of a
mansion that was once home to **Laurinda Santos Lobo**, a Brazilian heiress at
the centre of a circle of artists and intellectuals, who campaigned for women's
right to vote in the first half of the twentieth century. After her death in 1946,
the mansion fell into disrepair, but in the 1990s the ground floor was renovated
to house art exhibitions, and the surrounging grounds were landscaped for use
as a cultural centre. The sweeping panorama of Rio visible from here is
wonderful, and a pleasant on-site café is located alongside children's swings and
a space where classical recitals and theatre productions take place at weekends.

Museu Chácara do Céu

Next door to the ruins is the **Museu Chácara do Céu** (daily except Tues
noon–5pm; R$2; Rua Murtinho Nobre 93; ☎21/2507-1932, ⊛www
.museuscastromaya.com.br), located in a modernist stone building erected in
1957, and housing half of the three thousand-piece collection of Raymundo
Ottoni de Castro Maya, the French-born aristocrat in charge of the reforestation of Tijuca (1894–1968; the rest of the collection is at the Museu do Açude
at Alto da Boa Vista, see p.126). The museum made headline news during
Carnaval 2006 when it was subject to a daring raid in broad daylight. Armed
thieves took four paintings by Matisse, Picasso, Dali and Monet, collectively
valued at over US$50 million, before melting into the crowd – impeccably
timed to hold arriving police behind hordes of revellers at a carnival *bloco*.
Despite these important losses, it remains one of Rio's better museums, holding
a good European collection including sketches by Picasso as well as works by
famous Brazilian artists Cândido Portinari and Emiliano Di Cavalcanti. Old
canvases of Santa Teresa and Rio harbour illustrate just how much the city has
developed, while in the upper hall, two screens depict the life of Krishna.

Carmelite Convento e Igreja de Santa Teresa

From the **Parque das Ruínas**, a left turn onto Rua Dias de Barros brings you
to cobbled-street Ladeira de Santa Teresa, home of the 1750 **Carmelite**

ito de Santa Teresa (courtyard and chapel open at inconsistent times)
ound a simple hillside chapel dating from 1629. The *convento* also marks
t where a Duclerc-led French force was defeated by the city's inhabitants
10; thankfully, it has long since become a peaceful place, away from the
ub of Lapa and Centro. From this historic location there's also a great view
of the modern downtown sights. Just below the convent you can ascend a flight
of steps back up to Rua Joaquim Murtinho at the southern end of the Lapa
arches – and take a tram either southwards back up into Santa Teresa or across
the arches to Centro.

Largo do Guimarães to Largo das Neves

The streets west of Largo do Guimarães are the prettiest in Santa Teresa, though
they can be maze-like and disorientating if you don't know your way around
– if in doubt don't stray far from the tramline. A particularly interesting
street – **Rua Triunfo** – is reached by climbing the steps just north of Largo do
Guimarães; an especially wealthy road with stunning architecture which loops
back around to the tramline by Santa's Anglican church. A little farther, a couple
of the city's best *botecos* are great spots for lunch or a beer, while Brazil's
independence history is illuminated at the **Casa de Benjamin Constant**,
former home of the main instigator of the overthrow of the Brazilian monarchy.
Other attractions are the **Centro Cultural Laurinda Santos Lobo**, housed
in a striking old building and home to quality art exhibitions, and a short
diversion off the tram route is Santa's small but well-tended Catholic church.
Trams on this route terminate at village-like Largo das Neves, a quiet square
with beautiful houses and a couple of bars for a cool drink or bite to eat.

Casa de Benjamin Constant

Continuing west, Rua Carlos Magno passes the popular *boteco Bar do Mineiro*
(see p.182) before meeting Rua Monte Alegre, which heads downhill towards
the *bairro* of Fátima. A short way down this street is the **Casa de Benjamin
Constant** (Wed–Sun 1–5pm; R\$2; Rua Monte Alegre 255; ☎21/2242 0062),
the former residence of the military man and teacher declared in the Brazilian
Constitution as the Founder of the Republic on account of his role as War
Minister during the overthrow of the monarchy in 1889. The house itself is
fairly plain with a few paintings and pieces of period furniture (the bathroom
was considered state of the art in the nineteenth century), but the gardens are a
peaceful and shady spot in the heat of the day.

Centro Cultural Laurinda Santos Lobo

Along Rua Monte Alegre the other way (heading south) is Santa Teresa's small
library and adjoining it, the **Centro Cultural Laurinda Santos Lobo** (Tues–
Sun 9am–5pm; free; Rua Monte Alegre 306; ☎21/2224333), a grand house
where Laurinda (of Parque das Ruínas fame) hosted such great musicians as
Heitor Villa-Lobos and which served as a meeting place for arts and political
figures in the early twentieth century. Today, the centre hosts exhibitions of
most types of visual art often featuring local artists, as well as occasional jazz or
samba concerts in its lovely garden and terrace.

Rua Áurea and onwards to Largo das Neves

Beyond here, at the foot of Rua Áurea is the wonderful, friendly *Bar de Gomez*
(see p.182) (officially *Armazém São Thiago*), one of Santa's most popular drinking

haunts. If you look carefully at the numerous photos on the wall you might spot British ex-fugitive train-robber Ronnie Biggs, who made the bar his second home during his years here. A short diversion uphill on Rua Áurea takes you to the small, beautiful **Igreja de Santa Teresa**, the *bairro*'s Catholic church, notable for its stained-glass windows with a saint on each.

Northwestwards along the tramline from Rua Áurea (a ten-to fifteen-minute walk) on Rua Oriente, lies **Largo das Neves**, the final tram and (#214) bus stop. The square's three bars are slow and relaxed places in the heat of the day, putting their tables out onto the street on busier evenings when they draw a small crowd of locals. The largo has something of a village feel, with evenings and weekends given over to children playing and socializing fuelled by good food and *cerveja* (beer). In the light of a full moon, tradition dictates that *capoeiristas* perform here – to the delight of spectators.

Rua Almirante Alexandrino and Morrinho

Heading southwards and sharply uphill from Largo do Guimarães, the Dois Irmãos tramline twists and turns along Rua Almirante Alexandrino, passing luxury *Hotel Santa Teresa*, brightly-painted grand residences and, on the left, a modern supermarket imaginatively designed to imitate the Maracanã football stadium. Next to the supermarket is the stall of well-known artist **Getulio**, who sculpts all kinds of figures from random junk. A little farther up is the unmistakeable shape of **Castelo Valentim**, one of Santa Teresa's landmark buildings, which looms dramatically over the *bairro*. Designed by owner-architect Antonio Valentim and built in 1879, it wasn't until the 1920s that his son added the distinctive Gothic-esque turrets that set the building apart. Now divided into apartments, rooms are available to rent through B&B network *Cama e Café* (see p.168).

Opposite the castelo is a terrace of bars, shops and the evening Baianan street-snack bar *Acarajé da Nega Teresa* (see p.182). A little farther uphill is the entrance to *favela* Perreira da Silva and its art project Morrinho (see below). Along this stretch, Rua Almirante Alexandrino offers a series of dramatic views over central Rio and a group of neighbouring *favelas* between Santa Teresa and the *bairros* of Catumbi and Rio Comprido. Trams stop at the Dois Irmãos junction (at the road entrance to large *favela* Morro das Prazeres, or "Hill of Pleasures"), the site of the old reservoir where water began its descent down to the Arcos da Lapa, and where there's now a police post. The tramline itself (though without trams) continues to **Silvestre** below the Corcovado and above Cosmo Velho. To continue from here take any bus heading along Rua Almirante Alexandrino past the Corpo dos Bombeiros (Fire Station), which finish up a twenty-minute walk from Mirante Dona Marta (see p.81).

Morrinho

Though officially lying in Laranjeiras (see p.89), the remarkable *favela* art and NGO project **Morrinho** (Rua Pereira da Silva 826; R$30; ⓦwww.morrinho .com; call in advance ☎21/2246-1010, or arrange it as part of an itinerary with Santa Teresa Tour, with hotel pick-up or meet at Largo do Guimarães, see p.76; no fixed hours) is most easily visited from Santa Teresa, where a path leads from the side of the school at Rua Almirante Alexandrino 2024, through a gap in the rock to the Laranjeiras side of the hill and down through *favela* Pereira da Silva.

The extraordinary scene below places you as a giant within a highly realistic **model favela**, constructed from hollow bricks and painted in bright colours.

Started in the late 1990s as a playful reconstruction by a group of boys eager to act out the realities of community life, Morrinho grew into thousands of model homes, and, with an appearance in *National Geographic Brazil* in 2002 its profile was raised enough for the project to expand into a community development enterprise. The young architects of the project, now all in their mid-twenties, have built Morrinho into an NGO offering local people (funding allowing) courses in literacy, art and audiovisual production.

A visit here gives you time to see the art project, look around the *favela* (deemed safe due to the location of BOPE police headquarters at nearby Catete) and view the project's hilarious videos of *favela* role-plays performed with tiny Lego figures.

The Corcovado

The most famous of all images of Rio de Janeiro is that of the vast statue of *Cristo Redentor* (Christ the Redeemer) gazing across the bay from the **Corcovado** ("hunchback") hill, arms outstretched in welcome, or as if preparing for a dive into the waters below. The Art Deco **statue** (daily 9am–7pm; R$20), 30m high and weighing over 1000 tonnes, was scheduled to be completed in 1922 as part of Brazil's centenary independence celebrations, but this symbol of Rio wasn't, in fact, finished until 1931. The French sculptor Paul Landowski was responsible for the head and hands, while the engineers Heitor Silva Costa and Pedro Viana constructed the rest.

In clear weather, fear no anticlimax: climbing to the statue is a stunning experience by day, and nothing short of miraculous in the early evening. In daylight, the whole of Rio and Guanabara Bay is laid out before you; after dark, the floodlit statue can be seen from everywhere in the Zona Sul, seemingly suspended in the darkness that surrounds it and often shrouded in eerie cloud. Up on the platform at the base of the statue, the effect of the clouds, driven by warm air currents, and the thousands of tiny winged insects clustering round the spotlights, help give the impression that the statue is careering through space out into the blackness that lies beyond the arc of the lights – dramatic, and not a little hypnotic.

The **view** from the statue can be very helpful for **orientation** if you've just arrived in Rio. On a clear day, you can see as far as the outlying districts of Zona Norte, while on the south side of the viewing platform you're directly over the Lagoa Rodrigo de Freitas, with (beyond) Ipanema on the left and Leblon on the right. On the near side of the lake, Rua São Clemente is visible, curving its way through Botafogo, towards the Jardim Botânico and the racecourse, and on the lake's left side, the small *bairro* of Lagoa can be seen tucked in beneath the Morro dos Cabritos, on the other side of which is Copacabana.

Visiting the statue is, of course, a thoroughly exploited tourist experience with all the usual facilities for eating, drinking and buying souvenirs.

Getting to the Corcovado

Most people choose to go on the **cog-train** from the Corcovado train station, **Estação Cosmo Velho** (every 20–30min 8.30am–6pm; 20min; R$45 including entrance to Cristo; Rua Cosme Velho 513; ⓦ www.corcovado.com.br). Bear in mind that in high season the train is rammed with passengers, there's a long line

Botecos

Found on every city block, Rio's welcoming *botecos* – traditional bars – are atmospheric places to take in the flavour of a neighbourhood. Many are little more than holes in the wall; others have a carefully nurtured spit-and-sawdust look, while at more formal establishments, you'll be served by smartly dressed and respectful waiters who have worked the tables for decades. However smart or scruffy, *botecos* attract a real cross-section of *Cariocas* – who come together to socialise over cold, refreshing glasses of *chopp*.

Adega Flor de Coimbra, Lapa ▲

Music session in a Santa Teresa *boteco* ▼

Past and present

Before the advent of the **boteco** in the early twentieth century, social life in Rio was largely centred on the home, with occasional excursions to dances, musical soirées or the opera. Until the cramped colonial city was levelled in the late nineteenth century and replaced by grand avenues, elegant new buildings, shops, cafés and theatres – all inspired by the Belle Époque of Paris, the street was considered the place of the poor, slaves, former slaves, prostitutes and criminals.

The first *botecos* developed from grocery stores established by Portuguese immigrants, the word most likely derived from *botica*, the Portuguese term for a small warehouse or food store. Alongside basic supplies, these stores sold snacks and drinks, gradually becoming fully-fledged **bars** as they grew in respectability. While many of these early *botecos* were merely informal corner bars, still often referred to as **"pé-sujos"** (literally "dirty feet" – the term's origin reflecting the state of the bartenders' and clients' footwear or bare feet), drawing men from the surrounding block, others were purpose-built with Art Nouveau or Art Deco flourishes and waiters dressed in starched shirts and bow ties. As the twentieth century progressed, *botecos* developed into spaces for both men and women. This trend has continued with the emergence of so-called **"pé-limpos"** ("clean feet") *botecos*: more comfortable settings, typically with a traditional look, which offer rather more elaborate food and also function as venues for **live music**. Just as the beach is the main daytime meeting point for *Cariocas*, the city's lively *botecos* are where - for generations – friends have gathered to round off the day.

Chopp gelado

In Rio's tropical climate, it's hardly surprising that ice-cold lager – **chopp gelado** – is the tipple of choice for most *boteco* regulars. Connoisseurs of the drink have certain expectations of a glass of *chopp*: as it's unpasteurized, it must be consumed within ten days of production; it must be served chilled, just to the point of freezing ("*bem gelado*"); and finally it must have a head of at least three fingers in height. But given the industrial nature of most *chopp* consumed, it's sometimes hard to understand the seriousness with which the drink is taken. Thirst quenching it may be, but this watery beverage certainly isn't flavoursome. The biggest local brands – **Antarctica**, **Brahma**, **Bohemia** and **Skol** – are all similarly insipid in taste.

▲ Adega do Timão, Centro

▼ *Chopp gelado*

▼ Bar do Serafim, Larenjeiras

The best botecos

▸▸ **Adega Pérola** (Copacabana; see p.186). One of the most extensive ranges of *petiscos*, laid out tapas-style along the extended bar.

▸▸ **Adega Portugália** (Catete; see p.183). The *boteco* to taste the best *bolinhos de bacalhau* you're likely to find outside Portugal.

▸▸ **Bar de Gomez** (Santa Teresa; see p.182). This bar-cum-Portuguese-grocery-store preserves the spirit of an original *boteco*.

▸▸ **Bar Lagoa** (Ipanema; see p.189). Respectful, white-coated waiters set the tone of this family-friendly *boteco* with views onto the lagoon.

▸▸ **Cosmopolita** (Lapa; see p.181). Attracting a Bohemian crowd, *Cosmopolita's* Portuguese origins are clearly apparent in its menu.

▸▸ **Villarino** (Cinelândia; see p.180). Bossa nova fans may encounter the ghosts of Vinicius de Morães and Tom Jobim here.

Adega Pérola, Copacabana ▲

Cachaça ▼

Caipirinhas ▼

Cachaça

While *chopp* is the mainstay of *botecos*, **cachaça** – distilled sugar-cane juice – is the most popular spirit. Until the 1990s middle-class Brazilians were often dismissive of *cachaça*, viewing it as the preserve of the poor and desperate, and even substituting vodka for the spirit in the national cocktail, the **caipirinha**. Today, though, sweet-tasting *cachaça* (or *pinga*, as it is also often called) rightly generates immense national pride: aged in barrels, connoisseurs insist that the best artisanal *cachaças* are in the same league as fine single-malt whiskies. Although the state of Rio (especially around Paraty) has a long tradition of *cachaça* production, few local brands are worth trying, though **Coqueiro** is great in a *caipirinha* and **Maria Izabel** makes fine sipping.

Petiscos

Without exception, all *botecos* offer a range of **petiscos** (finger snacks), which, eaten over the course of an evening, can be as substantial as a full, modestly-priced meal. *Pé-limpos botecos* also usually have full menus, often of extremely attractive and tasty dishes. To encourage patrons to linger and continue drinking while simultaneously preventing a hangover, *petiscos* are typically either deep-fried or salty – and sometimes both. The delicious *bolinho de bacalhau* (cod croquette), a quintessentially Portuguese snack that recalls the Portuguese roots of many *botecos*, perfectly meets this criteria, as do the fried or grilled sardines served in the **Triângulo das Sardinhas** around Largo de Santa Rita (see p.180). More typically Brazilian *petiscos*, such as *carne-de-sol* (sun-dried beef jerky) and fried manioc, are almost always on offer, while *filé* (thinly sliced steak) is deservedly popular too.

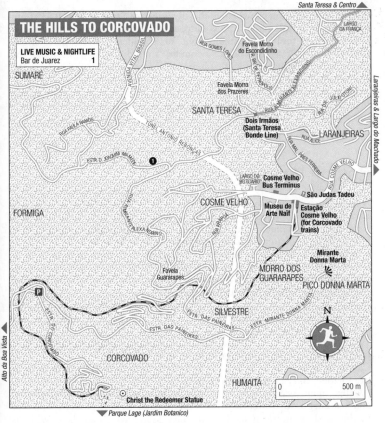

THE HILLS TO CORCOVADO

LIVE MUSIC & NIGHTLIFE
Bar de Juarez   1

SUMARÉ

Favela Morro
do Escondidinho

RUA GOMES LOPES

AVENIDA VITA BRASIL

R. DE PETRÓPOLIS

RUA ALMIRANTE ALEXANDRINO

RUA DE JÚLIO OTONI

Favela Morro
dos Prazeres

SANTA TERESA

RUA PAULA RAMOS

TÚNEL ANTONIO REBOUÇAS

ESTR. D. JOAQUIM AMAREDE

Dois Irmãos
(Santa Teresa
Bonde Line)

RUA ALICE

RUA AL. PIRES FERREIRA

LARANJEIRAS

RUA COSME VELHO

LARGO DO
BOTICÁRIO

Cosme Velho
Bus Terminus

São Judas Tadeu

FORMIGA

RUA MONTE ALEGRE

RUA ALEXANDRINO

COSME VELHO

RUA ARAPUÃ

Museu de
Arte Naïf

Estação
Cosme Velho
(for Corcovado
trains)

Mirante
Donna Marta

Favela
Guararapes

MORRO DOS
GUARARAPES

PICO DONNA MARTA

ESTR. DO CORCOVADO

P

SILVESTRE

ESTR. DAS PAINEIRAS

ESTR. DAS PAINEIRAS

ESTR. MIRANTE DONNA MARTA

N

CORCOVADO

HUMAITÁ

0   500 m

Christ the Redeemer Statue

Parque Lage (Jardim Botanico)

for tickets, and then a further wait to catch your train – consider going early in the morning or last thing in the afternoon to avoid the rush.

To get there by **metrô**, buy a *superficie* ticket (currently R$3.50) to Cosmo Velho, which entitles you to the onward **metrobus** from Largo do Machado station. **Buses** run direct to the station in Cosmo Velho from elsewhere, too – take the #422 or #497 from Largo do Machado, the #583 from Leblon or the #584 from Copacabana.

If you want to **walk**, there is an excellent though arduous two- to three-hour hiking trail from the Parque Large at Rua Jardim Botânico (most buses heading west from Botafogo on Rua São Clemente stop here, as does #583 from Leblon or metrobuses from Botafogo or Gávea) – ask the park staff where the start of the trail is. Similarly, you can also walk (or cycle) to the Corcovado from **Cosme Velho** or **Santa Teresa**, taking first Rua Almirante Alexandrino and then Estrada do Corcovado – and it's definitely worth making a stop at dramatic look-out point **Mirante Dona Marta** on the way. Make sure you travel in a group on both these routes and use common sense; though most people tackle them without problems, there have been reports of assaults and robberies in the past.

All major hotels and tour companies (see p.27) organize **excursions** which often include stops in Santa Teresa en route. Alternatively, the easiest way to get there by yourself from elsewhere in the city is to take a **taxi** – about R$35 from the Zona Sul, a little more from Centro, or R$20 from Largo do Machado. If you're feeling flush, you might want to consider a **helicopter flight** (☎21/2511-2141; ⓦwww.helisight.com.br) around the city, including the Corcovado – a six-minute flight costs around R$150; longer flights make a stop at **Mirante Dona Marta**.

However you choose to get there, keep an eye on the **weather** before setting out: what ought to be one of Rio's highlights can turn into a great disappointment if the Corcovado is shrouded in clouds.

Cosme Velho

A small *bairro* clinging to the Corcovado hillside, **Cosme Velho** lies between Laranjeiras and the upper slopes of Santa Teresa. There's not a great deal to it – though a two-minute walk uphill from the cog-train station on Rua Cosme Velho will take you to the **Museu Internacional de Arte Naïf** (closed at time of writing but supposed to reopen in 2009; Tues–Fri 10am–6pm, Sat, Sun & public holidays noon–6pm; R$5; ☎21/2205-8612, ⓦwww.museunaif.com.br), which boasts the world's largest naive art collection. Although most of the work displayed is by Brazilian artists, the museum also features paintings from throughout the world, with Haiti, the former Yugoslavia, France and Italy well represented. Among the collection are a number of attractive paintings of Rio and the Corcovado.

Directly across the road is the remarkable modern rotund, the **Igreja São Judas Tadeu**, notable mainly for its bare interior in contrast to the city's other Catholic churches; the congregation and surrounds are particularly animated in late October in celebration of the saint.

A five-minute walk further uphill (past the bus terminus) is the much-photographed **Largo do Boticário**, named after the nineteenth-century apothecary to the royal family (Joaquim Luiz da Silva Santo) who lived here. With its pebbled streets and a fountain set in its small courtyard, this is a particularly picturesque little corner of Rio. However, as old as the largo might appear to be, the original mid-nineteenth-century houses were demolished in the 1920s and replaced with colourful Neocolonial-style homes, some with fronts decorated with *azulejos*. Interestingly, many of the materials came from demolished colonial homes in the path of Avenida Presidente Vargas in Centro; the facades hint at how pretty and historic much of old central Rio was.

From here, large through-route Túnel Rebouças surfaces for about 200 metres between the mountains, and residential Cosmo Velho continues up to Santa Teresa and the steep hillsides of Corcovado. In typically *Carioca* fashion, the area is divided between extremely luxurious properties and the large and problematic *favela*, Morro dos Guararapes. A remarkable job has been done of hiding the *favela's* existence from visiting tourists; trees and walls shield it almost entirely from the ascending roads and railtrack to the Christ statue.

Flamengo, Botafogo and the Sugar Loaf

Stretching from Centro down through the Zona Sul, the *bairros* of **Flamengo**, **Botafogo**, **Glória** and **Catete** are calm residential areas with appealing and unpretentious street life. Busy during the day, the tree-lined streets come alive at night with residents eating top-notch Brazilian food in excellent local restaurants. Completing the loop around Botafogo Bay, the spectacular **Sugar Loaf mountain** overshadows the *bairro* of **Urca** below, a peaceful and affluent neighbourhood with a gorgeous beach wedged between the mountains.

Hugging the coastline south of Centro the **Parque do Flamengo** is an extensive area of reclaimed land transformed into a public recreation area and beach. The old shoreline is marked by the hills a few hundred yards inland – and most immediately by the unmistakeable landmark of **Nossa Senhora da Glória do Outeiro**, a whitewashed church high on a wooded hill. A visit to Catete's **Museu da Republica** is worthwhile for its sumptuous interior and a reminder of presidential excess at the beginning of the twentieth century. Until the 1950s, Flamengo and Catete were the principal residential zones of Rio's wealthier middle classes, and, although there are still many discreetly well-off streets and properties, they seem to co-exist reasonably happily with lower level apartments and hillside *favelas*.

In Botafogo, one of Rio's best museums - the **Museu do Índio** – successfully explores the culture, experience and knowledge of Brazil's Amerindian tribes. Innumerable cheap and good-value hostels have opened up across these areas – their pleasant atmosphere and proximity to Centro and the southern beaches make them enjoyable places to base yourself.

Glória and Catete

Bordering Lapa to the north, Santa Teresa to the west and the Parque do Flamengo to the east, Glória and its neighbour Catete are attractive residential neighbourhoods with a number of interesting museums. While Copacabana and Ipanema outclass them in the excitement stakes, Glória and Catete have a stronger community feel and a lively street atmosphere. South of Glória's

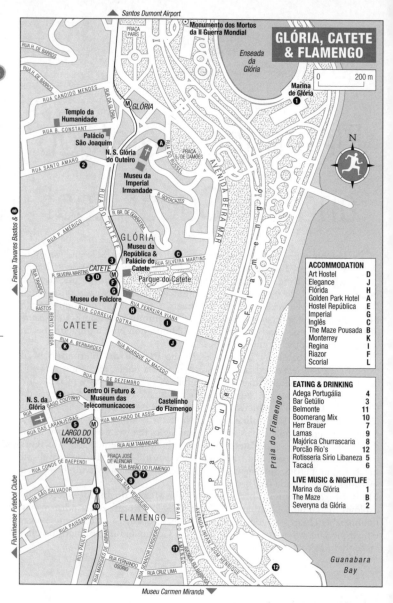

GLÓRIA, CATETE & FLAMENGO

0   200 m

ACCOMMODATION

Art Hostel	D
Elegance	J
Flórida	H
Golden Park Hotel	A
Hostel República	E
Imperial	G
Inglês	C
The Maze Pousada	B
Monterrey	K
Regina	I
Riazor	F
Scorial	L

EATING & DRINKING

Adega Portugália	4
Bar Getúlio	3
Belmonte	11
Boomerang Mix	10
Herr Brauer	7
Lamas	9
Majórica Churrascaria	8
Porcão Rio's	12
Rotisseria Sírio Libaneza	5
Tacacá	6

LIVE MUSIC & NIGHTLIFE

Marina da Glória	1
The Maze	B
Severyna da Glória	2

famous Igreja da Nossa Senhora da Glória do Outeiro, the main street, Rua do Catete, passes the Palácio da Catete and its museum, the **Museu da República**, while to the building's rear lies the attractive Parque do Catete and to the side the atmospheric **Museu de Folclore Edison Carneiro**. Westwards, rising up towards Santa Teresa, the Nova Cintra hill holds Rio's safest *favela*, **Tavares Bastos**. Neighboured by the headquarters of elite police unit BOPE, the hillside is renowned as a safe area and has a popular *pousada* and monthly jazz night (see p.87 & p.173). In the intersecting streets between the Parque do Flamengo, Rua do Catete and Rua Bento Lisboa are numerous cheap hotels and a good choice of hostels.

A block north of the largo bordering Catete you'll find the technology museum and art gallery **Centro Oi Futuro**, and east towards Flamengo beach the strange gothic shape of **Castelinho do Flamengo**, now an arts centre, between the apartment buildings.

The Morro da Glória

Across from the Glória *metrô* station, a five-minute walk up the quiet and peaceful Morro da Glória leads you to the early eighteenth-century **Igreja de Nossa Senhora da Glória do Outeiro** (Mon–Fri 9am–5pm, Sat & Sun 9am–noon; Ⓦ www.outeirodagloria.org.br). Painstakingly renovated, the church, quite simply the prettiest in Rio, is an absolute gem. It is notable for its innovative octagonal ground plan and domed roof, the latter decked with excellent seventeenth-century blue-and-white *azulejos* tiles and nineteenth-century marble masonry. Behind it you'll find the **Museu da Imperial Irmandade de Nossa Senhora da Glória** (Tues–Fri 9am–5pm, Sat & Sun 9am–noon; free), which contains a small collection of religious relics, *ex votos* and the personal possessions of Empress Teresa Cristina. The hill's winding cobbled streets reveal an affluent mix of modern apartments and colonial and early twentieth-century houses, alongside the odd mini cable car to aid residents in climbing to their houses from the park below.

Though now a calm spot within the inner city, the hilltop has a violent history; it was here in 1567, after two years of fighting, that the Portuguese founder of the city of Rio de Janeiro, **Estácio de Sá**, finally defeated formidable French forces to take control of the region (see p.247). In a remarkable example of the colonial powers' deftness at employing divide-and-rule tactics, both sides had indigenous allies alongside them. The Portuguese triumphed, but Sá himself suffered an arrow to the eye and died later from his wound.

▲ Igreja de Nossa Senhora da Glória do Outeiro

It's hard to imagine today, but in the nineteenth century the tree-covered hill was surrounded by water on its northern and eastern sides, small boats bobbing beside it. Even the grand 1920s *Hotel da Glória* (closed until 2011) at the hill's eastern foot was right on the seafront until the gradual land reclamations of the 1950s.

The Palácio do Catete and Museu da República

On the Rua do Catete, adjacent to the Catete *metrô* station, the **Palácio do Catete** is home to the atmopsheric **Museu da República** (Tues–Fri noon–5pm, Sat & Sun 2–6pm; R$6, free for under 10s and over 65s, and for all Sun; ☎ 21/3235 2650, ⓦ www.museudarepublica.org.br). The *palácio* was used as the presidential residence from 1897 until 1960, and it was here, in 1954, that Getúlio Vargas shot himself, believing he had been betrayed. The building was erected in the 1860s as the Rio home of the Barão de Nova Friburgo, a wealthy coffee *fazenda* owner.

As a historical museum, the *palácio* continues where the Museu Histórico Nacional (see p.51) leaves off, with the establishment of the first Republic in 1888 and the signing of the presidential constitution in 1891. The collection features both period furnishings and presidential memorabilia – including Vargas's bloodied pyjamas – though it's the opulent marble and stained glass of the building itself that make a visit so worthwhile. The immaculately preserved Art Deco and Neoclassical-style ceilings and stairwell make the building's interior the most appealing of any of Rio's historical attractions, and the Moorish Hall, modelled on the Spanish Alhambra in Granada, is spectacular. Period furniture is displayed throughout, while paintings from the Italian Renaissance depict the Greek myths. Downstairs, the space is used for temporary exhibitions, usually relating to modern Brazilian politics and history.

Parque do Catete

Behind the palace lies the **Parque do Catete** (daily 8am–6pm), whose birdlife, towering palms and quiet walking trails are good for an hour's break. Its pond with ducks and other waterfowl, playground and tricycles for hire make it a nice place to take small children. The grounds also include a new exhibition space, small theatre and art gallery called the Galeria do Lago (Tues–Fri 10am–6pm, Sat & Sun 1–6pm) and there are occasionally exhibitions, theatre productions or film screenings happening here at night, when the beautiful venue is illuminated by floodlights.

Museu de Folclore Edison Carneiro

Divided between two buildings, one inside the grounds of the *palácio* and the other in an adjacent house, the **Museu de Folclore Edison Carneiro** (Tues–Fri 11am–6pm, Sat & Sun 3–6pm; R$4; Rua do Catete 179; ☎21/2285 0441), part of the National Centre for Folklore and Popular Culture (ⓦ www.cnfcp .gov.br), is a fascinating folkloric collection that displays pieces from all over Brazil. Carneiro was a prolific historian and collector of Brazilian popular art, especially that influenced by West Africa such as carnival character figures, Afro-Brazilian cult paraphernalia, costumes, photographs and *ex votos*. The well-presented collection also includes a range of leatherwork, musical instruments,

Tavares Bastos: a favela on film

Arriving in **Tavares Bastos** *favela* in Catete you may well see armed police and drug traffickers, but they're almost certainly actors working on a Brazilian **novela** (soap opera) or a big-budget film. Over the past eight years the *favela* has been used as a set in many films including *The Incredible Hulk, Onibus 174* (*Bus 174*; see p.264), Jonathan Nossiter's *Gringos of Rio* (working title), starring Bill Pullman, as well as music videos by Snoop Dog, Pharell and the Black Eyed Peas. All film companies using the *favela* have to make a handsome contribution to the residents' association.

The reason for the film crews' sense of security in Tavares Bastos is simple; since 2000 the Rio de Janeiro police special operations unit, **BOPE**, has been based in the large building next door. The result of years of lobbying by resident Bob Nadkarni – a larger than life Londoner, artist and former war cameraman who moved to the *favela* to join his Brazilian wife – BOPE's move to Tavares Bastos resulted in the rapid departure of the dealers and a sharp rise in prosperity and opportunity. In a strangely ironic twist, the *favela* was also used as a set for the hit 2007 Brazilian feature film, *Tropa de Elite* (translated as *Elite Squad*; see p.265), a title highly critical of BOPE's behaviour across Rio's poorer communities.

If you're interested in visiting Tavares Bastos, Bob's self-designed, Gaudi-like *pousada The Maze* (☎21/2558-5547, ⊛www.jazzrio.com.br; see p.173) is an eccentric but smart accommodation option, bar and art exhibition space, which provides a great opportunity to experience *favela* life. It also has excellent monthly **jazz nights** (usually the first Friday of each month). At other times, phone in advance to go up for a drink and marvel at the view.

ceramics and toys. The soft lighting and traditional music throughout make for a distinctly eerie atmosphere that will please older children, though small ones may find it a little frightening. An audio guide is available in English, and the ground floor gift shop is a good place to pick up some souvenirs.

Centro Oi Futuro

A block from the Largo do Machado, the name of this imaginative techno-cultural centre which focuses on the future of human communication says it all. Imaginatively blending the arts with science, the Centro Oi Futuro (free; Rua Dois de Dezembro 63; ☎21/3131 3060, ⊛www.oifuturo.org.br) has space on its lower two floors for multimedia **exhibitions**, which have previously engaged with scientific or global themes like the ice caps or the virtual city. A **theatre** promotes self-reflective plays on communications and the media – and runs a good children's theatre programme, too. The main draw, however, is the third floor **Museu das Telecomunicações** (Tues–Sun 11am–5pm), arguably Rio's most interactive museum. As you enter you're given headphones with an attached electronic sensor so you can listen in to stories about communication dotted around the large room (English translations usually available; confirm in advance). The stories bring to life the histories of technologies such as TV, telephone and the internet. The introduction and impact of technology in a country the size of Brazil is also covered – with video footage of the first telephones and TVs in rural areas and interviews with children about how the internet makes them feel closer to distant parts of the country. Models and old appliances reveal how quickly things have changed – a topic also taken up in closed booths where you can sit in front of 3D screens projecting famous Brazilian personalities like architect Oscar Niemeyer suggesting what changes the future might hold. The roof terrace has a small café and good view if it all gets a bit too sci-fi for you.

Castelinho do Flamengo

East along Rua Dois de Dezembro from here is an incongruous Rio oddity, the **Castelinho do Flamengo**, or "Flamengo's Little Castle" (free; Praia do Flamengo 158; ℡21/2205 0655), built in 1916 and officially housing the Odovaldo Vianno Centre for the Arts. Most visitors to the city drive past this pink neo-Gothic castle wedged between two tall apartment buildings without ever going inside – but it is worth looking at close up, too – if only for its peculiarity. Inside, a number of rooms house temporary exhibitions on the plastic and video arts, there's also a good view across the park to the beach, as well as an extensive video reference library.

Flamengo and Laranjeiras

Flamengo, perhaps confusingly, gives its name both to the residential area between Catete and Botafogo and to the **Parque do Flamengo**, a narrow 5km-long stretch of prime seafront that starts at Santos Dumont airport and sweeps round as far as Botafogo Bay. Inaugurated in 1965, the park was the biggest land-reclamation project in Brazil; today it's hard to imagine waves crashing close to houses in Flamengo and Catete on its western side. Now one of Rio's most important public spaces, the park offers a decent beach, numerous species of trees and plants (chosen by master landscaper/designer Roberto Burle Marx), and walking trails – the latter admittedly somewhat overawed by transecting busy roads. At the southern end of the park, the **Museu Carmen Miranda** offers a brief insight into the life of Rio's most famous showbiz star.

You'll probably pass through the park many times by bus as you travel between Centro and Zona Sul's beach zone, but a diversion into Flamengo-proper and the *bairro* of Laranjeiras beyond yields rewards of good street life, bars and restaurants – especially around the **Largo do Machado**. There's also a couple of interesting historical sights and palaces, and the home of Rio's first football team, **Fluminense**, an old and affluent club which remains among Rio's top four.

The Parque do Flamengo

Known to most *Cariocas* (residents of Rio de Janeiro) as **o Aterro** – "the Landfill" – Parque do Flamengo was the brainchild and obsession of city landscaper **Carlota de Macedo Soares** (see p.268), a former student of famous painter Portinari, also well known as the girlfriend of American poet Elizabeth Bishop. 'Lota' reportedly took her friend, then governor of Rio, Carlos Lacerda, to the window of her Flamengo apartment overlooking the water, and explained to him her dream of a large city recreation space. The area now comprising Santos Dumont airport and the Museu de Arte Moderna (see p.47) had already been reclaimed using rock and earth from the levelling of the Castelo hill (see p.50), but the ambitious new plan included flattening another city-centre mound, the Morro Santo Antonio, now the site of the Nova Catedral Metropolitano (see p.49). Great Brazilian landscape architect and gardener **Roberto Burle Marx** was drafted in to complete the designs and undertake the extensive planting – though the two powerful personalities had an uneasy relationship.

The park today is mainly popular with local residents who use it for sports and exercise: there are countless tennis courts (open 9am–11pm), cycle tracks, and most importantly from the *Carioca* perspective, 24-hour **football pitches** (adjacent to Catete) which even at 4am are booked up far in advance, on account of Rio's huge night security workforce. The **beach** here is also worth visiting, running along the park for a kilometre and a half between Glória and Flamengo and offering excellent views across the bay to Niterói – though unfortunately it's not a place for swimming given the pollution in Guanabara Bay (a far better bathing option is at Ipanema beach). You might choose to eat at huge restaurant *Porção* (see p.184) at the park's southern end, being Rio's largest and most exclusive *churrascaria* ("steak-house") with more cuts of meat than you're ever likely to have seen. Otherwise the best day to visit is Sunday when one of the park's through-routes is closed and used instead for competitive runs and cycling – the beach is much more peaceful without the noise of passing traffic. A good walking option would be to start at Cinelândia or Glória *metrô* stations and continue south through the park finishing near the multitude of buses passing Botafogo beach.

Clearly visible at the northern end of the park is the modernist structure, the **Monumento aos Mortos na Segunda Guerra Mundial** (Monument to the Dead of World War II). The park is in some ways very typical of 1960s development – a space crisscrossed with high-speed roads – but a later 1980s addition, the calmer **Marina da Glória**, has added a mooring facility for many beautiful boats and is also the venue for numerous music concerts and dance music events, including the excellent Brazilian and international **Tim Music Festival** held here in October (see p.222).

Museu Carmen Miranda

In front of Av. Rui Barbosa 560, at the southern end of the park, is the **Museu Carmen Miranda** (Tues–Fri 10am–5pm, Sat 2–5pm; free; ☎21/2299 5586), located in a curious concrete bunker-like building. Born in Portugal but raised in Lapa, Carmen Miranda (see p.90) made it big in Hollywood following the seminal 1941 film *That Night in Rio* and subsequently became a major force in taking samba and *Carioca* culture to the wider world. She later became the patron saint of Rio's Carnaval transvestites; tributes to her can be seen at the city's gay festivals and regularly at Lapa clubs. The museum contains a wonderful, if small, collection of kitsch memorabilia including posters, some of the star's costumes – most notably one of her famed fruit-laden hats – and jewellery. Perhaps best of all it's an opportunity to sit back and see snippets of her most famous performances – bold and often outrageous songs and dances like *Tutti-Frutti Hat* and those from 1939 hit film *Banana da Terra*.

Largo do Machado and west to Laranjeiras

The *bairros* of Flamengo, Laranjeiras and Catete meet at **Largo do Machado**, an attractive square lined with palm trees and surrounded by a mix of tall modern office buildings and malls alongside Neoclassical-inspired remnants such as the private school on the largo's northern side. The church at the square's head is confusingly called the Igreja Matriz de Nossa Senhora da Glória – no connection to the *bairro* of the same name – and the paved, central area offers a relaxed ambience of flower stalls, open-air gamblers and pavement-style restaurants and *botecos*. The small mall on the southern side of the largo (known unofficially as Condo) contains an internet centre, national bus booking office, as well as Rio's best Arabic fast-food restaurant, *Rotisseria Sírio Libaneza* – stop in for an *esfiha* or *kibe do forno* with freshly-squeezed juice.

3

Carmen Miranda

Born in northern Portugal in 1909, **Maria do Carmo Miranda da Cunha** – better known as Carmen Miranda – moved, at 4 years of age, with her family to Rio de Janeiro, where her father had opened a barber's shop in the Bohemian inner-city *bairro* of Lapa (see p.69). While working as a milliner, the young Carmen pursued a musical career. At the age of 20, she made her first recordings, a samba and a *choro*, and had her first hit in 1930 with a *marchinha* (a typical Carnaval rhythm), *Taí – Eu Fiz Tudo Pra Você Gostar de Mim (There It Is, I Did Everything for You to Like Me)*.

Carmen's emergence at the centre stage of Brazilian popular culture was boosted by the support of the régime of Getúlio Vargas, which was eager to develop a new nationalist culture by making the samba tradition of poor blacks and *mulattoes* accessible to white elite and middle-class consumers. Less than fifty years after the abolition of slavery, a white woman had been discovered to showcase popular black rhythms and lyrics that spoke of poverty, the importance of music, and race and patriotism, while evoking an ideal of Brazilian sexuality and black *mulatto* sensuality. In translating black samba for a white audience, Carmen was seen as fun – her extravagant appearance key to her image. By the mid-1930s she had adopted an exaggerated form of colourful **Bahian dress**, which became increasingly flamboyant; featuring exotic plumage, sequins and incredible turbans adorned with tropical fruit bowls.

After achieving domestic stardom, Carmen turned her attention to the United States, bringing samba to an international audience. On Broadway and in Hollywood, she personified a south-of-the-border allure that was so culturally and geographically vague it could come from anywhere between Mexico and Argentina. Dubbed "the **Brazilian bombshell**" and starring in fourteen Hollywood movies between 1940 and 1953, Carmen became, and remains – even after her death in 1955 – a cultural icon in the US and Europe.

Brazilians have long held mixed feelings towards Carmen Miranda. Many felt that her departure for the United States was a betrayal, that she became too Americanized and that her Hollywood image – not least the "tutti-frutti" hats – lampooned Brazil, and presented her as a Latin caricature. Some Brazilians were keen to remind themselves that Carmen was not merely Portuguese by birth but never even adopted Brazilian nationality, but others were immensely proud of the international acclaim she achieved as Brazil's first global superstar. Her legacy has endured; her sense of humour and extravagant performances influencing a host of Brazilan artists, including Ney Matogrosso, Elis Regina, Gal Costa, João Gilberto and Caetano Veloso.

At the southern side of the Igreja, busy Rua das Laranjeiras heads west in the direction of Corcovado. Meaning literally "Orange groves", **Laranjeiras** is one of Rio's oldest *bairros*, populated by Europeans as early as the seventeenth century when farmers found fertile land around what was later named the Rio Carioca. The first building you come to of note, however, has a more recent past; the **Mercado São José das Artes** (locally known as the Mercadinho), on the right side of the street a block west of the Largo, was used as a storage facility for the nearby large sugar estate belonging to Eduardo Guinle before becoming a food market in the 1940s. These days you'll find a group of great food stalls inside ranging from Japanese to Bahian cuisines as well as a lively bar in the evenings – celebrated *Carioca* musician Tom Jobim obviously had a good time here, declaring it "one of the most characteristic and friendly points of the city of Rio."

A right turn here onto Rua Gago Coutinho is the **Parque Eduardo Guinle**, a truly beautiful spot hidden behind very busy surrounding roads. Should you find yourself in this part of town in the heat of the day it's an ideal spot to cool

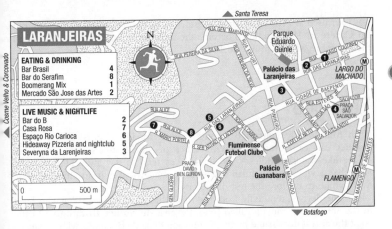

down in, with plenty of shady trees and hummingbirds flying around, as well as having a duck pond and small waterfall. Above the park on the western side is the **Palácio de Laranjeiras**, constructed in 1914; you can just about see its grand spires through the trees, but unfortunately the property functions as the governor's residence and is closed to the public. Above the park on the other side is a group of striking modern apartment buildings designed by popular Brazilian modern architect Lúcio Costa.

Rua das Laranjeiras continues west up to the *bairros* of Cosme Velho and Santa Teresa (see p.82) and to the Estação Cosme Velho for trains to Corcovado. A short way west of the Parque Eduardo Guinle, Rua Pereira da Silva cuts upwards into the hills to the *favela* of the same name and its remarkable art project, Morrinho (see p.79). Another point of note along this stretch of road is the Saturday morning **market** at Rua General Glicério, which heads southwards off Rua das Laranjeiras a kilometre further west. Stalls sell fruit and vegetables, souvenirs, clothing and delicious pastels – good for a late breakfast – and proceedings are usually accompanied by a live band playing *chorinho* classics.

Fluminense Football Club

Walking south along the main road Rua Pinheiro Machado is not an enjoyable exercise given the four busy lanes of traffic – but it is worthwhile if you have an interest in Brazilian football, as the home ground of **Fluminense Football Club** (Mon–Fri 11am–noon and 2–4pm, Sat 2–4pm; free; Rua Alvaro Chaves; ☎21/2553-7240, ⒲www.fluminense.com.br;) is based here. Even though all senior home games have been played at the Maracanã (see p.141) for decades and training is now held out of town, it's interesting to have a look at the club's old 4000-capacity stadium and its packed **trophy room**. Fluminense was the first football club to be founded in Rio de Janeiro – mainly by the British-Brazilian elite at the turn of the last century. It wasn't until well after 1950 that the sport became the inclusive and unifying competition it is today (see p.256).

Palácio Guanabara

Just south of the football club is one of Rio's grandest buildings, the bright cream-coloured Neoclassical **Palácio Guanabara** – now unfortunately closed to the public. Completed in 1863 it became the home of Princess Isabel, the daughter of Emperor Dom Pedro II, who was deposed in 1888. The building was later used as Presidente Vargas's residence before he moved to the **Palácio do Catete in 1937**, and then became the state governor's office in 1960 when the federal legislature moved to Brasília.

Botafogo

With four heavily congested through routes, foreign visitors staying at the beaches can easily miss Botafogo's quiet tree-lined streets with numerous village-like watering holes – and hence they tend to stay away. However, the *bairro* has a vibrant, bohemian atmosphere, which makes it an attractive base from which to explore the rest of the city.

Its name derives, reputedly, from the first white Portuguese settler who lived in the area, a ship captain called **João Pereira de Souza Botafogo**. On the coast the area is dominated by the wide-open Praia de Botafogo, which extends for a kilometre or so around the golden sand. The beach is great to look at, with its backdrop of the Sugar Loaf mountain and yachts bobbing on the bay, though its location close to busy traffic and its vulnerability to water pollution from the northern part of Guanabara Bay mean that only the brave or foolhardy swim here. Still, the stupendous view is best taken in from mall **Botafogo Praia Shopping**, at the corner with Rua Prof. Alfredo Gomes – the terrace of its eighth-floor café is a prime spot.

Away from the ocean, many of Botafogo's streets make for good urban walks – you can try to spot the remaining mansions built in the nineteenth century when it was Rio's outermost suburb and the preserve of the city's elite. Most enduring distinguished buildings have been converted for use as offices or to house **museums**, while to the southwest of the *bairro*, Rio's grand old cemetery São João Batista is where many of the city's rich and famous are buried. Botafogo has a good selection of **restaurants** in its well-known **Poló Gastronômico** – easily the best place in Rio to enjoy good quality Brazilian foods at very reasonable prices. The area is also becoming a really popular hostel district, cheaper than the beaches and appealing for its local street atmosphere.

Rua São Clemente and around

Heading west from Botafogo *metrô* station towards Humaita and the Lagoa, Rua São Clemente is the *bairro's* oldest street – with a few interesting buildings hinting at its history, as well as two excellent museums. Running along its length are a number of gated yet very attractive old colonial streets, among them Rua Estácio Coimbra, with many more turning north from the main drag. At no. 117, two blocks from the *metrô*, is one of the street's historic buildings, incongruously preserved amidst the modern blocks. Built in 1880, it currently houses the **Centro de Architectura e Urbanismo**, a small and vaguely interesting museum space if you happen to be passing. It's focused on the construction of Rio and has some enlightening maps and photos of old Rio.

Museu Casa de Rui Barbosa

From Botafogo *metrô* station, walk away from the ocean along Avenida São Clemente to reach the **Museu Casa de Rui Barbosa** at no. 134 (Tues–Fri 10am–5pm, Sat & Sun 2–6pm; R$6; ☎21/3289-4600, ⓦwww.casaruibarbosa .gov.br), set amidst the lush bowers of a garden with well-kept paths and

BOTAFOGO & URCA

NIGHTLIFE & LIVE MUSIC

Bar da Rampa	6
Casa da Matriz	13
Canecão	22
Cannequinho Café	22
Cinemateque	7
Far Up	15
Pista 3	11

ACCOMMODATION

El Misti	B
Panda	A
Real	D
Rio Party Hostel	E
Vila Carioca	C

EATING & DRINKING

Adega do Valentim	16
Adega de Velha	8
A Mineira	23
Aurora	2
Balcão da Urca	18
Botequim-184	20
Cobal do Botafogo	15
Estrela do Sul	10
Churrascaria	21
Eccellenza Pizzeria	5
Garota da Urca	3
La Mole	1
Miam Miam	17
Ovelha Negra	4
Champagneria	
Praia Vermelha Bar	19
e Restaurante	9
Raajmahal	12
Vegan Vegan	14
Yorubá	

Pão de Açúcar
(Sugar Loaf Mountain)
(396m)

N

URCA

MORRO DA URCA

Praia Vermelha

Praia da Urca

Enseada de Botafogo

Praia de Botafogo

Iate Clube do Rio de Janeiro

Teleférico
Cable car Station

BABILÔNIA

URUBU

LEME

Copacabana

Botafogo Football Club

Rio Plaza Shopping

Shopping Rio Sul

Clube Guanabara

Mirante do Morro do Pasmado

Botafogo Praia Shopping

Museu Casa de Rui Barbosa

Centro de Architectura e Urbanismo

Museu Villa-Lobos

Museu do Índio

Favela Morro Santa Marta

VILUVA

SÃO JOÃO

Cemeterio São João Batista

HUMAITÁ

Jardim Botânico & Ipanema

500 m

children's toys spilling out from a nursery across the grounds. Built in 1850, it became the home of Rui Barbosa, jurist, statesman and author, in 1893. The federal government established a museum here after his death. Born in Bahia state, Barbosa (1849–1923) graduated as a lawyer in São Paulo and, later, as a journalist and critic of the monarchy, founded the (now long-since folded) liberal newspaper *A Imprensa*. He became senator of Bahia and in 1905 and again in 1909 made unsuccessful attempts to be elected as the country's president.

The museum is basically a collection of Barbosa's possessions – beautiful Dutch and English furniture, Chinese and Japanese porcelain, and a library of 35,000 mostly leatherbound volumes, amongst which are two-hundred works penned by Barbosa himself. Additionally, the music room and ballroom both have impressive Art Deco finishing, and the bathroom was one of the first in Rio to be plumbed. Barbosa conferred a title on each room in the house – the Sala Bahia, Sala Questão Religiosa, Sala Habeas Corpus, Sala Código Civil – all of them identified with some part of his life.

Museu Villa-Lobos

A few blocks west, at Rua Sorocaba 200, is the **Museu Villa-Lobos** (Mon–Fri 10am–5.30pm; free; ℡21/2266-3894, ⓦwww.museuvillalobos.org.br). Established in 1960 to celebrate the work of the great Brazilian composer, Heitor Villa-Lobos (1887–1959), it's largely a display of his personal possessions such as baby-grand pianos, original music scores and a full programme of his life's concerts. You can also buy CDs of his music here.

Museu do Índio

Botafogo's main museum, the **Museu do Índio** (Tues–Fri 9am–5.30pm, Sat & Sun 1–5pm; T$5; Rua das Palmeiras 55; ℡21/2286-8899, ⓦwww .museudoindio.org.br;), is located a block west of the Museu Villa-Lobos. Housed in a beautiful colonial mansion dating from 1880, the museum was inaugurated on April 19, 1953, the commemoration of Brazil's "Day of the Indian" – not that there were many around by then to celebrate. Its an excellently put together collection, which succeeds in bringing alive some of the experiences of Brazil's indigenous peoples in the interactive format which is missing from the Museu Histórico Nacional. An extensive section on the Wajãpi (from Amapá state) contains reconstructed ceremonial areas, videos of traditional body painting and ceramics work, and areas with dimmed lights and atmospheric noises from the rainforest (you can only speculate on how the long shift-working security guards cope with it). Elsewhere, there are displays on the Amerindian construction of the universe, current challenges and future aspirations, as well as musical instruments, traditional costumes and other ritual devices.

Opportunities to try out body-painting designs and to enter a full-sized shelter of the Guaraní and Xingú – not to mention the giant carved crocodiles – will appeal enormously to many children. The attached shop is also worth visiting, selling a quality range of carefully sourced original artefacts at reasonable prices.

Morro Santa Marta and around

Back on Rua São Clemente, the street atmosphere changes very briefly at the top of Rua da Matriz where a glance upwards towards the Christ statue reveals the expansive **Morro Santa Marta favela**. The community takes its name from the existence of a small chapel containing the image of Santa Marta near the hill's summit. Urban legend dictates that in around 1680 a resident – Father Clemente – bought the surrounding land and baptized the hill in honour of his late mother,

Marta (thus it became the Morro Santa Marta), and placed her image in the chapel. Father Clemente, of course, has since been rewarded eternally through the inscription of his name on Botafogo's major east-west artery. The *favela* is now often referred to as **Dona Marta** following a period of confusion in the 1980s when evangelicals denying the saint's existence renamed their community.

Established in the 1930s with the arrival of migrants from the northeastern state of Paraíba, the *favela* today is notable for the bright colours of its buildings and a cable car which carries residents up to the community's summit. As a larger *favela* (around 7,500 residents) in the heart of the Zona Sul, Santa Marta has been well documented in books and films over the years. In 1996 Michael Jackson caused immense excitement with the filming of music video "They Don't Care About Us" here, and a couple of years later it was used as the case study for highly-rated documentary film *Notícias de uma Guerra Particular* (*News from a Private War*, 1999), the first Brazilian film to delve into the world of Rio's *narco-traficantes* from *favela*, police, and independent perspectives. Santa Marta is, at the time of writing at least, free from the Comando Vermelho gang of drug traffickers that used to control it, and now has a police presence. Nonetheless, Rio is unpredictable and visits without a local resident are inadvisable.

Continuing west along São Clemente, two further buildings of note (though both closed to visitors) are the 1949 artistic **Palácio da Cidade** (at the head of Rua Real Grandeza), which was formerly the British Embassy and now functions as the official residence of the Mayor; and the **Palácio São Clemente**, a block beyond, distinguished by its European orthodox-esque spire and now home to the Portuguese Consul.

Humaitá and south to the Cemitério São João Batista

The area of Botafogo west of Rua Conde de Irajá is called **Humaitá**, a mainly residential sub-*bairro* towards Lagoa that contains a great group of restaurants – collectively referred to as the **Poló Gastronômico de Botafogo**. The **Cobal de Humaitá** is a partially covered "market" of some twenty restaurants and bars off Rua Humaita and Rua Voluntários da Pátria. Its lively, animated atmosphere and regular live music means it attracts crowds most nights. A group of bars/restaurants around **Rua Visconde de Caravelas** and Rua Capitão Solomão are also good bets at pretty much any time.

A few blocks south and east of here on Rua General Polidoro is the **Cemitério São João Batista**, the Zona Sul's largest resting place for the full mix of its population. Extravagant house-like tombs for the city's super-elite lie on the level ground nearer the entrance, with large blocks of simple drawers higher up the hill – just like the *favelas*, in fact – in which the poor that can afford it are buried. Amongst the numerous stars buried here, look out for Tom Jobim and Carmen Miranda – both buried in the central area - while to find Clara Nunes and Vinicius de Moraes you'll need to ask the numerous ground staff for directions.

Morro do Pasmado and Clube Guanabara

Back on Botafogo's main north-south drag, just past the southern end of the beach and right in the middle of the busy road junction (cross via the footbridge) is a sports complex called **Clube Guanabara**. Non-members are allowed to use the facilities, but the most interesting thing here is its bayside *Bar da Rampa*, reached via an underpass from inside the club; it's an inviting spot by water with excellent seafood and regular samba parties attracting a diverse spirited crowd (see also p.198).

...sing up behind the Clube in the middle of the *bairro* is the **Morro do Pasmado** (Pasmado Hill), a wooded mound that is one of very few Rio hills without a *favela*. The summit's *mirante* (viewpoint) is reached via Rua General Severiano on the hill's southern side – a winding road arrives at a small shaded car park with snack huts, benches and a stunning view back across Botafogo Bay to Flamengo and Centro beyond.

Just south of here before you enter the Tunel Novo to Copacabana is one of the Zona Sul's biggest malls, **Shopping Rio Sul**, a giant construction of top brand shops and expensive, often overrated, restaurants. Nextdoor, the famous Rio concert hall, the **Canecão** (see p.198), is one of the top places to see big name MPB performances.

Botafogo Football Club and Rio Plaza Shopping

On an "island" in the centre of the busy road junction between Shopping Rio Sul and the Pasmado Hill is another mall, **Rio Plaza Shopping** – a much better bet for eating than its larger neighbour. Outside the mall at its southern end, partially hidden by trees, is the grand 1912 gold-coloured building General Severiano, home to **Botafogo Football Club** (Av. Vencesláu Brás 72; ☏21/2543-7272, ⓦ www.botafogonocoracao.com.br), which contains the club's trophy room and social club (closed for refurbishment at the time of writing).

Urca

The best bet for beaches in the Zona Sul outside of Copacabana and Ipanema is around **Urca**. There are sands on each side of the promontory on which this small, wealthy *bairro* stands – its name an acronym of Urbanizador Construção, the company that undertook its construction. Facing Botafogo, the Praia da Urca, only 100m long, is frequented almost exclusively by local inhabitants, while in front of the Estacio de Teleférico (cable car station) beneath the **Pão de Açúcar**, beautiful Praia Vermelha is a cove sheltered from the South Atlantic, whose relatively gentle (and clean) waters are popular with swimmers.

For a post-beach drink or bite to eat, visit either the *Restaurant Praia Vermelha*, located inside the army's compound (see p.185), or alternatively hang out at the **Balcão da Urca**, a stretch of wall near a bar at the end of Avenida João Luís Alves that draws a big crowd on sunny (especially weekend) evenings; the bar will even bring you beer or food when you're sitting a good distance down the road.

Pão de Açúcar

You should come to Urca at least once during your stay to visit the **Pão de Açúcar**, which rises where Guanabara Bay meets the Atlantic Ocean. In Portuguese the name means "**Sugar Loaf**", referring to the ceramic or metal mould used during the refining of sugar cane. Liquid sugar cane juice was poured into the mould and removed when the sugar had set, producing a shape reminiscent of the mountain. The name may also originate from the native Tamoyan Indian word *Pau-nh-Açuquá*, meaning "high, pointed or isolated hill" – a more apt

▲ Praia Vermelha from the Sugar Loaf mountain cable car

description. Intriguingly the first recorded non-indigenous ascent to the summit was made in 1817 by an English nanny, Henrietta Carstairs. Today, mountaineers scaling the smooth, precipitous slopes are a common sight, but there is a cable-car ride to the summit for the less adventurous.

The **cable car** system has been in place since 1912 – though absolute disbelief was the reaction from many locals when it was first proposed. Sixty years later the present Italian system, which can carry 1360 passengers every hour, was installed – and has since been used as the daredevil site for a number of long tightrope walks and cycles. By cable car, however, the 1400-metre journey is made in two stages, first to the summit of **Morro da Urca** (220m), where there is a theatre, restaurant and shops, and then on to the top of the Sugar Loaf mountain itself (396m) – the latter section famously used for the climatic scene in the James Bond film *Moonraker*. The cable cars have glass walls, and the glorious view from the top does not disappoint. Facing inland, you can see right across the city, from Centro and the Santos Dumont airport all the way through Flamengo and Botafogo; face Praia Vermelha and the cable-car terminal, and to the left you'll see the sweep of Copacabana and on into Ipanema, while back from the coast the mountains around which Rio was built rise to the Tijuca National Park.

Practicalities

Try and avoid the busy times between 10am and 3pm: the ride is best at sunset on a clear day, when the lights of the city are starting to twinkle. The base station is in Praça General Tibúrcio (daily 8am–10pm, every 30min; R$44; ⓦ www.bondinho .com.br), which can be reached by buses marked "Urca" or "Praia Vermelha" from Centro, #107 from Centro, Catete and Flamengo, or #511 and #512 from Zona Sul (be careful when returning to Copacabana to take buses heading directly there rather than the 90-minute route via Botafogo, Leblon and Ipanema).

An alternative (and probably the best) way to ascend the Morro da Urca (you can buy an onward ticket to the Sugar Loaf from there) is via the path from the eastern end of Praia Vermelha. A safe, **wooded trail** winds upwards around the hill along which you'll encounter curious small marmosets.

On the Morro da Urca, occasional **samba school** performances, balls and dance-music events liven up the summer months preceding Carnaval (see ⓦ www.veraodomorro.com.br).

The Zona Sul beaches

The world-famous **Zona Sul beaches**, stretching from **Leme** in the east to **Leblon** in the west, and including the *bairros* of **Copacabana** and **Ipanema**, cover almost seven kilometres of golden sand. The atmosphere is simply amazing; families, friends and couples crowd the palm-fringed bays, while on the wide pavements beach *quiosques* (kiosks) vend coconut water and *cerveja* to people-watchers amused by a constant flow of joggers, cyclists, posing muscle men and lycra-clad women. A far cry from the peace and quiet of the past, since the 1930s this stunningly beautiful stretch of coastline – backed by the São João and Cabritos hills and the Lagoa Rodrigo de Freitas – has grown to become Rio's most desirable area. Though Copacabana's glamour has somewhat faded, along with chic Ipanema and Leblon, it has for decades been considered by the outside world as the heart of the Brazilian good life.

Rio's sophisticated **beach culture** emerged as the city's famous sights started appearing in Hollywood movies and film stars such as Fred Astaire and Ginger Rogers began to grace Copacabana. Rio was one of the first destinations for the newly established jet set: "flying down to Rio" became an enduring cliché, celebrated in music, film and literature ever since (see p.100). While the term **Zona Sul** demarcates the whole area of the city south of Centro, above all it is the beaches that define the Zona Sul way of life. From the fashionable boutiques of Ipanema to the swanky bars of Leblon, the glamour of international stars at the *Copacabana Palace Hotel* to the stylish homes of Rio's most prosperous citizens, Zona Sul culture flaunts a kind of affluence, hedonism and carefree joy which other parts of Rio – often described as "*suburbio*"– can only dream about. And the area's influence extends far beyond the city. Across Brazil images of gorgeous *novela* (soap opera) actors and volleyball stars in Ipanema and Leblon are broadcast daily, whilst worldwide Copacabana and Ipanema have long since *become* Brazil; no introduction needed as the sexiest beaches on Earth. Most Zona Sul residents would simply never dream of living anywhere else.

From Botafogo, the **Túnel Novo** leads to Leme, a small *bairro* whose kilometre of beach sweeps into another almost-three kilometres of sand at Copacabana. Now one of the world's most densely populated areas, Copacabana is less classy than it once was, with four *favelas* having rapidly expanded on its hillsides, adding a remarkable contrast to the wealth below. Street traders are a permanent presence – revealing the significant disparity in social status and wealth that also makes the area one of Rio's most dynamic and unpretentious. Elegant Ipanema and Leblon

On the beach

In good weather the Zona Sul's beaches are alluring – many *Cariocas* pass much of their spare time here, sunbathing, swimming, jogging and playing beach **games** (see *Beach life* colour section). The beaches are divided into informal segments, each identified by **postos** (marker posts) assigned a number and located by the pavement a little over half-a-kilometre apart. Postos 1–6 run from the Morro do Leme along Copacabana beach to the Forte do Copacabana, and postos 7–12 continue from Arpoador along Ipanema and Leblon beaches to Avenida Niemeyer. While most parts of the beach attract a mix of people, gay men, families, beach-sport aficionados and even social classes loosely claim specific segments. It won't take you long to identify a stretch where you'll feel comfortable. Ipanema's posto 9 attracts a young, affluent and trendy crowd (see p.108), the areas between postos 2–3 and 8–9 are predominantly gay (see p.209), and postos 1, 7, and 11–12 are more family-oriented – the latter distinctly more affluent than the others.

Between the postos, *quiosques* (kiosks) set out chairs and tables on the pavement at regular intervals – ideal meeting points – selling anything from coconuts to fast food and full meals. Dotted along the sand itself, the staff of makeshift *barracas* (canopies) rent beach chairs and offer an informal waiter service for drinks at their patch of beach. **Beach vendors** offer an impressive array of goods including fresh pineapple, sweets, ice cream, *matte* (iced tea), grilled meats, corn and cheese on sticks, *caipirinhas*, as well as beach equipment, clothing, and even art work. Coconut water (*agua de coco or coco verde*) is sold everywhere and is a favourite hangover cure. Food here is generally quite safe to eat but be careful if you have a delicate constitution – especially with the trays of "fresh" shrimp.

In terms of beach **safety**, be aware of strong currents; the Atlantic waves are often strong and Copacabana in particular can be dangerous – look out for red flags which indicate that bathing is prohibited. Lifeguards are based at beach postos and there are also helicopters present on especially rough days. In general, however, there are few problems. **Pollution** is not an issue at Copacabana and Ipanema, the exception being after a prolonged period of heavy summer rain when the city's drainage system can become strained. Natural dangers aside, you should certainly be aware of security on the beach – take only the clothes and money that you'll need – it's also quite acceptable to use public transport while dressed for the beach. Buskers and beach sellers are almost always harmless – but there are a few tricksters who occasionally try to distract your attention while whipping away your bag.

have gained ground on Copacabana, their more chic streets lined with luxury boutiques, restaurants, bars, gyms and nightclubs. Their popular beaches also provide another four kilometres of sand and surf. All along the Zona Sul beaches, the seafront is backed by prestigious, high-rise hotels and luxury apartments that have sprung up since the 1940s – on Sundays and holidays something of the old ambience returns when the busy roads **Avenida Atlântica** in Copacabana and **Avenida Vieira Souto** in Ipanema are closed to allow room for joggers, cyclists and musicians – in Carnaval season live samba bands add to the excitement.

Leme and Copacabana

Bairros dominated to the east by the Sugar Loaf mountain and circled by a line of hills that stretch out into the bay, peaceful **Leme** and frenetic **Copacabana** are different stretches of the same three-and-a-half-kilometre beach divided by

Avenida Princesa Isabel. The Praia do Leme occupies the eastern kilometre up to the **Morro do Leme**, while the Praia de Copacabana runs southwest for close to 3km to the **Forte de Copacabana**. The seafront atmosphere is distinctly over the top, with exercising locals accompanied by party-hungry foreigners, and the bars and restaurants lining Avenida Atlântica packed day and night. Even the pavements are larger than life with vast **mosaics** designed by Burle Marx (see p.135) exhibiting the image of rolling waves, and the road's central reservation displaying a complex design best observed from the top of a hotel or from the Forte de Leme (see p.102). Contrastingly, the beaches at both Copacabana and Leme are marginally lower key than at Ipanema, with fewer vendors, more families and a greater cross-section of *Cariocas*. At night, on the floodlit beach, football is played into the early hours. Reading on the beach here is also a more realistic prospect than attempting to settle down with a novel on its more select, but busier, neighbour.

Copacabana emerged as a fishing village in the nineteenth century, finally connecting to the rest of the city in 1892 when the Túnel Velho link with Botafogo was inaugurated, later joined by the larger Túnel Novo (to Avenida Princesa Isabel) in 1904. The open sea and strong waves soon attracted beach-goers, though it remained a quiet, sparsely populated *bairro* until the splendid Neoclassically-styled *Copacabana Palace Hotel* opened its doors in 1923, its famous guests publicizing the beach and alerting enterprising souls to the area's

Flying down to Rio

My Rio, Rio by the Sea-o,
Flying down to Rio where there's rhythm and rhyme.
Hey feller, twirl that old propeller,
Got to get to Rio and we've got to make time.
You'll love it, soaring high above it,
Looking down on Rio from a heaven of blue.

The 1933 **Hollywood musical** *Flying Down to Rio* transformed the North American perception of the city. Starring Ginger Rogers, Fred Astaire and Dolores del Rio, its breathtaking finale featured chorus girls dancing on the wings of airplanes high above tourists' heads at a Copacabana beach hotel.

The opening of the sumptuous **Copacabana Palace Hotel** (see p.171) in 1923, marked Rio's first steps towards securing a glamourous international reputation. Nowhere in the city was more alluring at this time than the quiet, modern beach suburb of Copacabana, which was in the midst of an enormous real estate boom. Mansions, built only a couple of decades earlier, were being replaced by Art Deco hotels and apartment buildings designed to appeal to tourists and a growing middle-class. But although the *Palace* and the access enabled by Pan American Airways "Clipper" (or flying boat) service – which began running between Miami and Rio in 1930 – had started to attract wealthy US tourists, *Flying Down to Rio* firmly established the city as an international travel destination, identified in the minds of millions as a place of tropical sensuality, samba and non-stop carnival.

The arrival of **Carmen Miranda** (see p.90) and her Banda da Lua in the United States in 1940 further boosted Brazil's exotic image abroad. Tourism declined during World War II, and although the appeal of Copacabana remained strong in the immediate post-war period, other, closer Latin destinations – in particular Havana and Acapulco – successfully lured away American visitors. This contributed to Copacabana's gradual decline, a process that was hastened further with Ipanema's emergence as the Zona Sul suburb most favoured by Rio's rich and fashionable in the 1950s.

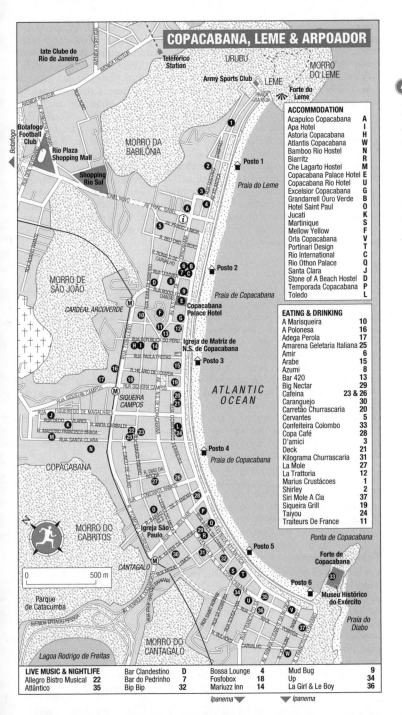

COPACABANA, LEME & ARPOADOR

Iate Clube do
Rio de Janeiro

Teleférico
Station

URUBU

MORRO
DO LEME

Army Sports Club

LEME

Forte do
Leme

PRAÇA
DA VIGIA

Botafogo
Football
Club

Rio Plaza
Shopping Mall

Shopping
Rio Sul

Botafogo

AVENIDA PASTEUR

AVENIDA PASTEUR

MORRO DA
BABILÔNIA

Posto 1

Praia do Leme

TUNEL NOVO

AV. PRINC. ISABEL

R. BELTRÃO SEIXAS

R. PRADO JUNIOR

R. RONALD DE CARVALHO

MORRO DE
SÃO JOÃO

CARDEAL ARCOVERDE

R. DUVIVIER

R. RODOLFO DANTAS

Praia de Copacabana

Copacabana
Palace Hotel

Igreja de Matriz de
N.S. de Copacabana

Posto 2

Posto 3

ATLANTIC
OCEAN

R. REPÚBLICA DO PERU

RUA PAULA FREITAS

R. HILÁRIO DE GOUVEIA

RUA SIQUEIRA CAMPOS

SIQUEIRA
CAMPOS

R. FIGUEIREDO DE MAGALHÃES

R. DÉCIO VILARES

R. MAESTRO FRANCISCO BRAGA

RUA SANTA CLARA

R. ANITA GARIBALDI

COPACABANA

MORRO DO
CABRITOS

Parque
de Catacumba

Lagoa Rodrigo de Freitas

Igreja São
Paulo

CANTAGALO

AVENIDA ATLÂNTICA

R. BARATA RIBEIRO

R. TONELEROS

AV. N.S. DE COPACABANA

R. CONSTANTE RAMOS

R. DIAS DA ROCHA

R. SANTA CLARA

R. XAVIER DA SILVEIRA

R. SÁ FERREIRA

AV. HENRIQUE DUMONT

AVENIDA EPITÁCIO PESSOA

AV. PRINCESA ISABEL

MORRO DO
CANTAGALO

Posto 4

Praia de Copacabana

Posto 5

Posto 6

Ponta de Copacabana

Forte de
Copacabana

Museu Histórico
do Exército

Praia do
Diabo

0   500 m

Ipanema ▼   ▼ Ipanema

ACCOMMODATION

Acapulco Copacabana	A
Apa Hotel	I
Astoria Copacabana	H
Atlantis Copacabana	W
Bamboo Rio Hostel	N
Biarritz	R
Che Lagarto Hostel	M
Copacabana Palace Hotel	E
Copacabana Rio Hotel	U
Excelsior Copacabana	G
Grandarrell Ouro Verde	B
Hotel Saint Paul	O
Jucati	K
Martinique	S
Mellow Yellow	F
Orla Copacabana	V
Portinari Design	T
Rio International	C
Rio Othon Palace	Q
Santa Clara	J
Stone of A Beach Hostel	D
Temporada Copacabana	P
Toledo	L

EATING & DRINKING

A Marisqueira	10
A Polonesa	16
Adega Perola	17
Amarena Geletaria Italiana	25
Amir	6
Arabe	15
Azumi	8
Bar 420	13
Big Nectar	29
Cafeina	23 & 26
Caranguejo	30
Carretão Churrascaria	20
Cervantes	5
Confeiteira Colombo	33
Copa Café	28
D'amici	3
Deck	21
Kilograma Churrascaria	31
La Mole	27
La Trattoria	12
Marius Crustáceos	1
Shirley	2
Siri Mole A Cia	37
Siqueira Grill	19
Taiyou	24
Traiteurs De France	11

LIVE MUSIC & NIGHTLIFE

Allegro Bistro Musical	22	Bar Clandestino	D	Bossa Lounge	4
Atlântico	35	Bar do Pedrinho	7	Fosfobox	18
		Bip Bip	32	Mariuzz Inn	14

Mud Bug	9
Up	34
La Girl & Le Boy	36

commercial potential. Rapid growth followed, precipitated by tramlines running from Centro through the tunnels and right along the coast; a landfill project was undertaken along which the two-lane **Avenida Atlântica** was built, with the beach expanded even further in the 1970s.

Now a popular residential area in a thoroughly impressive setting (around one fifth of the population are retired, having moved here in the 1950s when the area was at its most fashionable), Copacabana's expansion has been restricted by the Morro de São João, which separates it from Botafogo, and the Morro dos Cabritos, which forms a natural barrier with Lagoa to the west. Consequently, it's one of the world's most densely populated areas, as well as a frenzy of sensual activity – where looks are all important and the nightlife scene ranges from straight and gay chic through to – inevitably – sex tourism. Some say that Copacabana is past its prime, and certainly it's not as exclusive as it once was. But ultimately, despite a tourist-based economy Copacabana somehow manages to maintain its residential and commercial feel, and many foreigners love it for exactly that. Its vibrant street mix is much more representative of the whole city than Ipanema's is – and it's a brilliant place to sit and watch the Brazilian world go by.

Leme

Leme is a good deal less frenetic than its neighbour, its beach melting into Copacabana's between postos 1 and 2. It tends to attract families – people from the Zona Sul on weekdays and a greater number from Zona Norte at weekends – you can spot the difference by the elaborate picnics that people coming from further afield seem to bring. Linking Leme and Copacabana with Botafogo (and giant mall Shopping Rio Sul) at the end of Avenida Princesa Isabel is Túnel Novo – avoid walking through here as it's a favourite place for tourists to be relieved of their wallets (hundreds of buses pass through instead). Also on the Avenida – halfway up – is a branch of RioTur, the tourist information centre (Mon–Fri 9am–6pm; Av. Princesa Isabel 183 ☎21/2542-8080, ⓦwww.rio.rj.gov.br/riotur/en). At night the Avenida Princesa Isabel and the two to three blocks west into Copacabana turn into the Zona Sul's main red-light district. Backing onto Leme itself is the Morro da Babilônia, home to a large *favela* of the same name.

At the far end of Leme's beach is the Praça do Vigia, lined with park benches. From here a concrete path leads a short way along the cliffside, a brief and pleasant diversion from the beach with its rows of line fishermen and daring cliff divers at weekends. Most notably, however, the walk offers a wonderful photo opportunity back across the whole of the bay, with the Christ statue gazing down from the Corcovado beyond.

Forte do Leme

For the best view in the *bairro*, walk the trail to the **Forte do Leme** (8am–5pm daily; R\$4). Entering through the gate behind Praça do Vigia and following the road through the army's sports club, a cobblestone lane leads around the Morro do Leme and up to the fort. It takes about thirty minutes to walk through rainforest to the top, and the reward is a staggering view of both the Zona Sul beaches and the Sugar Loaf mountain over Guanabara Bay – it's also the ideal place to gain some perspective on Burle Marx's fabulous seafront pavement designs. Dating from 1776 and reconstructed in 1919, the fort originally monitored movements in and out of the bay. Today its ruins contain some eerie passages and modern ramparts, which you're free to explore.

▲ Walking the Copacabana seafront

Copacabana

Called Praia de Socopenapan by Rio's indigenous Tupi (see p.247), the name Copacabana is thought to have come from Lake Titicaca in Bolivia where it means "view of the lake". According to legend, Nossa Senhora appeared there; shrines were produced in her honour, one of which ended up in Rio – probably brought by merchants trading Peruvian silver in the eighteenth century. A chapel was promptly built for this new Nossa Senhora, though it was later demolished and replaced by Copacabana fort. The name survives only at the church Matriz de Nossa Senhora de Copacabana (see below).

Through the centre of Rio's most famous *bairro* runs the busy arteries **Avenida Nossa Senhora de Copacabana** and **Rua Barata Ribeiro**. The former is the smarter of the two and is lined with assorted clothing stores, supermarkets, *por kilo* (pay by weight) restaurants, and *lanchonetes* (snack bars). Many of the more hip shops have been pushed out of business by the boutiques of trendy Ipanema and the shopping malls of the wider Zona Sul, though there's still no shortage of quality gear around, and you'll certainly pay less for it here.

Some fine examples of Art Deco architecture can be seen throughout the *bairro*, none more impressive than the **Copacabana Palace Hotel** at Avenida Atlântica and Rua Rodolfo Dantas, built in 1923 and considered one of Rio's best hotels. With a long list of famous former guests – from Fred Astaire to Madonna and Lady Di to Theodore Roosevelt – it has a stylish and exclusive ambience and is well worth stopping by for a drink or meal in any of its three bars and restaurants during your stay. While Copacabana's churches can't be compared to those downtown, the most appealing are the attractive yet unremarkable **Matriz de Nossa Senhora de Copacabana** at Praça Serzedelo Correia off Rua Siqueira Campus, with a replica painting of the original Virgin Mary who gave her name to the *bairro*, and the **Igreja de São Paulo Apóstolo** at Rua Barão de Ipanema close to Rua Barata Ribeiro, a somewhat grander and brighter church with a large fresco behind the altar.

Broadly speaking, Copacabana has differences in both street and beach atmosphere as you move from one part to another. The area of the *bairro* close to Leme and down to Rua Duvivier – all around posto 2 – is unofficially the red-light district and contains numerous strip clubs and seedy bars, though there are also a few very good local places around here of which *Cervantes* bar/restaurant is the most famous (see p.187). Also at this end of Copacabana, lying behind Metrô Cardeal Arcoverde is the attractive hillside road, Ladeira do Leme, which leads to Botafogo and is *favela*-free on account of an army base at its summit.

The large central area from Rua Rodolfo Dantas down to blocks around Rua Miguel Lemos is Copacabana's busy commercial heartland, with plentiful shops, restaurants and hotels. North towards Botafogo are the quiet streets of **Bairro Peixoto**, a more tranquil residential area with an artistic, affluent feel, and an attractive central square with a children's playground and a Wednesday morning **feira** which has a variety of food stalls. At the southern end of the *bairro* towards the Forte de Copacabana, businesses are thinner on the ground and the streets a little calmer in the daytime - though there are a number of nightclubs. Copacabana's largest *favela* also lies on the hillside above – separated into three communities (from east to west): Pavão, Pavãozinho and Cantagalo – which can be noisy if you're staying close by. Well-established as a part of Copacabana, these communities stretching right up the hillside are an arresting site from nearby hotel rooftops – their populations serve the Zona Sul's huge demand for shop, hotel and restaurant workers. Cantagalo also has a well-known nightspot for *baile funk* dances (see p.262), though you should only contemplate going if you're familiar with the city and are taken by a local that you trust.

Praia de Copacabana

Probably the most famous stretch of sand in the world, gorgeous Copacabana beach is the setting for intense activity year-round. Joggers, football stars, models, prostitutes, millionaires and *favela* dwellers can all be found strutting their stuff along the Copacabana beach front. Along much of the beach's length, from postos 1 through to 5, you'll see beach football and volleyball galore, and a cross between the two, **footvolley** (*futevôlei*), was created here in the 1960s. Beach football had been temporarily outlawed on the grounds of disturbance, and allegedly football stars such as the infamous Almir gathered by Rua Bolivar near posto 4 and started kicking a football on the beach volleyball court to escape the law and impress passing crowds. It soon caught on, and these days you can see competitions in progress at any point along the beach. Look out also for the children's **Beach Soccer** (see p.244) school near to **posto 3**, which is run by famous former Flamengo footballers Junior, Juninho and Robertinho.

Aside from sports, other areas of the beach which attract particular cliques or atmospheres include the blocks around **posto 2**, which tends to be animated and touristy, as well as having more than its fair share of sun-tanning prostitutes on the look out for rich foreign pickings. Many of Avenida Atlantica's seafront bars – here and elsewhere – also attract sex workers in greater numbers than elsewhere in the city. Right opposite the *Copacabana Palace*, between postos 2 and 3, the *Quiosque Arco-Íris* and surrounding beach – marked by a rainbow flag – attracts a mature gay crowd, though not as large as posto 8 in Ipanema. The southern end of the beach from **postos 5** to (unmarked) **posto 6** near the *forte* is the quietest part of Copacabana's beach, and traces of the former fishing community that dominated the area until the first decades of the twentieth century remain. Early each morning the boats of the *colônia de pescadores* set sail from the far end of the beach, returning by 8am to sell their fish. If you're up at that time (or haven't gone to bed yet), it's a lovely sight to see them arrive.

Copacabana beach reaches its peak capacity each year for **Reveillon** (New Year) when up to two million people gather for fireworks, music and dance (see p.222). At other times, too, the beach is used for huge **concerts**; the free Rolling

Stones event in 2006, where they arrived on stage via a specially built aerial walkway from the *Copacabana Palace Hotel* across the road, reportedly attracted a crowd of a million and a half. Copacabana was also the beach of choice for events, including beach volleyball, at the Pan-American Games in 2007.

The Forte de Copacabana and Museu Histórico do Exército

Perched on a spit of land at Copacabana's southern end, the **Forte de Copacabana** (Tues–Sun 10am–5pm; R$4), inaugurated in 1914, was built to protect the entrance to Guanabara Bay. It's mainly worth visiting for the impressive views of Copacabana from the roof – but a diversion into the somewhat dingy rooms holds some interest for the military hardware on display; the workings of a giant 305mm cannon can be seen below, with the gun itself up on the fort's roof. However, the highlight is a branch of the excellent *Confeitaria Columbo* (Tues–Sun 10am–8pm) tearoom – you can sit out on attractive tables and enjoy the view with an assortment of fine cakes or savouries.

The entrance to the **Museu Histórico do Exército** lies above the tearooms. The museum houses a mildly interesting exhibition on soldiers through the centuries and the role of the army in Brazil's independence. The army's more controversial achievements such as the Expedições Bandeirantes, which aimed at indigenous genocide in the seventeenth and eighteenth centuries, or the military's twentieth-century role in bringing dictators to power and ruthlessly crushing any opposition, however, are glossed over without any reference to the horrific reality.

Ipanema

The trendiest and most desirable area of Rio, Ipanema also undoubtedly boasts the most fashionable beach. With gentler waters than Copacabana, it really is stupendous and tends to dominate the *bairro*'s life even more than its larger and slightly less salubrious neighbour. Together with Leblon just to the west, the two *bairros* have an exclusive air, expensive stores mingling with sushi bars, luxurious gyms and appealing *botecos* with yards of terrace space to watch the world go by. The seafront itself has little in the way of restaurants (except for the ever-present beach kiosks), which means everyone heads back into the *bairro* after the beach, re-energizing the streets and keeping bars and nightclubs busy until dawn. On Sunday, the seafront **Avenida Vieira Souto** is closed to traffic and the whole area is taken over by strollers, skateboarders, rollerbladers and posers of an especially toned and beautiful variety.

Ipanema came into its own in the 1960s following a decade of rapid development as then-chic Copacabana became rammed to bursting. Sand dunes were transformed into high-rise apartment buildings and dirt tracks into concrete roads. By the 1960s intellectuals, musicians and artists had created a relaxed, affluent and distinctly Bohemian ambience. It was from this alternative atmosphere that Bossa Nova emerged, catapulted onto the world stage by the genre's major proponents – Tom Jobim and Vinícius de Moraes, whose track *The Girl from Ipanema* became an instant hit (see p.108). These days, Bohemia has given way to a real estate and tourism boom, but the *bairro* nonetheless retains some of its carefree and artistic 1960s vibe. It now has a reputation as a fashion centre second-to-none in Latin America. Although many in São Paulo and Buenos Aires would dispute this, the *bairro* is packed with bijou little boutiques flogging the very best Brazilian names in fine threads.

IPANEMA

ACCOMMODATION

Arpoador Inn	M
Caesar Park	K
Che Lagarto Hostel	G
Fasano	C
Ipanema Beach House	B
Ipanema Hotel Residência	I
Ipanema Inn	J
Ipanema Plaza	D
Karisma Hostel	H
Mango Tree Hostel	A
Margarida's Pousada	E
São Marco	F
Vermont	

EATING & DRINKING

Bar Lagoa	3	Chaika	14
Bazzar	5	Deliro Tropical	23
Bazzar Café	13	Expand Wines	6
Benkei	17	Felice Café	32
Bofetada	26	Frontera	15
Cafeina	21	Garota de Ipanema	25
Casa de Feijoada	28	Gula Gula	20
Carretão Churrascaria	16	Lord Jim	22
		Market Ipanema	18
		New Natural	10
		Palaphita Kitsch	1
		Satyricon	9
		Sorvete Mil Frutas	12
		To Nem Aí	27
		Via Sete Grill	11
		Zazá Bistrô Tropical	29

LIVE MUSIC & NIGHTLIFE

Baronneti	7
Casa da Lua	8
Conversa Afiada	19
Dama de Ferro	4
Empório	24
Galeria Café	30
Mistura Fina	33
Nuth Club	2
Vinicius Show Bar	31

ATLANTIC OCEAN

▲ Sunset at Arpoador

Looking at Ipanema today you would never guess that it was founded as a village as recently as 1894. Maintaining the beach's Amerindian name – meaning "dangerous water" – a bridge over the channel from Copacabana was built in 1918 but the later development extended a beachfront road all along the coast, swallowing up the rocky outcrop now known as the **Pedra do Arpoador**. Just six blocks lie between the sea and the inland lake Lagoa Rodrigo de Freitas (see p.112) tucked between the surrounding green hills and preserving Ipanema as a separate entity from much of the rest of the city. At its western end, the *bairro* is divided from Leblon by a narrow strip of canal and parkland called the **Jardim de Alah**, which links Lagoa to the ocean.

Around Ipanema

Dominated by the Pedra do Arpoador – the huge rock at the eastern end of the Ipanema and Arpoador beaches (near to Copacabana) – the Parque Garota de Ipanema is a truly gorgeous place to spend a couple of hours. Try to get to Arpoador before sunset on a clear day as you'll enjoy a fine view across to Leblon and the Dois Irmãos mountains – in summer a setting sun on the horizon is traditionally greeted with mass applause. At the Pedra's eastern side, the tiny but beautiful **Praia do Diablo** also draws a crowd, though swimming here is a little rougher than at the Praia do Arpoador on the other side. Beginning at **posto 7**, the **Praia do Arpoador** itself is popular with families and the elderly as the ocean here is slightly calmer than neighbouring Ipanema's beach. At weekends, direct buses from Méier in Zona Norte bring hundreds of day-trippers to Arpoador, and a good number set up for the day between postos 7 and 8, with picnics and stereos – to the annoyance of some of the Zona Sul's well-to-do.

A block inland from the beach, behind Rio's most deluxe hotel, *Fasano*, is Ipanema's busiest square, **Praça General Osório**. Surrounded by innumerable restaurants, bars and shops, it has finally been linked by *metrô* to the rest of the

The Girl from Ipanema: bossa nova in its natural habitat

It was at a bar called *Veloso* in 1962 that master musicians and composers **Tom Jobim** and **Vinicius de Moraes** sat down and wrote **Garota de Ipanema** (*The Girl from Ipanema*), a song inspired by passing beauties which put Ipanema and the bossa nova style (see p.261) on the world map. A dreamy, contemplative piece with jazz-samba undertones and lyrics exploring fading youth, the recording – sung by **Astrud Gilberto** and with **Stan Getz** on sax – was an instant hit, winning a Grammy in 1965. Hundreds of subsequent cover versions by the likes of Frank Sinatra, Shirley Bassey and even Madonna have kept the song alive. *Bar Veloso* was renamed the *Bar Garota de Ipanema* in its honour (see p.189), the street renamed Rua Vinicius de Moraes, and Jobim's name endows Rio's international airport.

Today bossa nova has given way to samba, funk and imported sounds, but the jazzy genre can still be sought out, most notably at the *Bar do Tom, Vinicius Show Bar, Alegro Bistrô Musical* and the *Canecão* (see pp.198–200).

city, which will also provide added business for its so-called **Feira Hippie** (see p.234), a market of affordable clothes and assorted oddments held between 9am and 6pm every Sunday. The quality of the goods here – leather, jewellery, cushion covers, hammocks and crocheted tablecloths – varies, but there's always a good atmosphere. Ipanema's main transecting street, **Rua Visconde de Pirajá**, heads west from here and is the principal place to shop, with numerous small and elegant malls along its route (see p.229). On Friday another large *feira* takes place on the Praça de Paz three blocks west, though just food and flowers are on offer here.

Ipanema's Rua Farme de Amoedo and the large stretch of sand directly in front of it (a block west of Praça General Osório between postos 8 and 9) is Rio's most well-known gay area, with a collection of bars, clubs, gay-friendly cafés and a giant rainbow flag on the beach.

H. Stern World Headquarters

With its claim to fame as Ipanema's only museum of note, the ostentatious **H. Stern World Headquarters** (Mon–Fri 9am–6pm, Sat 9am–2pm; Rua Garcia D'Ávila 113) fits in well with its surroundings. Essentially a showroom of absurdly expensive – some extremely attractive – jewellery, it also guides you briefly through the process of gem excavation, cutting and processing in Brazil. Once a translated recording has established that "through the headphones we can control the customer mind process", you learn about the cutting and polishing of jewels from diamonds to imperial topaz, watching a series of craftsmen and women behind glass windows. As staff are on commission, it's very much sales-oriented, but if you're interested in jewellery then the showroom does make a visit worthwhile. Ignoring the $25,000 watches and $13,000 diamond-encrusted rings, move on to get a good look at the collection inspired by Carmen Miranda (colourful, brash, but attractive), the Brazilian modern collection (symmetries and curves surely inspired by the likes of Niemeyer) – and the exceptionally beautiful, though perhaps controversial, collection based on Amazonian Amerindians' designs, including eighteen-carat-gold feather necklaces.

Praia de Ipanema

Perhaps even more than at Copacabana, Ipanema's beach is unofficially divided according to the interest or desires of its users. A block west of Rua Farme de Amoedo's gay area is neighbouring **posto 9**, where young, hip, party (and arty)

people make camp. On sunny weekends you'll have to get here early
decent space as it's the most popular spot of all the Zona Sul beache
for books here, its all about *cerveja*, *caipirinhas* – and looking go
chunky barbecued meat sandwiches from the locally famous
Uruguayan *barraca*, denoted by a blue and white Uruguayan fl...
posto 9, the beach becomes marginally more tranquil, with more room for ...
beautiful people to sunbathe, stretch and enjoy vigorous beach sports – posto
10 is known for volleyball and attracts a smart and fashionable Ipanema crowd.

Leblon

Inhabited by the wealthy and chicly dressed, **Leblon** has more of a community
and residential feel than Ipanema. Locals gather in the upmarket cafés scattered
throughout the *bairro*, and Rio's most exclusive malls display designer clothes in
lavish surroundings. With the dramatic Dois Irmãos mountains dominating it from
above, Leblon's setting really is quite stunning, a situation all the more remarkable
when contrasted to *favela* Vidigal, on the slopes of Dois Irmãos beyond.

On the beach east of **posto 11**, a free gym – "**Muscle Beach**" – is based here
in the summer, tending to be used by the already hunky and well-toned, while all
around this posto are volleyball courts – informal classes take place here in the
mornings (look out for advertising boards). West of posto 11 is a play area and
facilities for young children, and the whole strip towards posto 12 attracts families.

Leblon's central artery, Avenida Ataulfo de Paiva, is lined with boutiques and
restaurants, and around the junction with Avenida Alfrânio de Melo Franca
you'll find the Zona Sul's two most exclusive malls, the large **Shopping
Leblon** and the smaller but even pricier **Rio Design** opposite – both offer free
wi-fi, the latter in a room with comfy sofas and a café. Just north of here
opposite the Lagoa Rodrigo de Freitas is the home of Brazil's biggest football
club **Clube de Regatas do Flamengo** (not to be confused with the *bairro* of
the same name. Mon–Sat 9am–6pm; R$10; Av. Borges de Medeiros 997;
☏21/2159- 0100, ⓦwww.flamengo.com.br), which has sports facilities and a
shop where you can buy Flamengo merchandise including shirts and bikinis.
The trophy room upstairs is strangely disappointing for Brazil's most popular
club, even though their 1981 Libertadores Cup triumph is there.

A block behind Clube Flamengo on Rua Gilberto Cardoso is the **Cobal**, a
collection of food market stalls and bars which at night becomes a huge,
bustling eating and drinking area. A little further to the west, Leblon's main strip
of bars and restaurants lies on Rua Dias Ferreira and the final two blocks of
Avenida Ataulfo de Paiva – a great place to come for a night out.

A hidden gem in Leblon, little visited by tourists, is the **Parque do Penhasco
Dois Irmãos**, accessed on the hillside beyond Avenida Visconde de
Albuquerque, from Rua Aperanã. A road winds up through landscaped gardens,
with a path continuing up to the base of the mountain, which provides grand
vistas of the whole beach area of the Zona Sul.

Vidigal

Back at the end of the beach, Avenida Niemeyer winds it way along the coast.
Almost immediately you reach the **Mirante do Leblon**, another good viewpoint
(and slightly less tiring to reach than the Parque, above), looking back along the
beach. A few hundred yards further is the **Praia do Vidigal**, tucked under the dual

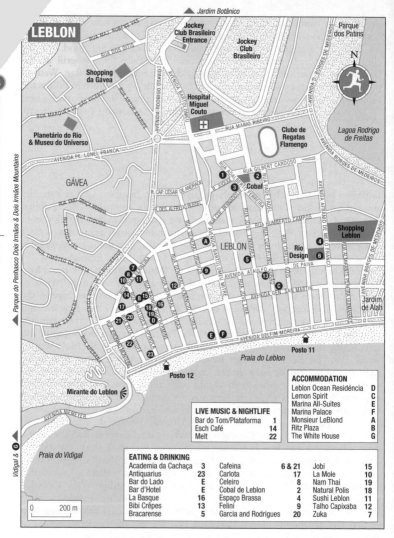

LEBLON

Jardim Botânico ▲

Jockey Club Brasileiro Entrance

Jockey Club Brasileiro

Parque dos Patins

Shopping da Gávea

Hospital Miguel Couto

Clube de Regatas Flamengo

Lagoa Rodrigo de Freitas

Planetário do Rio & Museu do Universo

GÁVEA

Cobal

LEBLON

Shopping Leblon

Rio Design

Jardim de Alah

Praia do Leblon

Posto 11

Mirante do Leblon ◀

Posto 12

Praia do Vidigal

Vidigal & ◀

ACCOMMODATION

Leblon Ocean Residéncia	D
Lemon Spirit	C
Marina All-Suites	E
Marina Palace	F
Monsieur LeBlond	A
Ritz Plaza	B
The White House	G

LIVE MUSIC & NIGHTLIFE

Bar do Tom/Plataforma	1
Esch Café	14
Melt	22

EATING & DRINKING

Academia da Cachaça	3	Cafeina	6 & 21	Jobi	15
Antiquarius	23	Carlota	17	La Mole	10
Bar do Lado	E	Celeiro	8	Nam Thai	19
Bar d'Hotel	E	Cobal de Leblon	2	Natural Polis	18
La Basque	16	Espaço Brassa	4	Sushi Leblon	11
Bibi Crêpes	13	Felini	9	Talho Capixaba	12
Bracarense	5	Garcia and Rodrigues	20	Zuka	7

0   200 m

peaks of the Morro Dois Irmãos and Vidigal *favela* on the mountain's lower slopes – one of the Zona Sul's largest shantytowns. The beach is only about 500m long and used to be the preserve of the *favela*'s residents until they lost it to a fencing plan by the *Rio Sheraton Hotel* – built in the 1970s long after the emergence of the *favela* and an odd choice of place to stay considering the hotel's inland *favela* view. Vidigal is also home to the rather rustic theatre of successful group Nos do Morro (see p.206), who have supplied actors for some of Brazil's most famous films.

If you're interested in seeing more of Vidigal or in climbing the Dois Irmãos mountains – only accessible from the *favela* – contact Turismo Alternativo (☏21/3322-8765 or 9392-9203, ⓦwww.turismoalternativo.com.br), who can arrange a day or half-day tour (R\$75–100).

5

Lagoa, São Conrado and the Floresta da Tijuca

S
et back from Ipanema and Leblon's plush beaches is the supremely attractive **Lagoa Rodrigo de Freitas**, always referred to simply as **Lagoa**. Together with its neighbouring *bairros* of **Jardim Botânico** and **Gávea**, these are Rio's most wealthy suburbs, where the seriously rich and status-conscious have chosen to live since the 1920s. The south-eastern shores of the lake close to Ipanema and Copacabana offer an ideal half-day diversion from the beach, where you can climb through the Parque da Catacumba to gain a stunning view of the area – followed by refreshments on Lagoa's shores. To the north and west of Lagoa, and backed by dense forest, Jardim Botânico and Gávea are dominated by beautiful **botanical gardens**, some of the city's best restaurants, as well as by the city's racecourse, the **Jockey Club Brasileiro**.

Nowhere are Rio de Janeiro's famous contrasts illustrated more sharply than on the steep hillside between wealthy Gávea and coastal São Conrado's condos and apartment blocks. *Favela* **Rocinha** is Rio's largest shantytown and home to some of the city's poorest residents, its location within the Zona Sul makes it the most frequent destination for **favela tours**. Jardim Botânico, Gávea and **São Conrado** all have an access point to the **Parque Nacional da Tijuca**, dominated by the **Floresta da Tijuca** – Rio's immense "urban forest" – an oxymoron that seems fitting in a city of extremes. If the beach madness of Ipanema and Copacabana has left you in urgent need of peace and tranquillity – then look no further than the beautiful waterfalls and hiking trails within the park's boundaries.

Gávea developed as a prosperous residential area after the arrival of electric trams in 1904, which trundled from Centro all the way up Rua Marques de São Vicente to where Rocinha now begins. Some of Rio's finest **modern architecture** can be found in the area, including Gávea's excellent cultural centre, the **Instituto Moreira Salles**, and, further afield, architect Oscar Niemeyer's former house in São Conrado, an early example of the innovative curved designs that he later became so famous for. Also in Gávea, the

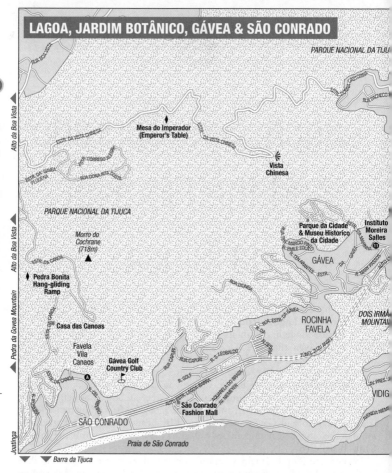

LAGOA, JARDIM BOTÂNICO, GÁVEA & SÃO CONRADO

PARQUE NACIONAL DA TIJU...

Alto da Boa Vista

Mesa do Imperador
(Emperor's Table)

Vista
Chinesa

PARQUE NACIONAL DA TIJUCA

Alto da Boa Vista

Morro do
Cochrane
(718m)

Parque da Cidade
& Museu Histórico
da Cidade

Instituto
Moreira
Salles

GÁVEA

Pedra da Gávea Mountain

Pedra Bonita
Hang-gliding
Ramp

Casa das Canoas

ROCINHA
FAVELA

DOIS IRMÃ
MOUNTAI

Favela
Vila
Canaos

Gávea Golf
Country Club

São Conrado
Fashion Mall

VIDIG

Joatinga

SÃO CONRADO

Praia de São Conrado

Barra da Tijuca

Planetário is a great spot for children and sky gazers, while the **Museu da Cidade**, set amidst the forest, has a small but interesting exhibition on the building of the city.

Lagoa

A lagoon linked to the ocean by a narrow canal that passes through the **Jardim de Alah**, dividing Ipanema from Leblon, attractive Lagoa is fringed by the **Parque Tom Jobim** (named in memory of Rio's famed bossa nova composer, see p.261). The area comes alive each evening and at weekends as people walk, rollerblade, jog or cycle along the 9km perimeter pathway, play tennis or baseball, or just gaze at passers-by. Summer evenings are especially popular when, on the west side of the lagoon in the area known as the **Parque dos**

Parque Lage 1

JARDIM BOTÂNICO 3

Jardim Botânico

Jardim Botânico Entrance

Planetário do Rio (Rio Planetarium) & Museu do Universo

Shopping da Gávea

PUC University

GÁVEA

Cobal

Hospital Miguel Couto

Clube de Regatas Flamengo

Jockey Club Brasileiro

Parque dos Patins

Jockey Club Entrance

Lagoa Rodrigo de Freitas

Parque de Catacumba

LAGOA

Fundação Eva Klabin

Parque do Cantagalo

Ilha dos Caiçaras

Shopping Leblon

Rio Design

Museu H. Stein

LEBLON

Posto 11   Posto 10   Posto 9   Posto 8

Praia do Leblon

Posto 12

Mirante do Leblon

Praia de Vidigal

Praia de Ipanema   Praia do Arpoador

ATLANTIC OCEAN

N

0   500 m

LIVE MUSIC & NIGHTLIFE	
00 (Zero Zero)	10

ACCOMMODATION	
Favela Receptiva	A
Sinless	B

EATING & DRINKING	
Arabe da Lagoa	8
Café Galeria	11
Café du Lage	1
Casa da Táta	9
Couve-Flor	6
Da Graça	4
Guima's	7
Mil Frutas	3
Olympe	2
Yumê	5

Patins (Skaters' Park), there is a row of food stalls and restaurants, including the *Arabe da Lagoa* (see p.192). Most have live music and dancing on summer evenings, too. On the opposite side of the lake, closer to Copacabana and Ipanema, is the **Parque Cantagalo**, which has a lower-key group of restaurants including rustic-chic *Palaphita Kitsch* (see p.189), with cushions scattered across its section of lakeshore. You can also hire peddle boats here (R$15 for thirty minutes) – but don't get in the way of the speedy rowers from sports clubs Vasco, Flamengo and Botafogo, also based around the shoreline. On Lagoa's steep eastern hillsides the land behind the wealthy apartment buildings is well forested, hiding the fact that until relatively recently *favelas* covered their slopes. A part of this area now holds the beautiful Parque da Catacumba.

Lagoa is now almost half its original size; land reclamation since the 1930s took back chunks of the surrounding area before the construction of Ipanema and Leblon. Until recently, the water was badly polluted, but a programme to clean it up has been partially successful and its mangrove swamps are slowly recovering. The ecology of the lake is quite complex: microorganisms in the

▲ Lagoa and the Jockey Club at night

lake's muddy depths produce sulphur which is only released when an exceptionally high tide connects the lake to the ocean every few years, causing sudden mass death of fish life.

Fundação Eva Klabin

One of the few remaining original homes at the southeast corner of the lagoon (and just five minutes' walk from Copacabana) contains the **Fundação Eva Klabin** (guided visits Wed–Sun 2.30pm & 4pm; ☎21/3202-8550, ⓦwww .evaklabin.org.br), a cultural centre with a museum offering cultural-historical activities (see the website) at Av. Epitácio Pessoa 2480. Built in 1931, the house is typical of the resort-style Norman architecture popular at the time – with affluent owners favouring smaller properties that tried to recreate the stepped passageways, pillars and alcoves deemed emblematic of the Norman period. The house became the family residence of Eva Klabin, a wealthy art collector of Lithuanian origin. The wide-ranging art collection is beautifully displayed in elegant, wood-panelled rooms and includes original pieces by Botticelli, Pizarro and Rembrandt. Eva's impressive international wardrobe is also fascinating and will appeal to anyone interested in period dress.

Parque da Catacumba

Parque da Catacumba (daily 8am–7pm) on Avenida Epitácio Pessoa is a wonderful, shaded place, within walking distance from Copacabana and Ipanema. The dense tropical vegetation forms an excellent backdrop for one of Rio's few sculpture parks; modern, abstract pieces that contrast sharply with their surroundings are scattered along a steep and winding cobblestone path. There is also now an adventure centre here, Lagoa Adventures (ⓦwww .lagoaaventuras.com.br; see p.224), offering a raised walkway and zip line, most suited to children and families. Continuing uphill beyond the highest-placed sculpture, a rough path leads all the way to the summit (20–30min) from where there is an astonishing view of Ipanema, Leblon and Lagoa at an unusual angle – the Lagoa is normally only looked down upon from the Corcovado. The narrow width of Ipanema is more apparent from here than elsewhere, and you can also gain a clearer idea of the lake's original boundaries.

Catacumba means catacomb, deriving from the hill's location as an Amerindian burial site before the Portuguese conquered in the seventeenth century. In the 1940s the hill slopes became smothered by *favela* da Catacumba, eventually home to 10,000 people and cleared away in 1970 to make way for apartment buildings. Many displaced people were moved to a new development in Zona Oeste called Cidade de Deus, far from the Zona Sul's employment – which led to social chaos, well documented in the film of the same name (see p.268).

Jardim Botânico

To the north of Lagoa lies the *bairro* of **Jardim Botânico**, a wealthy residential area dissected by busy Rua Jardim Botânico. Home to Rio's botanical gardens, Jardim Botânico has also developed a reputation for gastronomic excellence, with a fine group of restaurants both in the *bairro*'s centre and on quieter Rua Pacheco Leão. The latter street is lined with attractive cobbled side streets, many of which are now gated communities, before it heads upwards and westwards into the Parque Nacional da Tijuca. Jardim Botânico has an artistic feel – largely thanks to the presence of the headquarters of Globo, Brazil's largest media company – and is populated by film-makers, designers and other affluent artists. It's one of the few *bairros* not to have a *favela* on its hillside; instead, mansions stretch up into the forest. At the eastern end of the *bairro* **Parque Lage** is a tremendously beautiful spot away from the traffic.

Parque Lage

Directly to the north of Lagoa is the magnificent **Parque Lage** (daily 8am–5pm), designed by the English landscape gardener John Tyndale in the early 1840s, and which – remarkably – holds the last-remaining section of primary **Mata Atlântica** (Atlantic forest; see p.124) in Rio. Consisting of thirty-five hectares of forest stretching up the steep slopes of the Corcovado (a two to three hour trail leads upwards to the Christ statue, see p.80; ask park security to direct you to the start), as well as seventeen hectares of landscaped gardens containing breadfruit, almond and mango trees, the area's conservation was enabled by its longstanding private ownership. Containing a labyrinthine path network and seven small lakes, it's now a popular picnic location and romantic spot for couples.

At the park's centre is a palatial house which became the home of Commander Antônio Lage and his opera-singer wife in 1959; less than ten years later Lage passed the whole property to the Banco do Brasil who declared it a protected area. It is now home to the **Escola de Artes Visuais** and has a stunning colonnaded central courtyard surrounding a pool, with a few open rooms exhibiting the students' abstract work. The superb *Café do Lage*, a great place to relax in the shade, is also located here; the café and its surroundings frequently appear in *novelas* (TV soap operas) and music videos.

Jardim Botânico

Heading southeast from Parque Lage, at no. 1008 Rua Jardim Botânico, is the eponymous garden itself (daily 8am–5pm; R$5, over 60s free; free guided visits each hour except noon; electric car for the elderly and disabled; ☎21/3874-1808, Ⓦwww.jbrj.gov.br). Over half of it is natural forest (it's an important research centre for the Mata Atlântica Biosphere Reserve), while the rest is laid out in impressive avenues lined with immense imperial palms dating from the garden's 1808 inauguration. Dom João used the gardens to introduce foreign plants into Brazil – tea, cloves, cinnamon and pineapples among them – and they were opened to the public in 1890. Regarded as one of the world's finest botanic gardens, it contains five thousand plant species, and monkeys and parrots are amongst the wildlife that call the gardens home.

The building near the entrance which now contains the **visitor centre** dates from 1576; it has an interesting exhibition on the park's ecology, as well as a cafeteria and shop, while the adjoining building imaginatively exhibits environmental themes from across Brazil. The **history trail** is the best way to see the park, following a route which takes in a number of nineteenth-century buildings, arches and fountains alongside labelled trees, plants and sculpture – notably Mestre Valentim's *Ninfa do Eco* and *Caçador Narciso* (dating from 1783), the first metal sculptures cast in Brazil.

A newly opened cultural centre, theatre and cinema, the **Espaço Tom Jobim** (☎21/2274-7012; Ⓦwww.amigosjb.org.br), is set within a stunning garden and has a regular programme of plays, music and film.

Gávea

Stretching from the shores of Lagoa up into the *floresta* and *favela* Rocinha, **Gávea** is a mix of very affluent houses and an equally wealthy commercial area. Rio's racecourse, the **Jockey Club Brasileiro**, lies close to the lake – an obvious landmark often noticed from the Corcovado's Christ statue – while opposite its main entrance, **Praça Santos Dumont** is better known as "Baixo Gávea", a popular night-time hangout and street party area, packed with various bars and restaurants. **Shopping da Gávea** is one of the city's best malls, with a range of stores, good eating options and small **theatres**, while the city's domed **planetarium** is nearby next to Rio's Catholic University. Higher up the hill the **Instituto Moreira Salles** is an art gallery, café, and film and photo archive, located within a grand modernist structure – one of Rio's most significant sites. Nearby, the **Parque da Cidade** offers a small museum on the construction of the city and a series of forest trails, before the road climbs into *favela* Rocinha.

Jockey Club Brasileiro

On the Gávea side of Lagoa, the **Jockey Club**, also known as the **Hipódromo da Gávea** (Praça Santos Dumont 31, Gávea ☎21/2274-9720, Ⓦwww.jcb.com .br), can be reached on any of the countless buses marked "via Jóquei"; get off at Praça Santos Dumont at the end of Rua Jardim Botânico on the western side of the track. Racing in Rio was introduced by the British and dates back to

1825, though the Hipódromo wasn't built until 1926. Today, it attracts people from all walks of Rio life, serious gamblers accompanied by business executives and those just out for some entertainment – the atmosphere can range from extremely competitive to lighthearted, depending on the crowd. A night at the races is great fun in good weather, especially during the floodlit evening races when the air is a little more balmy – you can eat or sip a drink as you watch the action.

Races take place three to four times a week throughout the year (Mon 6.30–11.30pm, Fri 4–9.30pm, and most Sat & Sun 2–8pm), with the international Grande Prêmio Brazil taking place on the first Sunday of August. Foreign visitors can get into the palatial central members' stand (on the third floor) for just a few *reís* or sometimes for free, depending on how busy it is and on the mood of door staff – long trousers are essential for men. Races are normally at thirty-minute intervals, with ample time in between to order food or drinks; the ground floor bar is much younger and less formal than the overrated restaurant upstairs. You don't have to bet to enjoy the experience – the betting system can be a little confusing in any case.

Planetário do Rio de Janeiro

Half a kilometre along Rua Marquês de São Vicente from Praça Santos Dumont, just west of plush mall Shopping da Gávea are the twin domes of Rio's **planetarium**, which contains the interactive and child-friendly **Museu do Universo** (Tues–Fri 9am–6pm, weekends and public holidays 3–7pm; entry to both museum and film R$12, half price for students, under 21s, over 60s, and for all at weekends/public holidays; Rua Vice-Governador Rubens Berardo 100 ⓣ21/2274-0046, Ⓦwww.rio.rj.gov.br/planetario). Permanent exhibitions cover the wider universe as well as human "space conquest"; upstairs there are displays on the significant astronomical knowledge of both ancient peoples and living Brazilian Amerindian tribes: the creators of Stonehenge, Mayan pyramids and Incan temples, and, interestingly, the Brazilian Guarani people's construction of whole communities around positions of sun and moon.

In the planetarium's domes themselves, a lively **film** on the night sky, constellations and the calendar is shown with two versions, one for children (4pm) and the other for adults visiting without kids (6pm). **Telescope viewing** is available on Tuesday and Thursday evenings (7.30 & 9.30pm). At the back of the planetarium is the restaurant and nightclub *00*, which attracts an affluent Ipanema and Leblon crowd (see p.203).

PUC and Olaria da Gávea

A couple of minutes further west along Rua Marquês de São Vicente brings you to the campus of one of Rio's major universities, the **Pontifícia Universidade Católica**, better known as **PUC** (pronounced "poo-key") and inaugurated in 1955. Housed in unremarkable modern structures, the one older building on the campus, located right on the main road (at no. 225) is the **Solar Grandjean de Montigny**, an attractive house better known as Olaria da Gávea. Former home of French architect Grandjean de Montigny (see p.56) who is widely credited with bringing Neoclassical architecture – the style which had such a profound effect on the city – to Brazil. The house was built in 1826 and now serves as PUC's cultural centre, hosting regular public exhibitions.

Instituto Moreira Salles

About 2km southwest of the **Jockey Club**, dwarfed by apartment buildings at Rua Marquês de São Vicente 476, the **Instituto Moreira Salles** (Tues–Sun 1–8pm; free; ☏21/3284-7400, ⊛www.ims.com.br) is one of Rio's most beautiful private cultural centres. Located in the former home of the Salles family (the owners of Unibanco, one of the country's most important banks; Moreira's son Walter became Brazil's most famous film director following 1998's *Central Station* – see p.264), the centre is worth a visit just to get a glimpse into the lives of Rio's wealthy. Designed by the Brazilian architect **Olavo Redig de Campos** and completed in 1951, the house is one of the most refined examples of modernist residential architecture in Brazil; it's built around a courtyard and lush gardens landscaped by **Roberto Burle Marx**, who also created a stunning tile mural alongside the terrace. Among the beautiful plants and ponds are tall, striking *pau-mulato* trees – their white flowers which blossom in May and June contrast sharply with the ebony wood.

Unibanco is a major collector of Brazilian art, and, since the cultural centre opened in 1999, it has hosted significant exhibitions of nineteenth- and twentieth-century painting, sculpture and photography. The *Café Galeria* overlooking the marvellous tiled mural serves high-quality light lunches (R$13–18), cakes and ice creams and, at R$42 per person, a good, but expensive, high tea. Also located in the grounds are large and important **archives**, housing 450,000 photographs from the nineteenth and twentieth centuries, as well as a **music reference centre** devoted to the preservation of **MPB** (see p.262); both are free to access, and catalogues are available on the centre's website. There's also a **cinema** which shows high-quality contemporary films.

It's a half-hour walk to the Instituto Moreira Salles from the Jóquei Clube; alternatively, take **bus** #170 from Centro (Av. Rio Branco), Catete, Botafogo, Humaitá or Jardim Botânico, or the #592/3 from Ipanema, Copacabana or Leblon. Get off the bus just after the Praça Augusto de Lima taxi rank; if you find you've already entered Rocinha then you've gone half a kilometre too far.

Parque da Cidade and Museu Histórico da Cidade

If you turn right as you leave the Instituto Moreira Salles and walk for ten minutes up Estrada Santa Marinha, you'll reach the entrance to the attractive **Parque da Cidade** (daily 7am–6pm; buses as above), a former coffee plantation that since 1939 has effectively become a small and accessible chunk of Mata Atlântica (see p.124) below the Parque Nacional da Tijuca. Although it doesn't have the mountains, rivers and organization of the Parque da Tijuca, its lakes, waterfalls, trails and children's playground make it a good choice for half a day's forest relaxation just outside of the urban clamour. Another ten-minute walk from the park's entrance is the **Museu Histórico da Cidade** (Tues–Fri 10am–4pm, Sat & Sun 10–3pm; free), housed within a two-storey nineteenth-century mansion once owned by the Marquês de São Vicente. The entire collection is related to the history of Rio from its founding until the end of the Old Republic in 1930. All the exhibits – paintings, weapons, porcelain, medals and the like – are arranged in chronological order. The first salon deals with the city's foundation and has some interesting models of the Zona Sul before urban development, while other rooms cover the colonial period and the city's connection with São Sebastião. Near the mansion is the Capela de São João Batista (open only on weekends), a chapel which at the start of the millennium added unusual paintings by various modern artists of historical figures with the faces of contemporary Brazilians, among them Pele and Gal Costa.

São Conrado and Rocinha

The beautiful beach at **São Conrado**, dominated by numerous apartment buildings and high-rise hotels, is hidden from the rest of the Zona Sul by the jagged twin peaks of Pedra dos Dois Irmãos – and has at its western end an immense flat-topped mountain, 844-metre Pedra da Gávea. **São Conrado** is frequented by the famous and packed with hang-gliders and surfers at weekends. People flaunt their wealth without shame, though many are uncomfortable with the encroachment of enormous *favela* **Rocinha**, the residents of which share the beach and represent perhaps the starkest contrast in social-economic status to be found in Rio.

Away from both Rocinha and the beach, São Conrado is home to **Gávea Golf Club** (see p.238) and Oscar Niemeyer's former residence, the small **Casa das Canoas**, remarkable for its early-modernist design.

Most people arrive in São Conrado via the Lagoa-Barra highway through long Tunel Zuzu Angel, which was a frequent target for hold-ups in the 1980s and 1990s – given the often slow pace of traffic and the vast *favela* above – though these days Rocinha has calmed significantly. The other arrival routes are along the coast from Leblon on Avenida Niemeyer (see p.109) or, if on a bus from Gávea or a *favela* tour, you may arrive via the Estrada da Gávea, which winds its way over the hill from near the Parque da Cidade and down through Rocinha itself. **Bus** #500 (originating in Urca) will take you to São Conrado via Avenida Atlântica (Copacabana), Avenida Vieira Souto (Ipanema) and Avenida Delfim Moreira (Leblon).

Rocinha

Glistening in the tropical sun on the slopes between the Tijuca mountains and the peaks of Pedra dos Dois Irmãos sits Rio's largest *favela*, **Rocinha**, home to over 200,000 Brazilians – and still growing. Rocinha dominates the hill above São Conrado and extends into the upper reaches of Gávea – it literally means "small clearing", a reference to 1930s vendors at the market in Gávea, who used the hillside dirt track Estrada da Gávea to clear small patches of forest for cultivation. Makeshift wooden houses – now largely replaced by red bricks and even large

▲ Rocinha: Rio's largest *favela*

Dubbed as "slum safaris" or "poorism" by some, **favela tours** are big business in Rio. In the worst cases, visitors pay large sums to wealthy operators who treat *favelas* like an African game park, ferrying groups in open-topped camouflaged jeeps who gawp at poorer people going about their daily lives. The flip side is that visiting a *favela* sensitively can break down stereotypes and contribute to development and security. Many residents want outsiders to understand that *favelas* are not terrifying and lawless ghettos, but inhabited by decent hard-working people. Most middle-class *Cariocas* would have you believe that entering a *favela* guarantees being robbed or murdered; yet some now realize that addressing old social divisions might actually require a more innovative and inclusive approach.

While it's true that *favelas* are often controlled by organized drug gangs, it's simply not in their interest to create trouble for visitors as this would attract the attention of the police, who normally stay clear. Alone, you're liable to get lost and you may run into opportunistic thieves. But if you're accompanied by a resident you'll be perfectly safe and typically received with friendly curiosity.

There are many organizations working across Rio's more than eight hundred *favela* communities, several of which offer **volunteer opportunities**. Aside from those listed below, there are a range of others focusing on everything from football (see p.257) to surfing (see p.240) and education (see p.255).

Recommended favela tours

Many operators offer tours, some using jeeps, others minibuses or cars, and a few use motorbike-taxis or go on foot. Guides and content vary tremendously. Some highly dubious tours actually play up violent images in an effort to please tourists only interested in finding a scene straight out of *City of God*. Whichever one you opt for, make your own arrangements rather than going through an agent or hotel whose recommendations are usually influenced by the prospect of commission. Some operators also contribute to **social projects** – but a few of these efforts are negligible or even suspect.

Architectour (Half-day, flexible times; R$55, part of which goes to the foundation; T21/8115-3703, W www.favelaarchitectour.com). Proud Rocinha residents quadrilingual Rogério and his friend Daniel founded the Architectour in 2008 in response to seeing *favela* tourism exploited by outside interests. Each tour group has five people, and you are collected from your hotel or pre-arranged point. You travel like a *favela* resident – by van and motorbike-taxi – to reach Rocinha's summit, from where you

---

apartment blocks – appeared in 1932, followed by a slow influx of people from the region around Rio de Janeiro in the 1940s. The population increased again in the 1950s and 1960s as thousands from Brazil's poor Northeast arrived to construct and service the new Zona Sul (see p.255). Between 1933 and 1952 Rocinha's early residents enjoyed noisy entertainment in the form of the "Circuito da Gávea" car racetrack, which used the Estrada da Gávea and the coastal Avenida Niemeyer to form a circuit – the deadly winding section through Rocinha has famously been called "**Trampolim do Diabo**" (Devil's Springboard) ever since.

Though São Conrado below existed as a farm and country club from 1912, it didn't become a residential area until the 1970s, meaning many of Rocinha's families pre-date those of São Conrado. The *favela* continued to grow rapaciously until 1990 – growth has since slowed – but it wasn't until the new century that the state-led *favela-bairro* project made tentative efforts to integrate Rochina into legitimate city life. Even today families are arriving in search of a better life, often taking the poorest quality accommodation on the steepest

walk down through the community, taking in far more than *just* architecture. The Architectour gives a real sense of residents' ingenuity and *favela* life. Refreshments are offered at the **Two Brothers Foundation** (Ⓦwww.2bros.org), which provides educational opportunities in Rocinha.

Favela Tour (9am and 2pm; R$65, part of which is donated to projects in Vila Canoas; ☏21/3322-2727 or 21/9772-1133, Ⓦwww.favelatour.com.br) Marcelo Armstrong runs this insightful, well-respected and long-established tour. Guides are thoroughly trained, speak excellent English and provide fascinating commentaries on *favela* development; politics, drug trafficking, education, the future and achievements are all covered – without romanticizing inhabitants' lives. The two-hour tour visits Rocinha and Vila Canoas by minibus, with short sections on foot. Hotel/pre-arranged pickup; stops include craft stalls, day-care centre, junior school and a bar.

IBISS (Ⓦwww.ibiss.info, bookings by email only ✉ibiss@ibiss.com.br) One of Rio's largest NGOs, IBISS is funded by the Brazilian and Dutch governments to implement sixty large-scale health and education programmes across some of the city's most troubled communities. If you have a group of eight or more, their central office will coordinate a day tour for you, most often to *favelas* in the Zona Norte. With a large, knowledgeable staff working across the city, safety is paramount. Tours can include an IBISS-sponsored *favela* art project close to Penha in the Zona Norte (see p.144).

Morrinho (R$30; ☏21/2246-1010, Ⓦwww.morrinho.com; see p.79) A remarkable model *favela* in Laranjeiras, conceived by children as a life-like playground and built from multi-coloured bricks on the fringe of their home *favela* community. A tour includes a walk through the hillside neighbourhood and a video – you gain an insight into *favela* life from a child's perspective.

Staying in a favela

Staying in a favela is highly recommended thanks to three good, safe options that are changing the face of accommodation in Rio. Each provide you with an insight into Rio that a tour can only touch on, allowing you to meet local residents and contribute directly to the local economy. For full details see p.173. **Favela Receptiva** is an innovative network of host homes close to São Conrado; **Favelinha Pousada** has more of a hostel feel, located in *favela* Pereira da Silva close to Santa Teresa; and **The Maze** (see also p.87) is a highly original (and smarter) option in Catete's Tavares Bastos *favela*, with a phenomenal view.

slopes. On the other side of the district yet more forest is being cleared for attractive – though still illegal – new lots for Rocinha's wealthier class. Given Rocinha is governed locally by a residents' association who have known nothing but exclusion from formal legal channels for the best part of a century, illegality is a low concern. For many families incomes of under R$200 a month (sometimes significantly less) are as much as can be expected – as long as the gap with affluent shoppers at São Conrado's Fashion Mall remains stark, drug-trafficking is likely to remain a major part of community organization.

Rocinha has a lively commercial life, especially around its central square, **Largo do Boiadeiro**; prices are a good deal lower here than in the rest of the Zona Sul – there was even a *McDonalds* until it became clear it couldn't compete with nearby national chain *Bob's Burgers* in the popularity stakes. Rocinha has a range of bars and nightspots, including a huge venue for *baile funk* dances (not always the safest location), as well as a lively samba school at the foot of the hill (see p.215). Roadside stalls at its Gávea side are a good option for buying reasonably priced souvenirs and *favela* artwork.

Around São Conrado

São Conrado began life as an exclusive retreat, thanks to the creation of the **Gávea Golf and Country Club** – and though it's now dwarfed by its less salubrious neighbour, Rocinha, it has remained exclusive ever since. The *bairro* was named by landowner Conrado Niemeyer, who built a chapel in 1916 in honour of his namesake saint. In the same year, Conrado also completed his cliffside road to Leblon, naming it Avenida Niemeyer in tribute to himself, and not – contrary to popular belief – to famous architect Oscar Niemeyer (no relation), who much later built a house, **Casa das Canoas**, in São Conrado (see below). In the 1970s development took off along the **beach-front** and in the 1980s the **Fashion Mall** was added on the southern side of the main road, the Auto-Estrada Lagoa-Barra, at the community's eastern end. The mall contains luxury stores, a theatre, cinema and (expensive) food court. If you choose to **swim** at São Conrado, do so at the western end of the beach, away from the polluted streams tumbling down the hill through Rocinha straight into the ocean.

At the western end of the golf club, Estrada das Canoas heads steeply northwards to the Parque Nacional da Tijuca, passing a series of wealthy condominiums, small *favela* **Vila Canoas**, and at 520m above the beach, the **Pedra Bonita** hanggliding ramp (see p.238), from where adrenalin-fuelled flights descend right down to the ocean.

Casa das Canoas

A fifteen-minute uphill walk from Vila Canoas at Estrada das Canoas 2310 is the **Casa das Canoas** (Tues–Fri 1pm–5pm; R$10; ☏21/3322-3581 or 2509-1844, ⓦwww.niemeyer.org.br), **Oscar Niemeyer**'s small former home which he designed in 1951. Built using part of the jagged mountain's rockface as one wall and featuring his trademark curved walls and glass elsewhere, it's not hard to imagine how futuristic and revolutionary this must have appeared when first constructed. The house indicates the direction this master designer was to take in Brasília ten years later – revealed by scale models of buildings in Brasília displayed inside. Also on show are pieces of Niemeyer-designed curvy furniture and some fascinating drawings, including a proposed alteration to the Maracanã stadium that was never carried out.

Parque Nacional da Tijuca

If you look up from the streets of the Zona Sul, the mountains running southwest from the Corcovado are covered with exuberant forest. This is the periphery of the **Parque Nacional da Tijuca**, an incredible resource for the city, providing forty square kilometres of moist, atmospheric rainforest and 100km of hiking trails (daily 8am–6pm; ☏21/9691-3877, ⓦwww.terrabrasil .org.br). One of the largest "urban forests" in the world, the park divides Rio into its three respective zones (Sul, Oeste and Norte) and is made of up three separate areas of conservation within a wider forested area of a hundred square kilometres: the first close to the Corcovado; the second between São Conrado and Barra da Tijuca (containing flat-topped mountain Pedra da Gávea); and the largest section, the Floresta da Tijuca, lying in the centre of the park's wider area and offering the best range of hiking and touring options.

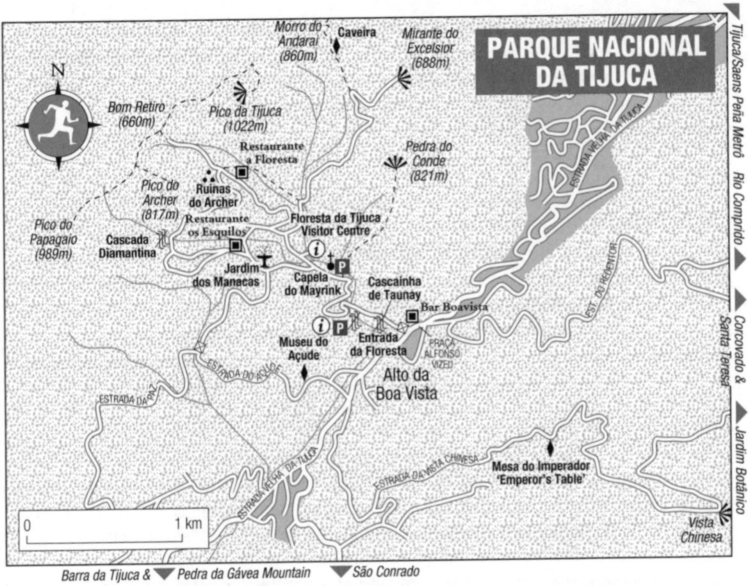

A very appealing place to get away from the city for a few hours or even a whole day, the park has numerous marvellous **drives**, and **hiking** and **cycling** options to suit all levels (see p.124). It can be visited most easily on an organised tour, though independent trips are certainly feasible if you have a little more time and don't mind using public transport.

At the centre of the park is the village and *bairro* of **Alto da Boa Vista**, an attractive rural setting from which you can enter the Floresta da Tijuca – which contains restaurants, a visitor centre and a multitude of trails surrounding Rio's highest mountain, the **Pico da Tijuca**. Nearby are the phenomenal forest gardens surrounding the art gallery **Museu do Açude**. Closer to the ocean, between São Conrado and Barra da Tijuca, lies the park's smallest section which contains its second largest mountain, the **Pedra da Gávea** – its summit arguably provides the very best view of Rio. The final section lies closer to the Zona Sul and is most easily accessed via Rua Pacheco Leão, which runs up the side of the Jardim Botânico and leads through the gateway Entrada dos Macacos to the **Vista Chinesa**, from where there's a marvellous view of Gávea's Parque da Cidade, Guanabara Bay and the Zona Sul. Rua Pacheco Leão eventually arrives in the *bairro* of Alta da Boa Vista. If you have a **car** (useful if you plan to do an extensive tour), you can also go in via Cosme Velho *bairro*, climbing up the Corcovado (see p.80) on Estrada das Paineiras and continuing along Estrada Redentor. If you're interested in **cycling** contact Paulo Celani (Ⓣ21/9985-7540, Ⓔjustfly@alternex.com.br), who rents bikes and will drop you off at an ideal location in the forest, such as picnic spot **Bom Retiro** or the Vista Chinesa.

History, flora and fauna

When the Portuguese arrived, dense green tropical forest covered what is now the city. As Rio grew, the trees were felled and the valuable hardwood was used in construction or for charcoal. In the seventeenth century the forests of Tijuca farther inland were cut down and replaced by sugar cane and, later, by coffee plantations and small-scale agriculture. In the early nineteenth century a shortage of pure water and landslides on the Tijuca slopes alarmed city authorities. Eventually it was decided a concerted effort was needed to restore Rio's watershed, and in 1857, a **reforestation project** was initiated; by 1870 over 100,000 trees had been planted and the forest was reborn. Most of the seeds and cuttings planted were native to the region; the rich tropical biosphere that remains is home to some 2200 species of birds, mammals, reptiles and amphibians, and around 20,000 species of plants – an amazing eight percent of the Earth's total. The park is a remarkable example of the potential for the regeneration of the Mata Atlântica that once covered much of Brazil's coastline.

Following the success of the forest's regeneration, Brazil's state institute of forestry (IBDF) has gradually reintroduced **fauna**, and the forest is once again the home of insects, reptiles, ocelots, howler monkeys, agoutis, three-toed sloths and other animals. Most successful has been the return of **birdlife**, such as bellbirds, sparrowhawks, tanagers and guans, making Floresta da Tijuca a paradise for birdwatchers. Yet at the same time, overstretched park rangers have been struggling in recent years to keep residents of the (at least) ten neighbouring *favelas* from hunting wildlife for food or trade. Areas of the park are also used as *terrenos*, places where Afro-Brazilian originating *candomblé* and *umbanda* ritual ceremonies are performed. In the past forest fires have been caused by these rituals.

Hiking Tijuca

Guided tours and walks

Joining a guided tour is the simplest way of getting around and allows you to take in two areas of the park as well as to do a guided hike. For **Pedra da Gávea** a guide is essential. The **Floresta da Tijuca** can be hiked independently, though it will be worth your while buying a decent map in a city bookstore and following the advice of the park visitor centre. Most tours offered by hotels and travel agents involve nothing more strenuous than a short walk outside of the bus, but more personal – and infinitely more rewarding – are the tours run by two of the following highly reputable Rio tour companies. Rio Hiking and Crux Eco-Aventura both pick you up and drop you at your hotel and guides speak fluent English. If you're happy getting to the park on your own (follow advice below), then free guided hikes are also offered by a third operator – from the Floresta visitor centre (see p.126).

Rio Hiking (☏21/2552-9204 or 21/9721-0594, ⊛www.riohiking.com.br) Offers hikes for small groups along the park's many trails, most often to the **Pico da Tijuca**, but also to caves or on tailor-made itineraries. Full-day tours also normally include lunch and a site in Santa Teresa. Half-day R$190, full-day R$155.

Crux Eco-Aventura (☏21/3322-8765 or 9392-9203, ⊛www.cruxecoaventura.com.br) Similar hiking itineraries to Rio Hiking, including an excellent guided hike to the summit of Pedra da Gávea; they also specialize in **rock climbing** and **rappelling** down waterfalls. Split adventure/cultural tours are also offered. R$140–200.

Rio Trilhas Ecoturismo (☏21/2492 2252-3, ⊛www.riotrilhas.com.br) Offers a programme of free, guided walks in the Floresta da Tijuca, Tues–Sun throughout the year, depending on the weather. Covers all big peaks as well as easier trails, with very friendly guides, and provides a good opportunity to meet like-minded Brazilians. Walkers normally meet at 9am at the visitor centre or the Entrada da Floresta; phone for confirmation. They'll also organize a free private hike if you have over five people.

The best hikes

Some forest trails – especially the easiest ones – are well marked, but if you want to take a harder route you're best off joining one of the guided tours listed above. There

Alto da Boa Vista and into the Floresta

A collection of grand and beautiful homes sprawling across the nearby lower hillside, **Alto da Boa Vista** is the main community in the forest and centred on Praça Alfonso Viseu. Surrounded by eclectic architecture, the square has a good restaurant (see listings, p.193) and a spring now built over with a fountain. To get here independently, you're best off taking a bus or taxi. By public transport, the easiest way is to go by *metrô*, changing to a bus (#221, #233 or #234) at the end of the line at Saens Peña station in the *bairro* of Tijuca (Zona Norte). Cross over the main road and catch the bus in the direction of Barra da Tijuca (Zona Oeste), getting off at Praça Alfonso Viseu after 20 minutes. Alternatively you can also catch bus #221 from Praça Tiradentes in Centro. Be warned that if you're intent on walking to Alto de Boa Vista from the Zona Sul, even the shorter trip from the Entrada dos Macacos above Jardim Botânico will mean a hot, dehydrating climb for over 10km.

The entrance to the Floresta da Tijuca, the **Entrada da Floresta**, with its distinctive stone columns, is on Praça Alfonso Viseu's western side. A few hundred metres farther is the unbelievably picturesque, 35m high, waterfall, Cascatinha de Taunay, with a car park, restaurant and information point close by. A good twenty-minute inclined walk beyond is the **Capela do Mairynk**, a chapel constructed in 1860, but almost entirely rebuilt in the 1940s for aesthetic

are numerous great walking and hiking options – here are a few of the best, rated according to their level of difficulty.

Museu do Açude If you're looking for an easy, gentle forest walk, this is it. The grounds of the museum are stunning and have a network of short trails leading into and around the surrounding forest (see p.126).

Cachoeira das Almas Another easy hike. After a thirty-minute walk above the visitor centre (where you should pick up a map), leave the road and begin a three-hour round trip following a river valley up to attractive waterfalls before looping back via the road, passing the *Restaurante a Floresta* on the way.

Mirante do Excelsior You won't need a guide for this medium-difficulty, four-hour hike starting at the visitor centre and following Estrada do Excelsior along a river valley for much of its route before beginning a steady incline up to this well-kept viewpoint (611m) of the Zona Oeste, part way up a mountain. You can opt to return (or hike the reverse) via a trail, the Trilha do Anhanguera.

Caminho da Saudade Another medium-difficulty hike that consists of a mix of road, forest and river trail in the centre of the park. It takes about four hours to complete and has two separate (though not lengthy) inclines, passing the excellent *Restaurante os Esquilos* between the two.

Pico da Tijuca Reaching Rio's highest peak (1021m), in the far north of the forest above Bom Retiro, is a medium-to-difficult hike, with a steady incline and two separate steep sections; hiring a guide is advised.

Pedra da Gávea This hike, at the coast in the park's southern section, is the most difficult of the ones we've listed – and a popular favourite. Allow yourself between two and four hours (depending on your fitness level) to complete the ascent, and be prepared for the final section, which requires basic climbing; a guide is essential. An astonishing view of the Zona Sul and Zona Oeste is a just reward, with beaches, lakes and mountains spread out before you.

purposes. Its most interesting feature is the reproduction of three altar panels painted by Cândido Portinari, one of Brazil's greatest twentieth-century artists; the originals are part of the much-depleted collection of the Museu de Arte Moderna (see p.47).

Behind the chapel is a car park, picnic area and popular bathing spot, with a couple of marked trails leading off into the forest. Following the trail along the side of the river for a few minutes brings you to the helpful park **Visitor Centre** (℡21/2492-2252; 8am-6pm), an excellent resource for finding out more about the area and starting a **guided hike** (see box, p.124); the centre is also accessible by road if you continue past the chapel and double back farther on. It sells maps and books and shows videos in different languages on conservation, flora and fauna.

Museu do Açude

A hidden gem that appeals as much to lovers of art as of the outdoors, the wonderful **Museu do Açude** (Wed–Mon 10am–4pm; R$2; Est. do Açude 764, Alto da Boa Vista; ℡21/2492-5443, ⓦwww.museuscastromaya.com.br;) is located a fifteen-minute walk south of Praça Alfonso Viseu; if going by bus direct from Saens Peña *metrô* station (see p.125), ask to be let off by the Corpo de Bombeiros (fire-station), from where it's a ten-minute walk uphill. Raymundo Ottoni de Castro Maya, a wealthy aristocrat and coordinator of the reforestation of Tijuca, purpose-built the main house to hold half of his impressive art collection; his other house in Santa Teresa, the gallery Chácara de Céu (see p.77), now displays his collection of paintings.

The highlights here are a series of Chinese and Hindu bronze **sculptures** dating from as far back as the eighth century, including splendidly modelled Tang-dynasty era "Grou" birds (symbolizing immortality) and Chinese ceramics from the Ming and Qing dynasties. Also on display are attractive porcelain dinner services (one is a three hundred-piece set from England), which suggest Castro Maya may well have used a different one at each of his renowned sumptuous receptions for Rio's elite. Upstairs is less interesting, displaying mainly antique furniture; the one piece of note – a brightly coloured nineteenth-century ceramic painting of riders on horseback from Rhodes – is easily missed at the top of the stairs.

The **garden**, however, probably holds the most interest. One of the best in Rio, it's a small landscaped section of rainforest, with an aura of peace and tranquillity as monkeys and birds call each other through the trees. A few easy, marked trails reveal ponds, rich plant life and – most surprisingly – modern **art installations**; look out for the giant canopy walkway by Eduardo Coimbra. Surrounding the house are five hundred painted vases collected by the artist Jean Baptiste Debret – a friend of Castro Maya.

6

Zona Oeste

io's **Zona Oeste** is an enormous area stretching 40km through an expanse of apartment blocks, beaches, *favelas*, mountains and scenic rural landscapes. Arriving from the Zona Sul in **Barra da Tijuca**, the stunning 25km beach stretching out into the distance, backed by high-rise residences and the wide avenue Avenida das Américas, you could think you'd arrived in Miami. Aside from the beach, Barra's main attraction is its numerous shopping malls, but the areas beyond – **Recreio**, **Grumari** and **Barra de Guaratiba** – all provide access to the dramatic and ecologically rich natural environment that formerly defined the whole region.

The nature parks of **Marapendi** and **Chico Mendes** in Recreio are entry points to the inland lagoon system of the Barra-Recreio area, while more dazzling beaches appear in the form of **Prainha** and **Grumari**, especially attractive to seclusion-seekers and surfers. A short way inland, the wonderful folkloric museum **Casa de Pontal** and the landscaped gardens of **Sítio Roberto Burle Marx** make a day or two's trip to these far-reaching areas more than worthwhile. While a car is almost essential to explore the region in any depth, with a little planning you can visit the main areas by bus too – and there are always guided tours if you don't fancy visiting alone.

Most of inland Zona Oeste has little to offer outside visitors – **Jacarepaguá** has a mixed middle- and working-class population while poorer areas such as **Cidade de Deus** and **Rio das Pedras** have large populations living in a mix of *favela* and purpose-built low-income housing. Even further inland, Rio's suburban sprawl weaves its way from **Bangu** through a gap in the mountains to **Campo Grande** and finally on to the city boundaries at **Santa Cruz**.

Barra da Tijuca

Since the 1960s, Zona Oeste's flat coastal plain has developed apace as Rio's new middle- and upper-class residential area, pushed further along the coast as the Zona Sul became ever more crowded and expensive. The eastern end of this plain, **Barra da Tijuca**, is sandwiched between the enormous inland lagoon **Lagoa da Tijuca** and the white sandy shoreline – always called just **Barra** (pronounced "ba-ha"). Exhibiting the kind of car-oriented development synonymous with the era, Barra resembles a large North American city, and unlike the Zona Sul, its residents are rarely to be seen walking anywhere, aside from within the vast shopping malls which line its central artery, the Avenida

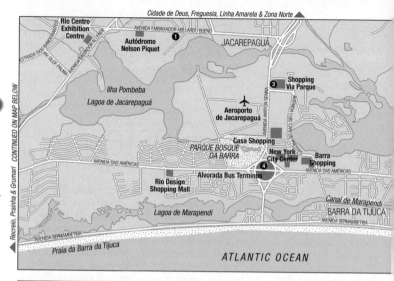

Cidade de Deus, Freguesia, Linha Amarela & Zona Norte

Rio Centro Exhibition Centre

Autódromo Nelson Piquet

JACAREPAGUÁ

Ilha Pombeba

Lagoa de Jacarepaguá

AVENIDA EMBAIXADOR ABELARDO BUENO ➊

Shopping Via Parque ➌

Aeroporto de Jacarepaguá

Casa Shopping

PARQUE BOSQUE DA BARRA

New York City Center

Barra Shopping

AVENIDA DAS AMÉRICAS

Alvorada Bus Terminus ➍

Rio Design Shopping Mall

Lagoa de Marapendi

Canal de Marapendi

BARRA DA TIJUCA

AVENIDA SERNAMBETIBA

Praia da Barra da Tijuca

ATLANTIC OCEAN

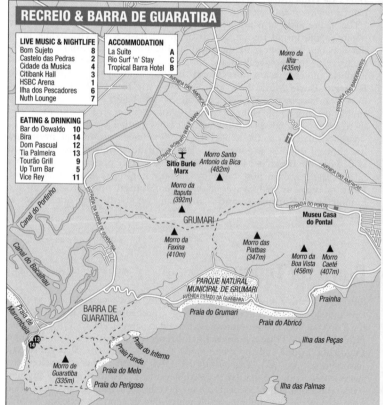

RECREIO & BARRA DE GUARATIBA

LIVE MUSIC & NIGHTLIFE
Bom Sujeto	8
Castelo das Pedras	2
Cidade da Musica	4
Citibank Hall	3
HSBC Arena	1
Ilha dos Pescadores	6
Nuth Lounge	7

ACCOMMODATION
La Suite	A
Rio Surf 'n' Stay	C
Tropical Barra Hotel	B

EATING & DRINKING
Bar do Oswaldo	10
Bira	14
Dom Pascual	12
Tia Palmeira	13
Tourão Grill	9
Up Turn Bar	5
Vice Rey	11

Morro da Ilha (435m)

Sitio Burle Marx

Morro Santo Antonio da Bica (482m)

Morro da Itaputa (392m)

GRUMARI

Museu Casa do Pontal

Morro da Faxina (410m)

Morro das Piatbas (347m)

Morro da Boa Vista (456m)

Morro Caeté (407m)

PARQUE NATURAL MUNICIPAL DE GRUMARI

AVENIDA ESTADO DA GUANBARA

Prainha

BARRA DE GUARATIBA

Praia do Grumari

Praia do Abricó

Ilha das Peças

Canal do Portinho

Canal do Bacalhau

Praia de Marumbaia

Morro de Guaratiba (335m)

Praia do Inferno

Praia Funda

Praia do Melo

Praia do Perigoso

Ilha das Palmas

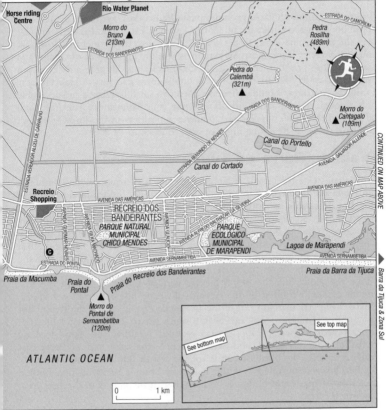

das Américas. If the *bairro* was to have a "central" street, it would probably be Avenida Olegário Maciel, which runs from the main highway down to the beach, lined with a few shops and restaurants.

Barra's most affluent residents choose to build their grand homes in **Joátinga**, the hillside area closest to São Conrado; with its discreet and attractive beach at their disposal. However, most people heading into Barra from the Zona Sul will miss Joá altogether, passing through the tunnel beneath the *bairro* and emerging to cross the mouth of the lagoon. The multilane main road continues in a more or less straight line through Avenida Ministro Ivan Lins into Avenida Armando Lombardi and then the **Avenida das Américas**, surrounded by high-rise offices and apartment blocks. The one building of interest, the **Cidade da Música**, is Rio's newest cultural addition and one of the city's most striking modernist constructions.

You can reach Barra da Tijuca by many **buses** from Copacabana, Ipanema or Botafogo, including #553 and #524 – though the speedy, air-conditioned **metrôbus** is the quickest and easiest option; it currently departs from Siquera Campos station in Copacabana, though with the opening of the new station General Osório in Ipanema in 2010 it is expected to move. If you want to head straight to the beach, consider catching the **Surf Bus** (see p.134).

Joátinga

Where the mammoth flat-topped mountain **Pedra da Gávea** rises up from the ocean between São Conrado and Zona Oeste, the Estrada do Joá passes up and over the mountain's lower slopes – an alternative to the tunnel below should you have your own transport. An extremely wealthy hillside area of condos and mansions, Joá's private member's *Clube Costa Brava* juts out onto a rocky ocean outcrop, an easily identifiable marker. A little known and very attractive beach, **Praia da Joátinga**, is hidden here between two small headlands and accessible only through the condominium above (leave your name at the gate and you'll be granted entry). It's popular with residents and surfers-in-the-know – though you have to negotiate a long flight of steps to reach it.

Praia da Barra da Tijuca

More than twice the length of Copacabana and Ipanema's beaches combined, the **Praia da Barra da Tijuca** and its continuation, the **Praia do Recreio dos Bandeirantes**, are amazing stretches of white sand and surf with enough busy and deserted sections to fulfil any preference. These clean waters are hugely popular at weekends both with people from Barra itself and the distant suburbs. There's a lot more space here than in the Zona Sul, ample for playing football and volleyball, and tournaments are frequently held along its length. As with the rest of the city, the waves and currents are very strong here.

Like the Zona Sul, the beach here is divided into postos with the first stretch of beach fronted by the Avenida do Pepê home to postos 1 and 2. **Posto 2** in particular, in front of the *Barraca do Pepê* is seen as the trendy hot spot, with the section eastwards back towards **posto 1** Rio's major location for kitesurfing (see p.240). Barra's young, wealthy and good-looking sunbathe, pose, eat, drink and exercise here – the only part of Barra that really resembles the outdoor culture of the rest of Rio. Heading westwards, the beach is accompanied its whole length by Avenida Sernambetiba, fronted by a mix of apartment buildings and hotels as it disappears in the heat haze towards Recreio.

Barra blues: from mangrove to condo

Only fifty years ago Barra da Tijuca and Recreio, characterized by their rich diversity of **flora** and **fauna**, were just a series of sandy tracks devoid of any development. With the area's complex mix of saline and landlocked **lagoons** and **restinga** land areas (sandy and acidic coastal soils rich in low-level shrubs and trees), sensitive ecosystems coexisted, promoting an amazing range of vegetation including orchids and bromeliads, cacti, pitanga trees and varieties of mangrove. Giant anteaters and capivara rodents roamed the sandy soils, while innumerable fish species, caymans, crabs, scarlet ibis, spoon-billed *colhereiros* and even *guaxinim* (Brazilian racoons) could be found in and around the boggy waters.

As housing and business development took off around the lakes' shores in the 1950s and 1960s, mangroves were gradually forced out and the lakes became heavily polluted – particularly as malls were built at the edge of **Lagoa da Tijuca** in the following decades. The *restinga*, too, was pushed to near-extinction by the 1970s as the relentless construction of housing and roads enveloped the coastline.

Nonetheless, by the 1980s an environmental plan was finally put into place, too late for much of the wildlife, but soon enough to enable the prosecution of polluters and to conserve the **Bosque da Barra** (see p.132) and the massive million-square-metre **Lagoa de Marapendi** – still home to the endangered Papo Amarelo cayman. Today, the **Parque Ecológico de Marapendi** and **Parque Chico Mendes** in Recreio (see p.133) offer the opportunity to discover more about these fascinating ecosystems.

Avenida das Américas

Barra's multilane thoroughfare, Avenida das Américas, has little to recommend it to visitors – though most Barra residents consider the twelve shopping **malls** that line it the *bairro*'s de facto centre. **Downtown** is the most significant mall, located at Av. das Américas 500. It's an outdoor extravaganza of shopping, eating and drinking, shaded by trees and extremely popular in the evenings – though amazingly its design resembles a *favela* more than a temple of consumerism. Close to Downtown at Av. das Américas 1510, is the **Hipermercado Extra**, which hosts the excellent monthly market **Babilônia Feira Hype** (2–11pm; R$5; Ⓦ www.babiloniahype.com.br) – you'll find a good selection of handicrafts, as well as clothes and jewellery by young designers – it's vastly preferable to the surrounding shopping options.

Continuing west along the Avenida for 3km you reach **Barra Shopping**, over half a kilometre of clothes shops and food courts. If the stores don't appeal then its one saving grace is the outlet of bookshop Livraria Travessa with an attached branch of *Copa Café*, which serves tasty cappuccinos and gourmet burgers. 2km west, as Barra merges with Recreio, **RioDesign Barra** is the strip's most exclusive mall; it has a children's play area, cinema and numerous high-class boutiques and restaurants.

Cidade da Música

You can't miss the startling modernist **Cidade da Música**, smack bang in the middle of Avenida das Américas at the junction with Avenida Ayrton Senna just west of Barra Shopping. The building was designed by French architect **Christian de Portzamparc**, a self-confessed admirer of Niemeyer, whose style is clearly identifiable in the futuristic, curved ramp walkways used to enter the building. Constructed between 2003 and 2008 at a cost of over R$500m, it features giant rounded side panels that resemble the overlapping feathers of a crouching bird,

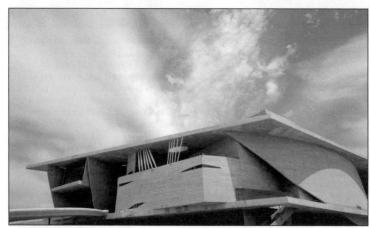

▲ Cidade da Música

while inside, the major auditorium is planned to be an opera house and the new seat of the Orchestra Sinfônica Brasileira, with 1800 seats. There are also three cinemas, ten practice rooms, a restaurant and shops (for a programme, consult Friday's *O Globo* or *Jornal do Brasil* newspapers). Next to the Cidade da Música is the **Alvorada bus terminus**, with services to all over the city.

Bosque da Barra

Across the road from the Cidade da Música to the northwest, the attractive **Bosque da Barra** (Tues–Sun 8am–5pm) provides welcome respite from the surrounding malls and traffic. Founded in 1981 with the intention of preserving a small patch of beachside *restinga* vegetation (see opposite), it's a lovely 50-hectare park primarily of interest for the numerous giant guinea-pig-like **capivaras** that can be seen feeding here. If you're lucky, you might spot a sloth, too. It's a great spot to take children – with trails around a series of small lakes, though you never quite escape the noise of traffic and aircraft at nearby Jacarepaguá airport.

North towards Jacarepaguá

The northern part of inland Barra da Tijuca around Avenida Ayrton Senna is home to a number of large developments, only reachable by car. **Shopping Via Parque** lies 2km north of Barra Shopping and the Cidade da Música, and contains Rio's largest indoor concert venue – **Citibank Hall** – which has hosted Nina Simone and Pavarotti, among others (see p.200 for details).

West of here along the northern fringes of the Lagoa de Jacarepaguá towards Estrada dos Bandeirantes is the **Cidade dos Esportes** – a series of complexes used for the 2007 Pan American Games which are now in severe danger of becoming white elephants – to be revitalized only in the unlikely event Rio's Olympic bid for 2016 is successful. One still-functioning exception is the indoor sports stadium – now renamed the **HSBC Arena** – which hosts music events (see p.200). Bob Dylan, Queen and REM have all performed here.

Just west of here are the car race track **Autódromo de Nelson Piquet**, and Rio's enormous exhibition and conventions complex **RioCentro**, which famously hosted the 1992 Earth Summit.

Recreio and around

Continuing west along the coast from Barra da Tijuca is **Recreio dos Bandeirantes**, always referred to as just Recreio, a further stretch of beautiful beach with slightly lower-rise residential development than its neighbour. The *bairro's* name originates from the *bandeirantes* – effectively colonizers who cleared the countryside to claim it from the Amerindians and begin planting. The beach here was the *bandeirantes* favoured playing-spot – "recreio" means "recreation" – though today the term better applies to the bands of surfers roaming the beaches in search of the best waves.

The **Praia do Recreio** is separated from the **Praia do Pontal** and **Praia da Macumba** by the tree-covered (and monkey-inhabited) ocean outcrop **Morro do Pontal**, linked to **Recreio** at low tide. The beach on both sides is popular, with numerous vendors and perfect white sands, though the sea can be rough and has dangerous currents at times – immediately west of the morro the water is calmer and often crystal clear. West along the coast from Recreio, peaceful beaches **Prainha** and **Grumari** rival the world's best for picturesque beauty.

Away from Recreio's beach a short way inland, the protracted **Lagoa de Marapendi** is a haven for wildlife; it has an ecological park where you can view some of the region's native flora and fauna at its western end, while another smaller park, the **Parque Chico Mendes**, is dedicated to preservation of native fauna. Farther inland, the winding Estrada do Pontal passes through lush forest to the **Museu Casa de Pontal**, which has a fascinating folkloric collection. North of Recreio on the other side of Avenida das Américas, semi-rural **Vargem Grande** is located along the Estrada dos Bandeirantes at the foot of the mountains, of interest only for its horseriding opportunities and – in the unlikely event you fancy water-based fun away from the beach – fun park **Rio Water Planet**.

Parque Municipal Ecológico de Marapendi

An inviting and well-organised park dedicated to preserving the sensitive 1.2 square-metre Lagoa de Marapendi ecosystem, the **Parque Municipal Ecológico de Marapendi** (Av. Alfredo Baltazar da Silveira, Recreio ☎21/2497-7088; free) is a ten-minute walk from both the beach and Avenida das Américas at the lake's far western end. It has a visitor centre, library, walking trails and plans for boat trips along the lakeshore. The helpful park staff are extremely knowledgeable about native flora and fauna, much of which has become locally extinct as a consequence of the Zona Oeste's rapid development (see p.131). The area surrounding the lake is native *restinga* – sandy soils with low-level vegetation – while the murky water itself is home to rare endangered caymans, not too hard to spot if you're with one of the guides. One of the park's biggest challenges is to convey the importance of mangrove preservation to maintain fish stocks and cleanse the water. Close to the visitor centre, there's a large children's playground.

Parque Natural Municipal Chico Mendes

Dedicated to the conservation of fauna formerly inhabiting Zona Oeste's *restinga* (see p.131), the **Parque Natural Municipal Chico Mendes** (Av. Jarbas de Carvalho 679, Recreio; ☎21/2437 6400) has a network of short trails from which you can see native *capivaras* (large guinea-pig like rodents), tortoises, *papo amarelos* (yellow-bellied caymans), giant anteaters and various birds of prey.

The small visitor centre is not as comprehensive as the Parque da Marapendi's, but the park – which also contains a playground – is a good place to take children. It was named in tribute to famous Brazilian trade unionist and Amazonian anti-logging campaigner **Chico Mendes**, who was killed in 1988 as a result of his work, but whose death resulted in a far higher worldwide profile for the rainforest conservation movement.

Museu Casa do Pontal

Turning inland onto the Estrada do Pontal at the far end of Praia da Macumba brings you to the superb **Museu Casa do Pontal** (Tues–Sun 9.30am–5pm; ☎21/24903278, ⓦwww.museucasadopontal.com.br; Estrada do Pontal 3295), a truly magical place that will easily keep you occupied for a couple of hours. Founded by a Frenchman who toured Brazil in search of folkloric figures, the collection demonstrates his love for all things Brazilian. The museum is a journey through rural crafts and customs with thousands of colourful exhibited wooden figures arranged in everyday life scenes, such as undertaking agricultural tasks or travel, at worship or in festivals. The displays become progressively more outlandish and impressive, with figures gradually increasing in size, culminating in a number of moving scenes both from city and country. Even heaven and hell, pregnant women and Carnaval are vividly illustrated.

Prainha and Grumari

Stunningly attractive beaches just west of Recreio, both **Prainha** and its longer neighbour **Grumari** attract many day-trippers at weekends, but on weekdays they remain secluded and peaceful – visited by just a few surfers and couples. There are no lifeguards here though, so do be aware of strong currents. Both beaches are backed by thick forest – and in Grumari's case by banana plantations high above which add a slightly lighter tone of green to the hillsides. There are low-key fresh fish restaurants along both stretches of sand – at the far end of Grumari seek out great seafood at beach shack *Bar dos Poetas* – it's a popular part of the beach to hang out at, too, with a small river offering freshwater bathing. Back at the other end of Grumari, its extension, **Praia do Abricó** is designated for nudists.

If you don't have your own transport, the best way to get to Prainha is on the **Surf Bus** (☎21/2539 7555, ⓦwwwsurfbus.com.br), which leaves from Largo do Machado *metrô* station at 7am, 10am, 1pm and 4pm, and stops along the way in Copacabana, Ipanema, São Conrado, Barra and Recreio, before finishing up at Prainha to return again ninety minutes later. The bus has a DVD player and a good surfer's vibe. At weekends the bus terminates at Macumba beach, to avoid traffic along the narrow stretch towards Prainha. There is no service onwards to Grumari, though you could walk there in about half an hour.

Vargem Grande

Heading inland from Recreio, the original road through the Zona Oeste, Estrada dos Bandeirantes winds its way around the base of the hills for over 30km from close to Guaratiba all the way to Jacarepaguá and beyond. Despite being in the countryside here, you're still very much within the city boundaries, with built-up areas on the other side of the mountains that continue 20km to the west. Nonetheless, **Vargem Grande** is semi-rural with small-scale farmers and a mix of middle- and lower-class housing spread all the way along the

Estrada. This is horseriding territory, home to a number of local stables (see p.239) which offer trips around the nearby hills, forests and rivers. Strangely, a handful of good restaurants attract visitors from across Zona Oeste on weekend evenings. Also along this stretch is **Rio Water Planet** (see p.224), the city's one and only water-park, a huge outdoor affair that seems to attract as many adults as children.

Barra de Guaratiba and around

Further west again and reached by **bus** along Avenida das Américas, or by **car** over the mountain from Grumari, is the quiet village of **Barra de Guaratiba**. Nestled at the end of a promontory beneath the mountains, it's a picturesque spot with a tremendous view of the **Praia** and **Restinga da Marumbaia**, a stunning stretch of sand, low vegetation and mangrove which disappears west into the horizon – a natural gem which is conserved as an army base, sadly out of bounds to anyone else. The countryside around the village is popular amongst *Cariocas* (Rio's residents) seeking a discreet retreat – and most tourists only come to visit the **Sítio Burle Marx**, the beautiful landscaped gardens of one of Brazil's most famous designers.

Barra de Guaratiba is also famous for its numerous **fish restaurants**, scattered all along the Estrada da Barra de Guaratiba – most serve North-eastern coconut-based *moquecas* at cheap prices (R$20 for two people), but if you want to splash out head for the justifiably celebrated *Tia Palmeira* (daytime) or *Bira* (night-time), located in the village, fifteen minutes by bus from the Sítio (see p.193).

Sítio Roberto Burle Marx

The hugely influential landscape gardener and painter **Roberto Burle Marx** bought this forty-hectare former banana plantation, the **Sítio**, in 1949 and converted it into a nursery for the plants that he collected on his travels around the country. In 1973 he moved here permanently, staying until his death in 1994.

Today the Sítio is used as a botany research and teaching centre, and **tours** (daily 9.30am and 1.30pm; R$5; 90min; ☎21/2410-1412) of the property and grounds are given to the public, in broken English – if available the day you visit (check by telephone). It's essential to book in advance. Burle Marx was not only a collector of plants, but also of Brazilian folk art and Peruvian ceramics – his vast collection is on display inside the house, along with his own paintings and textiles. A small **Benedictine chapel**, dating from 1610, and the Sítio's original colonial-era farmhouse are also located within the grounds.

To get to the Sítio, take **bus** #387 ("Marambaia–Passeio") from the Passeio Público in Centro, which passes along the Avenida Atlantica in Copacabana at around 7.20am (then at two-hourly intervals), Ipanema (7.30am) and Barra de Tijuca (8am), and will leave you right outside the Sítio's entrance gate – allow ninety minutes from Copacabana. Alternatively, the air-conditioned "Santa Cruz Via Barra" or "Campo Grande Via Barra" buses follow the same route, but will leave you at the Ipiranga petrol station in Guaratiba from where you should ask for directions; the Sítio is a fifteen-minute walk away.

7

Zona Norte and Niterói

U rban **Zona Norte**, stretching almost 20km northwards and westwards from Centro, is home to over fifty percent of Rio's population. Most of the area between the international airport and the city centre is given over to *favelas* and other low-income housing, though the church at **Penha** stands out beacon-like on a hilltop, unremarkable in itself but striking in its place amidst the northern slums. Close to Centro, the area of **São Cristóvão** is certainly worth visiting, its history of critical importance to Rio and its **Museu Nacional**, Brazil's foremost archeological and ethnological museum – housed within Rio's royal palace, is fascinating. Nearby the world-famous **Maracanã football stadium** is the most visited site in northern Rio, while elsewhere **samba schools** offer some of the city's best night-time entertainment, many located close to the Zona Sul in the Zona Norte's more affluent *bairros*: Tijuca, Andarai and Vila Isabel (see p.215). The parts of Zona Norte you'll have seen on the way from the airport or on the bus coming into the city aren't very enticing and though they don't reflect the region as a whole, they do provide a general flavour of northern Rio.

To the east of Zona Norte, **Baía de Guanabara** (Guanabara Bay), stretches inland for thirty kilometres, its narrow mouth enclosing Rio on the one side and the city of **Niterói** on the other. Thought to be a river by the first European explorers – hence the name Rio – the bay is now traversed by the Rio-Niterói bridge, opening up sites such as the **Museu de Arte Contemporânea**, housed in an astonishing building designed by Oscar Niemeyer. Niterói shares little culturally with Zona Norte, its wealthier population having much more in common with Rio's Zona Sul – and it is most easily reached by boat from Centro.

São Cristóvão and the Maracanã

São Cristóvão – though in parts rundown – is one of Rio's oldest areas, its history closely connected with Portuguese colonization and Brazilian independence. Situated immediately west of Centro and easily reached due to its good *metrô* connection, the *bairro* first developed when a ground concession for agriculture (known as a *sesmaria*) was granted to the Society of Jesus in the

SÃO CRISTÓVÃO & THE MARACANÃ

EATING & DRINKING
Quinta da Boa Vista 1

N

Estádio São Januário Vasco da Gama Football Club

Feira Nordestina (Centro Luis Gonzaga)

Favela Morro do Telegrafo

MORRO DE TELEGRAFO

Museu da Fauna

Jardim Zoológico

Favela Mangueira

Mangueira Samba School

Palácio de São Cristóvão & Museu Nacional

Quinta da Boa Vista

MARACANÃ

Maracanã Stadium (Estádio Mário Filho)

Maracanãzinho

Museu do Primeiro Reinado de Santos

São Cristóvão Football Club

SÃO CRISTÓVÃO

0   500 m

Tijuca — Túnel Rebouças & Zona Sul

sixteenth and seventeenth centuries. The Jesuits used the area as a sugar plantation divided into *chácaras* (smallholdings), one of which, the Chácara do Elias,
became the home of wealthy Portuguese merchant Elias Antônio Lopes, who
built his grand residence on a mound with a superb view as far afield as
Guanabara Bay. The whole property later became the country seat of the Portuguese royal family when Elias presented his now renamed **Quinta da Boa
Vista** ("the Good View Quarter") to Dom João VI in 1808. Now a leafy park,
the Quinta is home to the fascinating scientific institution – the **Museu
Nacional** – and the much-improved **Rio Zoo**, though São Cristóvão as a
whole has remained associated with the Portuguese ever since. To the north of
the *bairro*, old colonial streets lead to the **Vasco da Gama Football Club**, the
Portuguese-built stadium of one of Brazil's biggest teams, while nearby a small
but beautiful royal "*palacete*" holds the **Museu Primeiro Reinado**.

Following colonialism, São Cristóvão deteriorated and many of its wealthier
families moved to the Zona Sul as Brazil attempted to distance itself from the
Portuguese past. From the 1940s industrial development took over the district and

the construction of factories, warehouses and a series of huge road overpasses further demolished its formerly chic demeanour. Next to the Linha Vermelha overpass is the **Feira Nordestina**, a huge marketplace hosting a marathon 24-hour extravaganza of great northeastern music, shopping, food and drink every weekend of the year. On the western fringes of São Cristóvão at the Morro de Telégrafo, immigration and a chronic housing shortage led to the appearance of *favela* **Mangueira**, which later became home to one of Rio's biggest and most famous samba schools, hosting weekend events all year round (see p.215).

Once you're in the area you may as well make a day of it and see a number of the sights here, which also include (most importantly) Brazil's giant temple to football, the **Maracanã stadium**. If you're interested in either football or the story of modern Brazil, a visit to its **Museu des Esportes** is a must.

You can reach São Cristóvão by **metrô** (line 2, changing at Estácio) or by **bus**, express #462, #463 or #473 from Copacabana (via Tunel Rebouças; catch from Rua Tonelero heading west), #472 and #474 from Flamengo, #460 from Leblon and #461 from Ipanema.

Quinta da Boa Vista and around

Zona Norte's most attractive park, the **Quinta da Boa Vista** (daily 9am–6pm) stands in stark contrast to the surrounding region. The Avenida Dom Pedro II leads to its grand gates for over a kilometre, hinting at just how important and opulent the setting was in the days of the monarchy. Within the gates, the Avenida is lined with indigenous sapucaia trees, blossoming beautifully pink in October/November and providing much-needed colour to industrial São Cristóvão. Following a huge Neoclassical facelift in 1820, the home of Dom João at the park's centre became the **Palácio de São Cristóvão**, and though the architecture does not quite deserve its alias as the "Tropical Versailles", it's certainly impressive. It remained in the hands of the royal family through the nineteenth century; Dom João's grandson, Dom Pedro II, was born here and lived in the palace until his exile when Brazil became a republic in 1889.

Surrounding the palace, which now hosts **Museu Nacional**, are well-landscaped grounds. Rio's zoo occupies a substantial area, while two lakes have pedalo boats for hire, and Chinese pagodas provide space for occasional recitals and samba sessions. It's an excellent place for a stroll and a snooze under the trees, though the weekend crowds are more energetic, practising sports and playing games. If you're looking for **refreshments**, the good Portuguese *Restaurant da Quinta da Boa Vista* is opposite the zoo (see p.194), while a basic *por kilo* (pay by weight) restaurant is located at the rear of the Museu Nacional and there's a further option inside the zoo itself.

Museu Nacional

In the centre of the park, on a small hill, is the commanding Neoclassical **Museu Nacional** (Tues–Sun 10am–4pm; R\$3; ☏21/2562-6042, ⓦwww .museunacional.ufrj.br), the oldest scientific institution in Brazil and certainly one of the most important. It contains extensive archeological, palaeontological, zoological and botanic collections – and also has an excellent ethnological section and a good display of artefacts dating from classical antiquity. Altogether, an estimated one million pieces are exhibited in 22 rooms, though for the next few years at least, while the palace undergoes major renovation work to restore the royal living room (and gold and stucco works in Empress Teresa Christina's quarters), it looks likely that only half the collection will be on display at any one time.

The **archeological** section covers the human history of Latin America, displaying Peruvian ceramics, the craftsmanship of the ancient Aztec, Mayan and Toltec civilizations of Mexico and mummies excavated in the Chiu-Chiu region of Chile. In the Brazilian room, exhibits of Tupi-Guarani and Marajó ceramics lead on to the indigenous **ethnographical** section, uniting pieces collected from the numerous tribes that once populated Brazil. The genocidal policies of Brazil's European settlers, together with the ravages of disease, reduced the indigenous population from an estimated six million in 1500 to the present-day total of less than two hundred thousand. The **ethnology** section has a room dedicated to Brazilian folklore, centred on an exhibition of the ancient Afro- and Indo-Brazilian cults – such as *macumba, candomblé* and *umbanda* – that still play an important role in modern Brazilian society.

The mineral collection's star exhibit at the museum's entrance is the **Bendigo Meteorite**, which fell to Earth in the state of Bahia and has a plaque at its front with the date 1888 on it (for sign-seekers, the year slavery was abolished) – but on closer examination a second plaque at its side reveals it arrived in 1784 – and moved to Rio over a century later. Its original weight of 5360kg makes it the heaviest metallic mass known to have fallen through the Earth's atmosphere. And beyond the rich native finds you'll also come across Etruscan pottery, Greco-Roman ceramics, Egyptian sarcophagi and prehistoric remains.

Jardim Zoólogico and the Museu da Fauna

Rio Zoo, also called the **Jardim Zoólogico** (daily 9am–4.30pm; R$6; ☎21/2567 9732), is located to the rear of the palace. Founded in 1888, the zoo appears to be slowly modernizing, with monkeys, orangutans, hippos and hundreds of birds given "plenty" of space, but some enclosures are still old-fashioned with cages patently too small for elephants, bears and lions. A pleasing recent addition has been the construction of an aerial **fauna walkway** just outside of the zoo proper (tickets valid for both), which leads across a large open enclosure with ponds and trees and a variety of animals including hefty rodent *capivaras* and emus. To the side are large pools with seals.

Whatever its flaws, the zoo serves an important scientific role in Brazil, managing some prominent breeding programmes for endangered native animals and offering hundreds of school groups from deprived neighbour-hoods the chance to understand more about their natural environment. The **Museu da Fauna** (Tues–Sun 9am–4.30pm; guided tours by appointment only; free), neighbouring the zoo, has a collection of stuffed birds, mammals and reptiles from throughout Brazil; worth a look for those especially inter-ested in Brazilian species.

Museu do Primeiro Reinado de Santos

A short walk east from the Quinta along Avenida Dom Pedro II is a former royal property, which, through its shabby grandeur, amply demonstrates the decline of São Cristóvão. The **Museu do Primeiro Reinado de Santos** (Tues–Fri 11am–5pm; R$2; Av. Dom Pedro II 293; ☎21/2332 4513) is primarily of historical interest. This Neoclassical "*palacete*" was reconstructed in 1826 on the orders of Emperor Dom Pedro I to house his lover, the Marquesa de Santos. Though now crying out for restoration, the interior is lavish; paintings and wooden carvings portray the Greek myths while a beautiful harp is profiled on the ceiling of the music room. The entrance hall and stairwell is one of Rio's most beautiful, and a peaceful shaded courtyard at the rear has an attractive water fountain at its centre.

Close enough to the Palacio Imperial, the house proved a perfect location for Dom Pedro to entertain guests at dances – though the Marquesa herself couldn't have had much time to join in, as less than four years later she'd had four more children by Dom Pedro and the affair was over; she returned to São Paulo and later married.

North to the Feira Nordestina and São Januario

Ten minutes' walk from Rio Zoo northeast along Avenida de Exército, the Campo de São Cristóvão looms into view, home to the excellent **Feira Nordestina** (Mon–Thurs 10am–4pm & nonstop Fri 10am to Sun 10pm; Ⓦwww.feiradesaocristovao.com.br) – the best of Rio's regular **markets**. Its roots extend back to the late nineteenth century and the first large-scale migration of impoverished Northeasterners to Rio, but since 2003 it has been held in a vast, purpose-built stadium in the shadow of the Linha Vermelha highway overpass. A replica of the great Northeastern markets, it comprises **seven hundred stalls** (many run by people in traditional costume) selling typical handicrafts and caged birds next to huge slabs of sun-dried beef and an amazing array of food and drink from *tapioca* to *cachaça* – while *forro* music from the parched Northeastern backlands fills the air.

The best buys are beautifully worked hammocks, leather bags and hats, *literatura de cordel* (illustrated folk literature pamphlets), herbal medicines and spices.

▲ Feira Nordestina

Weekends are a great time to go along with visiting migrants and their descendants enjoying their day off and listening to live music in the evenings (see p.200). See p.25 for bus numbers.

Heading northwest from here, though best reached by bus (#472 and #473 from the Zona Sul), is football stadium **São Januário**, home to club Vasco de Gama (visits mostly Saturdays; arrange a tour or to see a game with football guide Rob Shaw – see below; ☎21/2176-7373, ⓦ www.crvascodagama.com). This is by far the most interesting club to visit in Rio. The intimate 1927 stadium seats around 32,000 and was built by the São Cristóvão Portuguese community with fans of the club contributing money in a story of major importance both for Brazilian football and wider society (see p.256). Reminiscent of an older British stadium within a close-knit community of terraced houses, the building features a grand entrance and facade with extensive Portuguese tiling, while inside a bust of explorer Vasco de Gama himself is a reminder of the club's links to the Portuguese past. Next to the bust, the trophy room is packed with bright and polished trophies, while at the southern end of the pitch itself, behind the goal, is a Catholic chapel with a full-time priest who conducts regular services.

Maracanã Stadium

The **Maracanã Stadium** or, more formally, the **Estádio Jornalista Mário Filho**, is the biggest football stadium in the world. It is located to the west of Quinta da Boa Vista, a short walk across the rail line, over the Viaduto São Cristóvão. Built in two years by 10,000 labourers in time for the 1950 World Cup, it now holds over 100,000 people – though at the final match of the 1950 tournament 199,854 spectators crammed in to watch Brazil lose to Uruguay (see p.257) in what was deemed a national catastrophe. Built first and foremost as a monument to demonstrate Brazil's arrival as a nation to the rest of the world, the Maracanã is today the country's major statement of footballing prowess.

Attending a **game** here is one of the most extraordinary experiences Rio has to offer; even if you don't like football – it's worth going just for the theatrical spectacle. The stadium is the home ground of local clubs Flamengo and Fluminense, and almost all local derbies are played here including those of Botafogo and Vasco. Well over 100,000 fans attend games like the colourful "Fla-Flu" – Flamengo v Fluminense – fixture, and with various tournaments throughout the year the only break is for a few weeks over Christmas. Huge **concerts** are also held at the stadium, in the past featuring stars such as Sting, Madonna, Paul McCartney and even Frank Sinatra, which all attracted crowds in excess of 150,000.

The **2014 World Cup** final will be played here, though the stadium will close in advance of the tournament for a major refurbishment expected to last well into 2011. When the Maracanã is closed, games will be held at **Engenhão** to the west (see p.142) and **São Januário**, see above. It seems likely that the stadium's interesting one-room **Museu dos Esportes** (daily 9am–5pm, match days 8–11am; R$30; ☎21/2299-2941) will remain open. From here, you can join a **guided tour** which offers a chance to see the stadium's extensive collection of Brazilian sporting memorabilia, experience the view from the presidential box, wander through the changing rooms and tread on the hallowed turf itself. Alternatively, visit the stadium as part of a half- or full-day football **tour** by highly knowledgeable guide Rob Shaw (☎21/9874-8962 or 21/2275-8811, ⓔ brazsoc@hotmail.com; see also p.240), which on request can also take in Vasco or Fluminense's grounds, Ronaldo's first club São Cristóvão, or even an organized match with some Brazilian semi-pros.

The Maracanã is an easy and inexpensive destination to reach by **taxi** (around R$30 from the Zona Sul beaches), but if you come by **metrô** (line 2 changing at Estácio) get off at the Maracanã station and walk across the overpass right to the museum's entrance at Gate 18. By **bus**, take #464, #434 or #435 from Leblon (Ataúlfo Paiva), Ipanema (on Visconde de Pirajá) or Copacabana (Av. N.S. de Copacabana); the first two also go via Flamengo.

Beyond São Cristovão

Outside of São Cristóvão and the Maracanã, Zona Norte is likely to have interest only for longer-term visitors who want to get off the beaten track and see how the majority of the city's inhabitants live outside of the Zona Sul. That said, visits to samba schools Portela and Imperio Serrano in the *bairro* of **Madureira** are occasionally organized by tour groups as a great and less-touristy alternative to often-visited Mangueira and Salgueiro schools, while further north the grand neo-Moorish palace of the Fundação Oswaldo Cruz seems an unlikely addition to the urban spread. The **Igreja da Penha** is well worth a visit for its hilltop location alone – and to see (or join) its steady stream of pilgrims – though its enormous surrounding *favela* means that at times security can be an issue. The gateway to much of suburban Zona Norte is by **train** from station Central do Brasil (journeys vividly portrayed in the wonderful film of the same name, see p.264), while long **bus** journeys also ply the routes, leaving from the Castelo and Praça Tiradentes areas of Centro.

Engenhão and around

Some 7km west of the Maracanã in the *bairro* of **Engenhão de Dentro**, is Rio's other big sports stadium, **Engenhão** (officially the Complexo Esportivo João Havelange), built for the 2007 Pan American Games and now serving as Rio club Botafogo's ground (see p.96). Engenhão will also be the venue for the majority of Flamengo and Fluminense games when the Maracanã is closed for refurbishment in preparation for 2014. Brazil's most modern stadium, it is strikingly spacious and minimalist; about as far from the design of the Maracanã as you could get, with a 45,000 capacity and room for expansion. Engenhão is most easily reached by **train**; take the *metrô* as far as Central and change to an overground train destined for Belford Roxo or Deodoro, getting off at Engenho de Dentro (check it's stopping there before boarding at Central; *integração* tickets available for combined *metrô* and train). About a kilometre and a half north of Engenhão on Avenida Dom Helder Câmara is major Zona Norte shopping mall, **Norte Shopping** – unremarkable enough, though it can be a much-needed air-conditioned break from the heat if you happen to be in the area.

Madureira

The *bairro* of **Madureira**, another 5km or so further west, has been the heart of Zona Norte since the building of its market, the **Mercadão de Madureira** (Av. Ministro Edgard Romero 239; @www.mercadaodemadureira.com; close to Madureira train station) in 1914. First farmed by the Portuguese in around 1700, the area was further developed by the arrival of trains at the turn of the twentieth century. In its early years the market made the *bairro* the major point of food distribution for the whole of Rio – food factories are still the major local employer – but with the formation of the **Portela** samba school in nearby Oswaldo Cruz in the 1930s, followed by **Imperio Serrano** by impoverished black dock workers in 1947, Madureira has remained the entertainment and cultural heart of northern Rio ever since with music ranging from samba to *forró* to hip hop and house music for straight and gay crowds each and every week (see p.211 & pp.214–215).

The original **market** suffered a disastrous fire in 2000 but has now been rehoused in what can only be described as a modern shopping mall – something that, to most outsiders at least, appears entirely incongruous. The market "stalls" spill out into the mall's walkways, their bizarre assortment of bric-a-brac, carnaval costumes, foods, herbs, live animals and religious oddities offering constant sensual surprises. The Afro-Brazilian spiritualist cult *macumba* is widely practised in the north of the city and the *mercadão* is the faith's centre for purchasing associated *ex votos* and other offerings. Stalls sell human-size models of *macumba* deities, as well as candles, paintings, bells and ribbons, while models of Catholic saints or Nossa Senhora herself are all available too – many *macumba* practices overlap with tenets of the Catholic faith. The market also has small cages packed with all kinds of animals for sacrificial purposes – best avoided if you might find this difficult to cope with. The streets around the market, such as Rua São Geraldo, also offer good shopping.

Nearby, at Rua Conselheiro Galvão 130, is the home of Rio's fifth football club, **Madureira** (☎21/3359-2232, ⓦwww.madureiraec.com.br), an unexpect-edly sophisticated place with a neat, tricolour-painted ground and an equally well-presented trophy room. Known as the "*celeiro de craques*" (store of talent) on account of its excellent youth system and repeated production of star players, it's worth a visit if you're interested in Brazilian football (see p.243).

Most trains heading west from Central do Brasil stop at Madureira; look for lines to Belford Roxo or Deodoro (*integração* tickets available for combined *metrô* and train). Buses #355 from Praça Tiradentes and #298 from Castelo also pass here.

Fundação Oswaldo Cruz

Rising up impressively on a tree-covered hillock next to major Zona Norte artery Avenida Brasil (3km north of São Cristovão), the glorious Pavilhão Mourisco is home to the **Fundação Oswaldo Cruz** (Tues-Sat 10am-4pm; free; Av. Brasil 4365, Manguinhos; ☎21/2598-4242, ⓦwww.fiocruz.br), since the mid-1980s dedicated to the study and promotion of biomedical sciences. It's the building itself that's of most interest, however: Rio's only neo-Moorish style construction, the fort-like building was designed by Portuguese architect **Luiz de Moraes Júnior** and completed in 1906. The red and sand-coloured facade features a series of balconies set within mosaic-covered arches, with two distinctive domed minaret-like towers above. Inside, visitors are allowed to wander around much of the building, including into the third-floor library which is decorated with carved ceiling mosaics and French-made tiled floors reminiscent of arabic tapestries. At the heart of the building, an ornate tower holds the oldest elevator in Rio.

Igreja de Penha and around

Perched dramatically on a clifftop some 12km north of São Cristóvão, the **Igreja de Nossa Senhora da Penha de França** (☎21/2290 0942, ⓦwww .santuariopenhario.org.br) is a late nineteenth-century, colonial-style church, which most visitors to Rio only see from their bus or taxi on the way to and from the international airport. Penha is nonetheless an organized, shaded and peaceful oasis on the edge of one of Rio's most troubled areas – and while visits here are unlikely to result in any danger, they should be undertaken in that knowledge.

An important place of pilgrimage, it has 382 steps (and a tiny tram if you don't fancy the climb) and attracts many thousands of worshippers during the month-long Festa da Penha in October, and many more throughout the rest of the year. According to a legend surrounding the church's construction, the area's mid-seventeenth-century landowner was surveying his property from the hilltop when confronted by a large snake; – he was saved through the appearance of Nossa Senhora and consequently built a chapel which began attracting pilgrims – it wasn't until 250 years later that the church was built. Close-up, the church is thoroughly unremarkable, though its setting amidst the Zona Norte urban chaos is magnificent. The sanctuary below the church has a shop selling postcards, refreshments, and – most intriguingly – wax moulds of body parts, from hearts, pancreases and lungs to penises which you can "sacrifice" (burn) in case of your (or your partner's) malfunction.

To reach the church take a taxi from Centro direct, or buy an *integração* ticket and switch from the *metrô* (line 2) to the train at Triagem, going onward in the direction of Saracuruna or Gramacho. At Penha station exit via Rua dos Romeiros and take a taxi to the sanctuary. If you're in need of lunch or evening drinks afterwards, take a taxi onward to *Boteco Original* in the nearby Bras de Pina *bairro* – one of Zona Norte's finest *botecos* which is full of photos of *sambistas* (see p.194).

Vila Cruzeiro

An alternative way to arrive at the church of Penha is to visit during a tour of the *favela* bordering on the church grounds – **Vila Cruzeiro** – though like many *favelas* the community has serious security issues and on no account should you arrive here without arranging a visit first. It's a part of the group of communities that make up the Complexo do Alemão and Vila da Penha; these *favelas* stretch over four and a half square kilometres and are home to over 100,000 people. Infamous for all the wrong reasons, following a decade of sporadic and extreme violence between rival drug gangs and police – including a notorious incident where nineteen innocent people (including children) were killed by police in advance of the 2007 Pan American Games – Dutch-Brazilian NGO IBISS has responded by opening a remarkable community centre in the heart of Vila Cruzeiro, offering a range of programmes to residents (see box opposite), from health to education and sports to the arts. A 2008 **painting project** (Ⓦwww.favelapainting.com) has changed the face of one street, and another project provided an opportunity for outsiders to visit on tours guided by newly trained young people from the community. Impressively, the 2008 Nobel-supported International **Children's Peace Prize** was awarded to 16-year-old Vila Cruzeiro student Mayra Avellar for her work mobilizing children to fight for their right to attend school in the face of extreme odds (see Ⓦwww.faveladocumentary.com).

If you would like to visit, contact the IBISS head office (by email only Ⓔibiss@ibiss.com.br; English spoken). The community can be reached at the end of bus route #313 from Praça Tiradentes.

Niterói

Across the bay from Rio and linked to the north of Centro by the impressive 14km Rio-Niterói bridge, officially called the **Ponte Presidente Costa e Silva**, much of the neighbouring city of Niterói is populated by middle-class residents who enjoy the lower cost of living here. *Cariocas* have a tendency to sneer at **Niterói**, typically commenting that the only good thing about the city is its views back across **Guanabara Bay** to Rio. It's certainly true that the vistas are absolutely gorgeous on a clear day, but Niterói has much more to offer than this comment might suggest, not least for admirers of the work of the architect **Oscar Niemeyer**, whose **Museu de Arte Contemporânea** (**MAC**) is the major draw.

MAC aside, Niterói does have a few other sights worth seeing, but they are spread widely across the city. In the centre, almost next to the ferry terminal, Niemeyer admirers will instantly recognize the wave-like lines of his 2007 creation, the **Teatro Popular** (Ⓦwww.teatropopular.com.br). Also next to the ferry terminal is the the **Mercado do Peixe** (Tues–Fri 6am–4pm, Sat & Sun 6am–noon), the main fish market for Rio. As well as seeing an incredible variety of seafood, you can also eat here – there are some forty simple, but wonderful, restaurants of various sizes serving delicious fish creations.

Niterói's **beaches** are every bit as good as those of Rio's Zona Sul. **Praia de Jurujuba**, long and often crowded, is reached from the centre along the beautiful bayside road by bus #33 ("via Fróes"). On the way, it's worth taking a look at the pretty, late sixteenth-century church of **São Francisco Xavier**. The church is often closed, but the priest lives next door and will open it on request.

A short distance northeast along the coast, through Jurujuba, is the **Fortaleza de Santa Cruz** (Tues–Sun 9am–4pm; free), dating from the sixteenth century and still in use as a base of an artillery division of the Brazilian army. As the nearest point across the bay to Rio's Sugar Loaf mountain, it has particularly good views. If you have time, also check out the **Museu de Arqueologia de Itaipu** (Wed–Sun 1–5pm; R$2), in the ruined eighteenth-century Santa Teresa convent near Itaipu beach, for its collection of ceramics and other artefacts excavated from ancient burial mounds. Around here, to the east of Niterói, beyond the bay, there are numerous **restaurants**, **bars** and **hotels**, which all fill up with locals at weekends.

You can reach Niterói from Rio by **bus** (from the Menezes Cortes bus terminal or from Av. Nossa Senhora de Copacabana), or, for a more entertaining journey, by catching the passenger **ferry**. Ferries depart from the docks, close to Praça XV de Novembro, in Rio (every 15–30min; R$2.50). **Hydrofoils** (R$5) leave from the same dock at similar intervals and take just ten minutes. For the centre of Niterói, take a ferry or hydrofoil for "Estação Niterói" while a crossing to the Niemeyer-designed "Estação Charitas" is best for the beaches and the Museu de Arte Contemporânea. At both points there are helpful **tourist information** offices (9am–6pm).

With the notable exception of the 🐟 *Mercado do Peixe* Niterói cannot claim to have any particularly outstanding places to eat. But if fish (or a snack-bar) doesn't appeal, try *Coelho á Caçarola* at Av. Central 20, in Itaipu (closed Mon–Wed), which features some 25 rabbit dishes on its menu, or *Verdanna Grill* at Av. Quintino Bocaiúva 603 near the Estação Charitas ferry terminal, the best place in town to satisfy a meat craving.

Museu de Arte Contemporânea

Most visitors to Niterói head straight for the Oscar Niemeyer-designed **Museu de Arte Contemporânea** (Tues–Fri 10am–6pm, Sat & Sun 10am–7pm; R$4; Wed free; ⓦ www.macniteroi.com.br), or **MAC** as it is more commonly called. Opened in 1996, and located just south of the centre on a promontory by the Praia da Boa Viagem, the flying-saucer-shaped building offers a 360-degree perspective of Niterói and across the bay to Rio. The museum boasts an unexciting permanent display of Brazilian art of the second half of the twentieth century and also hosts temporary exhibitions, although these are rarely of much interest. Instead, the real work of art is the building itself, which even hardened critics of Niemeyer find difficult to dismiss out of hand. The curved lines of the gallery are beautiful, and the views of the headland, nearby beaches and Guanabara Bay from the interior are breathtaking.

8

Out of the city

Some of Brazil's most beautiful stretches of coast are easily accessible from the city of Rio, offering a completely different experience from the fun, but always crowded, beaches of Copacabana and Ipanema. Alternatively, the dramatic mountainous landscape and refreshing climate of the interior can provide a welcome break from the frenzy and often stifling heat of the city.

Only about three hours northeast of Rio on the aptly-named **Costa do Sol**, **Búzios** is firmly established as one of Brazil's most glamorous destinations. The attractions of the peninsula are straightforward: easy accessibility, a sunny climate, lovely beaches and sophisticated nightlife. While the feel is certainly that of a chic resort, even people who normally avoid resort-style tourism will at least appreciate Buziós' undoubted natural beauty.

The mountainous littoral and calm green waters of the **Costa Verde** ("Green Coast"), to the southwest of Rio, provide a marked contrast to the sand and surf of the Costa do Sol. Perhaps because they are just a few hours drive from the huge city, the unspoilt forest-clad Ilha Grande and the small picture-postcard colonial town of Paraty are all the more striking in their difference from the hectic *bairros* of Rio.

Heading off **inland** to the mountains where **Petrópolis**, Brazil's imperial summer capital, is nestled, is another excellent option. Although impressive mansions and other buildings from this period easily merit a day trip, the beautiful forested landscape of the nearby **Parque Nacional da Serra dos Órgãos** may tempt you to linger. With a little more time on your hands, head west from here into the Paraíba Valley where stately plantation houses are enduring reminders of Rio's nineteenth-century coffee boom.

If you plan on renting a **car** (see p.27), you'll find the coasts and mountains an easy drive from the city. Alternatively, comfortable inter-urban **buses** fan out to all points in the state from the Rodoviária Nova Rio (see p.24) or you can ask the hotel where you're staying to arrange transfers to and from Rio.

Búzios

Of the many beach resorts immediately north of Rio, undoubtedly the most sophistictated is **Armação dos Búzios**, or **Búzios** as it's more commonly known. A place of immense natural beauty with less than 35 days of rain a year, mostly falling in September and October, it's a bit like taking a step out of Brazil and into an upscale Mediterranean resort. Armação, the main village,

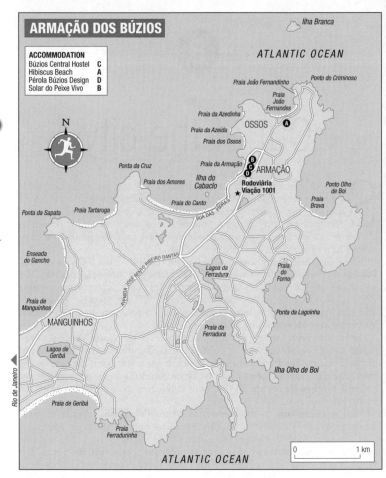

is built in a vaguely colonial style, its cobbled streets lined with restaurants, bars and chic boutiques. Now, during the high season (December to February), the population swells from a modest 22,000 to well over 150,000. A simple fishing village until the 1970s, the boats that once ferried the catch back to shore now take pleasure-seekers beach-hopping and scuba diving, and the roads connecting the town with the outlying beaches have been paved. This is the kind of place people either love or hate: if a crowded resort full of high-spending beautiful people is your thing, then you're sure to fall for Búzios; if not, give it a miss. Even so, outside of the summer peak season it's hard not to be taken in by the peninsula's sheer beauty, with March to May the best time to visit as there are relatively few tourists, prices are low and the weather is generally perfect.

Accommodation

Accommodation in Búzios is fairly expensive, and reservations are essential in high season – although the tourist office will try to find you a room in one of the resort's more than 300 hotels and *pousadas*. The lower-priced *pousadas*, mainly owned and run by Argentines, can be found in or near Armação or Ossos; they are generally the nicest and most friendly too.

Búzios Central Hostel Av. José Bento Ribeiro Dantas 1475, Armação ☎ 22/2623-9232; ⓦ www .buzioscentral.com.br. While the double rooms are small (R$112) and the dorms are equally cramped (R$40 per person), the pleasant common areas and relaxing gardens with a plunge pool makes this, a HI-affiliated hostel, one of the best budget options in Búzios.

Hibiscus Beach Rua 1, Praia de João Fernandes ☎ 22/2623-6221, ⓦ www .hibiscusbeach.com.br. Spacious bungalows, each with a small terrace and wonderful sea views, make this welcoming British-owned and-run *pousada* a good choice. There's a good-sized pool, and the area's best snorkelling beach is very close, while Armaçao's nightlife is a 5min taxi ride (or half-hour walk) away. R$220

Pérola Búzios Design Av. José Bento Ribeiro Dantas 222, Armação ☎ 22/2620-8507, ⓦ www .perolabuzios.com.br. All the facilities one would expect of a luxury hotel; including stylish modern furniture, a fitness centre and spa, and a large, beautiful pool. Although there's no sea view, the hotel is located just metres from Rua das Pedras. R$780

Solar do Peixe Vivo Rua José Bento Ribeiro Dantas 999, Armação ☎ 22/2623-1850, ⓦ www .solardopeixevivo.com.br. At this friendly, relaxed place, the guest rooms, in cabins in the garden, are simple but spacious; there's a pool and the beach is directly across the road. The main reception building is notable for being one of the oldest structures in Búzios. R$210

The town and its beaches

Búzios consists of three main settlements, each with its own distinct character. **Manguinhos**, on the isthmus, is the main service centre with a tourist office (24hr; ☎0800/24-9999), a medical centre, banks and petrol stations. Midway along the peninsula, linked to Manguinhos by a road lined with brash hotels, is the attractive village of **Armação**, where cars are banned from some of the cobbled roads. Most of Búzios's best restaurants and boutiques are concentrated here, along with some of the resort's nicest *pousadas*, and there's a helpful tourist office on the main square, Praça Santos Dumont (daily 9am–8pm; ☎22/2623-2099). A fifteen-minute walk along the Orla Bardot that follows the coast from Armação, passing the simple, but lovely, seventeenth-century Igreja Nossa Senhora de Sant'Ana on the way, brings you to **Ossos**, the oldest settlement, comprising a pretty harbour, a quiet beach (though don't swim in the polluted water here) and a few bars, restaurants and *pousadas*.

Within walking distance of all the settlements are beautiful white-sand **beaches**, 27 in total, cradled between rocky cliffs and promontories, and bathed by turquoise and crystal blue waters. A good way to get oriented is to hop on the **Búzios Trolley** (9am, noon, 3pm; 2hr; R$40 including drinks and snacks) at Praça Santos Dumont, which goes to twelve beaches and offers an English-language commentary on the peninsula's vegetation and history. You can also get from beach to beach by minivan ($R2), taxi (rarely more than R$15) or by foot. The beaches are varied; the north-facing ones have the calmest and warmest water, while Atlantic rollers come crashing onto those facing the south and east, making them popular with surfers. Though the beaches at Armação may look tempting, the water is polluted and swimming should be avoided. A short distance to the northeast, however, are the very clean waters of the small, rather isolated and extremely picturesque beaches of **Azeda** and **Azedinha** as well as the rather larger **João Fernandes**, the best place for snorkelling. Further east is **Praia Brava**, bordering a fine, horseshoe-shaped bay which is rarely overcrowded as there are few hotels close by. To the west of Armação, is the **Praia da Tartaruga**, where the water is pristine and, apart from some bars, there are few buildings. South of Armação, on the opposite side of the peninsula, the lovely bay of **Praia da Ferradura** is quite built up (and consequently crowded), but not nearly as bad as **Praia de Geribá**, which is solidly backed by condominium developments. Further out, the appealing **Praia de Tucuns** is a long stretch of sand that attracts surprisingly few people.

Eating, drinking and nightlife

Eating out is one of Búzios's great attractions with the best places concentrated in Armação; though standards are generally high, so too are prices. Superb seafood and sophisticated pasta are the specialities of *Satyricon*, an elegant and extremely expensive Italian restaurant at Rua das Pedras 500 (☎22/2623-2691). For first-rate moderate-expensive meat served to a demanding (mainly Argentine) clientele, 🍴 *Estância Don Juan* at Rua das Pedras 178 (☎22/2623-2169) is the best option. There are several good pizzerias, the best of which is *Da Vinci*, at Rua das Pedras 286 (☎22/2623-7098), with wood-burning ovens and 25 varieties of rather expensive pizzas. There are some cheaper options, including a few excellent *por kilo* (pay by weight) restaurants, in the town centre. One of the best for value, with an exceptionally varied choice of salads and hot dishes, is *Bananaland* at Rua Manoel Turíbio de Farias 50 (☎22/2623-2666), the road running immediately parallel to Rua das Pedras. Cheapest of all, and often excellent, are the beachside *barracas* (rustic beach bars) selling oysters, mussels and grilled fish.

Nightlife – which gets going at around 11pm and continues until dawn – is another one of Búzios' highlights and it's impossible to exaggerate how crowded Armação gets in January and February, while even in the off-season the bars along Rua das Pedras remain quite lively at weekends. The *Pátio Havana*, a rather upscale bar at Rua das Pedras 101, is well worth checking out for the often first-rate jazz hosted there. There are several nightclubs along Rua das Pedras and the Orla Bardot. Open from December to March, they easily match the best in Rio, with similar funk, hip-hop, pop and occasional Brazilian offerings. Popular with *Carioca* tourists is *Privilege* at Orla Bardot 500 (Fri & Sat, from 11pm) but, while twice as expensive, the Ibiza-based *Pacha*, at Rua das Pedras 151 (Fri & Sat, from 11pm), has become the venue of choice for trendy club-goers.

Ilha Grande

Ilha Grande comprises 193 square kilometres of mountainous jungle and stunning beaches; excellent for some scenic tropical rambling. It's also inhabited by a spectacular range of wildlife including parrots, exotic hummingbirds, butterflies and monkeys. The area is so unspoilt because until the late twentieth century it was notorious as the location of prisons and was either wholly or partially off-limits to the public. The prisons are now no more than ruins. Today almost the entire island is a state park, and the authorities have successfully limited development and enforced a complete ban on motor vehicles.

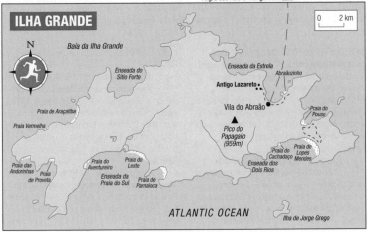

Ilha Grande offers lots of **walks** along well-maintained and fairly well-signposted trails, usually leading to wonderful beaches, but it's sensible to take some basic precautions. Be sure to set out as early as possible and always inform people at your *pousada* where you are going – in writing if possible. Carry plenty of water and remember to apply sunscreen and insect repellent at regular intervals. If you think that you might be out after around 6pm, it's best to carry a flashlight with you as darkness comes suddenly, and even on a night with a full moon the trails are likely to be pitch-black due to the canopy formed by the overhanging foliage.

Arrival and information

There are **boats** to Vila do Abraão, on Ilha Grande, from both Mangaratiba and Angra dos Reis, further along the coast towards Paraty. Just five **buses** a day run from Rio to Mangaratiba (5.30am, 9am, 12.30pm, 3pm and 6.45pm) – if you catch the earliest bus you'll make the ferry that sails from Mangaratiba daily at 8am (with an extra boat on Fri at 10pm); ferries make the return crossing at 5.30pm.

With hourly buses from Rio, Angra dos Reis is easier to reach and as ferries to Abraão leave later in the day (Mon–Fri 3.30pm, Sat & Sun 1.30pm; returning at 10am daily), there's less chance of not making the connection. Tickets cost R$6.50 during the week or R$14 on Saturdays, Sundays and holidays from both Mangaratiba and Angra; if you miss the ferry you can usually count on finding a small launch to do the crossing, charging around R$30 per person and taking around 90 minutes. During the summer there's a constant flow of these launches from both mainland towns, but at other times Angra is the best bet. If you have a car, get advice at the ferry terminals on where to find a secure, lock-up parking spot. Be sure to come with plenty of **cash**: changing dollars or traveller's cheques is impossible on the island, there's no ATM and not all *pousadas* and restaurants accept credit cards.

Accommodation

Pousadas in Abraão are mostly simple (though they tend to be more expensive than places of similar quality on the mainland), while those elsewhere on the island are often more exclusive and comfortable. Reservations in the high season, especially at weekends, are absolutely essential; in the off-season prices are halved.

Holandês Abraão ⏱24/3361-5034, ⊛www .holandeshostel.com.br. This always-popular youth hostel is located behind the beach, next to the Assembléia de Deus. Dorms (R$40 per person) sleep either four or eight guests and there are chalets with a double and a single bed (R$110). The garden, with dense vegetation and sitting areas, is exceptionally attractive.

Lagamar Praia Grande de Araçatiba ⏱24/9221-8180, ⊛www.pousadalagamar .com.br. The nicest of several charming *pousadas* located in a quiet fishing hamlet, offering generous seafood meals, *caipirinhas* and a wholesome breakfast served in as

beautiful a setting as can be imagined. R$220

Naturália Abraão ⏱24/3361-9583, ⊛www.pousadanaturalia.net. Although set on a hillside back from the beach, all the guest rooms have breathtaking sea views from their balconies. Breakfast is always a treat, and the friendly owner is usually on hand to offer advice on hikes or boat trips. R$200

Oásis Abraão ⏱24/3361-5116, ⊛www.oasis .ilhagrande.org. In a peaceful location at the far end of the beach, a 10min walk from the jetty. Simple, cosy rooms and excellent breakfasts. R$160

Around the island

As you approach the low-lying, whitewashed port of **Vila do Abraão**, the mountains rise dramatically from the sea, and in the distance lies the curiously shaped summit of Pico do Papagaio ("Parrot's Beak"), which rises to a height of 980m and can be reached in about three hours. There's very little to see in Abraão itself, but it's a pleasant enough base from which to explore the rest of the island. The ruins of the **Antigo Presídio** lie a half-hour walk along the coast west from Abraão. Originally built as a hospital, it was converted to a prison for political prisoners in 1910 and was finally dynamited in the early 1960s. Among the ruins, you'll find the *cafofo*, the containment centre where prisoners who had failed in escape attempts were immersed in freezing water. Just a fifteen-minute walk inland from Abraão and overgrown with vegetation, stands the **Antigo Aqueduto** that once channelled the island's water supply. There's a fine view of the aqueduct from the **Pedra Mirante**, a hill near the centre of the island, and, close by, a waterfall provides the opportunity for a cool bathe on a hot day.

For the most part the beaches – **Aventureiro**, **Lopes Mendes**, **Cachadaço** and **Morcegoare** to name a few – are still wild and unspoilt. They are most easily reached by **boat**; a typical day-long excursion costs R$25–35 per person, and the departure time from Abraão's jetty is 10.30am, with stops for snorkelling (equipment provided) before continuing on to a beach where you'll be picked up later in the day, arriving back in Abraão at around 4.30pm. Most beaches can also be reached on **foot**, and there are some lovely quiet beaches, such as **Grande das Palmas** and **Mangues**, within an hour's walk of Abraão. These and many of the other beaches have a *barraca* or two selling snacks and cold drinks, but it's always a good idea to bring basic supplies with you.

Insects

Bear in mind that right along the Costa Verde mosquitoes and *borachudos* – tiny, vicious gnats that bite without your hearing or, until later, feeling them – are an annoying presence. Be sure to bring plenty of insect repellent and mosquito coils with you.

For a longer hike, the exceptionally lovely coconut-fringed **Praia da Parnaioca** is an attractive destination. It takes about five hours to reach the praia, so it's no jaunt, but the trail through the forest is well marked. Alongside the glorious horseshoe-shaped praia is an old fishing village that was abandoned by its inhabitants because of their fear of escaped prisoners. If you want to stay over you should have little trouble finding a room to rent and something to eat, as the community is slowly re-establishing itself here.

Eating, drinking and nightlife

Summertime **nightlife** in Abraão is lively, with the *Bar Verdinho da Ilha* playing some eminently danceable *forró* music. Restaurants, predictably, concentrate on seafood (try the *Rei dos Caldos*, which specializes in tasty fish soups), but there are also a couple of reasonable pizzerias. **Carnaval** is well celebrated here – much more relaxed than the Rio experience – and watch, too, for the festival of São João (Jan 20).

Paraty

About 300km south of Rio is the Costa Verde's star attraction, the beautiful colonial town of **Paraty**. One of Brazil's first planned urban projects, the narrow cobbled streets of Paraty's historic centre – out of bounds to motorized transport – are bordered by simple churches and pretty houses adorned with bougainvillea and other brightly coloured plants and teeming with hummingbirds.

Inhabited since 1650, the centre of Paraty (or, officially, Vila de Nossa Senhora dos Remédios de Paraty) has changed little since its heyday as a staging post for the eighteenth-century trade in Brazilian gold, passing from Minas Gerais to Portugal (see p.157). Following the decline of the gold trade during the

▲ Paraty

nineteenth century, the economy revived with the port being important for the shipment of coffee. After the collapse of coffee production in Rio at the end of the century, Paraty entered a long period of stagnation; fishing, sugar farming and *cachaça* production were the area's only economic activities until the rise of tourism in the late 1970s. Nowadays, however, Paraty, which UNESCO has awarded world heritage status, is very much alive; the town and the surrounding area's population of 33,000 are actively involved in fishing, farming and tourism.

Arrival and information

There are nine buses a day between Rio and Paraty (4hr 30min). Paraty's **rodoviária** is located just outside the historic centre, a five-minute walk along Avenida Roberto Silveira, the main road that leads into town. The **tourist office** (daily 8am–7pm; ☏24/3371-1897) is near the entrance of the old town, on the corner of Avenida Roberto Silveira and Praça Chafariz , and can supply a good map of the town and the outlying area and a list of hotels and restaurants.

Some of the mainland beaches can be accessed by road – ask at the tourist office for details of bus times. If you're really feeling energetic, you can hire a **mountain bike** for R$35 a day from Paraty Tours at Av. Roberto Silveira 11, who also supply maps with suggested itineraries covering beaches, mountains or forests. They can also arrange **car rental** for around R$140 a day.

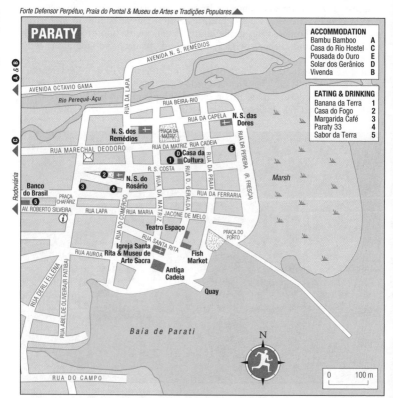

Forte Defensor Perpétuo, Praia do Pontal & Museu de Artes e Tradições Populares

Festa Literária Internacional de Paraty – FLIP

By far the most noteworthy of the many festivals that Paraty hosts each year is the **Festa Literária Internacional de Paraty** (FLIP; ⓦ www.flip.org.br), held annually since 2003. Thanks to remarkable international and Brazilian connections forged by FLIP's creator, Liz Calder (the co-founder of British publisher Bloomsbury), the festival immediately established itself as *the* literary event of the Brazilian calendar, as well as one of the most influential literary jamborees in the world. Held annually during the first two weeks of July, FLIP's programmes read like a who's who of world literature having featured the likes of Nadine Gordimer, Amoz Oz, Orhan Pamuk and Tom Stoppard, alongside important Brazilian writers such as Lygia Fagundes Telles, Milton Hatoum and Chico Buarque.

It's impossible to exaggerate the enthusiasm of the audience, mainly *Cariocas* and *Paulistas* – even talks or readings by obscure writers are packed solid. The main programme takes place in the magnificent *Tenda dos Autores* (Authors' Marquee) with the events shown on big screens around town. A lively fringe festival has also developed, featuring writing workshops, performances by top Brazilian musicians and events aimed at local children.

Accommodation

From late December to after Carnaval – and when special events are held, accommodation is hard to find: if you are without a reservation your best hope will be to find a room outside of the historic centre – ask the tourist office for advice. For the rest of the year, however, it's easy to track down good **accommodation** and rooms can be amazing value.

Bambu Bamboo Rua Glauber Rocha 9 ☏ 24/3371-8629, ⓦ www.bambubamboo .com. This British and Brazilian owned *pousada*, set in a peaceful riverside location 15min walk from the historic centre, is one of the most pleasant places to stay in Paraty. The guest rooms are spacious and there is a large pool in the attractive garden where breakfast is served. R$300

Casa do Rio Hostel Rua Antônio Vidal 120 ☏ 24/3371-2223, ⓦ www.paratyhostel.com. Cramped, but otherwise excellent, this youth hostel is located just a few minutes' walk from Paraty's historic centre. Helpful staff and a range of tours on offer. R$25 per person in a dorm and R$80 for a double room with private bathroom.

Pousada do Ouro Rua Dr Pereira 145 ☏ 24/3371-2033, ⓦ www.pousadaouro.com.br. The least expensive luxury *pousada* in Paraty's historic centre, boasting tastefully

furnished rooms – spacious and light in the main building, but rather small and dark in the annexe. There's a pretty walled garden and a good-size pool, too. R$290

Solar dos Gerânios Praça da Matriz ☏ 24/3371-1550, ⓦ www.paraty.com.br /geranio. This beautiful, superb-value *pousada* is packed with rustic furniture and curios. The rooms are small and spartan but impeccably kept; most have a balcony and all have a private bathroom. The multilingual owner and her cats are extremely welcoming. R$100

Vivenda Rua Beija-Flor 9 ☏ 24/3371-4272, ⓦ www.vivendaparaty.com. A 10min walk from the historic centre, this modern and immensely relaxing B&B has one double room (R$210) and two roomy bungalows (R$275) with kitchenettes, all set around an attractive patio garden and pool. The owner is a perfect host, providing local advice (and *caipirinhas*!).

The Town

Paraty is a perfect place to wander aimlessly, each turn of the corner revealing another picturesque view, but while as an ensemble the seventeenth- and eighteenth-century buildings appear absolutely stunning, there are no individual gems. Even so, there are a few churches and other buildings that are worth seeking out. As with most small colonial towns in Brazil, each of Paraty's extremely simple white-washed churches traditionally served a different sector of the population. Dating back to 1646, **Nossa Senhora dos Remédios** (daily 9am–5pm), on the Praça da Matriz, is Paraty's main church and the town's largest building. During the late eighteenth century, the church – built for local bourgeoisie – underwent major structural reforms, and the imposing exterior and austere interior have remained unchanged ever since. In 1800 Paraty's aristocracy had their own church built: the graceful **Igreja das Dores** (daily 1–5pm), which has a small cemetery, is located three blocks from the main church, by the sea. Along Rua do Comércio is the smallest church, the **Igreja do Rosário** (Wed–Sun 9am–noon & 1.30–5pm), constructed in 1725 and used by slaves. Finally, at the southern edge of the town, the **Igreja de Santa Rita** (Wed–Sun 9am–noon & 2–5pm) is the oldest and architecturally most signifi-cant of Paraty's churches. Built in 1722 for the freed *mulatto* population, it is notable for its Portuguese Baroque facade; the small **Museu de Arte Sacra**, a small, but interesting, repository of religious artefacts from Paraty's churches, is attached. Next to Santa Rita you'll find the late eighteenth-century **Antiga Cadeia**, now the public library, a building that looks more like a simple house than the feared jail that it once was, while opposite is the lively **fish market**. On the corner of Rua Dona Geralda and Rua Samuel Costa, the beautifully maintained **Casa da Cultura** (Wed–Mon 10am–6.30pm; R$5; Ⓦwww .casadacultraparaty.org.br); is well worth stopping at for the excellent locally inspired art and photography exhibitions.

To the north of the old town, across the Rio Perequé-Açu on the Morro de Vilha Velha, is the **Forte Defensor Perpétuo**, constructed in 1703 to defend Paraty from pirates seeking to plunder gold ships leaving the port. The fort underwent restoration in 1822 and today the rudimentary structure houses the **Museu de Artes e Tradições Populares** (Wed–Sun 9am–noon & 2–5pm; free), a permanent display of local fishing tools and basketware as well as handicrafts for sale.

Beaches and islands

Keeping yourself amused while visiting Paraty should be no problem. From the **Praia do Pontal**, on the other side of the Perequé-Açu River from town, and from the **port quay**, schooners leave for the beaches of Paraty-Mirim, Jurumirim, Lula and Picinguaba and some of the other 200 local beaches. Tickets typically cost R$30 per person; boats leave Paraty at noon, stop at three or four islands for swimming opportunities and return at 6pm. These trips can be rowdy affairs, with the larger boats capable of carrying several dozen people and usually blaring out loud music. Alternatively, for around R$250 (or R$150 in low season) you can easily charter a small fishing boat for three to five passen-gers by asking at the quay.

17km southwest of Paraty, 8km of it along an unpaved road (which should be avoided following heavy rains), is **Paraty-Mirim**, an attractive, calm bay ideal for swimming. Six buses head here from Paraty each day (45min). Although there are a couple of bars serving food, there's nowhere to stay at the beach. Roughly halfway between the beach and the main road, however, is the *Vila Volta* (Ⓣ24/9815-7689, Ⓦwww.vilavolta.com.br; R$110), a rustic *pousada* in an extremely peaceful setting.

Trindade, a lively village 21km southwest of Paraty (7 buses daily; 45min), is located between some of the Costa Verde's best beaches. The main beach is nice

During the seventeenth and eighteenth centuries, Paraty's harbour was [...] important in Brazil after that of Rio de Janeiro. The port developed to [...] Portugal, by way of Rio, gold and diamonds from Minas Gerais and to transp[...] supplies to the distant mining communities. Amongst these "supplies" were enslaved Africans, either shipped directly from Africa or from the plantations of more northerly parts of Brazil. Paraty was Brazil's most important slave trade centre south of Rio.

For decades the **Caminho do Ouro** was the only gold shipment route authorized by the Portuguese government, with mule trains taking up to six weeks to complete the steep and dangerous 500-kilometre journey to Ouro Preto, the most important mining centre. But due to attacks on Rio-bound ships by pirates hiding out in the nearby islands and coves, an alternative route was created to link Rio with the mines. In 1750 the Caminho Novo (the New Trail) was inaugurated, leading to a decline in Paraty's fortunes.

Today, the Caminho do Ouro can easily be accessed by car, bike or bus by following the Cunha road up into the Serra do Mar. The easiest place to head for is at Km 4 of the road, where there's a well-signposted side road leading 900m to the **Fazenda Murycana** (daily 10am–6pm; R$5), a farm complex that dates back to the seventeenth century. As well as a farm, Murycana originally served as an inn for travellers on the Caminho do Ouro and as a toll post where the royal tax of twenty percent on goods was levied. The restored buildings can be visited, the most interesting being the slightly ramshackle, yet still attractive, **casa grande**, now a museum. There's a restaurant serving typical country food (R$25 per person), and one can taste and purchase the *fazenda's* famous, but poor quality, *cachaça*. Be sure to note, however, that this is one of the most popular excursions and the *fazenda* can get unpleasantly crowded, especially at lunchtime, with the arrival of tour groups.

For a more rugged experience, consider hiking along a restored segment of the Caminho do Ouro. The trail's access point is at the Centro de Informações Turísticas do Caminho do Ouro, located at Km 8 of the Cunha road. Here you can head further inland along the partially cobbled trail. Beware: the trail is very slippery after the rain, and even in dry conditions you'll need good footwear to tackle the steep and uneven terrain. The landscape, which appears pleasantly pastoral at first, grows increasingly impressive, and you'll have spectacular views of the forested mountains, Paraty and the ocean. Be sure to bring water with you but after about an hour you'll reach a waterfall to shower under and a source of fresh drinking water.

enough, but you're better off walking away from the village across the rocky outcrops to Praia Brava or Praia do Meio, where a few bars are the only signs of development on these perfect mainland beaches.

Eating, drinking and nightlife

Paraty has plenty of watering holes to keep you amused in the evenings, though out of season you may find yourself drinking alone. Amongst the atmospheric bars with live **MPB** (popular Brazilian music) are *Paraty 33*, on Rua da Lapa alongside the **Nossa Senhora dos Remédios**.

For an unusual dining experience, sign up to a special gastronomic event at the **Academy of Cooking and Other Pleasures** (Rua Dona Geralda 211 ☎24/3371-6468, ⓦwww.chefbrazil.com) hosted by **Yara Castro Roberts**, a professional cook and restaurant consultant who has encouraged interest in Brazilian food through cookery classes, television appearances and writing. Several evenings a week, Yara gives demonstrations in her home, alternating between menus drawn from Rio, Bahia, the Amazon and Minas Gerais, her home state. The evening, which usually lasts from 7.30 to 10.30pm, costs R$130 per person, with groups limited to eight or so people.

One can eat well in Paraty and there's a good choice of **restaurants** in all price brackets. The cheapest places to eat are outside of the historic centre, along Avenida Roberto Silveiro – while none of these are remarkable, you won't have any difficulty finding a filling meal of fish, meat, beans, rice and salad for under R$20.

Banana da Terra Rua Dr Samuel Costa 198. Paraty's most interesting restaurant, with an emphasis on local ingredients (such as bananas and plantains). The grilled fish with garlic-herb butter and banana is delicious, as are the wonderful banana desserts. Expect to pay well over R$130 per person. Evenings only except Sat & Sun, when lunch is also served; closed Wed.

Casa do Fogo Rua Comendador José Luiz 390. Attractively presented, immensely flavourful vegetable, seafood and meat dishes, all flambéed – with local *cachaça* of course. R$60 for the three-course dinner special.

Margarida Café Praça Chafariz. Imaginative, well-prepared modern Brazilian cooking is the speciality here; the desserts are a special treat, especially the bananas flambéed in *cachaça*. There's a nice bar, plus remarkably good MPB on most nights. At least R$80 per person for a full meal.

Sabor da Terra Av. Roberto Silveira 180. Paraty's best *por kilo* restaurant, offering a wide variety of inexpensive hot and cold dishes that include excellent seafood. Located outside of the historic centre, next to the Banco do Brasil.

Petrópolis

Sixty-six kilometres directly to the north of Rio de Janeiro, high in the mountains, stands the elegant city of **Petrópolis**. Surrounded by stunning scenery, and with a gentle, alpine summer climate, Petrópolis became a favourite retreat of Rio's elite during the nineteenth century. Although slightly faded in appearance, the grand avenues lined with mansions and palaces still evoke imperial grandeur, making Petrópolis a favourite destination for foreign visitors and *Cariocas* seeking a short break from Rio.

It was Emperor Dom Pedro II who took a fancy to Petrópolis and in 1843 he designated the mountain resort as the summer seat of his government. As the

---

Imperial Petrópolis in republican Brazil

Although Brazil has been a republic since 1889, two branches of the **Brazilian Imperial House** – one headed by Prince Luís of Orléans e Bragança (who lives in São Paulo and Paraty) and the other by Prince Pedro Carlos of Orléans e Bragança (who lives in Petrópolis) – have been fighting over the line of succession to a nonexistent throne ever since. Their absurdly complicated argument concerns lineage and the legality of Emperor Dom Pedro II's renunciation of the throne. Few Brazilians today have the slightest interest in their hypothetical throne, though in 1993 when a constitutional plebiscite was held to decide whether Brazil should maintain its presidential system of government or adopt a parliamentary system, a surprisingly high eleven percent voted in favour of the re-establishment of the monarchy.

Now it is only in Petrópolis where any members of the redundant royal family, who returned to Brazil in the 1940s, exert any real influence. Aside from the squabbling Imperial House collecting a 2.5 percent tax on all real estate transactions within the historic city limits, Prince Pedro Carlos and his branch of the family own a range of local businesses including a brewery that produces the very decent Cerveja Itaipava range, the daily local newspaper, the *Tribuna de Petrópolis,* and an upmarket antique shop, the Antiquáio da Princesa at Av. Koeller 42 – once the home of Princess Isabel, the wife of Dom Pedro. It's a fanciful possibility that the imperial house will rule Brazil again, yet a few nostalgic monarchists continue to campaign for the rival claimants to the throne.

PETRÓPOLIS

◄ Corrêas, Parque Nacional da Serra dos Órgãos (A) & ❶

ACCOMMODATION
Albergue da Quitandinha	E
Hotel Casablanca	C
Pousada 14 Bis	D
Pousada da Alcobaça	A
Pousada Imperial Koeller	B

EATING & DRINKING
Alcobaça	1
Imperatriz Leopoldina	2
Paladar	3

Casa do Barão de Mauá

Palácio de Cristal

Palácio de Princesa Isabel

Catedral São Pedro de Alcântara

Palácio de Cultura

Palácio Amarelo

Casa de Rui Barbosa

Igreja Luterana

Casa da Ipiranga

Jardim Glaziou

Museu Imperial & Palácio Imperial

Colégio Santa Isabel

Local bus terminal

Casarão do Viscunde de Ubá

Forum

Casa Santos Dumont

Trono de Fátima

▼ Quitandinha, Palácio Quitandinha, (E), Rio de Janeiro & Rodoviária

0   200 m

❽ **OUT OF THE CITY**

159

royal family moved to Petrópolis to escape Rio's torrid heat, Brazilian aristocrats, politicians and business leaders as well as foreign diplomats followed – building residences appropriate to their status. The annual mass flight to Petrópolis continued well into the twentieth century, only really coming to an end in 1960 with the inauguration of Brasília as the new capital of Brazil.

The Town

Any visit to Petrópolis should begin at the **Palácio Imperial** on the tree-lined Rua da Imperatriz, the remarkably modest summer residence of Emperor Dom Pedro II. Built in the late 1840s, the Palácio is a fine Neoclassical structure set in beautifully maintained formal gardens. Open to the public as the Museu Imperial (Tues–Sun 11am–5.30pm; R$8; Ⓦwww.museuimperial.gov.br), it contains a fascinating collection of the royal family's possessions. On entry, you're given felt overshoes in which to slide around the polished floors, and inside there's everything from Dom Pedro II's crown (639 diamonds, 77 pearls, all set in two kilos of finely wrought gold) to the regal commode. In the former stables the royal railway carriage is displayed, while other buildings in the garden serve as space for temporary exhibitions and an excellent **tearoom**. Three nights a week the former palace is illuminated for a **sound** and **light show** (Thurs–Sat 8pm; R$20) – well worth attending for the classical music and sound effects even if you don't understand the Portuguese narration.

From the Palácio, walk along Rua da Imperatriz to the **Catedral São Pedro de Alcântara** (8am–6pm), a rather overbearing neo-Gothic style structure built between 1884 and 1939. Inside its mausoleum lie the tombs of Emperor Dom

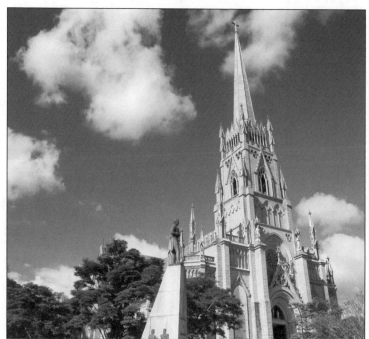

▲ Catedral São Pedro de Alcântara, Petrópolis

Coffee country

To many people, coffee and Rio de Janeiro are synonymous, a legacy of the nineteenth century when Brazil completely dominated the trade. But Rio's **coffee boom** was actually shortlived, starting in the 1820s and collapsing suddenly in 1888, when slavery – on which plantation-owners were completely dependent – was abolished. Many of the more resourceful farmers migrated south to São Paulo to take advantage of immigrant labour and the availability of fertile, well-watered land. Furthermore, single-crop farming on the hilly terrain of the **Paraíba Valley** resulted in serious levels of soil erosion, while the felling of the forest to plant coffee bushes altered the climate, causing drought. The "coffee barons" either abandoned their *fazendas* (plantations) or looked for other uses of their land. Dairy farming was eventually found to work and now almost all the former plantation land is given over to cattle grazing. Today, the Paraíba Valley, some 200km west of Petrópolis, is a peaceful backwater, with evidence of the coffee boom most apparent in the **fazenda houses** that are left standing in various states of repair.

With a few days and, ideally, a car, a visit to the Paraíba Valley can be fascinating. The area can be reached in two hours from Rio, and is a convenient stop-off if travelling between Petrópolis and Paraty, or other points on the coast. A particulary attractive place to make for is **Rio das Flores**, a sleepy little town with a population of less than 8000. From whatever direction you approach the town, you're sure to notice some grand *fazenda* houses either right alongside the road or in the distance; many others lie hidden from view off side roads. **Visting these houses** (usually R$35 per person) involves scheduling appointments, something that the tourist information office (Mon–Fri 9am–5pm; Rua Cesar Nillares 120; ☎24/2458-1162) can usually help with. Accommodation is available right in the centre of town at the modern and very simple *Pousada das Flores* (☎24/2458-1037; R$70). More expensive, but certainly much more pleasant, is staying at the *Fazenda Santo Antônio* (☎24/2488-2148, ⓦwww.fazendastoantonio.com; R$260, half-board), some 22km southeast of town. The six guest rooms are either in the impeccably preserved *casa grande*, or plantation house, that dates back to 1842, or in the former *senzala*, or slave quarters. The buildings are set amidst beautiful gardens with a row of stately imperial palms, and there's a pool and horses available to ride. The English-speaking owner and his wife could not be more helpful and will make arrangements for visits to neighbouring properties.

Pedro I, Princess Regent Dona Isabel and several other royal personages. From here one can easily stroll past the city's most elegant nineteenth-century mansions, especially those along **Avenida Koeller** and on **Avenida Ipiranga**, where you'll also find the German **Igreja Luterana** (open only for Sunday services at 9am). Most of the mansions have been converted into offices, but one of the most extravagant of properties, the French-style **Casa da Ipiranga**, at Av. Ipiranga 716 (Thurs–Tues noon–6pm; R$5; ⓦwww.casadaipiranga.blogspot.com), with its impressive exterior and lavishly decorated interior, has remained virtually unchanged since being built in 1884 for a wealthy Portuguese coffee merchant.

Other historic buildings worth tracking down are the **Casa Santos Dumont** at Rua do Encanto 22 (Tues–Sun 9.30am–5pm; R$5), an alpine chalet built in 1918 and the home of the Brazilian aviator of the same name, containing personal memorabilia; the **Casa do Barão de Maurá** at Praça da Confluência 3 (Mon–Sat 9am–6.30pm, Sun 9am–5pm; R$5), featuring displays devoted to the baron best known for his role in constructing Brazil's first railway; and the grand, half-timbered Norman-style **Palácio Quitandinha** on the Estrada de Quitandinha, just outside of town. Once the Quitandinha Casino, it stopped receiving the rich and famous when the Brazilian government prohibited gambling in 1946, and was eventually converted into a luxury apartment building. Nearby, at Rua Cristóvão Colombo 1034, the **Museu Casa do Colono** (Tues–Sun 9.30am–5pm) is a simple house dating back to 1847 with a small collection of curios, tools and pictures relating to the German immigrants who settled in and around Petrópolis in the early nineteenth century.

Practicalities

Buses for Petrópolis leave Rio's Rodoviária Nova Rio (see p.24) every fifteen minutes and take just over an hour. In fine weather, the journey is glorious: for the best views of the mountain scenery sit on the left-hand side of the bus. Petrópolis's *rodoviária* is located some 10km from town. From there you can take a bus to the municipal bus terminal, a short walk to most sights. There are helpful branches of the tourist office (℡0800-241-516) at the *rodoviária* (daily 9am–6pm) and at Praça da Liberdade (daily 9am–6pm).

You can easily visit Petrópolis as a day-trip, but spending a night or two can be a relaxing escape. Centrally located, the *Pousada 14 Bis* (Rua Santos Dumont 162 ℡24/2231-0946, ⓦwww.pousada14bis.com.br; R$140) offers tastefully furnished bedrooms, a lounge full of Santos Dumont (the Brazilian aviator) memorabilia and relaxing gardens. The ♣ *Pousada Monte Imperial Koeller* at Av. Koeller 99 (℡24/2237-1664, ⓦwww.pousadamonteimperial.com.br; R$250), a nineteenth-century mansion around the corner from the Museu Imperial, has comfortable rooms decorated in period-style. Many people prefer staying in the beautiful countryside, but this is only really practical if you have a car. Especially attractive is the ♣ *Pousada da Alcobaça* at Rua Dr Agostinho Goulão 298 (℡24/2221-1240, ⓦwww.pousadadaalcobaca.com.br; R$350), located near the entrance of the Parque Nacional da Serra dos Órgãos. The cosy rooms, lovely gardens and superb meals (also available to non-residents) makes this the most delightful place to stay around Petrópolis.

There are some reasonable restaurants in and around town. Located within a nineteenth-century mansion, *Paladar* (Tues–Sun 11am–4pm) at Rua Barão do Amazonas 25 offers an inexpensive *por kilo* buffet with a varied choice of salads and Brazilian hot dishes with tables both indoors and on the terrace overlooking Praça da Liberdade. For elegant dining, there's the *Imperatriz Leopoldina*, housed within the regal *Solar do Império* hotel at Av. Koeller 376 (℡24/2103-3000). The chef has created a wonderful menu inspired by Empress Leopoldina's supposed love of Brazilian ingredients and flavours; expect to pay around R$90 per person.

Parque Nacional da Serra dos Órgãos

One of Brazil's most beautiful mountain regions, the **Parque Nacional da Serra dos Órgãos** (Tues–Sun 9am–5pm, or camping by advance reservation ℡21/2152-1119), straddles an area of highland Atlantic rainforest immediately to the east of Petrópolis. The main features of the park are dramatic rock formations that resemble rows of organ pipes (hence the range's name), dominated by the towering **Dedo de Deus** ("God's Finger") peak. There are tremendous walking possibilities in the park; the favourite peaks for those with mountain-goat tendencies are the Agulha do Diablo (2050m) and the Pedra do Sino (2263m) – the latter has a path leading to the summit, a relatively easy three-hour trip (take refreshments).

It costs R$3 per person to enter the park, including a map with the main trails marked. There are some campsites, too, but no equipment for rent, so you'll need to come prepared or join a day or longer hike organized by Serra Trekking (℡24/2242-2360, ⓦwww.serratrekking.com.br). To reach the park from Petrópolis, take one of the frequent buses to Corrêas (30min, R$3) and change to a number 616 "Pinheiral" bus (hourly, 35min, R$3) that will leave you near the park entrance.

Listings

Listings

Accommodation

There's no shortage of **accommodation** in Rio, a city long associated with glamour and international tourism, though there are considerable seasonal variations in terms of demand and prices. **High season** is from December to the end of February, when it's worth booking in advance – either through a tourist office or leave your luggage in the *guarda volumes* (baggage offices) at the *rodoviária* or the airport while you look. During **Carnaval** and **Reveillon** (New Year), prices triple, accommodation is harder to find and most hotels accept bookings for a minimum of five nights (at Carnaval) and three nights (at Reveillon). During **low season**, many hotels decrease their prices by around thirty percent – ask for a *desconta* (discount) if it is not obviously forthcoming, and check that you are able to pay with a **credit card** – some establishments don't accept them and discounts often apply only to cash payment. **Prices** in this chapter, unless stated otherwise, refer to the cheapest double room in high season outside of Carnaval – or for **hostels**, the cheapest single dorm bed.

The quality of **hotels** has generally improved in Rio over the past ten years – budget options forced to compete with rapidly multiplying hostels (which now number around eighty, most of which also offer private rooms), and exclusive options contending with a new trend in **boutique hotels**, often in stunning hillside locations. For much of the year you should be able to find a reasonable double room, usually with air-conditioning, for around R$120, dropping to as little as R$70 in less-favoured locations. Some of the cheaper traditional hotels are still a little stuffy, but most are learning that modern renovation is the only way to stay in business for the long term. Mid-range hotels at the beaches tend to cost upwards of R$200, with the higher quality places costing between R$300 and R$700 – boutique hotel rates generally start at around R$600, and offer great value away from the coast, though transport can be slow. As you would expect, luxury-class hotels have facilities to match the best in the world – and even many smaller establishments have swimming pools, especially away from the beaches.

Tours

In recent years Rio's guided-tour business has become unhealthily competitive, with hotel management and staff switching companies to gain maximum commission. In hostels you'll find ready-made lists of **tours** for guests to sign up to – and while these might be with reputable operators, they may also be with overpriced, unprofessional outfits who have little interest in their subject matter. This is especially relevant for **favela tours** where the tour subject is people's lives (see p.120) rather than a mountain or museum. To avoid ending up on the wrong tour or paying over the odds – book direct with the operator and make the phone call yourself. All speak English.

Backpackers stay all over Rio's **Zona Sul**: the majority of hostels lie in Copacabana and Ipanema, though Botafogo, Catete and Santa Teresa all offer great-value **dorm accommodation** for those looking for more than just beach life. Bunks go for between R$25 and R$45, depending on location, quality and size of dorm, and most properties also offer a few private rooms for between R$80 and R$130. Triple and quad rooms in many hotels represent particular value for money, in some cases as cheap as dorms.

All listings include breakfast – *café da manhã* – except at most **aparthotels** (usually for longer stays) where you're expected to use your private kitchen. It ranges enormously in quality; at basic places it always includes fruit, bread, ham, cheese and coffee, while better establishments lay on extravagant buffets.

Centro

Business travellers may choose to stay in **Centro** close to Santos Dumont airport and downtown offices. While a little journey from the beaches, foreign travellers, too, are starting to realize that they can get more for their money closer to the centre of the city. At all costs avoid the cheap *pensões* in the north of the city centre near Central do Brasil train station as they're mostly inhabited by full-time (male) residents, and the area is far from safe. Centro borders on nightlife district Lapa, and all three listed options provide easy access to the *bairro*. For locations, see map on p.42.

Hotels

Belas Artes Av. Visconde do Rio Branco 52, Centro ☏ 21/2252-6336 ⓦ www.hotelbelasartes .com.br. A small, highly respectable city-centre hotel, a couple of blocks from Lapa with simply furnished, clean rooms with a/c and parking. If you don't mind the location these are the best-value private rooms in Rio. R$70

Ibis Rio Santos Dumont Av. Marechal Camara 280, Centro ☏ 21/3506-4500 ⓦ www.ibishotel .com. Located just 200m from Santos Dumont airport, this is ideally located for a late arrival or early departure. The 330 rooms are compact, simple yet very comfortable and offer excellent value, while the staff are extremely efficient. R$120

Windsor Asturias 14 Rua Sr Dantas, Centro ☏ 21/2195-1500 ⓦ www.windsorhoteis.com.br. Right in the heart of Cinelândia, close to Santos Dumont airport and Lapa, this 166-room luxury business hotel has excellent facilities including rooftop pool, bar and gym, a smart restaurant and business centre. R$200

Lapa

Samba hot spot and down-at-heel red-light area, **Lapa** may be rough around the edges but also has a few small hotels – perhaps surprisingly most of them are clean and respectable, and situated at the edge of Centro it's ideally placed for enjoying the pandemonium of Carnaval. Avoid Lapa's two hostels due to serious recent security issues. For locations, see map on p.70.

Hotels

Arcos Rio Palace Av. Mem de Sá 117, Lapa ☏ 21/2242-8116 ⓦ www.arcosriopalacehotel .com.br. Rooms at this business-like and popular 120-room hotel are secure and inexpensive. Well equipped with internet, rooftop pool and bar, and a decent buffet breakfast. Perfect for enjoying Lapa's nightlife and near to Santos Dumont airport. The owners have two similar hotels nearby, one marginally cheaper. From R$145

Marajó Rua São Joaquim da Silva 99, Lapa ☏ 21/2224-4134 ⓦ www.hotelmarajorio.com.br.

Yards from the Lapa mayhem and the Escadaria Selarón, you may not get much sleep here at weekends but the rooms are comfortable and the hotel reliable, making this a good-value choice. R$65

Santa Teresa

Bohemian **Santa Teresa**, on the hills above Lapa and Glória, is a favourite for travellers interested in Rio's history, arts scene and lively mix of *favelas* and opulent residences. The area's beautiful, leafy aspect and atmospheric restaurants, bars and street life make it one of the most pleasant places to stay in Rio. Rooms are almost all of a high standard and a striking contrast to the many uniform options elsewhere – it's also in the heart of the action for Carnaval. Two Santa Teresa *pousadas* listed below also offer dormitory accommodation. For locations, see map on p.70.

Hotels

Castelinho Rua Triunfo, 38, Santa Teresa ☎21/2252-2549 ⓦwww.castelinho38.com. Located in the centre of the *bairro*, the prime attraction of this 1866 hotel/guesthouse is its large rear terrace with built-in breakfast/bar area, perched on the side of Santa Teresa's hillsides. Atmospheric and charming, the main hall hosts art exhibitions and occasional samba parties, though bedrooms are a mixed bag – stay upstairs for the view and smarter bathroom. R$230

Hotel Santa Teresa Rua Almirante Alexandrino 660, Santa Teresa ☎21/3380-0200 ⓦwww.santateresahotel.com. An impressive, environmentally-conscious, 44-room hotel in a nineteenth-century mansion featuring contemporary tropical design. The large suites have modern interiors, wi-fi, stone-tiled bathrooms (presidential suites have baths) – and most have panoramic views across Rio. There's a fine restaurant (see p.183) and bar, as well as a pool and spa. From R$500

Solar de Santa Ladeira do Meireles 32, Santa Teresa ☎21/2221-2117 ⓦwww.solardesanta .com. This tranquil 1890 hillside villa offers five comfortable, quirkily-decorated rooms with a shared kitchenette, and a family bungalow, all with a/c, some with an attractive veranda. Excellent buffet breakfast and wi-fi throughout. The garden has a bar and plunge pool, and a stunning swimming pool with fabulous views of Flamengo beach and the Sugar Loaf mountain is provided at the adjoining property. Also available to rent as whole villa. R$220–500

Pousadas and Bed and Breakfasts

Casa Áurea Rua Áurea 80, Santa Teresa ☎21/2242-5830 ⓦwww.pousada-casa -aurea-rio.com. A beautifully-restored nineteenth-century house in a central location; offering doubles, twins, trebles and a six-bed dorm with or without a/c and private bathroom. The relaxing terrace with open kitchen, hammocks, rocking chairs and tropical plants is a highlight – and a small pool is planned. From R$130, call for dorm price.

Casa Beleza Santa Teresa ☎21/2224-7403 ⓦwww.casabeleza.net. An upscale B&B located amidst tranquil gardens with a swimming pool and fruit trees that attract monkeys. Once the official residence of the governor of the state, the turreted 1960s Spanish colonial style house offers two tastefully decorated suites with a/c and wi-fi – one can be rented as a double, one as a twin apartment complete with giant

▲ Hotel Santa Teresa

Cama e Café

A novel bed and breakfast network, **Cama e Café** (various locations ☏21/9638-4850, ⓦwww.camaecafe.com.br) is a refreshing development which offers considerable comfort as well as opportunities to meet local residents. Network members are a fascinating cross-section of the Santa Teresa community; usually painters, sculptors, teachers, musicians, academics or business people. Many speak English and all are tremendous sources of local knowledge and advice – some also offer tours. On request, Cama e Café staff will do their best to match you to residents with similar backgrounds or interests (including to gay hosts). All forty houses have been carefully vetted and graded to three levels according to style and comfort. Simpler houses have doubles (R$100) with fan and shared bathroom, mid-range properties (R$145) are generally more spacious and comfortable, and superior rooms (R$200) are available in some of the area's grandest residences. Amongst the fantastic (and best value) options in the latter category is **Castelo Valentim** dating from 1879; it towers over Santa Teresa with magnificent views taking in the Maracanã and Sambódromo, and there's also an eerily-special entrance through an underground tunnel. Artist Ana Durães' grand 1860 house, despite its lack of view, offers the most luxurious accommodation.

bathroom. A wholesome breakfast is served, and the helpful owners are a good source of local advice. From R$200

Casa Mango Mango Rua Joaquim Murtinho 587, Santa Teresa ☏21/2508 6440 ⓦwww.casa-mangomango.com. Conveniently located close to Lapa, this imposing house has large airy rooms (without a/c), each decorated with a distinct theme, such as samba or Afro-Brazilian art, while there's also a two-bed chalet with kitchenette. The huge garden (with a pool), lounge and shared guest kitchen are great places to meet fellow travellers. From R$90, or R$35 per person in the ten-bed dormitory.

Pousada Pitanga Rua Laurinda Santos Lobo 136, Santa Teresa ☏21/2224-0044 ⓦwww.pousadapitanga.com.br. A charming newly-opened property, with a large terrace and swimming pool, surrounding a courtyard with a giant mango tree, *Pitanga*

is close to bars and restaurants and offers smart but plain doubles; the cheapest (and best value) rooms are upstairs with fan (R$100), with the remainder offering private bathrooms and a/c for between R$150 and R$200.

Hostels

Rio Hostel Rua Joaquim Murtinho 361, Santa Teresa ☏21/3852-0827 ⓦwww.riohostel.com. A small, friendly hostel with a sister property in Ipanema (you can divide your time between them with an eighth night free) with lockers, attractive communal areas and a small pool. Though its location is a bit isolated, it's near Lapa and close to Santa Teresa's bars and restaurants. R$37 in a dorm room or R$120 for an attractive double with private bathroom and view.

Glória, Catete and Flamengo

Flamengo, Catete and Glória lie between Botafogo and the city centre, all offering (admittedly non-swimmable) beach access and easy bus and *metrô* links both north and south. **Catete** and **Flamengo**, centred on the Largo do Machado, were once the chic residential *bairros* of the middle-classes – they are now bustling, diverse areas, better served by cheaper hotels and hostels than Copacabana. While neighbouring **Glória** is not entirely without its share of prostitution, the *bairro* is not a dangerous area and has an appealing, slightly faded grandeur. Lapa is also a short bus ride away. For locations, see map on p.84.

Hotels

Flórida Rua Ferreira Viana 81, Flamengo
☎21/2195-6800 ⓦwww.windsorhoteis.com.br.
This highly recommended, long-established hotel retains a traditional atmosphere in its long ornate public rooms and in the adjoining business centre in the former guardhouse of Catete Palace. The 300 rooms, divided between the original hotel and a new building, are spacious and well equipped and there's free wi-fi access in most rooms. Amenities include a good restaurant, a large rooftop terrace with pool, a sauna and a gym. R$280

Golden Park Hotel Rua do Russel 374, Glória
☎21/2556-8150 ⓦwww.hotelgoldenparkrio
.com.br. This medium-sized hotel has a business-like feel with parking, modern facilities and a small rooftop pool. Rooms are simple but nonetheless comfortable and air-conditioned – request one at the front, where you'll get more light and have a park view. Very close to the Marina da Glória and Flamengo beach. R$150

Imperial Rua do Catete 186, Catete
☎21/2112-6000 ⓦwww.imperialhotel.com.br.
Good value, spacious and comfortable rooms housed in an attractive, renovated 1880s building located near the *metrô* station and the park. Some rooms are slightly more luxurious with jacuzzis. Parking is available and there's also a decent pool, which is unusual for a hotel in this price category. R$120

Inglês Rua Silveira Martins 20, Catete
☎21/2558-3052 ⓦwww.hotelingles.com.br.
This 30-room, long-established hotel is one of the best places to stay in Catete, featuring spacious rooms, all with bathrooms, a/c, TV and *frigobar*. Ask for a front-facing room as they have good views over the Catete Palace gardens. R$125

Monterrey Rua Artur Bernardes 39, Catete
☎21/2265-9899. A safe and quiet budget option close to Largo do Machado, with basic rooms with tiny ensuite, TV and a/c from 8pm–8am. A simple breakfast is brought to your room in the morning – great if you're reluctant to get out of bed during Carnaval. An almost identical hotel, the *Rio Lisboa*, is located next door. R$70

Regina Rua Ferreira Viana 29, Flamengo
☎21/3289-9999 ⓦwww.hotelregina.com.br.
Rooms are on the small side but they are well maintained and have comfortable beds, minibars and a/c. With pleasant public areas, friendly staff and an excellent location close to Catete, one block from the beach, this is a highly recommended spot. R$140

Riazor Rua do Catete 160, Catete ☎21/2225-0121 ⓦwww.hotelriazor.com.br. This basic and welcoming place right next to the *metrô* and Catete Palace has clearly seen slightly better days, though it's clean and good value. Some rooms have a/c and TV; many have a fair amount of street noise so go for the quieter ones at the back. R$80

🏃 **Scorial** Rua Bento Lisboa 155, Largo do Machado ☎21/3147-9100 ⓦwww
.scorialriohotel.com.br. This modern, somewhat soulless,140-room 4-star business hotel tucked away behind the Largo do Machado (close to the *metrô*), offers exceptional value in terms of facilities and service. Rooms are very comfortable and there's a sauna, gym and business centre, as well as a rooftop pool with views of *Christo* and the Tavares Bastos *favela*. An excellent breakfast and a city tour for weekend guests are included. R$180

Hostels

🏃 **Art Hostel** Rua Silveira Martins 135, Catete ☎21/2205-1983 ⓦwww
.arthostelrio.com. Located in a nineteenth-century building near the *metrô*, this artistic hostel has bags of atmosphere. The ten-bed dorms vary; some are a little cramped and some have fans while others have a/c for the same price. The reception area has a café with wi-fi. The friendly staff often accompany guests to sample nightlife in nearby Lapa, or you can relax in hammocks on the roof terrace or lounge on floor cushions in the video room. R$29, private room R$105

Hostel República Rua Silveira Martins 139, Catete ☎21/2556-2315 ⓦwww.hostelrepublica
.com.br. This new, spotlessly clean hostel is one of Rio's largest with 120 beds in rooms (with fans or a/c) sleeping 4 to 17 people. Though it feels rather institutional, the hostel is well equipped with modern bathrooms, a large communal area with wi-fi, leather sofas, pool table and bar and a tiny guest kitchen. R$30, private rooms with a/c, TV and bathroom R$120.

Botafogo

Botafogo strangely has few hotels, but has become a hostel hotspot due to its proximity to the beaches (via bus or *metrô*) and its affordability. A contrasting neighbourhood of busy throughfares and village-like leafy cross-streets, this is also one of Rio's best eating and drinking districts with a lively, alternative atmosphere. For locations, see map on p.93.

Hotels

Real Rua Real Grandeza 122, Botafogo
☎21/2286-3093. This pleasant, inexpensive no-frills hotel is a bit of a trek from the *metrô* but convenient for catching buses heading downtown and to the beaches – it's also very close to Botafogo's excellent eating and drinking options. Rooms are clean if slightly on the small side; all have a/c, TV and private bathrooms. R$150

Pousadas and Bed and Breakfasts

O Veleiro Botafogo ☎21/2554-8980 Ⓦwww.bb.oveleiro.com. Located a 30min walk to Botafogo bus stops and *metrô* (or short taxi-ride), this gorgeous hillside B&B is set amidst lush gardens attracting parrots, hummingbirds and toucans. Accommodation ranges from a comfortable cabin (R$145), to a suite with lounge, a/c and TV (R$230). The large breakfast includes Brazilian specialities and is usually served on the outdoor patio, by the small outdoor pool. The genial Brazilian/Canadian hosts offer expert guided tours in and around Rio.

Hostels

El Misti Praia de Botafogo 462, casa 9
☎21/2226-0991 Ⓦwww.elmistihostel.com.

Very reasonably priced option close to the *metrô* and buses to Copacabana and Centro, though a longish walk from Botafogo's best bars and restaurants. The hostel has a pleasant lounge and bar as well as a patio adjoining the guest kitchen. Most dorms are six or eight-bed; a little crowded but comfortable and most have a/c. R$25, private rooms R$86.

Rio Party Hostel Rua Henrique de Novais 71, Botafogo ☎21/2246-9120 Ⓦwww.riopartyhostel.com.br. Linked to several bars and nightclubs, this 50-bed hostel is comfortable, clean and spacious, with lockers and free internet. It also has an attractive outdoor area and offers a good wholesome breakfast. Close to some great bars and restaurants, the young and friendly staff advise on all things fun-filled and lay on a "Love Machine Van" to take you to the beach. R$30

Vila Carioca Rua Estacio Coimbra 84, Botafogo ☎21/2535-3224 Ⓦwww.vilacarioca.com.br. Located on a quiet street in a beautiful, rambling nineteenth-century house typical of Botafogo, the hostel has a sedate, family feel. The brightly decorated dorm rooms are cramped, but all have a/c, and there are attractive communal areas. Close to the *metrô*, internet available. R$29

Copacabana and Leme

Copacabana's energetic street life makes it the kind of place you either love or hate, but while the area has seen better days, it seems to be on the up once again and offers the widest range of accommodation in Rio, from hostels to luxury hotels. **Leme** – really a continuation of Copacabana – is less frenetic due to its location at the end of the stretch of beach in the opposite direction of Ipanema.

If you're staying for a month or more an apartment could be a good option: Rio Star Imóveis Ltda (☎21/3275-8393), Rio Flat Service (☎21/3512-9922) and Copacabana Holiday (☎21/2542-1525) all have buildings in Copacabana, Leblon and Lagoa; prices range from R$2000/month for a studio or one-bedroom unit with a communal swimming pool. For locations, see map on p.101.

Room for romance

In a society where most people live at home until they marry, **motels** – a Brazilian national institution – are a favourite of young (or old) lovers with nowhere else to go. These abundant short-stay accommodations (usually available for 4–8 hours) range from basic rooms with bathrooms and garages through to sophisticated suites with pools, saunas, dancefloors, cable TVs and gourmet meals delivered to your door. Some motels are so popular that married couples might even visit them for a change of scene, while their discreet bookings are useful for liaisons of an extramarital variety. It's also not unknown for tourists at Carnaval to use motels as accommodation options – though you'll have to make sure you don't oversleep and get charged for another period.

Most motels in Rio are on the edge of the city in purpose-built complexes – the Estrada da Barra da Tijuca in Zona Oeste has numerous options – but reliable choices within the Zona Sul (with a variety of room levels) include the hilariously named **Sinless**, at Vidigal close to Leblon (Av. Niemeyer 214 ⊕21/2512-9913, ⓦwww.sinless.com.br; from R$30), **Panda** in Botafogo (Rua São Clemente 298 ⊕21/2537-3134, ⓦwww.pandahotel.com.br; from R$80), and **Elegance** in Catete (Rua Correia Dutra 19 ⊕21/3235-9000 ⓦwww.elegancehotel.com.br; from R$95).

Hotels

Acapulco Copacabana Rua Gustavo Sampaio 854, Leme ⊕21/3077-2033 ⓦwww.acapulcohotel.com.br. A comfortable, peacefully situated hotel. The guest rooms, a few with beach view, are modern and well decorated; some have balconies and all have private bathrooms and cable TV. The *luxo* rooms (R$230) are well worth the extra R$20 above the standard category while the spacious suites are great value for three or four people. Very stylish lobby with free internet use and helpful staff on hand.

Apa Hotel Rua República do Peru 305, Copacabana ⊕21/2548-8112 ⓦwww.apahotel.com.br. A dreary-looking, dated but nonetheless perfectly respectable hotel with simple, clean rooms (all with a/c, TV, mini-bar, free wi-fi access and balconies) in a central area of Copacabana three blocks from both beach and *metrô*. The rooms that sleep four people are excellent value. R$180

Astoria Copacabana Rua República do Peru 345, Copacabana ⊕21/2545-9090 ⓦwww.astoria.com.br. Next door to the *Apa*, the *Astoria* is notable for its good-value (tiny) single rooms, ideal if you're travelling alone but want a full and smart hotel service at reasonable cost – with pool, gym and excellent breakfast. R$120

Atlantis Copacabana Rua Bulhões de Carvalho 61, Copacabana, ⊕21/2521-1142 ⓦwww.atlantishotel.com.br. In an ideal location just a block near the Praia do Arpoador and Copacabana beach, the *Atlantis* offers

straightforward, compact but clean rooms and has extremely helpful staff. The small rooftop pool has great views, though you pay for the location here. R$200

Biarritz Rua Aires Saldanha 54, Copacabana ⊕21/2287-6086 ⓔbiarritzhotel@terra.com.br. Just one block from Av. Atlântica and the beach, this simple but clean and friendly place is located in a quiet backstreet and has rooms at back and front, with just R$20 difference in price. Notably, the *Biarritz* has reduced its prices in recent seasons, reportedly "due to the rain" – hopefully this does not mean inside the building. R$160

Copacabana Palace Hotel Av. Atlântica 1702, Copacabana ⊕21/2548-7070 ⓦwww.copacabanapalace.com.br. Anyone who's

▲ *Copacabana Palace Hotel*

anyone has stayed in this glorious Art Deco landmark, which, despite Copacabana's general decline, remains the place to stay in Rio. Although every possible facility is on offer, there's a lack of communal areas, apart from the large pool in a central courtyard with its two (excellent) surrounding restaurants. A great place to relax if you can afford to do so. Starting at R$900 for smaller city-view rooms.

Copacabana Rio Hotel Av. Nossa Senhora de Copacabana 1256 ☏21/3043-1111 ⓦwww .copacabanariohotel.com.br. Excellent value option in the heart of Copacabana, a block from the beach. Rooms are large and comfortable, though the rooftop pool, gym and sauna are unexpected highlights, with staggering views along the beach, to Ipanema, and of hillside *favelas*. R$200

Excelsior Copacabana Av. Atlântica 1800, Copacabana ☏21/2195-5800 ⓦwww .windsorhoteis.com. A reasonable upper-end choice in the middle of Copacabana's beachfront, next door to the Copacabana Palace. The 230 rooms are well equipped, and the rooftop pool has spectacular views. One of the oldest hotels on the Avenida (opened in 1950), it tries to maintain the atmosphere of a bygone age – and appeals to a more mature crowd.

Grandarrell Ouro Verde Av. Atlântica 1456, Copacabana ☏21/2543-4123 ⓦwww.dayrell .com.br. Externally this 1950s hotel is nothing special, but inside it's discreetly elegant with spacious and well-kept rooms – go for the more expensive ones with sea views. Offering excellent service and value. R$196

Martinique Rua Sá Ferreira 30, Copacabana ☏21/2195-5200 ⓦwww .windsorhoteis.com. The best value choice in its price category and rightly popular, the hotel is located near the quiet, western end of Copacabana, close to the Forte de Copacabana and Ipanema. Modern rooms have large, exceptionally comfortable beds and there's a small rooftop pool and gym. There's also wi-fi throughout and some rooms have a partial sea view. R$241

Orla Copacabana Av. Atlântica 4122, Copacabana ☏21/2525-2425 ⓦwww.orlahotel.com.br. Great value at the Ipanema end of Copacabana's beachfront, the *Orla* has good, comfortable rooms, plus a gym, a sauna and a small rooftop pool with great views. Also a gay-friendly option, with a good number of

gay and lesbian visitors, especially at Carnaval. R$290 (sea view R$367)

Portinari Design Rua Francisco Sá 17, Copacabana ☏21/3222-8800 ⓦwww .portinaridesignhotel.com.br. Less than a block from the beach, this is one of Copacabana's few hotels that dares to be a bit different. Each floor has been conceived by a different Brazilian designer. All the rooms are exceptionally comfortable, if a little on the small side – some have a partial sea view. The rooftop restaurant has memorable views – of two of Copacabana's *favelas*. There's a gym and sauna, but no pool. R$300

Rio International Av. Atlântica 1500, Copacabana ☏21/2546-8038 ⓦwww .portobay.com. Among Rio's best hotels due to its attention to detail (champagne check-in, room gifts and home newspapers provided at no extra cost) and the quality of the rooms – with a good balance between functionality and design and many of which have stunning 180-degree views of the beach. There's also a marvellous rooftop pool and a stylish restaurant. R$460

Santa Clara Rua Décio Vilares 316, Copacabana ☏21/2256-2650 ⓦwww.hotelsantaclara.com .br. This simple but well-maintained hotel offers attentive service and good value. Most rooms have twin beds – ask for a double bed when booking if you want one. Located in a tranquil spot in the Bairro Peixoto part of Copacabana, it's eight blocks from the beach and close to the Túnel Velho leading to Botafogo's attractions. Wi-fi throughout and good discounts for longer stays. R$150

Toledo Rua Domingos Ferreira 71, Copacabana ☏21/2257-1990 ⓦwww.hoteltoledo.com.br. There are certainly better hotels available at this price in Copacabana, but this is just one block from the beach. Rooms are adequate but feel a little small, mainly due to the fact that most have an extra bed. Breakfast is taken on a high floor with a beautiful ocean view. R$195

Aparthotels

Jucati Rua Tenente Marones de Gusmão 85, Copacabana ☏21/2547-5422 ⓦwww .edificiojucati.com.br. Inexpensive and highly recommended, set seven blocks from the beach in a residential part of Copacabana, right on a square with fountain, children's playground and a Wednesday morning

Staying in a favela

Staying in a **favela** is a great option and far from the "roughing it" experience you might expect. Many of the city's shanty towns are no-go areas, but two comfortable and secure options lie near Santa Teresa and Catete, while a third offers a friendly bed and breakfast experience in host homes in São Conrado.

Favela Receptiva (Estrada das Canoas 610, São Conrado ☎21/9848-6737 ⓦwww.favelareceptiva.com.) If you want to experience *favela* life first-hand in a safe and friendly environment, this is Rio's best option. Genial organizer Eneida has gathered a great group of hosts within the small **Vila Canoas** community, whose homes are all clean, attractive and comfortable with TV and free internet – though they are small. Located at the western end of São Conrado on the edge of the forest, the beach is a fifteen-minute stroll, and Leblon and Ipanema are twenty minutes away by bus (VW combi vans ply the route between Vila Canoas and Rocinha *favela*). Single and double rooms with fan are available – and you can even rent a whole house – with good breakfasts included and the option of eating other meals at the community's various simple restaurants. Eneida looks after guests herself, too, and offers excellent tours to samba, *forró*, and funk dances, as well as organizing trips into the Floresta da Tijuca and to nearby mountain Pedra da Gávea – with the option of hang-gliding from the platform close-by. Professional massages and dance classes are also on offer in the community. R$55 per person.

Favelinha (*Favela* Pereira da Silva, Laranjeiras ☎21/9225-0618 ⓦwww.favelinha .com.) Residents of Zona Sul's hillside *favelas* have the city's best views and this small, peaceful community has the pick of the bunch – not to mention the impressive art project *Morrinho* (see p.79) as an added attraction. The hostel/*pousada* itself has seven small, simple rooms, some with dorm beds and each with veranda and hammock – and though it lacks in joviality, the extraordinary location and stunning view compensate. Five minutes walk from Santa Teresa (from Rua Almirante Alexandrino, 2023), Largo de Machado *metrô* station is a combi-van ride or thirty-minute walk away. R$75; dorms R$35.

The Maze Inn (Rua Tavares Bastos 414, Casa 66, Catete ☎21/2558-5547 ⓦwww.jazzrio.com see p.87.) Tavares Bastos is no ordinary *favela* and *The Maze* is certainly not a run-of-the-mill *pousada*. One of Rio's best accommodation options, it features a large, comfortable open hall/bar with a staggering view across Botafogo Bay to the Sugar Loaf mountain, while crazy-tiled passageways, spiral staircases and small roof terraces add to the Gaudi-esque confusion. Rooms are small but very attractive, some with private bathrooms and verandas – and all with a fridge and decorated with talented owner Bob Nadkarni's impressionist paintings. The large British-Brazilian breakfast is a major selling point, as are the monthly **jazz nights**. Appealing to young travellers as much as to older people with a sense of adventure, the location enables you to experience *favela* life in a safe environment. There's wi-fi throughout and doubles start at R$100 (five-day block booking preferred), small dorm R$50.

market. The large apartments are simple; most containing a double bed and two bunkbeds, a bathroom, kitchenette, TV and wi-fi access. R$120 (4 people R$140)
Hotel Saint Paul Rua Barao de Ipanema 95 ☎21/3544-8110. A well-maintained aparthotel three blocks from the beach. Each apartment has a bedroom with two single beds (some doubles available), a lounge, kitchen and bathroom with a balcony overlooking a courtyard with swimming pool. All are simple but modern, with microwave, a/c and TV. R$200 (minimum 3 days), good discounts for longer periods; each additional person in apartment R$20 up to a maximum of five people.
Temporada Copacabana Edificio Av. Atlantica 3196 ☎21/2255-0681 ⓦwww.temporada copacabana.com.br. Though the hotel *Debret* was always the firm favourite for independent

travellers desperately wanting to stay on Av. Atlântica on a budget, renting an apartment here is a cheaper and less drab option – though with no breakfast. Bedrooms are small but adequate and clean, with a/c, bathroom, a small sitting room with TV and tiny kitchen. Minimum three-day stay. Full beach view, R$150 (four people R$200)

Hostels

Bamboo Rio Hostel Rua Lacerda Coutinho 45, Copacabana ☎ 21/2236-1117 ⓦ www.bamboorio .com. Attractively positioned in a quiet residential street in central Copacabana, a short walk from the *metrô* and beach, the hostel offers five- to twelve-bed mixed dorms, the best of which are upstairs away from the often-noisy reception. There's a/c, free internet use, a small pool and a bar. R$35

Che Lagarto Hostel Rua Santa Clara 304, ☎ 21/2257-3133 ⓦ ww.chelagarto.com. Located in central Copacabana five blocks from the beach, this relaxed but friendly hostel in an older house amidst apartment blocks is the cheapest and most basic of Che Lagarto's three Rio hostels. Dorms

sleep four to eight and there's a smart pool-table room, an attractive patio with hammocks, free internet access and dinner available. R$35

Mellow Yellow Rua General Barbosa Lima 51 ☎ 21/2547-1993 ⓦ www.mellowyellow.com.br. A large hostel, with a maze of dorm rooms and stairways, you could easily get lost after a few *caipirinhas* at the lively roof bar. The a/c dorms range from six- to fourteen-beds (the latter overpriced and the former a little cramped); one free night's accommodation is offered per week stayed. The great facilities include free internet, a jacuzzi and a playstation room. R$35

🏃 **Stone of a Beach Rua Barata Ribeiro 111, Copacabana** ☎ 21/3209-0348 ⓦ www .stoneofabeach.com. An unpretentious hostel that, despite having ninety beds, maintains a friendly atmosphere. Wooden bunks are spaciously arranged with locker space below; all dorms have a/c and free wi-fi, while bathrooms and the guest kitchen are large. Upstairs there's a cinema in one room, a bar and Jacuzzi on the roof and adjoining the hostel is the popular *Clandestino* bar/club. R$32

Ipanema and Leblon

Ipanema is without doubt the most fashionable place to stay in Rio, with the liveliest section of beach, too – though you'll pay for the privilege. There's upscale shopping and dining as well as numerous bars – including more than a few ex-pat and hostel hangouts – so if you're looking for traditional *Carioca* culture you'd be better off elsewhere. Just beyond Ipanema lies **Leblon**, an exclusive residential neighbourhood with fewer accommodation options and no *metrô* access, but it does have some of the city's best restaurants and bars *and* its beach equals Ipanema's in beauty.

If you're looking for **apartments** in Ipanema, call Ipanema Sweet (☎ 21/8201-1458 ⓦ www.ipanemasweet.com), who have one- and two-bedroom apartments near the beach beginning at R$220 per day (longer stays negotiable). Accor Hotels (ⓦ www.accorhoteis.com.br) have very good properties in Botafogo, Arpoador, Ipanema and Leblon; one- and two-bedroom apartments with a pool start at around R$180 per day, depending on the location. For locations, see maps on p.106 and p.110.

Hotels

Arpoador Inn Rua Francisco Otaviano 177, Arpoador, Ipanema ☎ 21/2523-0060 ⓦ www .arpoadorinn.com.br. The only hotel in Rio right on the beach promenade without a road in front, this is a popular choice peacefully located on the edge of Ipanema closest

to Copacabana. Rooms are comfortable though overpriced, but the location and sunsets here are unbeatable. A great breakfast is served on promenade tables. R$210, beachfront rooms cost double.

Caesar Park Av. Vieira Souto 460, Ipanema ☎ 21/2525-2525 ⓦ www.caesarpark.com.br. One of Rio's finest and most expensive beachfront hotels, featuring all the comforts its celebrity guests would expect. Even the most basic rooms (all completely sound-proof) are large with elegant furniture and huge beds, and though you pay extra for a beach front room, those to the side are equally grand. The rooftop restaurant and gym are amongst Rio's best, and there's a variety of bars and two restaurants. Beach security and lifeguards provided. R$1060

Fasano Av. Vieira Souto 80, Ipanema ☏21/3202 4000 ⓦwww.fasano.com.br. Rio's most stylish and exclusive hotel boasts a roof terrace with a 360-degree view from the beach to Corcovado. There's a spa, a stunning infinity pool and a gym with a complimentary personal trainer. Designed by Philippe Starck, the open bedroom-lounges ooze exclusivity with soft colours, onyx light fittings, balconies and large bath tubs. Fantastic Italian (primarily) seafood restaurant and a chic British 1960s-styled *Bar Londres*. It's also Rio's most expensive choice, starting at R$1120.

Ipanema Inn Rua Maria Quitéria 27, Ipanema ☏21/2523-6092 ⓦwww .ipanemainn.com.br. This excellent-value hotel is just a block from the beach, in the best part of Ipanema between beach postos 9 and 10. The comfortable rooms with all the usual facilities, while small, can squeeze in an extra (fold-out) bed, while the double-priced superior rooms just about have a sea view. Good craft shop on the ground floor. R$200

Ipanema Plaza Rua Farme de Amoedo 34, Ipanema ☏21/3687-2000 ⓦwww .ipanemaplazahotel.com. A discreetly luxurious property small enough to provide individual attention, with fine facilities including a gym, saunas, rooftop pool and a pan-Asian restaurant and 24hr bar. "Superior" suites are tastefully furnished, while the hipper "Ipanema" floor offers higher levels of service (champagne check-in, in-room breakfast on request, free internet). Popular with gay visitors due to its location a block from the beach's gay strip. R$450

Marina Palace and Marina All-Suites Rua Delfim Moreira 630 & 696, Leblon ☏21/2172-1000 ⓦwww.hoteismarina.com.br. These neigh-bouring beachside hotels are both great places to stay; although the *All-Suites* is the more exclusive, the *Palace* offers better value and almost equal service. The main differences are the designer style of the *All-Suites* rooms – some are hip and

modern while others have a more traditional look – and the *Palace* rooms/suites are a little smaller with slightly softer beds. Both have business centres, restaurants (see p.191) and pools – for which the *Palace* wins hands down due to the phenomenal views. R$400 (*Palace*), R$700 (*All-Suites*)

Ritz Plaza Hotel Av. Ataulfo de Paiva 1280, Leblon ☏21/2540-4940 ⓦwww.ritzhotel.com .br. The *Plaza's* suites are spacious and offer unadorned yet classy furnishings and wood-panelled floors, kitchens, large TVs and small bathrooms. There's a tiny pool with a mini-waterfall at the rear of the property, while the restaurant has mosaic-tiled walls. Steps from great bars and restaurants and two blocks from the beach. R$350

São Marco Rua Visconde de Pirajá 524, Ipanema ☏21/2540-5032 ⓦwww.sanmarcohotel.net. A good deal for its location, on the main shopping street just a few minutes from the beach. The small rooms with a/c, TV and tiny bathrooms come in three categories, the mid-range standards are easily the best value (R$218) as the *superiors* offer barely greater comfort and the *econômicos* (R$183) have barely any space aside from the bed. Go for an internal room as there's lots of street noise at the front.

Vermont Rua Visconde de Pirajá 254, Ipanema ☏21/2522-0057 ⓦwww.hotelvermont.com.br. Simple though perfectly clean and adequate rooms with small bathrooms in a central location. The "special" rooms (some of which sleep three people) are much larger and lighter and well worth the modest additional cost. All rooms have a/c but they're not likely to suit those bothered by street noise. Breakfast is served until 11am and there's wi-fi and a business centre. R$220

Aparthotels

Ipanema Hotel Residencia Rua Barão da Torre 192, Ipanema ☏213125-5000 ⓦwww .ipanemahotel.com.br. Spacious, stylish apartments and friendly staff make this a great option for longer stays and at Carnaval – otherwise it's pricey. All have stone-tiled floors, balconies, king-size beds and a small kitchen. The attractive pool on the sixth floor has a fine view of the Ipanema rooftops with the Lagoa and Corcovado behind. R$280 plus bills

Leblon Ocean Residéncia Rua Rainha Guilhermina 117, Leblon ☏21/2523-5959 or 2512-9897. Two blocks from the beach, in

Leblon's dining and drinking quarter, this smart aparthotel offers attractive serviced suites, most with two beds and an extensive leisure area with pool, decking and sauna. Minimum stay five nights (R$1000, normally booked for one month at R$4500), which is good value especially at Carnaval – book well in advance.

Monsieur LeBlond Av. Bartolomeu Mitre 455, Leblon ☎ 21/3722-5050 ⓦ www.protel.com.br. Popular and reasonably spacious apartments with two to four beds, a breakfast bar and a small balcony. Around R$200/night if you book by the month (R$400 walk-in rate), including breakfast and car parking. There's a pool and gym, and views of either hills, Lagoa or beach – make sure you get the one you want. Good family option. Buses go everywhere from outside the building.

Pousadas and Bed and Breakfasts

Margarida's Pousada Rua Barão da Torre 600, Ipanema ☎ 21/2239-1840 ⓔ margaridacarneiro @hotmail.com. One of very few B&B options in the Zona Sul, *Margarida's* claims a great location on the corner of Rua Aníbal de Mendonça with friendly service. The clean rooms are equal to hotels at the same price (beds are slightly on the soft side), with tiled floors, a/c, TVs, fridges and small, clean bathrooms. Shared kitchen available. The best choices are the back rooms away from the street noise (from R$150) – or the bargain large triples (R$200).

The White House Estrada do Vidigal, Leblon ☎ 21/2249-4421, ⓦ www.riowhitehouse.com. Attracting a mix of long-stay young foreigners and short-stay older backpackers drawn to the relaxed atmosphere and upscale location, *The White House* offers a large dorm with eight single beds and a number of simple double rooms, most have a gorgeous sea view and there's a veranda and comfortable lounge that's used for late-night music sessions and weekend *churrascas*. Close to Vidigal *favela* and the Praia do Vidigal, Leblon is a short walk away. R$40 dorm, R$80 double room (monthly stays negotiable); no breakfast.

Hostels

Che Lagarto Hostel Rua Paul Redfern 48, Ipanema ☎ 21/2512-8076 ⓦ www.chelagarto .com. One of several Che Lagarto hostels, a

block from the beach and an easy walk to the nightlife of Ipanema and Leblon. Excellent facilities include laundry, kitchen, a/c and Internet, plus the staff are helpful and there's a ground floor bar with occasional live music. R$38 per person in a twelve-bed dorm (more for five- or six-bed rooms), double rooms with private bathroom also available.

Karisma Hostel Rua Barão da Torre 175-7, Ipanema ☎ 21/2247-7269 or 21/2523-1372 ⓦ www.hostelipanema.com. A welcoming and relaxed hostel among many in the same very safe courtyard three blocks from the beach. Lockers, internet access and laundry facilities are offered, a/c is available in some rooms and there are bikes for rent. R$45 per person in dorms sleeping three to six people. Airport pick-up can be arranged.

Ipanema Beach House Rua Barão da Torre 485, Ipanema ☎ 21/3202-2693 ⓦ www .ipanemahouse.com. An attractive hostel with a garden with outdoor pool and bar area, great for nigh-time socializing. Dorm rooms are reasonably spacious and the hostel has numerous facilities such as a pool table, TV room, kitchen and lockers. Three blocks from the beach towards Ipanema's western end. R$45

Lemon Spirit Rua Cupertino Durão 56, Leblon ☎ 21/2294-1853 ⓦ www.lemonspirit.com. Just a block from the beach, this is one of the Zona Sul's best hostels, with clean and spacious a/c accommodation in a friendly, simple environment. There's a bar, TV lounge and kitchen downstairs, alongside a small and secure veranda. Some of the city's best bars and restaurants are nearby, and the location five blocks from Ipanema with easy bus access further afield is an advantage. R$40

🏃 **Mango Tree Hostel** Rua Prudencio de Moraes 594, Ipanema ☎ 21/2287-9255 ⓦ www.mangotreehostel.com. Spacious dorm rooms are in one of Ipanema's very few remaining houses, complete with large bathrooms with extra-powerful showers. The relaxing overgrown back garden with breakfast terrace and hammocks is another highlight. A block from the beach vibes of postos 8 and 9, this 26-bed hostel is an oasis amidst busy streets. Dorms with a/c are a little expensive (R$45), but outside of the peak summer heat those with fans are a bargain (R$35). Double rooms on offer, too (R$140).

Beach life

Rio's inspirational beaches may be a magnet for international tourists, but they're first and foremost the preserve of *Cariocas* – rich and poor, young and old – from the families that descend on Copacabana every Sunday to the muscle hunks and skimpy bikinis of Ipanema. The city's golden sands are training grounds for the volleyball and football stars of the future to perfect their skills – you'll even see locals combining both sports in the fashionable new game, *futevôlei* – and surfers and kitesurfers take advantage of the coastal currents. But relaxing and people-watching are the principal pursuits for most, ideally complemented by a *caipirinha* or *cerveja* purchased from one of the innumerable beach vendors.

Women's beach fashion ▲

Havaianas, Ipanema ▼

Beach style

Cariocas enjoy looking good – especially on the beach, where they model distinctive local swimwear that makes *gringos* seem instantly prudish. Your best bet for blending in is to buy your swimsuit in Rio – fashions change regularly and you'll pay considerably less in Brazil than in Europe or North America (see p.230). You might, however, find that the most conservative **bikini** you come across is one of the skimpiest you'd see back home – though rest assured that anything more demure would be out of place at Ipanema's **posto 9** (see p.108). The young, trendy and beautiful people who base themselves here take breaks from swimming and *cerveja*-drinking by strutting their stuff along the shoreline (see p.98).

Bikini tops and bottoms are usually mixed and matched. Many women of all shapes and sizes choose to sport the **fio dental**, the "dental-floss" G-string bikini, yet strangely enough, in this culture of revealing nearly all, going topless is just not the done thing. For men, the **sunga** is *de rigueur*, a pair of tight, enlarged speedos, which mostly come in darker colours. The look is perfected with a pair of **Havaianas**, the most popular brand of brightly coloured flip-flops, for sale on every street.

Beach towels are a rare sight, instead *Cariocas* usually lie on **kangas** (sarongs). After all, it's far easier to dry off after a swim with a game of batball or *futevôlei*. It's certainly not unusual to see *Cariocas* dressed for the beach (read: undressed) on buses from other city *bairros* – there's no room for shyness, so leave the bag and book at home and get out there!

Men wearing *sungas* ▲

Beach vendor selling *kangas*, Ipanema ▼

The body as project

Plastic surgery is big business in Rio de Janeiro, and many people choose to get nipped, tucked, lipo-sucked or implanted to improve on the probably already taut body they've developed from daily running along the seafront. Many *Cariocas* treat their body as a project – to be developed, flexed, tanned, waxed, and ultimately flaunted. If a little manipulation along the way has helped, they're usually more than willing to talk about it. The beach is the catwalk for this especially Brazilian kind of vanity – **beleza** ("beauty") – which is admired as a form of self-respect, though there is no criticism of those who haven't yet engaged in the body project themselves.

▲ Plastic surgery clinic

▼ Ipanema beach

The best beaches

The city of Rio de Janeiro has over 30km of accessible beach, each one known for distinctive atmosphere, clientele or favoured beach sport. Out of the city, in surrounding Rio state, you'll find hundreds more enticing beaches (see p.147).

▸▸ **For beach football**
Copacabana beach, see p.104.

▸▸ **For kitesurfing**
Praia do Pepê, see p.130.

▸▸ **For palm-fringed paradise**
Ilha Grande, see p.150.

▸▸ **For people-watching**
Ipanema beach, see p.108.

▸▸ **For seclusion**
Grumari beach, see p.134.

▸▸ **For sunset**
Arpoador beach, see p.107.

▸▸ **For surfing**
Praia de Macumba, see p.133.

▸▸ **For swimming**
Leblon beach, see p.109.

▸▸ **For views**
Praia do Flamengo, see p.89

▲ Praia do Flamengo at night

▼ Copacabana beach

Surfing, Barra da Tijuca ▲

Cycling along Copacabana beach ▼

Playing on Ipanema beach ▼

Beach sports

Maintaining an even tan and tight musculature is the principal occupation for most of Rio's beachgoers. Joggers swarm up and down the pavements, bronzed types flex their muscles on parallel bars at Arpoador and Flamengo, and **beach football** at Copacabana is as strong a tradition as legend would have it. Certainly, there's no problem getting a game (try around posto 4), though playing on loose sand with skilled practitioners of Brazil's national sport does have the potential for great humiliation. A faster seven-a-side game has taken off, too – **beach soccer** – it even has its own international championship, usually held on Copacabana beach (see p.244).

Volleyball is also incredibly popular. You'll see the most impressive skills displayed at Ipanema, Leblon and Barra da Tijuca beaches. A cross between volleyball and football developed in the 1980s and 1990s, **futevôlei** is played by a pair of two-player teams on a volleyball court, using only the feet, head and chest. It's a game of remarkable skill, best observed when professional footballers are showing off the talents they've developed during a lifetime practising on the beach. If you're seeking a slightly less energetic beach experience, pick up a set of **frescoball** (or batball), played by devotees all along the shoreline.

Gaining rapid ground as a major **surfing** and **kitesurfing** destination, Rio also offers some of the best breaks in South America, coupled with the attractive prospect of nightlife yards from the sands. The **Surf Bus** will transport you and your board all along the coastline to find the best waves (see p.240).

Zona Oeste

Further afield near to the magnificent beach and not-so-magnificent apartment blocks of **Barra da Tijuca** is one excellent boutique option, a smattering of standard beach hotels and a surfers' hostel. For locations, see map on p.128.

Hotels

La Suite Rua Jackson de Figuereido 501, Joatinga ☎21/2484-1962. The owners of boutique hotel *La Suite* are keen to maintain mystery – not least by eschewing a website. Located in Rio's most affluent gated community, the seven rooms have tremendous views of coast, forested mountains, apartment blocks and sprawling *favelas*. The design mixes elegant kitsch and out-and-out opulence, each room colour-themed and with a matching marble bathroom. There's a dazzling infinity pool, a celebrated French chef, and easy access to beautiful Joatinga beach. From R$300

Tropical Barra Hotel Av. do Pepê 500, Barra da Tijuca ☎21/2158-9292 ⓦ www.tropicalbarra hotel.com.br. Not many visitors opt to stay in Barra – but the *Tropical*'s location right on the beach is appealing – attracting many business execs to its conference facilities. Rooms vary from standard to luxury suites; all have tiled floor with rugs, and bedspreads and light fittings which give the place a slightly 1970s feel. R$310

▲ *La Suite*

Hostels

Rio Surf and Stay Rua Raimundo Veras 1140, Recreio ☎21/3418-1133 ⓦ www.riosurfnstay .com. A perfect location for a surfers' hostel, two blocks from the waves. There's a friendly family feel to the hostel, with one six-bed dorm room (R$38) and three double rooms with private bathroom (R$110). Also offers internet, lockers, mosquito nets and a pool table and bar. Camping available.

Niterói

Across the bay from Rio, **Niterói** offers a selection of business–oriented hotels and *pousadas*. Few tourists choose to stay here as Rio's accommodation options are within day-visiting distance, but Niterói's few museums, federal university and long stretches of beach are all attractions which all make it a pleasant city to visit for a couple of days.

Hotels and pousadas

Hotel Village Icaraí Rua Mariz e Barros 97, Icaraí ☎21/2611-7753 ⓦ www.hotelvillage icarai.com.br. A block from the beach at Icaraí and 10min from downtown Niterói, the *Village* is a mid-range option with large rooms or suites with soft lighting, veranda, a/c, TV and spacious bathrooms. Its rooftop pool, gym, bar and jacuzzi make it a good-value choice. R$190

Pousada Luar de Camboinhas Av. Cinco, Casa 638, Camboinhas ☎21/2619-1634 ⓔ cemoi@bol .com.br. This well-appointed house offers a selection of suites with hotel-style service, such as minibar, a/c and TV, while there's a small pool at the rear. Ten minutes' drive from the beach and downtown area. R$130

Eating and drinking

A
s Brazil's most significant tourism centre with one of its largest middle-class populations, Rio is well served by **restaurants** offering a wide variety of cuisines. At night, eating and drinking are almost always done together and at leisure – meeting friends in a **bar** or **boteco** (see *Botecos* colour section) is a fundamental Brazilian tradition, with drinks accompanied by **petiscos** (finger foods of various sizes) or even full meals. Many restaurants allow for a night's drinking, too – most would never dream of hurrying their customers out.

The majority of *Cariocas* eat well at lunch, often in a self-service *por kilo* restaurant where you pay for the weight of your plate – and many options in office areas such as Centro only open in the middle of the day. Evening eating tends to be lighter and slightly more adventurous, with Brazilian dishes alongside (most typically) French, Italian and Japanese cuisines, though other Asian options now exist too. Whatever the food, it is almost always accompanied by either bottled **cerveja** (lager-beer) or draught **chopp** (pronounced "shopee"), and often continues into the early hours. That said, night-time fine dining with **wine** is certainly on the up – most often European, Argentinian or Chilean, with cheaper and lower quality Brazilian wines also available (*reserva* options are the safest bets). Most restaurants start to fill up around 9pm and last orders are generally taken at around midnight. We detail places known primarily for their food and drink, while coverage in the following chapter, "Live music and nightlife" lists venues known for music or dancing – though there is some overlap as many of those options also serve food.

Table **reservations** are rarely needed in Rio, though where advisable (or if there's home delivery) telephone numbers are provided. The best areas for eating – where there are a few options in close proximity – are at the western ends of both Botafogo and Leblon, in the centre of Santa Teresa, in Jardim Botânico, close to Praça XV in Centro – and of course Ipanema and Copacabana also have a good variety dotted around. In general, eating out in Rio is not cheap, and can, in fact, be very expensive (mains between R$20 and R$60 per person are typical) – especially along the Zona Sul beach strip. Nonetheless there's no shortage of low-priced places (R$8-R$20) to grab a basic meal or just a snack and a drink (see opposite). **Vegetarians** won't have any serious problems in Rio, although the lists of meaty *petiscos* may well get tedious. A few of the best vegetarian options are listed, though most decent *por kilo* restaurants serve excellent salads, and beans and rice are always available. You can also try asking the waiter to have the kitchen prepare something a little tastier.

Aside from beer the other omnipresent drink is the delicious, strong **caipirinha** (see p.190), a cocktail made from limes and *cachaça* (Brazilian cane sugar spirit). These normally come so heavy in sugar it's worth ordering *com pouco açucar* ("with just a little sugar") or even *zero açucar* and adding an artificial sweetener they'll provide you with.

Cheap eats, fast food, juices and ice cream

Throughout Rio, especially in Centro and Copacabana, you'll see numerous snack and juice bars and hamburger joints. The omnipresent **Bob's Burgers** remains more popular than its American counterparts – perhaps solely due to its excellent, rich milkshakes (the "ovalmaltine" is recommended) as the burgers are poor. You'll get better, more authentic and cheaper food at any *galeto* or *lanchonete* – Brazilian **snack bars** where you normally eat diner-style, at the counter, a range of snacks, burgers or very cheap **combined plates** (*pratos feitos* or *pratos executivos*) of meat, beans and rice – generally costing under R$12. Another favourite dish is the *bauru* (pronounced "bow-roo"), a simple steak normally served with cheese, fried egg, chips and salad. The symbol "X" listed alongside burgers simply means cheese. You won't need any guidance to find these places, but given the food in most cheap eating joints is very average our listings highlight some superior options. Served in *lanchonetes* and in many bars, *salgados* are ubiquitous savouries, of which the most common varieties are: deep fried *pasteis* (plural of *pastel*) – pastries filled with heart of palm (*palmito*), cheese or minced beef; *pães (pão) de queijo* – small and succulent cheese breads; *joelhos* (literally knees) – ham and cheese pasties; and *coxinhas* – conical-shaped fried cornmeal dough with chicken at the centre. Other fast-food chains worth looking out for are **Habib's**, which offers reasonable quality Arab-influenced fast food and **Kone**, a popular and reliable sushi chain, most of whose restaurants open through the night.

Juices (*sucos*), available in most *lanchonetes* and restaurants, are another highlight. Much of the fruit used comes from the Amazon, the most famous of which, *açai*, is a tasty and health-giving berry, juiced and converted into a sweet ice cream-like drink, while combinations using *manga* (mango), *acerola* (vitamin c-heavy cherry), *limão* (lime), and *morango* (strawberry) are all popular. **Vitaminas** are juiced fruits and vegetables (like beetroot), generally mixed with milk. Sugar is added to juices automatically; if you don't want it (or prefer an artificial sweetener), make sure you ask *sem açucar* ("seng asoo-ka"). **Sorvete** (ice cream) is perennially popular, especially on warm summer evenings. The best parlours are in Leblon, Ipanema and Copacabana, and flavours include unusual tropical tastes like *maracuja* (passion fruit), *pitanga* (Brazilian red cherry) and *jabuticaba* (Brazilian grape).

Centro

The restaurants in the city centre cater largely for people working in the area – most are *por kilo* and at lunchtimes service is sometimes rushed. That said, there are a number of options catering to those visiting Centro's sites, and you can find really good Brazilian, Portuguese and Lebanese cuisine. There are lots of cheap eating places and bakeries around Praça Tiradentes and Saara market, while after work office workers flock to the pedestrian zone close to Praça XV (see p.52), centred on Travessa do Comércio and Rua do Ouvidor for early evening drinks and *petiscos*. Later on, the action shifts to burgeoning Lapa. If you're just looking for a good sandwich to take away, the simple *lanchonete* at the centre of Largo da Carioca is a good bet. Almost everywhere in Centro is closed from Saturday lunchtime until Monday morning. See map on p.42 for locations.

Snacks, juices, cafés and ice cream

Atelie Culinário Odeon Cinema, Praça Floriano, Cinelândia. Good-quality café with tables out on the praça where you can watch the world go by. The baguette sandwiches (R$18) are imaginatively named after films

made in Rio – such as *Madame Satá* or *Central do Brasil*. It also serves light meals.

Confeitaria Colombo Rua Gonçalves Dias 32, Centro (see also p.48). This Centro must-see has an impressive grand central hall lined with full-length mirrors –a perfect place for breakfast, morning coffee or tea and cakes; the adjoining *Salão Bilac* offers tasty and very reasonable Brazilian lunches such as steak or seafood (R$16) and the more formal *Salão Cristovão* (reached by elevator) has a traditional Franco-Brazilian menu (R$50) with great dessert buffet (men no shorts or sleeveless shirts). 9am–8pm; closed Sat at 4pm and all day Sun. There's also a branch at the Forte de Copacabana.

Bistro do Paço Praça XV de Novembro 48, Centro. An excellent coffee or lunch spot shaded under the thick stone ceiling-arches of the Paço Imperial, the *Bistro* serves imaginative sandwiches including vegetarian options, *carpaccio* and salads (under R$20) and an extremely inviting range of cakes and tortas. Tues–Sun noon–6pm.

Restaurants, bars and botecos

Alba Mar Praça Marechal Âncora 186, a short walk south of Praça XV de Novembro. Housed in the remaining octagonal tower of the old municipal market, this imposing restaurant was founded in 1933 and provides a superb view of Guanabara Bay. Stick with the moderately priced seafood, served by stern yet enthusiastic waiters in white uniforms. Lunch only, closed Sun.

Beduíno Av. Pres Wilson 123, Cinelândia. This relaxed, popular and inexpensive Arabic restaurant has great *kibe-crú* (raw spiced minced lamb) and *kafta* (ground lamb and parsley skewered kebab), though also offers a good falafel meal and mezze – both unavailable at most other Syrian/Lebanese restaurants in Rio.

Bar Luiz Rua Carioca 39, Centro (see p.48). This manic but essentially run-of-the-mill restaurant and bar, serving German-style food and ice-cold *chopp*, is quite an institution – having been a favourite watering hole for Rio's Bohemian and intellectual groups. The *filet mignon* is excellent, though the menu is overpriced (R$30-80). Closed Sun.

Gula Gula Rua 1 de Março and Rua Ouvidor, Centro. A large branch of this popular group of Rio restaurants (see p.189).

Mannita Rua do Ouvidor 45, north side of Praça XV de Novembro. Probably the best place for sushi and sashimi in Centro, this upstairs business-like eatery also serves noodle dishes. Mon–Fri lunch only.

Monchique Rua Visconde de Inhauma 62, Centro. Downtown Rio has hundreds of lunchtime *por kilo* restaurants, but a good meal costs under R$16 at *Monchique*. It has a great buffet, salad bar and grill and serves an excellent chicken casserole.

Paladino Rua Uruguaiana 226, Centro. Part Portuguese bar, part liquor store with thousands of bottles lining the walls, this is an excellent place to drink *chopp* and munch on steak sandwiches and delicious sardines, breaded and fried.

Rio-Minho Rua do Ouvidor 10, Centro. The *Rio-Minho* has been going strong for over 120 years, serving tasty mid-priced Brazilian dishes. The kitchen concentrates on seafood – try *badejo* fish, lobster in butter, prawn in coconut milk or the fried fish with red peppers. Mon–Fri lunch only.

Sabor Saúde Rua da Quitanda 21, Centro. An inexpensive, good restaurant and health-food store serving only organically grown produce, with the occasional fish-based dish too. Mon–Sat 11.30am–4pm.

Sentaí (O Rei da Lagosta) Rua Barão de São Felix 75, Centro (see p.64). A wonderfully atmospheric, long-established Portuguese seafood restaurant. Try the lobster *moqueca* (R$70 for two), though the prawn risotto and seafood spaghetti are also excellent (R$35 for two). Located in a rundown part of Centro, you may wish to take a taxi. Daytime only, Mon–Fri.

Sírio e Libanês Rua Senhor dos Passos 217, Centro. In the heart of the Saara Lebanese market, this traditional Arabic restaurant serves *kibe* and other kebab meats, alongside falafel and other vegetarian options. Good set-menu lunches and combination platters for two.

Triângulo das Sardinhas Rua Miguel Couto 124, Centro (see p.60). Several bars with outside tables on a small pedestrianized road by the Largo de Santa Rita. A great bet if you've been sightseeing at the northern end of Centro and fancy a few drinks and plate of fresh grilled sardines – open early evening until 10pm.

Villarino Corner of Av. Calógeras and Presidente Wilson, Cinelândia. Its walls lined with nostalgic photos, the *Casa Villarino* has clearly had its golden era as a meeting place for intellectuals, poets and musicians – Vinicius de Morães reportedly first proposed a partnership with Tom Jobim here in 1956 – though it's still a good after-work spot for a *chopp* and *petisco*.

Lapa

You won't have any trouble finding a good spot for a drink in **Lapa**, a Bohemian neighbourhood known for its wild nightlife. Avenida Mem de Sá, Rua do Lavradio, Rua Riachuelo and Rua Joaquim Silva are all crowded with bars that spill out onto the street, and many of the music venues in Lapa also offer food (listed under "Live music and nightlife"); those listed below serve particularly good food. For eating in the early hours try *Nova Capela* (see below); many people inexplicably head straight for *Pizza Guanabara* – a mystery given the pizza is poor and overpriced. See map on p.70 for locations.

Restaurants, bars and botecos

Cosmopolita Corner of Av. Mem de Sá and Travessa do Mosqueira, Lapa. An excellent Portuguese restaurant/*boteco* established in 1926 with a loyal, rather Bohemian, clientele – including many students from the music school opposite. Fish dishes – cod-based *bacalhau*, in particular – is the firm favourite, though all usual steaks and *petiscos* are served. Closed Sun.

Espírito Santa Empório Rua do Lavradio 34, Lapa. This newly opened venture by the owners of the tremendously successful Santa Teresa restaurant (see p.182) offers delicious Amazonian-themed dishes and a full range of *petiscos* to accompany a slow evening's drinking and conversation. Mon–Wed 12–6pm, Thur–Sat 12pm–1am.

Nova Capela Rua Mem de Sá 96, Lapa. Open until 6am, the best bet for early morning eating in Lapa, with white-coated waiters bringing good quality Portuguese meals to your table (R$30–60 for two people). A firm favourite is the chicken *canja* soup, purported to stop a hangover before it arrives.

Santa Teresa

If possible, make time for a visit up into the airy hills of **Santa Teresa** – an enjoyable ten-minute tram ride from Centro. The *bairro* is a centre of dining excellence with Sundays particularly popular with visitors from other parts of the city – most on the hunt for *feijoada*, the quintessentially *Carioca* pork and bean stew – though food from all over Brazil is represented, including fusions with French cuisine. Thursday through Saturday is also lively and people congregate until late in the Bohemian bars and restaurants around Largo do Guimarães and Largo das Neves. Many places close on Monday. See map on p.70 for locations.

Carioca cozinha

Traditional Brazilian *cozinha* (cuisine) revolves around *churrasca* (grilled meats), which are served everywhere – the choicest cut is *file* (filet steak) – but chicken, sausage and pork are also common. Visit a **churrascaria** for a meat feast, with "*rodizio*" referring to the type of unlimited eating where waiters bring food around from table to table – meat arrives on long skewers from which you choose the slice you want. The other key *Carioca* favourite is **feijoada**, a delicious pork and bean stew which traditionally uses almost every part of the pig. Historically eaten on Saturdays (now often on Sundays), a *feijoada* is a social event with music, dance and plentiful *cerveja*. **Feijão** (red beans) are eaten with rice at most meals, while a *caldo de feijão* is a flavoursome puréed bean soup. **Farofa**, toasted manioc flour which only Brazilians appear to appreciate, is also provided with most meals. Other specialities draw on Portuguese traditions such as cooking with **bacalhau** (dried, salted codfish), while you'll also come across typical Northeastern options like chunky manioc chips, Bahian **moqueca** (a fish and coconut casserole), or *carne assada*/*carne de sol* (smoked/sun-dried beef). Neighbouring Rio, the state of Minas Gerais is hotly rated for its cuisine (like its people, called **mineira**) – particularly its pork meat stews, mild ricotta-esque cheeses and vegetable dishes.

Snacks, juices, cafés and ice cream

Acarajé da Nega Teresa Rua Almirante Alexandrino 1458. Rio's best street food is available here between Wednesday and Sunday from 6pm until late when traditionally-dressed Bahian Teresa sets up her stall close to German bar *Mike's Haus*. Large, tasty snacks made from *manioca* (cassava) such as *acarajé* pockets filled with *feijão* and shrimp *vatapá*, or *caruru* with okra, are available. Try the sweet coconut and ginger for dessert.

Café Largo das Letras Rua Almirante Alexandrino 501. A simple café and bookshop serving cakes and coffees in one of Santa's historic buildings – a great spot overlooking the Largo do Guimarães. Tues-Sun 2–8pm.

Jasmin Manga Largo do Guimarães. This attractive café on the square has internet access/wi-fi, and an outdoor terrace. A good bet for coffee and cakes but avoid the unnecessarily small sandwiches. It also has a good Saturday *feijoada*. Open seven days.

Restaurants, bars and botecos

Adega do Pimenta Rua Almirante Alexandrino 296. Most people go to this German spot for the sausage and *sauerkraut*, but the duck with red cabbage is also excellent (R$35) and there's a weekend variation on *feijoada* using white beans and German sausage. Plus the apple strudel is to die for.

Aprazível Rua Aprazível 62 ☎21/2508-9174. A French-trained chef, family feel and gorgeous terrace with wonderful views make this an excellent, though fairly expensive, choice. Franco-Mineira dishes such as fish cooked in orange, coconut and *caju*, or *medalhau* steak with a spinach and banana cream are remarkable, while the heart of palm in pesto starter is delectable. Great dry Martini and frozen *cachaça* cocktails. Book in advance. Thurs–Fri 8pm–midnight, Sat noon–midnight, Sun and holidays 1–6pm.

Asia Rua Almirante Alexandrino 256. Bringing Soho chic to Santa Teresa, stylish *Asia* prides itself on its *Dim Sum* (ten-piece R$45) – though if you like it with green tea the latter will set you back R$16. It also has good stir fries and curries, but save room for the deep-fried ice cream and banana fritters in *maracuja*. Charming veranda. Mon–Thurs dinner only, Fri–Sun from noon.

Bar do Arnaudo Rua Almirante Alexandrino 316. Just along from the *Adega do Pimenta*, this is an excellent low- to mid-priced place to sample traditional food from Brazil's Northeast, such as *carne do sol* (sun-dried meat), *macaxeira* (sweet cassava) and *pirão de bode* (goat's meat soup). Sat & Sun closed from 8pm & closed Mon.

Bar de Gomez Corner of Rua Áurea and Rua Monte Alegre. A truly wonderful place to have a few *choppes* or a glass of wine, this bar-cum-Portuguese grocery always has a crowd of friendly locals – though *petiscos* are average for the price (R$16 upwards). Look out for the photo of British train robber Ronnie Biggs on the wall – his local bar during years of exile in Santa. On the Paulo Mattos tram line, a short walk from Largo do Guimarães.

Bar do Mineiro Rua Paschoal Carlos Magno 99. Recommended old bar that could be in any small town in Minas Gerais, with authentic country-style food. *Feijoada* is served all weekend, and all *petiscos* come in extralarge size, well worth the price (from R$20). Also has good beers and an excellent range of *cachaças*.

Espírito Santa Rua Almirante Alexandrino 264 ☎21/2508-7095. It didn't take long for *Espírito Santa* to become a firm local favourite with queues down the road at weekends; Amazonian fruits like *açai*, *bacuri* and *copuaçu* provide mouth-watering sauces for the *tabaqui* fish ribs and *file* (R$35), while a plantain-banana *moqueca* will please vegetarians. There's a great *caipirinha* list, too. Closed Mon.

Goia Beira Largo das Neves 13. If you're in Santa for more than one day you should certainly go for a drink or a bite at this attractive square, and *Goia Beira* is the most popular bar here – stick with *petiscos* like *carne assada* as the pizza here is very average. Evenings only till late; closed Mon.

Sobrado das Massas Rua Almirante Alexandrino 6, Largo do Corvelo. Most of the week this restaurant serves up heavy pasta dishes and reasonable pizza, but on Saturday it lays out an especially good *feijoada* – a portion for two costs just R$18.

Sobrenatural Rua Almirante Alexandrino 432 ☎21/2224-1003. A Santa institution due to enigmatic owner *Servula*'s legendary samba sessions in the 1990s, which drew huge crowds. Now lower-key, though live music still features at this deliberately rustic looking seafood restaurant; highlights are the *moquecas* and grilled *surubim*, a meaty freshwater fish, served with creamy coconut, plantain, and Brazil nut sauce (all dishes serve two; R$80).

Térèze Hotel Santa Teresa, Rua Almirante Alexandrino 660 ☎21/2222-2755. Smart restaurant with a French chef and huge windows with wonderful views overlooking Santa Teresa and Centro. Creations include seared tuna with quails eggs and aubergine crème, duck fettucine, or shrimp flamed in *cachaça* (from R$35).

Glória, Catete, Flamengo and Laranjeiras

There are some really great eating and drinking options across these bustling commerical and residential *bairros*. Numerous good-value budget pizza buffets, *por kilo* restaurants and *lanchonetes* surround the **Largo do Machado** at the centre of this wide area, while a short walk or bus ride in most directions will bring you to high-quality Brazilian and Italian food and excellent bars, all at affordable prices. See maps on p.84 and p.91 for locations.

Snacks, juices, cafés and ice cream

Boomerang Mix Rua Paissandu 122, Flamengo, and Rua das Laranjeiras 76. Both branches of this trendy café/*lanchonete* are 5min' walk from the Largo do Machado. If you can get over the lurid colour scheme there's a good range of sandwiches and burgers (R$10–15), and the shakes and iced-coffees are all superb.

Rotisseria Sírio Libaneza Largo do Machado 29 (inside Condo shopping mall), Catete. Perhaps an unlikely place to find three neighbouring Middle Eastern *lanchonetes*, but the food is great – from the best *esfihas* in town to full meals of lentils with rice and spiced mince and stuffed aubergine or *kafta* kebabs. Best washed down with a delicious fresh juice. Mon–Sat till 8pm.

Tacacá Rua Barão do Flamengo 39, Flamengo. Hailing from Belém, the owners of this speciality *lanchonete* bring tastes of the Amazon to Rio. Their claims to fame are the *açaí* (berry smoothie/ice cream) – the best in Rio, served in large bowls with tapioca or granola – and the *tucupi* shrimp and *manioc* yellow hot pepper soup – an extremely tasty appetizer, served in a *calabash*.

Restaurants, bars and botecos

Adega Portugália Largo do Machado 30, Catete. Easily the best restaurant/bar on the square, you can choose to sit at the bar or out on the street and drink *chopp* or good wine until 4am at weekends. Friendly staff serve large *petiscos* and mains sufficient for two, including good-quality meats and excellent *bolinhas de bacalhau* (cod and potato croquettes).

Bar Brasil Corner of Rua Senador Correia and Praça São Salvador, Larenjeiras. An excellent traditional *botequim* on a peaceful residential square three blocks from Largo do Machado. Offers a wide Portuguese *petisco* menu as well as a very good cheap *prato executivo* lunch served until the evening.

Bar do Serafim Rua Alice 24, Laranjeiras. If Laranjeiras had a centre the foot of Rua Alice would probably be it; throbbing at Carnaval, the few *botecos* located here are busy even at quieter times, and *Serafim* has the best food among them. Portuguese *bacalhau* is a speciality, fish or squid with vegetables is good. Mon–Sat lunch until 10pm, Sun until 6pm.

Bar Getúlio Rua do Catete 146. A simple yet very lively and popular *boteco* opposite the Palácio do Catete and close to many hostels and hotels. Good *chopp* and budget eats like the R$15 *file* steak.

Belmonte Praia do Flamengo 300. A Flamengo institution, this is the most popular of the *Belmonte* chain of *botecos* to be found all over Rio, spilling onto the street and open all night. If you can get anywhere near the bar to order food, then the prawn soup is one of the city's tastiest.

Herr Brauer Rua Barão do Flamengo 35, Flamengo. With 100 different traditional ales and other international beers, this smart and organized *cervejeira* will delight people looking for anything other than *chopp* – though you pay for the privilege. The food menu features *petiscos* and grilled salmon, steak or chicken main courses.

Hideaway Rua das Laranjeiras 308. Offering three separate areas – nightclub, lounge bar and restaurant – the best thing about *Hideaway* is its pizza, baked in a wood-fired oven and easily the best you'll get in this part of town (the Calzone is surprisingly good). It also has good burgers, a range of *petiscos* and decent wine and cocktail list. See also p.201.

Lamas Rua Marquês de Abrantes 18, Flamengo. This popular, highly recommended restaurant has been serving well-prepared Brazilian food since 1874 (the Oswaldo Aranha steak – pan-fried with lots of garlic – is a staple: R$32). Always busy, with a vibrant atmosphere and a clientele of artist and journalist types, *Lamas* is a good example of *Carioca* middle-class tradition. Open until 4am.

Majórica Churrascaria Rua Senador Vergueiro 11–15, Flamengo. Long-established, with an ambience of old Europe, this is a better-than-average place to tuck into some meat

(R$30–50) – the *picanha especial* (special rump steak) is the favourite. If you're not in the mood for beef, try excellent grilled trout from the mountains near Petrópolis or the seafood salad.

Mercado São João das Artes Rua das Laranjeiras 90. Near the Largo do Machado, this is Laranjeiras's answer to the Cobals in Botafogo and Leblon; a small converted marketplace now home to low-key eating and drinking options with indoor/outdoor tables and a youthful feel. Try the spicy fare at *Baiano* or the meat sandwiches at *Sarjeta* – though oriental spot *Bambu* makes a mean *caipi-sake*.

Porção Rio's Av. Infante Dom Henrique s/n, Aterro do Flamengo. A vast *churrascaria rodizio* offering, for R$80 per person, an abundance of red meat, chicken and fish, alongside a giant salad and sushi buffet. Although part of a chain, the food is top quality and service efficient. Located alongside the ocean with glorious views of Guanabara Bay and the Sugar Loaf mountain; there's also a branch in Ipanema at Rua Barão da Torre 218, though without the same view it seems overpriced.

Botafogo and Urca

Botafogo and its western sub-area **Humaitá** undoubtedly host some of Rio's most interesting restaurants, hidden away in back streets and often overlooked by tourists. At Humaitá's impressive indoor market, **Cobal**, you can take your pick of Brazilian, Italian, vegetarian and Japanese cuisines (alongside drinks), and on the surrounding streets there are a host of other options, too. Although there are few places to eat in **Urca**, one of Rio's quietest *bairros*, it's a pleasant place for a relaxing drink or meal. If you find yourself around the Praia de Botafogo at lunchtime, you could do worse than ascend to the top floor of Botafogo Praia Shopping – though the food is typical of mall food-courts, the panoramic view of Botafogo Bay, Sugar Loaf mountain and Niterói is fantastic. See map on p.93 for locations.

Restaurants, bars and botecos

Adega do Valentim Rua da Passagem 178, Botafogo ☎ 21/295-2748. A comfortable restaurant (especially the front salon) serving authentic Portuguese food. Expect to pay around R$35 per person for one of the many cod dishes, roast suckling pig or goat. The smoked meats are especially good (though expensive) and there's a nice wine list, too.

Adega de Velha Rua Paulo Barreto 25, Botafogo. A cheap, popular restaurant with tables on the street, which serves good food from the

Northeast of Brazil, including *carne seca*, goat, pork and *caldo de feijão*, as well as excellent steak sandwiches. Open until 1am Mon–Sat.

Á Mineira Rua Visconde de Silva 152, Humaitá ☎ 21/2535-2835. An excellent introduction to the food of Minas Gerais, with a superb value (R$23 per person) all-you-can-eat buffet, including soups, grilled meats, vegetarian dishes and desserts. Alternatively there's a meat-oriented *rodizio de petiscos* to accompany a night's drinking (R$18, not including drinks). Free minibus available to bring you to and from your hotel anywhere in the Zona Sul. Mon–Sat lunch and dinner till late; closes 9pm Sun.

Aurora Rua Capitão Salomão 43, corner with Rua Visconde de Caravelas, Humaitá. A traditional *boteco* dating from 1898, *Aurora* sits on a corner with two other *botecos* holding identical menus. The best options are the large portions of fried fish with rice and spinach crème, though the Portuguese-style meats are also good. A popular and lively meeting point for an evening's drinking.

Balcão da Urca Av. Luís Carlos. At the far end of this road in Urca, *Cariocas* gather along the seawall on fine evenings to drink *cerveja* and eat *petiscos* brought across the road by enthusiastic waiters from the nearby *botequim*. This Rio institution offers wonderful views across Botafogo Bay.

Botequim-184 Rua Visconde de Caravelas 184, Humaitá. More of an upmarket restaurant than a *botequim*, but the large menu is varied, from steaks – such as "a Diana", flambéed with mushrooms and vodka – and fish dishes like *moqueca* (R$40).

Cobal do Botafogo Rua Voluntários da Pátria 446, Humaitá. A huge range of moderately priced restaurants, bars and *lanchonetes* serving anything from pizza to German sausage and vegetarian savouries to Northeastern Brazilian meals. This is a popular lunch and dinner spot, many local residents meeting here for *cerveja*, sport on TV, or live music.

Eccellenza Pizzeria Rua Visconde de Caravelas 121, Humaitá. A very good quality and value Italian pizzeria with a massive menu of both traditional toppings and Brazilian creations including excellent sweet pizzas. Smart interior with open kitchen. R$20 upwards.

Garota da Urca Av. João Luiz Alves, Urca. This restaurant's claim to fame is having one of the best views in Rio, looking back towards Botafogo and the Corcovado. The food – Brazilian with an Italian twist – is fairly average, so you may just want to stop by for a drink, though the *peixe a garota* (fish of the house) serves two and is reasonable at R$30.

La Mole Praia de Botafogo 228, and throughout Rio. Inexpensive and very decent Italian food is served at *La Mole*, an upmarket chain long popular with both families and couples. It also has a smart interior and the large meals for two are especially good value (R$20–35).

Miako Rua Farani 20, Botafogo. Along with *Azumi* in Copacabana, this is the most traditional Japanese restaurant in Rio, a friendly and simple place serving reliable sushi, sashimi, *teppan-yaki*, tempura and *filé na chapa* (combination platters R$40), as well as a few Chinese dishes for good measure. The *yaki soba* is distinctly average; fried ice cream with chocolate sauce is the clear winner for dessert.

Miam Miam Rua General Góes Monteiro 34, Botafogo. An intimate, stylish and Bohemian atmosphere combines with an innovative menu – far beyond its self-defined "comfort food" label. Starters include duck samosa with orange honey sauce or curried chicken *bolinhos*, and mains (R$40) include hot-pepper-encrusted tuna with chutney or duck gnocchi. There are also excellent vegetarian options, desserts and a cocktail list – try the house Martini with lychees and sake.

▲ *Miam Miam*, Botafogo

Ovelha Negra Champanharia Rua Bambina 120, Botafogo ☎21/2226-1064. This small and friendly champagne bar has two long communal tables and an ice-cold selection. Great for meeting people, it gets lively later in the evening. Mon–Fri only; 6–11pm or midnight.

Praia Vermelha Bar e Restaurante Círculo Militar da Praia Vermelha, Praça General Tibúrcio, Urca ☎21/2275-7292. A perfect spot for a drink and quality thin-crust pizza overlooking the Sugar Loaf and Guanabara Bay. Daily noon–midnight.

Raajmahal Rua General Polidoro 29, Botafogo. Deserves a mention as the sole Indian restaurant in Rio, with a relaxing ambience. It's popular due to affluent Brazil's current vogue for all things Indian, though curry connoisseurs will find the food very average and prices extravagant (dahl R$40). Local preference is for mild curries so ask if you want a bit more bite. Closed Sun.

Vegan Vegan Voluntários da Pátria 402, Botafogo (corner with Rua Conde de Irajá). Rio's only vegan restaurant has two set menus each day (R$18), featuring imaginative use of local ingredients like *manioc* (cassava) and *palmito*, with great side salads and home-made mayonnaise. Desserts are also good, accompanied with vegan ice cream. Lunch only (until 5pm). Meat eaters will find it the perfect antidote to *churrasca* overkill.

Yorubá Rua Arnaldo Quintela 94, Botafogo. Friendly restaurant serving moderately priced Afro-Bahian cooking. The beautifully presented meals always take a long time to appear, but the *bobó* (a dish based on *mandioca* purée), *moquecas* and other Bahian specialities are well worth the wait. Closed Mon & Tues; dinner only Wed-Fri; lunch only Sat & Sun.

Copacabana and Leme

There is no shortage of restaurants in **Copacabana** and adjoining **Leme**, but many, unfortunately, are not particularly good – unless you enjoy sitting in a restaurant swamped with holiday-makers being shuttled about by tour companies. That said, there are a few good options for Brazilian and worldwide cuisine that attract more locals than tourists, ranging from budget to expensive. Well worth trying if you're prepared to look a little harder. See map on p.101 for locations.

Snacks, juices, cafés and ice cream

Amarena Geletaria Italiana Rua Barata Ribeiro 516. Opened in 2008, people quickly learned that *Amarena* was streets ahead of the Copacabana competition. A small but imaginative range of exquisite ice creams includes Tiramisu and Italian cherry flavours. Open until midnight at weekends; 11pm weekdays.

Big Nectar Corner of Av. N. S. de Copacabana and Xavier da Silveira. A cut above the average *lanchonete* in Copacabana, juices are pure and fresh and there's a range of good value cheap eats such as large pizzas (R$12) and tasty *pratos feitos* (R$9) of fish or meat, chips, rice and salad to eat there or take away and microwave.

Cafeina Rua Constante Ramos 44 and Rua Barata Ribeiro 507. An excellent chain of cafés that set the standard for cakes, pastries and coffees along the Zona Sul beaches, and whose menu also includes a hearty hot and cold breakfast with fresh orange juice and coffee (R$42 for two people).

Confeitaria Colombo Forte de Copacabana (closed Sat at 1pm and all day Sun). A miniature version of their Centro restaurant (see listing p.179), selling mainly teas, coffees, cakes and savouries to a crowd enjoying the stunning view of Copacabana from outdoor tables – for which there's nearly always a queue.

Restaurants, bars and botecos

A Marisqueira Rua Barata Ribeiro 232. For over fifty years this restaurant has been serving well-prepared Portuguese-style food, if a little unimaginative and pricey (from R$40). A good spot for seafood or the Sunday special of calf's foot and white bean stew.

A Polonesa Rua Hilário de Gouveia 116 ☏21/2547-7378. A small, attractive, white-washed restaurant where the menu features mostly reasonably priced, traditional (and rather heavy) Polish dishes, such as beetroot soup and fish in a horseradish sauce, suitable for a chilly winter's evening. For dessert, the soufflés and apple cake are a treat. Closed Tues–Fri lunchtime & Mon.

Adega Pérola Siqueira Campos 138. Tucked away a block north of the *metrô*, this traditional-looking *boteco* is popular with locals and theatre-goers who come for the excellent *petiscos* laid out along the extended bar. From oysters to rollmops and marinated aubergine and peppers to *caldo de feijão*, quality is always good and there are imported beers and wines, too.

Amir Rua Ronald de Carvalho 55 ☏21/2275-5596. Award-winning restaurant widely considered to be Rio's best Arabic eatery. The platters of falafel, *kafta* kebabs and delicious appetizers are certainly imaginative and tasty, and with outside tables and regular belly dancing it's a great (and not too expensive) option for lunch or dinner.

Arabe Av. Atlântica 1936 ☎21/2235-6698. One of very few good restaurants on Avenida Atlântica, *Arabe* is a reasonably priced Lebanese restaurant with an excellent value *por kilo* lunch buffet (around R$25). The evening menu includes mezze, Arabic pizza, couscous and *shwarma* (R$50-70 for two people). Heavy on meat choices, but vegetarians won't go hungry. There's another branch at Lagoa close to Gávea.

Azumi Rua Min. Viveiros de Castro 127 ☎21/2295-1098. Two blocks from the Copacabana Palace, this very traditional Japanese restaurant is a hidden gem, tucked away on a quieter street. Features superb sushi and sashimi platters alongside well-presented bento boxes, oysters, and deep bowls of noodle and seafood soups. Reasonably priced, from R$25.

Bar 420 Av. N.S. de Copacabana 420, by Rua Inhanga. A simple and small budget *á la carte* restaurant with friendly service and pavement tables. Simple chicken or meat dishes are all under R$12, with tasty tilapia with rice and salad costing a little more.

Carretão Rua Siqueira Campos 23. Unlimited *churrasca rodizio*, reviewed under Ipanema.

Caranguejo Rua Barata Ribeiro 771, corner of Rua Xavier da Silveira. Excellent, inexpensive seafood – especially the *caranguejos* (crabs) – served in an unpretentious environment with tables on the pavement and packed with locals and tourists alike. Various meals for two from R$75. Closed Mon.

Cervantes Av. Prado do Júnior 335 (restaurant) and Rua Barata Ribeiro 7 (bar). Few places in Rio draw a crowd from across the social spectrum, but this tiny restaurant and bar (linked at the rear) in Copacabana's red-light district manages to with queues down the road from lunch until 5am. The rush is for their exceptional sandwiches – thick wedges of cured meats with fresh pineapple in home-baked crusty bread; the garlic chicken is sublime. Also great steak meals (for two, R$40) and good *chopp*.

▲ *Cervantes*, Copacabana

Copa Café Av. Atlântica 3056 (corner of Rua Bolívar). This smart, dimly lit and intimate restaurant is in fact a glorified burger bar – though they are exceptionally good burgers (from R$30) and there are also meat, fish and pasta dishes. Open very late, this is a good spot for a few drinks, too.

D'Amici Rua Antonio Vieira 18, Leme ☎21/2541-4477. One of Rio's best – and most expensive – Italian restaurants where people go as much to see and be seen as they do for the food. The meals, though, are excellent; besides the pastas and risottos, the roast lamb is particularly good.

Deck Av. Atlântica 2316, corner of Rua Siqueira Campos. Probably the cheapest restaurant on the seafront, the food here won't win prizes but it is reliable, including a *prato executivo* set lunch and unlimited pizza *rodizio* (R$15), served from 6pm till midnight.

Kilograma Churrascaria N.S de Copacabana 1144 (by Rua Djalma Ulrich). A large, upmarket *por kilo* restaurant with a fantastic high-quality selection and excellent grill. At night there's also an unlimited pizza *rodizio* (under R$20).

La Mole Dias da Rocha 311. See review under Botafogo.

La Trattoria Rua Fernando Mendes 7. Cheap to mid-priced place (R$25-50) serving the best homely Italian food in Copacabana. Amongst the excellent range of pasta dishes, the fettuccine in a mixed seafood sauce is especially recommended. Pizzas are also reasonable.

Marius Crustáçoes Av. Atlântica 290, Leme ☎21/2543-6363. This unlimited seafood buffet resembles a tacky seaside theme park and tends to be filled with tourists gorging on oysters, crabs and crayfish along with numerous *cervejas*. Waiters have a tendency to be brusque, too – so it is best to opt for nearby *Shirley* instead.

Shirley Rua Gustavo Sampaio 610, Leme. A quality Portuguese seafood restaurant with austere white-jacketed waiters and, inevitably, a TV screening football and *novelas*. Inviting dishes include snapper in white wine, paella for two (R$50), lobster and wonderful giant shrimp.

Siqueira Grill Rua Siqueira Campos 16. Copacabana's most well-known *por kilo* restaurant, a varied and exclusive affair with massive choice of meats grilled before your eyes, salads, potato and fish dishes, sushi and dessert buffet.

Siri Mole e Cia Rua Francisco Otaviano 50 ☎21/2267-0894. One of the few really good Bahian restaurants in Rio mainly serving beautifully presented – and fairly expensive – seafood dishes (often spicy). Inside, the restaurant is quite formal, but to one side outdoors the excellent *Sirizinho* (little *Siri*) has a few tables where you order separately and munch on *acarajé* and other Bahian snacks.

Taiyou Marriott Hotel, Av. Atlântica 2600. A generally expensive but high-quality sushi and sake bar, which also has a nightly *rodizio Japonesa* with unlimited sushi and *chopp* beer for a very reasonable R$60 – just don't order the mineral water for R$8.

Traiteurs de France Av. Nossa Senhora de Copacabana 386. Simple cooking from one of the very few affordable and good French restaurants in Rio, at the back of a French bakery/*lanchonete.* Try the duck *magret* with cognac or the lobster risotto. Lunch only, closed Sun.

Ipanema

Ipanema has eating and drinking haunts to appeal to all its visitors – from thirsty beach-goers to the gay crowd of Farme de Amoedo (see p.210) to affluent residents seeking upscale fine dining. Though numerous Brazilian restaurants can be found here, there are more European options and sushi bars than elsewhere – most on the mid-range to expensive side, though limited budget eating is possible. There are also a couple of options listed on the Ipanema side of Lagoa, with views over the lake. See map on p.106 for locations.

Snacks, juices, cafés and ice cream

Beach Sucos Corner of Rua Farme de Amoedo and Rua Visconde de Piraja. Juices here are fresh and not watered down. For budget travellers there's a decent choice of meat or fish *pratos feitos* for under R$10 – a bargain in Ipanema.

Cafeina Rua Farme de Amoedo 43 (see review under Copacabana).

Chaika Rua Visconde de Piraja 321 (for home deliveries call ☎21/2267-3838). Though lunch and dinner is served here, *Chaika* is best known for the great range of mouth-watering tortas and cakes in its high tea – and its wonderful ice cream. The range of breakfasts include *Carioca* (cheese savouries, tortas and fruits), American, Argentinian and Miami. Coffees and English teas also available.

Felice Caffé at Rua Gomes Carneiro 30. This popular and loungey spot for coffee, light lunch and drinks until midnight draws a mixed gay and straight crowd. Wonderful Italian-style ice creams include green tea and white chocolate flavours.

Livraria da Travessa – Bazzar Café Rua Visconde de Pirajá 572. A version of the *Bazzar* restaurant (see opposite) located in Rio's best bookshop. Serves breakfast, sandwiches and very rich cakes in an unhurried envirnoment. Mon–Sat 9am–11pm, Sun noon–9pm.

Market Ipanema Rua Visconde de Pirajá 499. Located down an alley in the heart of the shopping area, *Market* is a fantastic option for breakfast and brunch (though there's full meals, too) with omelettes, yogurts, waffles and poached eggs washed down by good coffees and smoothies and served from 9am–6pm. Open Thurs–Sat until midnight, with a good cocktail list and a bar feel on the outdoor terrace.

Sorvete Mil Frutas Rua Garcia D'Ávila 134. *The* place to come for Rio's best (and equivalently expensive – R$15) ice cream and boasting dozens of flavours – including exotic Brazilian fruit such as *pitanga* and *jabuticaba*, as well as sandwiches, brownies and tortas.

Restaurants, bars and botecos

Bar Lagoa Av. Epitácio Pessoa 1674, Ipanema. The oldest (dating back to 1934) of the lakeside restaurants, the Art Deco *Bar Lagoa* is usually full of families from adjacent neighbourhoods, served by white-coated waiters delivering beer, German sausage and smoked pork chops the size of football boots to their tables. The apple strudel is also excellent. Arrive by 9pm and sit on the patio where there's a good view of the lake. Inexpensive and highly recommended.

Bazzar Rua Barão da Torre 538 ☎21/3202-2884. This modern, upscale restaurant is beautifully designed with wood finishing, terrace deck and large palms between the tables. Dishes include poached Buzios shark over *banana da terra* purée plus meats and lobster (R$35–70).

Benkei Av. Henrique Dumont 71, delivery available ☎21/2540-4830. The sushi and sashimi here is good quality and reasonably priced for the area. There's an evening sushi/sashimi *rodizio* (R$45) and unlimited lunchtime buffet (Mon–Fri, R$33). Hot *shimeji* mushrooms, tempura, *harumaki* and *gyoza* options.

Carretão churrascaria Rua Visconde de Pirajá 112, Praça General Osório. The Zona Sul's most reasonable *churrasca rodízio*, where an army of waiters deliver meats of all descriptions to your table for R$40, accompanied by a wide-ranging buffet. More spacious than *Carretão*'s Copacabana branch (and marginally more expensive), though still busy.

Casa da Feijoada Rua Prudente de Morais 10. Usually served only on Saturdays, a good *feijoada* has been offered seven days a week here for twenty years, along with other traditional, moderately priced and extremely filling Brazilian dishes – including seafood.

Delírio Tropical Rua Garcia D'Ávila 48. A block from the beach between postos 9 and 10, this is a cheap breakfast and lunch choice, co-owned by the coach of Brazil's volleyball team. Specializing in exciting vegetarian options like salads, quiches and couscous, alongside burgers and a couple of meaty mains, you can choose six buffet items for R$10 and watch the world go by.

Expand Wines Rua Barão da Torre 358 (Praça N.S. da Paz). Rio's best wine store combines with a fine-dining experience – choose a wine from among hundreds to accompany the excellent-value three-course *executivo* lunch (R$40, until 6pm) with starters like *carpaccio* or parmesan salad, followed by fillet of *namorado* fish, steak or risotto (vegetarian option available).

Frontera Rua Visconde de Pirajá 128. Close to Praça General Osório, this is a good restaurant with a choice of an unlimited *buffet libre* (R$37) or *por kilo* (around R$30 for a plateful). It also has a sushi bar, grill and good vegetarian options, though night-time eating is preferable due to its dimmed lights.

Garota de Ipanema Rua Vinícius de Morais 49. Always busy, this bar entered the folk annals of Rio de Janeiro when the bossa nova song *The Girl from Ipanema* was written here by Tom Jobim (see p.108). While certainly touristy (with unexceptional and overpriced food – from R$30), there are few better places in Rio for a beer.

Gula Gula Av. Henrique Dumont 57, Ipanema ☎21/2259-3084. A good choice of reasonably priced and very tasty salads and grilled dishes (R$20–40) makes this a firm local favourite. Steaks come with a choice of cheese sauces, while fish is grilled to perfection. Great tortas and fruit or ice cream options for dessert. Branches throughout Rio, though this is the most attractive one.

Lord Jim Rua Paul Redfern 44. This English pub, in a building with a mock-Tudor facade, serves steak and kidney pie, fish and chips, high tea and a good English breakfast at weekends. Well known for its dart board and snooker table, it's now infamous for gringo-hunting prostitutes. Mon–Fri from 6pm, weekends from noon.

New Natural Rua Barão da Torre 167, Ipanema. Not strictly a vegetarian *por kilo* restaurant as it serves fish and chicken too, but the food is really tasty, and fairly cheap. There's a wide range of hot and cold choices including vegetable and soya dishes; a decent health-food store is adjacent. Lunch only, closed Sunday.

Palaphita Kitch Quiosque 20, Parque do Cantagalo, Av. Epitácio Pessoa, Lagoa.

Caipirinha recipe

Cut a lime into thick wedges and place in a tall glass with four teaspoons of caster (or granulated) sugar. Using a pestle or wooden spoon, crush the lime and sugar together vigorously. Add crushed ice to the top of the glass, then fill with *cachaça* (Brazilian sugar cane spirit – white rum or vodka are acceptable alternatives). Stir briefly and serve with samba!

Wonderful relaxed lakeside spot a couple of minutes' walk from Ipanema. You may have to wait in a queue to be seated at one of the low outdoor sofas – but it's worth it. Great carpaccio and imaginative antipastis using Amazonian ingredients; it also serves fondue and has a good cocktail list; candles and soft music create a romantic atmosphere.

Satyricon Rua Barão de Torre 192 ☎21/2521-0955. Though excessively formal (and very expensive), the Italian food served here is understandably rated the best in Rio. Seafood is the restaurant's speciality; you can choose your lobster from the tank for thermidor (R$140). There are also plenty of meat dishes (try the ostrich), and there's an excellent range of pasta choices, too.

Via Sete Grill Rua Garcia D'Ávila 125, Ipanema. Good straightforward food at reasonable prices. Lighter options include wraps, burgers and salads while the *mahi mahi* or *filet* with baked potato and salad is best enjoyed on the street terrace looking across at Louis Vuitton and the other high-class boutiques of Ipanema.

Zazá Bistrô Tropical Rua Joana Angélica 40 ☎21/2247-9101 Light-hearted, imaginative fusion cuisine based on Brazilian, Peruvian, Thai, Indian, North African and European dishes. The colourful décor, the terrace with great views and the plush cushions and divans in the relaxing first-floor living room make this a popular spot with both tourists and trendy locals. Around R$70 per person. Evenings only.

Leblon

Considered Rio's most chic eating and drinking area, Leblon's bars and restaurants get very lively at weekends with more of a cross-section of the city's residents than you'd perhaps expect – and it's certainly more conducive to a good night out than Copacabana. Most options are situated in the area known as **Baixo Leblon**, essentially around the two streets Rua Dias Ferreira and Avenida Ataúlfo de Paiva, west of Avenida Bartolemeu Mitre and three or four blocks back from the beach. Locals of all ages also flock to Leblon's excellent **Cobal** market place for a night's drinking. See map on p.110 for locations.

Snacks, juices, cafés and ice cream

La Basque Rua Rainha Guilhermina 90. Leblon's best ice-cream parlour, the classic flavours like vanilla and chocolate are the top choices, though the hazelnut with chocolate brownie is divine.

Cafeina Av. Ataulfo de Paiva 1321, and inside Leblon Design mall. See Copacabana for review.

Garcia & Rodrigues Av. Ataulfo de Paiva 1251. A foodie's paradise: while the French restaurant at the rear is unimaginative and stuffy, there's an excellent bistro, wine shop, ice-cream parlour, bakery and

deli, with great fresh bread and an excellent choice of take-out sandwiches, salads, quiches and other prepared meals. Good option for breakfast, too. Sun–Fri 8am–midnight; Sat 8am–1am.

Natural Polis Corner of Rua Rainha Guilhermina and Av. Ataulfo de Paiva. One of many *lanchonetes*, but *Natural Polis* has good unwatered-down juices, espresso coffee, and a decent *prato feito* of chicken, chips, rice and salad for R$11 – probably the cheapest meal in Leblon.

Talho Capixaba Av. Ataulfo de Paiva 1022. Well-established as one of *the* Leblon spots to meet for a slow morning coffee or light bite, this deli-cum-café has tables on the street and is less of a restaurant than *Garcia & Rodrigues*, though equally exclusive. Good selection of sandwiches – especially cheese varieties – though for meats *Cervantes* in Copacabana is far better for the same price.

Restaurants, bars and botecos

Academia da Cachaça Rua Cde. Bernadotte 26, Leblon. A good place to sample Brazil's national drink, *cachaça* – this small and often crowded bar has three hundred brands to sample, mostly from southern and western Brazil. The strong spirit is to be treated with respect at all times and thankfully some *petiscos* and a reasonable *executivo* lunch are offered to line the stomach. Though the bar is on the edge of an uninspiring mall, the décor is great – look out for the creative Brazilian ceiling flag.

Antiquarius Rua Aristides Espínola 19 ☏21/2294-1049. Of Rio's many fine Portuguese restaurants, this is arguably its best. Especially good for seafood (not just cod), but goat and wild boar are other fine choices here, as are the rich desserts. Soft colours and traditional paintings create an intimate unstuffy atmosphere. Very expensive (main courses R$100), and definitely no shorts allowed.

Bibi Crepes Rua Cupertino Durão 81 ☏21/2259-4948. The *Bibi Sucos* Zona Sul empire has now expanded into chunky crepes – and they do them very well, filled with savoury fillings like meats and cheeses, and a variety of fruits and chocolate sweets. Burgers, juices and sandwiches also available; home deliveries.

Bracarense Rua Jose Linhares 85. Along with *Jobi* the most famous Leblon *botequim*. A popular place for a streetside beer, the *camerão* dishes and *bolinhos de queijo* are also good. Open till 10pm weekdays, midnight at weekends.

Carlota Rua Dias Ferreira 64 ☏21/2540-6821. Highly imaginative, expensive pan-Asian cooking with North African influences is served in a bright and cosy atmosphere. The seven kinds of spring rolls are noteworthy, as is the Thai prawn curry – though portions are a little on the small side. Mon–Thurs dinner only, Fri & Sat lunch & dinner, Sun lunch only.

Celeiro Rua Dias Ferreira 199, Leblon. A quite modest-looking but superb

lunchtime choice, Rio's most imaginative *por kilo* restaurant has good vegetarian options including an extremely varied salad bar, alongside excellent bread and delicious desserts. Well worth the sometimes long wait for a table and the price, twice the amount you'd normally expect to pay *por kilo*. Mon–Sat 10am–5.30pm.

Cobal de Leblon Rua Gilberto Cardoso and Rua Fadal Fadal. Abundant and affordable bars and *lanchonetes* next to a vegetable market, where everything from pizza and sushi to Brazilian regional fare is served until late at night, alongside copious amounts of cold *chopp*. Not quite as exciting as its Botafogo counterpart, but a good place for a drink nonetheless.

Espaço Brasa Av. Afrânio de Melo Franco 131. If *Porcão* is just too overwhelming but you're still looking for high quality *churrasca*, the meats brought to your table here are excellent and the ambience classy – if a little echoey in this giant hall. Buffet includes carpaccio, oysters and unusually, Middle Eastern salads and houmous. Good value on weekdays at R$54; Fri–Sun R$61 – including service.

Felini Rua General Urquiza 104. An excellent *por kilo* option in Leblon, Felini is renowned for delicious baked vegetable and fish dishes, though it also has the usual choice of *churrasca* and sushi – plus tempting *tortas* for dessert.

Jobi Av. Ataulfo de Paiva 1166. Wonderful yet small *pé limpa boteco* in the centre of Leblon, *Jobi* is decorated with chequered tablecloths and stays open until dawn at weekends. Getting a table can be tricky in this perennially popular bar – it becomes more raucous late at night. Menu highlights are the sandwiches, *carne seca* and Saturday *feijoada*. There's a cheap *executivo* lunch if you're on a budget.

Marina All-Suites Bar do Lado and Bar d'Hotel Av. Delfim Moreira 696 ☏21/2172-1100. Two surprising seafront options leading the way in hotel entertainment, the ground floor corner *Bar do Lado* (Tues-Sun) is open till 3am at weekends and has a good cocktail list, whereas the chic yet groovy upstairs *Bar d'Hotel* attracts as many locals as visitors, plays a wide range of music and gets going at 9 or 10pm Thurs–Sat. The inviting menu includes goat's cheese ravioli with almond pesto, and grilled seabass or steaks. Great cocktail and wine list, too.

La Mole **Rua Dias Ferreira 147.** Popular and affordable Italian-style eatery; reviewed on p.185.

Nam Thai Rua Rainha Guilhermina 95 ⊕21/2259-2962. Finding superb Thai food is an unexpected pleasure in Rio, and here it's hard to go wrong. The *Tom Yum* soup is excellent, the duck tender, curry sauces rich and delicious and ginger fish mouth-watering. Also offers a Chinese *Dim Sum* lunch most days. Service is friendly and the décor smart wood-finished. Mains from R$40, closed Mon. They also deliver.
Sushi Leblon Rua Dias Ferreira 256. Superb (but expensive) sushi and Japanese-inspired dishes such as grilled squid stuffed with shiitake are offered as this stylish restaurant – a well-known meeting point of actors, models and artists. Mon–Sat evenings only; Sun 1.30pm–midnight.

Zuka Rua Dias Ferreira 233 ⊕21/3205-7154. Food is grilled in front of your eyes, then doused in amazing sauces by a chef capable of creating unforgettable fusion cuisine: one of his specialities is seared tuna in a cashew crust, served with a potato-horseradish sauce; the giant garlic prawns are also incredible, as are the rich chocolate desserts. Around R$70 per person. Tues–Sun lunch and dinner; Mon dinner only.

Jardim Botânico, Gávea and the Floresta da Tijuca

Set slightly apart from Rio's main hotel and residential neighbourhoods, **Jardim Botânico** and **Gávea** are not obvious areas for restaurants but nonetheless offer an assortment of excellent options which attract people from all over the Zona Sul. Ideal following a morning stroll around the botanical gardens or after an evening at the races, the few evening fine-dining options are best reached by taxi. One option is also listed in the Floresta da Tijuca. See map on p.112 for locations.

Snacks, juices, cafés and ice cream

Café Galeria Instituto Moreira Salles, Rua Marques de São Vicente, Gávea. Surrounded by one of Rio's most impressive modernist buildings, a lavish (and expensive – R$40) high tea is offered here, along with light lunches and salads (see p.118).

▲ Café Galeria, Instituto Moreira Salles

Café du Lage Escola de Artes Visuais, Parque Lage, Jardim Botânico. A beautiful place for breakfast (until 1pm), coffee or afternoon tea with pineapple cake. The food is good but unexceptional, though the setting is tremendous – you can gaze out across the courtyard's central pool from the shade of historic pillars, before exploring one of Rio's best parks.

Casa da Táta Rua Professor Manuel Ferreira 89, Gávea ⊕21/2511-0947. Opening Mon–Sat at 8am and Sun at 9am, this is probably the best place in the city to eat breakfast. Juices, fruit, cold choices and *pães de queijo* (speciality cheese-breads) and chocolate are all on offer, with good coffee too. Unbelievably, they'll also deliver breakfast to you if you book the day before.
Mil Frutas Rua Seabra, Jardim Botânico (see review under Ipanema).

Restaurants, bars and botecos

Arabe da Lagoa Av. Borges de Medeiros, Quiosque 7, Parque dos Patins, Lagoa. The best option at the Gávea side of Lagoa, this is another branch of Copacabana's excellent *Arabe* (see p.113), with good food, gentle musical accompaniment and a wonderful lakeside outdoor setting – regrettably with equivalently high prices.

Bar Boavista Praça Alfonso Viseu, Alta da Boa Vista. Right at the entrance to the Parque da Tijuca, this is a very reasonable and friendly restaurant with a large overgrown pergola. All dishes are big enough for two, the best option is ostrich with Roquefort and potato *roesti* – also the most expensive at R$50.

Couve-Flor Rua Pacheco Leão 724, Jardim Botânico. One of Rio's most popular *por kilo* restaurants due to the quality of its inexpensive to moderately priced salads and hot meals. Brazilian dishes predominate but there's also roast beef, duck, pasta and crepes (the obligatory sushi is not that good). Surprising vegetarian options such as spinach soufflé, and the *bacalhau* roll with passionfruit are tremendous. Leave room for dessert.

Da Graça Rua Pacheco Leão 780. Part-bar, part-restaurant, part-café, *Da Graça* is very popular at weekend nights, serving simple, decent, mid-to-expensive fare such as falafel, couscous, *carne seca*, and pizza made with a tapioca base. It has a good cocktail list and is brightly decorated. Watch out for the artistic cover charge when they have a (usually average) singer/guitarist.

Guima's Rua José Roberto Macedo Soares 5. An intimate and reasonably priced restaurant, catering for an arty and intellectual crowd. The food is delicious, and unusually, the *couvert* (wholemeal bread and pâté) is worth the price. Try steak in mustard and pear sauce, and leave space for the delectable chocolate pudding.

Olympe Rua Custódio Serrão 62, Jardim Botânico ☎21/2539-4542. Celebrity chef Claude Trosgros makes regular expeditions to the Amazon and other remote regions in search of new ingredients and ideas. On returning, he reinvents dishes, fusing them with classical and *nouvelle* styles of French cuisine. Expect unusual combinations such as foie gras with baked heart of palm and a *jabuticaba* sauce, and quails stuffed with *farofa* and coriander and served with an *açaí* sauce. Try the *menu confiance* (tasting menu) at R$185 – the presentation is pure theatre. Somewhere for a special occasion. Mon–Sat evenings & Fri lunch.

Yumê Rua Pacheco Leão 758, Jardim Botânico ☎21/3205-7321. A top Rio choice for relaxing Japanese-style, either on rugs with low tables or around a bar in a striking overgrown courtyard with retractable roof. The sushi and sashimi are predictably good, and the range of Japanese hot food also excellent quality. Highly recommended.

Zona Oeste

Some truly excellent eating options lie a little further afield in **Zona Oeste**, especially known for their seafood and attracting day trippers from elsewhere in the city. Around Barra da Tijuca itself most eateries are located in uninspiring shopping malls (RioDesign Barra for upmarket eating and Downtown for cheaper options and popular bars), though a few surprisingly good ideas are listed closer to the beach, easy to reach from the Zona Sul. See map on p.128.

Restaurants, bars and botecos

Bar do Oswaldo Estrada de Joá 3896, Barra da Tijuca. The oldest *botequim in* Barra, Oswaldo opened up in 1946 and made his name by selling the best *batidas* in Rio – a moreish blended cocktail of sugar-cane juice or vodka with a variety of fruits. It's hard to leave without trying many of the options, which include coconut, peach, strawberry, cashew or coffee crème; popular after the beach until late.

Bira Estrada da Vendinha 68, Barra de Guaratiba. Owned by the son of Tia Palmeira (see p.194) Bira has sublime seafood, rustic charm and a hilltop location most restaurants in Zona Sul would envy. The exceptional coastal view is accompanied by monkeys in the trees and large portions of excellent *moqueca de camerão* or Robalo fish *calderada* (Brazilian bouillon) – expensive (R$120 for two) but definitely worth it. President Lula clearly thought so when he once saw in the New Year here. Thurs–Sun only, lunch and dinner.

Don Pascual Estrada do Sacarrão 867 Casa 12, Vargem Grande ☎21/2428-6237. If you have your own transport and a sense of adventure, track down this superb wood-panelled Italian restaurant in the most unlikely location (follow directions on Ⓦwww.donpascual.com.br), right in the rainforest with regular live music and an enormous outdoor pizza oven. It also serves imaginative seafood pasta dishes.

Tourão Grill Praça São Perpétuo 116, Praça do "0", Barra da Tijuca. This eat-all-you-can *churrascaria* is recommended for its good-quality succulent meats and significantly cheaper prices than in the Zona Sul (R$27).

Tia Palmeira Caminho de Souza 18, Barra de Guaratiba ☏21/2410-8169. Seriously worth thinking about if you're headed to the Sítio Burle Marx; together with her son's restaurant, *Bira* (see p.193), these are probably the best seafood restaurants in Rio. *Tia Palmeira* is only open at lunchtime and famous for its excellent *moqueca* as part of a varied and enormous set lunch for R$65 per person.

🏃 **Vice Rey Av. Monsenhor Ascâneo 5355, Praça do "0", Barra da Tijuca ☏21/2493-1683.** With an attractive stone and wood interior, this large seafood restaurant has a really lively atmosphere when full. The *Tabua de Frutos do Mar* is good value for two (R$89) while there's also meat and poultry available. They brew their own excellent bitter ale (try the Amber) on the premises in large tanks you can see behind the bar.

Zona Norte

Eating options in the north tend to focus on Brazilian and Portuguese cuisine, and if you're willing to hunt out interesting places you can eat as well as in the Zona Sul at half the price. Those listed below are ideal if you happen to be visiting the sites here, or are headed out to samba schools or the wonderful 24-hour Feira Nordestina (see p.140). This said, be advised that much of sprawling **Zona Norte** is unsafe if you don't know where you're going – best to go by taxi or with local friends. See map on p.137 for locations.

Restaurants, bars and botecos

Boteco Original Rua Guaporé 680, Brás de Pina, Zona Norte. Few visitors venture this far into *subúrbio*, but if you're visiting the *Igreja da Penha* (see p.144) and want to discover more of the area, this is one of Zona Norte's best *botecos*, with a large *cachaça* list and range of well-presented, weird and wonderful *petiscos* – try the *Rolé Pela Subúrbio*, rolled pot roast beef in a pastry shell. Open until midnight; this isn't an area you should wander around.

Petisco da Vila Av. 28 Setembro 238, Villa Isabel. With a large buffet and outdoor drinking terrace, this large *boteco* is one of Zona Norte's best known eating and drinking establishments, located in an affluent area. Excellent *caipirinhas*; well worth a visit if you're headed for a night out at nearby Villa Isabel or Salgueiro samba schools.

Quinta da Boa Vista São Cristovão, Zona Norte. This smart restaurant opposite Rio Zoo has a large glass-covered a/c dining area under the trees and offers a quality traditional Brazilian/Portuguese menu of meats and seafood (R$50–100 for two).

Live music and nightlife

C*ariocas* of all ages love to go out – day or night. Each evening, though especially Wednesday through Sunday, there's a choice of most kinds of Brazilian music – samba, *forró*, *pagode*, bossa nova, MPB (Música Popular Brasileira) and *baile funk* hold sway (see p.260) – but an international blend of jazz, rock, pop, hip-hop and dance music is on offer, too. The city is also home to the Orquestra Sinfônica Brasileira, which leads the way on the city's excellent **classical** music circuit (see p.45).

Consult either *Programa*, a section of Friday's *Jornal do Brasil* newspaper, or *Rio Show*, the equivalent supplement in Friday's *O Globo*, to find out **what's on** – both list music concerts and arts events across the city. A couple of websites are also worth checking – Ⓦwww.riofesta.com.br provides up-to-date details of what's on in many of the Zona Sul's clubs and music venues and Ⓦwww .samba-choro.com.br has a useful diary of samba sessions around town. Bohemian **Lapa**, is the city's nightlife heartland; check Ⓦwww.lanalapa.com.br for listings and local news. The listings to follow cover **live music** and **nightclubs** in each area – and though there are a few late bars listed which have some overlap with Chapter 10: Eating and drinking, those featured here have more focus on entertainment and in some cases an entrance fee. Rio's lively **gay scene** is covered on p.208.

Aside from Lapa, other highlights of Rio's nightlife include visiting a **samba school** in Rio's Zona Norte (see p.215) (mainly Sat nights Sept–Feb, though events also happen in the daytime and at other times of the year). Crowds are of refreshingly mixed ages and although the original purpose of these nights was to rehearse for the Carnaval parades some of the schools now more closely resemble nightclubs. Large **samba shows** in the Zona Sul are inevitably tourist affairs where schools perform glitzy music and dance routines – the best of these is at Centro's **Cidade do Samba** on Thursday evenings. Also in Zona Norte, the immense **Feira Nordestina** offers a programme of *forró* music – accordion-driven swing from Brazil's Northeast, while closer to the beaches in **Gávea**, street drinking en masse takes place into the early hours Thursday through Monday nights.

The various regionally rooted traditions in folk music remain alive and if you'd like to get into a bit of Brazilian swing, go in search of the more traditional dance halls. These **gafieiras** originally sprang up in the 1920s as ballrooms for the poorer classes, and today they remain popular places where *Cariocas* can listen to traditional dance music, from samba to *forró* and beyond.

The best of these are *Estudantina* in Centro and *Democraticos* in Lapa. For less traditional surroundings, there are fashionable **nightclubs** that attract both *Cariocas* and tourists in the Zona Sul.

Live music

Lapa (see p.69) is the best spot for *forró*, *choro*, samba and other kinds of fusion. Though tourists visit the *bairro* in increasing numbers, venues still mainly attract locals of all backgrounds – good places to make for are rough-around-the-edges Rua Joaquim da Silva – attracting a mix of residents and college students – or Rua do Lavradio, distinctly more upmarket but equally exciting. If walking, be alert and take care not to veer onto badly lit side streets. If you would like someone to guide you around, contact RioHiking (see p.239), who regularly take small groups bar hopping in Lapa (R$100 per person, excluding drinks) and to samba schools further afield. Beyond Lapa, options abound across the city, especially in Centro and along the Zona Sul beaches. **Santa Teresa** has plentiful live sessions in bars and restaurants, though as there's rarely any kind of timetable those venues are covered in chapter 10 (see p.182).

Look out for **street sambas**: top spots are the 🎭 *Samba do Ouvidor* (alternate Saturdays 2–6pm; Rua Ouvidor and Rua Commercio, Centro; ask around to check when it's on), 🎭 *Pedra da Sal* (Mondays 7pm–12am; Rua Argemiro at the base of the Morro de Conçeição), hidden away on a tiny praça in Gamboa and the 🎭 **Feira Rio Antigo** (see p.73), held all day on the first Saturday of each month at Lapa's Rua do Lavradio – the street is closed to traffic and dedicated to antiques, street music and drinking.

From December to February, excellent shows at the **Morro da Urca** feature Brazilian and international acts of all genres in a very impressive hilltop location – for more information visit ⓦ www.veraodomorro.com.br. Rio's big **concert venues** are located in Barra da Tijuca (Zona Oeste), Centro and Botafogo. The Zona Norte is home to the unmissable **Feira Nordestina** (see p.140), and a couple of other decent options if you're determined to hear music off the beaten track.

Centro

See map on pp.42–43 for locations.

🎭 **Centro Cultural Carioca Rua do Teatro 37** ☎21/2252-6468 ⓦ www.centrocultural carioca.com.br. The CCC, housed in a historical building with attractive décor is open Mon–Sat 8pm–late for samba, jazz and MPB aimed at a thirties-upwards crowd – listen out for Teresa Cristina, one of Rio's greatest female samba voices. Food available. Daytime *forró* and samba dance classes downstairs. R$20–30.

🎭 **Cidade do Samba Rua Rivadávia Correa 60, Gamboa** ☎21/2213-2503 ⓦ www .cidadedosambarj.com.br. The year-round Thursday night (from 8pm) show, *Samba in Rio*, is the best of the city's touristic presentations, with a mature crowd enjoying excellent music, famous singers, glittering costumes and awe-inspiring samba moves. A mini-Carnaval parade is staged with giant floats, while behind the complex is the backdrop of Providencia *favela* – the area partly responsible for samba's development. R$130, including *caipirinhas*, *cerveja*, soft drinks and a snack buffet.

Elite Rua Frei Caneca 4, by Campo de Santana ☎21/2232-3217. Hidden away behind the arches of a pretty pink nineteenth-century building near Lapa, bands at this traditional, intimate *gafieira* play less modern music (Fri–Sun 10pm–late) than other dancehalls, while patrons wear more formal attire (men: shirt and shoes). R$10.

🎭 **Estudantina Praça Tiradentes 79** ☎21/2507-8067. Close to Lapa, one of the oldest surviving *gafieiras* (established in 1928) has traditional décor and features up to 1500 animated dancers (Thurs–Sat

9pm–4am). Live samba bands – and slower *pagode* on Fridays – appeal to locals and visitors of mixed ages. R$15.

Rio Scenarium Rua do Lavradio 20, ☏21/2233-3239 🌐www.rioscenarium.com.br. Located over three floors in an antiques-filled townhouse, this is one of the area's liveliest and most popular venues. Samba and *choro* are performed on the main stage which attracts a crowd of all ages – while an adjoining hall has a young nightclub vibe. Arrive before 8pm for a table (food available), open till 3am. The venue is quirky and the music superb, but service can be slow and impolite. R$30–50.

🏃 **Samba da Luzia Av. Almirante Silvio de Noronha 300 ☏21/2508-9574 🌐www.sambaluzia.com.br.** One of Rio's best Friday night samba options, this "Samba do Aeroporto" next to Santos Dumont airport, attracts a large, regular clientele who enjoy a stunning view of the bay and Corcovado, great live music, cocktails and *petiscos*. Music from 10pm; R$15.

🏃 **Teatro Rival Petrobras Rua Alvaro Alvim 33, Cinelândia ☏21/2240-4469 🌐www.rivalbr.com.br.** An intimate cabaret-style theatre with tables, food and drink. Features a varied programme Tues–Sun from 7.30pm, from samba-singing old-timers (Nelson Sargento, Beth Carvalho) to modern MPB vocalists. Advance tickets recommended, R$20–40.

Trapiche da Gamboa Rua Sacadura Cabral 155, Saúde ☏21/2516-0868 🌐www.trapiche gamboa.com.br. A slice of sophisticated Leblon in seedy Gamboa might seem contradictory but this converted warehouse is a great spot for samba on Thursdays, while Wednesdays are strictly *forró*. Monthly promotions on Sundays. Tues–Sun from 9pm.

Vivo Rio Avenida Infante Dom Henrique 85, Parque do Flamengo 🌐www.vivorio.com.br. For tickets call ☏21/4003-1212. One of Rio's large music venues, located next to the Museu Arte Moderna (MAM). Showcases Brazilian acts and international DJs.

Lapa and Santa Teresa

See map on p.70 for locations.

Asa Branca Av. Mem da Sá 17, Lapa ☏21/2224-9358. An informal dancehall that's been deservedly popular for decades, attracting samba, *choro* and, especially, big-name *forró* bands Tues–Sat from 10pm, R$10.

Bar do Juarez Estrada Dom Joaquim Mamede, Santa Teresa. This lone open-air bar in the upper reaches of the *bairro* (by taxi turn northwards of Rua Almirante Alexandrino by the school) features a superb Friday night samba da mesa (from 10pm), wonderful views and strong *caipirinhas*.

Bar da Ladeira Rua Evaristo da Vega 149, Lapa ☏21/2224-9828 🌐www.matrizonline.oi.com.br. Informal, quality *choro* and samba (Tues–Sat from 7pm; R$10–15) in this low-key but friendly and popular bar with veranda and pool table right by the Arcos (close to *Semente*).

Café Cultural Sacrilégio Av. Mem da Sá 81, Lapa ☏21/3970-1461 🌐www.sacrilegio.com.br. A small townhouse with a great atmosphere and killer *batidas* (cachaça-based drinks). The place attracts some great *choro* singers as well as samba, fusion rock-samba, and occassionally *forró* artists Tues–Sun from 6pm till late.

🏃 **Carioca da Gema Av. Mem de Sá 79, Lapa ☏21/2221-0043 🌐www.barcariocadagema.com.br.** This popular bar-cum-pizzaria-cum-samba venue has a live programme almost every night. Monday features the excellent deep-voiced singer Rhichahs, while Fridays feature the Grupo do Semente with special guests from samba's old guard like Monarco and newer sensations like Teresa Cristina. From 6pm till late; R$20–50.

Circo Voador Rua dos Arcos s/n ☏21/2533-5873 🌐www.circovoador.com.br. A large permanent tent next to the arches, *Circo Voador* features live Brazilian and foreign bands playing rock, rap, MPB, reggae and samba, and also has a popular monthly (Fri) *baile funk* night.

🏃 **Democráticos Rua do Riachuelo 93, Lapa ☏21/2252-4611 🌐www.clubedos democraticos.com.br.** Rio's oldest *gafieira*, dating from 1867, offers a superb music policy to please the masses. There's a very popular *forró* night on Wednesdays samba between Thursday and Sunday and Friday is one of Rio's best promotions. It's essentially one large hall with a poor sound system, but it oozes atmosphere.

Estrela da Lapa Av. Mem de Sá 69, Lapa ☏21/2507-6686, 🌐www.estreladalapa.com.br. A rather upmarket spot in a restored late nineteenth-century house, it offers great samba as well as *choro* and MPB bands Thurs–Sun from 10pm. Features an upstairs balcony, and from midnight DJs recharge the dance floor with *forró* and eclectic sounds. Look out for samba diva Elza Soares. R$25–50.

Fundição Progresso Rua dos Arcos 24, Lapa ☎ 21/2220-5070 ⓦ www.fundicaoprogresso.com.br. An exciting complex with stage venues, a nightclub and workshop/practice space for drumming, circus and arts groups, and performances from artists and DJs. In the summer you'll catch the hottest samba school *baterias* (drum groups) and dancers here – while adjoining open air bar *Parada da Lapa* has rock music and football games on a big screen.

Santo Scenarium Rua do Lavradio 36, Lapa ☎ 21/3147-9007. Started up by Rua do Lavradio kingpins *Rio Scenarium*, *Santo* is a popular street-side bar with great live music. Principally of interest for its bossa nova and jazz, this is a place to come for a few drinks to soak up the Lapa atmosphere.

🏃 **Semente Rua Joaquim Silva 138, Lapa** ☎ 21/2242-5165. Top-quality samba and *choro* at this small Bohemian bar daily except Fridays from 8.30pm. Formerly *Comune de Semente*, it has churned out masses of musical talent and continues to impress. Monday hosts superb live guitar by Zé Paulo Becker and occasionally the great Yamandu Costa – who cut his teeth here – appears. Sunday features live samba.

Glória, Catete and Flamengo

See map on p.84 for locations.

🏃 **The Maze Rua Tavares Bastos 414, Casa 66, Catete** ☎ 21/2558-5547 ⓦ www.jazzrio.com. On the first Friday of each month the brilliant and eccentric *Casa de Bob* comes alive with the sounds of jazz, as more "daring" Zona Sul residents head to this small *favela* with a phenomenal view of the bay. The location is safer than Ipanema, the live jazz fuelled with ample *caipirinhas* and a media and arts crowd enjoy life to the fullest. See also p.87

Severyna da Glória Rua Santo Amaro 38, Glória (by Beneficência Portuguesa hosp.) ☎ 21/2224-6604. Fridays see this Northeastern-themed late bar/restaurant host a popular *roda de samba* (from 9pm, R$8) and on Saturdays Beatles cover bands and other rock and pop entertain a locals crowd. Open daily.

Laranjeiras

See map on p.91 for locations.

Bar do B Mercado São João das Artes, Rua das Laranjeiras 90. This tiny bar within the attractive Mercado close to Largo do Machado is a popular spot for beers and low-key live music, with rock and blues on weekdays and bossa/samba at weekends.

🏃 **Casa Rosa Rua Alice 550, Laranjeiras** ☎ 21/2557-2562, ⓦ www.casarosa.com.br. Sunday evening (from 6pm, R$18) here is one of Rio's best treats; mixing funk, hip-hop, a *roda de samba* and live rock/reggae. In a famous former brothel, it attracts a friendly 20s/30s crowd, and a great *feijoada* dinner is thrown for just R$2. Saturdays features MPB acts, while Fridays are a mix of Carnaval vibes and funk.

Espaço Rio Carioca Casas Casadas, Rua das Laranjeiras 307 ☎ 21/2225-7332. This tiny venue just inside a small shopping centre features more traditional *chorinho* and samba music from 8pm on certain nights (check newspaper listings).

Severyna de Laranjeiras Rua Ipiranga 54, Laranjeiras ⓦ www.severyna.com.br. A large Northeastern restaurant with bare-brick walls and a football screen, featuring a similar programme to its cousin in Glória (above) – but the upper floor is open at weekends (R$10) with samba and rock/pop, while Mondays are strictly *forró*. Daily from 7pm–late.

Botafogo

See map on p.93 for locations.

🏃 **Bar da Rampa Av. Nestor Morreira 42, Praia de Botafogo** ☎ 21/2295-2597. Accessed by passing under the main road from inside the *Clube Guanabara*, this is Botafogo's best-kept secret, in a gorgeous location with yachts bobbing lazily on the bay. Excellent samba sessions Wed night (from 10pm) and alternate Sunday daytimes. Great for food, too, with large plates of fresh prawns, fish or shrimp risotto.

Canecão Av. Venceslau Brás 215 ☎ 21/2105-2000 ⓦ www.canecao.com.br. Since the 1960s many top Brazilian artists, from Caetano Veloso to recent MPB stars, have performed at this concert hall (by Rio Sul shopping centre). Despite the often superb shows, the venue is a little formal, with up to 2000

Finding the best samba

Tracking down the best **samba** in town can mean just being in the right place at the right time – from the beach promenade in Copacabana to restaurants in Santa Teresa, some of the finest sessions happen spontaneously. The sambas here, however, are some of the hottest options in Rio.

Monday
Pedra da Sal – excellent street samba in Centro (see p.66).
Carioca da Gema – great Lapa music venue (see p.197).

Tuesday
Salgueiro samba school (Sept–Feb) (see p.215).
Bip Bip – legendary *botequim* in Copacabana (see p.200).

Wednesday
Bar da Rampa – Samba in a superb location (also bi-weekly Sun; see p.198).
Bar da Ladeira – Lapa bar fast building a name for great samba (see p.197).

Thursday
CCC and *Trapiche da Gamboa* – great venues in Centro (see p.196).
Cidade do Samba – touristic samba show (see p.196).

Friday
Democráticos, *Carioca da Gema* and *Rio Scenarium* – big name samba performers in Lapa.
Samba da Luzia – brilliant Centro samba hotspot (see p.197).
Bar do Juarez – excellent off-the-beaten track samba in Santa Teresa (see p.197).
Centro Cultural Carioca (CCC) – Centro bar renowned for top performers (see p.196).
Severyna da Glória – lively samba in a popular restaurant (see p.198).

Saturday
Rua Gliçerio market, Laranjeiras – fun street samba and *chorinho* (see p.91).
Rua do Lavradio – Lapa street samba, the first Saturday every month (see p.73).
Samba do Ouvidor – bi-weekly street samba in Centro (see p.55).
Samba schools (various) – joyous day and all-night events September–February (see p.215).

Sunday
Casa Rosa – Laranjeiras club with great samba, 6–9pm (see p.198).
Semente – Lapa bar with great late-night sessions (also Mon; see p.198).
Bom Sujeto – classic samba spot in Barra da Tijuca (also Mon; see p.200).

people seated at tables served by suited waiters.

Canequinho Café Av. Venceslau Brás 215 ☎21/2105-2000, ⊛www.canequinhocafe.com.br. Music, cabaret and comedy is the entertainment of choice (Tues–Sat from 9pm, R$20–60) at this 180-capacity sit-down venue adjoining the *Canecão*. MPB or soul hold sway and there's a good cocktail list, too.

Far Up Cobal, Rua Voluntários de Pátria 448 ☎21/2266-5599. A bar on the edge of the Cobal eating and drinking centre, open Mon–Sat 8pm–late, it offers live jazz on Mondays and eighties and nineties rock and pop – alongside inevitable Beatles cover bands – at other times.

Copacabana and Leme

See map on p.101 for locations.

Allegro Bistro Músical Rua Barata Ribeiro 502, Copacabana ☎21/2548-5005, ⊛www.modernsound.com.br. Within renowned music store Modern Sound, this dimmed-lights bistro has excellent bossa-jazz on Friday evenings 5–9pm and samba-jazz fusion nights on Saturdays from 4pm – at other times classical pianists and quartets feature. Closed Sundays.

Bar do Pedrinho Rua Ronald de Carvalho 57, Copacabana. A livelier-than average *boteco* with tables out on the street and great live samba and *choro* music at weekends and Carnaval.

Bip Bip Rua Almirante Gonçalves 50, Copacabana ☎21/2267-9696. With more space on the street than in the bar, this tiny *botequim* has a big reputation for samba. Sunday is the most famous night featuring appearances by famous old-time singers; Tuesday is quieter with mainly *choro* music.

Bossa Lounge Av. Atlantico 994, Leme ☎21/7857-0342, ⓦwww.bossaloungerio .com.br. A relaxed new bar that successfully mixes live bossa nova with modern DJs (from 10pm Tues–Sun, from R$10) playing jazz-tinted drum & bass and house. Also has good cocktails and an imaginative Mediterranean-South American food menu (R$20–40).

Ipanema

See map on p.106 for locations.

Conversa Afiada Rua Maria Quitéria 46, Ipanema ☎21/2247-8609. A large *boteco* downstairs has great *caipirinhas* and *picanha* steak, while the upstairs "club" is the best place in Ipanema to hear live bands (R$25). Saturdays are most popular, though Tuesday's *Terceira Movimento* features excellent comedy and poetry and Thursday attracts good bands, too.

Mistura Fina Rainha Elizabeth 769, Arpoador ☎2523-1703. A classy thirties upwards venue between Ipanema and Copacabana with a good restaurant/piano bar, now enlarged (200-plus capacity) and well known for its weekend samba and MPB nights like "*Doces Cariocas*" (Carioca Sweets).

Vinicius Show Bar Rua Vinicius de Morães 39 (upstairs), Ipanema ☎21/2287-1497 ⓦwww .viniciusbar.com.br. This exclusively bossa nova bar plays all the old classics (from 9pm) to a tourist crowd that remembers Vinicius's heyday. Performances are polished and the music good.

Leblon

See map on p.110 for locations.

Bar do Tom Plataforma, Rua Adalberto Ferreira 32, Leblon ☎21/2274-4022. At this Rio institution avoid the expensive and poor-quality tourist Carnaval show upstairs in favour of this really good cabaret-style venue in honour of the late Tom Jobim. Shows draw an almost entirely mature local crowd and feature bossa nova singers, with occasional MPB and samba dancing.

Esch Café Rua Dias Ferreira 78, Leblon ☎21/2512-5651. About as Leblon as you can get, *Esch* is a cigar-tobacconist and jazz bar with live musicians four evenings per week (normally around 10pm) who incorporate bossa nova and samba into their styles. Exclusive yet charming.

Zona Oeste

See map on p.128 for locations.

Bom Sujeto Estrada da Barra da Tijuca 18 ☎21/2491-8955. A traditional *boteco* located close to *Bar do Oswaldo* with numerous photos of old-time *sambistas* on the walls, and famed for its Sunday and Monday evening sessions, frequented by samba masters (R$15). Fri–Sat there's also live music.

Citibank Hall Av. Ayrton Senna 3000, Barra da Tijuca ☎0300/789-6846 ⓦwww.citibankhall .com.br. South America's self-proclaimed largest seated venue, the arena attracts both Brazilian and international stars. Buy tickets at ⓦwww.ticketmaster.com.br and expect to pay upwards of R$100.

HSBC Arena Av. Embaixador Abelardo Bueno 3401, Barra da Tijuca ☎21/3035-5200 ⓦwww.hsbcarena.com.br. A stadium-type arena left over from 2007's Pan-American Games, hosting sports and large-scale music events – in 2008–09 REM, Bob Dylan and Alanis Morissette played here.

Ilha das Pescadores Estrada da Barra da Tijuca 793 ☎21/2493-0005. Not considered as trendy as it used to be, *Isla das Pescadores* attracts a diverse mix from western Rio's suburbs, all out for a good dance, with live *pagode*, samba, funk and dance music, in an attractive lakeside setting.

Zona Norte

See map on p.137 for locations.

Feira Nordestina São Cristovão ⓦwww .feiradesaocristovao.com.br. A 48hr non-stop party in a stadium every weekend might sound far-fetched, but it has been hosted here for decades (see p.141). Dance to *forró*, funk and reggae and indulge yourself in *carne seca* (sun-dried beef) and *cerveja*.

Tendência Visconde de Abaeté 33, Villa Isabel ☎21/2577-6144. A late, smartish bar with live music and good food, this is a great place to go to before heading to the area's samba school. The clientele is more representative of Rio's diverse residents than most equivalent bars in the Zona Sul and there are often groups playing soul and reggae.

Nightclubs and DJ venues

Rio's best-known **clubs** are located in Ipanema, Copacabana, Leblon and Barra da Tijuca, though Lapa and Centro both have a few options and Botafogo's vibrant alternative-music-oriented Matriz venues are worth checking out. Going out in the beach areas tends to be pricier than elsewhere, but there are still **bars** and **clubs** to suit most tastes; a few are aimed directly at gringos, but most still attract a majority local crowd. Considering the number of hotels in Copacabana it has surprisingly few decent nightspots. While a handful of bars and clubs are low on snobbishness and can be really good fun, Copa as a whole is high on strip joints and clubs like the notorious seafront *Help Discoteque*, better known for working girls than for disco. If you're moving around the *bairro* at night you're best off going by taxi for safety. In Centro, the **Arco de Teles** area warms up early on Wednesday–Friday evenings, filled with locals drinking and eating after work, then staying on for nightclubs which open early and finish by 1am. Rio's biggest (gay) nightclub *The Week* is located at **Gamboa** beyond Centro's Praça Mauá – an area fast becoming a hot spot despite its sleazy strip joints.

Centro

See map on p.42 for locations.
Dito e Feito Rua do Mercado 21 ☎21/2509-1407 ⊛www.ditoefeito.com.br. Young, after-work crowds pack this double-level club where almost every night is "Ladies' Night"; women only from 6–8pm, with male strippers and drinks promotions. Electronic, pop, hip-hop and *baile funk* music. Mon–Fri till 1am, Sat 10–4am; R$10–40.
NuthCentro Rua Quitanda 51 ☎21/3861-8629 ⊛www.nuthcentro.com.br. This Centro branch of a top Barra nightspot opens Tues–Sat and draws an affluent crowd. There's a ground level "*botequim*", a second level champagne bar with full meals, and a dancefloor playing eclectic tunes. R$20–30.
The Week Rua Sacadura Cabral 154, Saúde ☎21/2253-1020 ⊛www.theweek.com.br. Rio's biggest club is predominantly gay (see p.211), though Friday nights also attract straight men and women. If you like house music this is the best place in town. The ground floor has a swimming pool and there are two DJ areas and four bars. R$50 entrance.

Lapa

See map on p.70 for locations.
Club Six Rua das Marrecas 38 ☎21/2510-3230, ⊛www.clubsix.com.br. Hip-hop, *baile funk* and trance/techno are on offer on Saturdays at this rustic townhouse club on three floors. Drawing a wider twenties crowd than most clubs in the Zona Sul, there's free beer once you get inside. A good place to end up after Lapa bar-hopping. Sundays feature *forró*, *zouk* and samba.
Febarj Av. Mem de Sá 37 A lively one-room hip-hop club at the heart of Lapa's strip of cheap bars, *Febarj* has Brazilian tunes earlier in the night and American later on, Thurs–Sat from 10pm. Girls get a lot of attention in here. R$5.
Alto da Lapa Av. Mem de Sá 25 ☎21/2224-7088. A newish cheap-but-reliable upstairs club playing very loud house/techno, hip-hop and *baile funk* – a good spot to call in for an hour if you're on a tour of Lapa's cheaper bars and clubs, Tues–Sun from 9pm until very late.

Glória, Catete, and Flamengo

See map on p.84 for locations.
Marina da Glória Av. Infante Dom Henrique, Glória ☎21/2555-2200. This spit of land poking into the bay from the Parque do Flamengo is more famous for music festivals than luxury boats (see p.220) – including October's Tim Festival and February's DJ Music Conference. At other times quality nights take place such as 15 June *forró* Festa Juninho.

Laranjeiras

See map on p.91 for locations.
Hideaway Rua das Laranjeiras 308 ☎21/2285-0921, ⊛www.hideaway.com. This evening (very good) pizzeria turns into a small, friendly club at weekends, playing dance

music, hip-hop and funk to an under 25s crowd. From 10pm; R$20.

Botafogo

See map on p.93 for locations.

 **Casa da Matriz** Rua Henrique Novaes 107 ℡21/2226-6342, Ⓦmatrizonline.oi.com .br. A stylish and happening club featuring more Brazilian music than is typical – though varying through the week. Thursday attracts a youngish crowd with pioneering Brazilian drum 'n'bass/crossover DJs, while Saturday has a slightly older clientele for pop, soul and electro. Wednesdays are reggae and dub, Mondays strictly rock. From 11pm; R$10–30.

Cinematéque Rua Voluntários de Pátria 53 ℡21/2266-1014, Ⓦmatrizonline.oi.com.br. Another cool nightspot from the Matriz crew featuring a bar with food and great cocktails (Tues–Sun 7pm–late), while the club upstairs has eclectic music for all ages with bossa-jazz, samba, MPB and dance DJs (free up to R$30).

Pista 3 Rua Sao Joao Batista 14 ℡21/2286-3389, Ⓦmatrizonline.oi.com.br. The definitive alternative Botafogo night out (Wed–Sun 9pm till late), this three-floor townhouse club offers eighties and nineties pop, punk-rock, indie and Brazilian sounds, and innovative cabarets combining theatre and comedy, with a mixed crowd (R$5–20).

Copacabana

See map on p.101 for locations.

Atlântico Av. Atlântica 3880 (corner of Rua Franciso Sá), ℡21/2513-2485. By posto 6, this late-night bar (7pm–4am) resembles a nightclub with its house/techno DJs and young crowd of locals and tourists. Mondays, Thursdays and Saturdays are especially lively, costing up to R$40.

Bar Clandestino Rua Barata Ribeiro 111. A brick-walled arty bar to one side of the *Stone of a Beach* hostel with great parties from 11pm on Wednesdays (hip-hop) and weekends (dance music), with good DJs, a cocktail list and mixed hostel and local crowd.

Fosfobox Rua Siqueira Campos 143 ℡21/2548-7498 Ⓦwww.fosfobox.com.br. Small and trendy basement weekend club; Saturday combines rock with disco/electro. Some nights – mostly Sundays – are aimed at the local gay crowd; check the programme in advance. R$25 entrance.

Mariuzinn Av. Nossa Senhora de Copacabana 435 (near Rua Paulo Freitas) ℡21/2545-7672 Ⓦwww.mariuzinn.com.br. R$40 with beer included, this packed club is popular with a twenties-thirties crowd Thurs–Sat 11pm–morning. It has sofas and two bars playing pop and electronic music.

Mud Bug Rodolfo Dantas 12 and Rua Paula Freitas 55 ℡21/ 2235-6847 Ⓦwww.mudbug .com.br. Two very popular sports bars featuring live rock and bossa music weekdays and a noisy mainly-Brazilian crowd with DJs Fri–Sat (till 3am), when there's also an entrance charge of R$15.

Up Av. Nossa Senhora de Copacabana 1144 ℡21/3202-9051. The smartest option in Copa, this brand new club at the Ipanema end of the *bairro* is decorated with 1940s–60s oddments and has a music policy of hip-hop on Fridays and dance music other nights. Open Thurs–Sun 10pm till late; R$20–40.

Ipanema

See map on p.106 for locations.

Baronneti Rua Barão de Torre 354 ℡21/2247-9100 Ⓦwww.baronneti.com.br. One of the city's most exclusive clubs (R$70) filled with Ipanema and Leblon's beautiful people, all getting down to some seriously good house music. In a sign of how far Brazil's ghetto music has come into the mainstream, Wednesday features *baile funk*.

▲ *Baronneti*, Ipanema

Empório Rua Maria Quitéria 37 ☎21/3813-2526. A fun bar, open daily till very late, for gringos and gringo-hunters. Features DJs and a small dancefloor, mostly playing rock music. It pulls a really big crowd at weekends.

Nuth Club Av. Epitácio Pessoa 1244 ☎21/3575-6850 ⓦ www.nuth.com.br. Brand new, this stylish lounge club (open daily till late) with dancefloor has an expensive, though not especially innovative, menu, but ample space for chatting and enjoying good cocktails whilst overlooking Lagoa. House and Brazilian fusion sounds.

Leblon

See map on p.110 for locations.

Melt Rua Rita Ludolf 47 ☎21/2249-9309. With a reputation to uphold as less snobby than some other clubs in the area, *Melt* is a stylish hipster haven with a good range of music – including some live shows. Hip hop, samba, funk and dance music is generally what's spinning; there's also a nice candlelit lounge upstairs. Entrance R$30–50.

Gávea

See map on p.112 for locations.

00 Av. Padre Leonel Franca 240 (within the Planetarium grounds) ☎21/2540-8041 ⓦ www.00site.com.br. Extremely stylish club frequented by a rich and trendy crowd. Some of Brazil's top DJs play an eclectic mix of music; Friday is hip hop, soul and funk; Saturday is disco/electro and Sunday is one of Rio's most popular gay house nights. There's an expensive, yet innovative restaurant.

Zona Oeste

See map on p.128 for locations.

Castelo das Pedras Favela Rio das Pedras, Jacarepaguá. Rio's most popular *funk Carioca* venue features DJs, MCs, stage dancers and a crowd of 3000 sweating, gyrating bodies. Currently safer than other city *favela funk bailes*, tourists tend to go on Sunday nights on an organized tour with Be A Local (ⓦ www.bealocal.com), though you can get here under your own steam if you're confident: take a van from Av. Bartolomeu Mitre/Rua Conde Bernadotte around 11pm (50min), returning in the morning. Alternatively, stay at Favela Receptiva and go with a *favela* resident.

Nuth Lounge Av. Armando Lombardi 999, Barra da Tijuca ☎21/3575-6868, ⓦ www.nuth.com.br. The original Nuth club is an exclusive and sometimes snobby affair, but you can't escape the beautiful surroundings, good-looking people and inventive music. Monday's "flashback" is more mature, Thursday mixes electronica, and Sunday's post-beach bash (7pm) is a superb way to round off a day on the Barra sands.

Theatre, dance and film

Brazil's artistic creativity shines through in Rio – from the theatrical complexity and remarkable designs of **Carnaval** to the city's imaginative plethora of interactive exhibitions. Rio is bursting with **theatres**: most areas within the Zona Sul have at least four, with many shopping malls also hosting nights of comedy and drama. **Cinemas** are spread across the city, screening American and European imports, arthouse productions and domestic releases (see p.207). In terms of **dance**, the city's ballet and contemporary dance scene is led by the Ballet do Theatro Municipal, though many other choreographers also run their own companies – one of the most internationally renowned is the Companhia de Dança Deborah Colker (Ⓦwww.ciadeborahcolker.com .br), whose style draws on circus as much as ballet.

For **what's on** information, *Programa* in Friday's *Jornal do Brasil* newspaper or the *Rio Show* supplement in *O Globo* both have full listings of arts, theatre and film events. The weekly magazine *Veja* also has a decent supplement profiling what's on in Rio. Pick up a copy of dedicated theatre guides *Aplauso* and *OFF* (available from tourist offices and all over town; Portuguese only) for more thorough reviews and listings, while the similar *Vairolar* guide (also on the web at Ⓦwww.vairolar.com.br) is a comprehensive guide to both theatre and film in the city. Theatre **tickets** for larger venues are available at their box offices or at Modern Sound in Copacabana (Rua Barato Ribeiro 502, near the junction with Rua Santa Clara, ☏21/2548 5005, Ⓦwww.modernsound.com.br; see p.234). Major upcoming shows are also listed on websites Ⓦwww.ticketronic .com.br and Ⓦwww.ticketmaster.com.br, though you'll need a Brazilian address (or to arrange delivery at your hotel) to purchase.

Theatre

Rio has a strong theatrical culture and plentiful venues for performances. Practically everything is in Portuguese, but even if you're not a speaker many plays are still enjoyable – particularly musicals at Centro's theatres. **Ticket prices** range from as little as R$10 in smaller venues to around R$25 at more established theatres; good seats at the Theatro Municipal, Rio's premier performing arts venue, can cost more than R$100.

Hybrid works mixing theatre, music and comedy are popular – Tuesday night's *Terceira Movimento* at *Conversa Afiada* in Ipanema is excellent (see p.200). If

Rio on stage

Theatrical traditions

Brazil's theatrical history long pre-dates Carnaval, from the elite's imports of European plays to slaves' anti-colonial resistance masquerades and African-based dances like *capoeira*. However, it found its distinctive voice in the nineteenth century, with dramatizations of novels by Rio literary master **Machado de Assis.** An immensely talented and self-educated *mulatto* writer, he emerged from poverty to teach himself fluent French and English, translate numerous works by Shakespeare into Portuguese and write comedies laden with social realism. His masterpiece *Dom Casmurro* is seen as the Brazilian *Othello*.

Contemporary talents

In the twentieth century **Nelson Rodrigues** was recognized as Brazil's greatest playwright. Rodrigues wrote about Rio's middle- and upper-classes. His psychologically insightful 1943 play *Vestido de Noiva* (*The Wedding Dress*) caused a stir and his subsequent play *Álbum de Família* (*Family Album*) was censored for two decades because of its exploration of marital infidelity.

Other important Brazilian theatrical figures include São Paulo-based adopted-Brazilian **Gerald Thomas**, known for his operatic collaborations with composer Philip Glass. His **Dry Opera** company attracts critical attention for its unconventional stagings of traditional operas. **Augusto Boal** has become Rio's most globally influential contemporary director, his interactive Forum Theatre, practised and studied worldwide, is part of his politically engaged **Theatre of the Oppressed** – now based in Lapa (Av. Mem de Sá 31 ⓦ www.ctorio.org.br).

Favela community theatre

Favelas have always been hotbeds of theatrical talent, harnessed occasionally by NGOs but most successfully by the Vidigal-based company **Nós do Morro** (ⓦ www .nosdomorro.com.br), whose community theatre has supplied a steady stream of actors to Rio's vibrant film and TV industry – some even featured in the cast of *Cidade de Deus*. With Brazilian TV actors typically coming from privileged backgrounds, the company's stars have broadened the social status of the profession.

---

you're looking for circus acts, Rio's pre-eminent group is Intrépida Trupe, based at Lapa's *Fundição Progresso* (see p.198). Their original and energetic shows combine circus with dance and theatre. They can also be seen performing at Carnaval with samba schools such as Salgueiro or Villa Isabel. Finally, if you're looking for a large-scale Carnaval show, bypass Leblon's touristy *Plataforma* in favour of the Cidade do Samba's weekly spectacle (see p.196) which features recent Carnaval performers, great costumes and a mock parade with floats.

Centro

Centro Cultural Banco do Brasil Rua Primeiro de Março 66, Centro ☏ 21/3808-2040, ⓦ www.bb.com.br/cultura.The top city cultural centre hosts arts events of all descriptions – often free. It has two theatres, with performances often combining music, drama and debate/lecture – though Shakespeare is sometimes staged, too. Tues–Sun 10am–9pm.

Teatro Carlos Gomes Praça Tiradentes Centro ☏ 21/2232 8701, ⓦ www.teatrocarlosgomes .com.br. One of the largest theatres in Rio, the state-run Carlos Gomes is renowned for musicals and large-scale theatre productions.

Teatro João Caetano Praça Tiradentes, Centro ☏ 21/2299-2141. This downtown theatre has seen better days, though its faded grandeur still provides a decent setting for comedies, classics and musicals.

Theatro Municipal ☏ 21/2299-1711, ⓦ www.theatromunicipal.rj.gov.br. Rio's grandest venue, modelled on the Paris Opéra, is the home of the Orquestra Sinfônica Brasileira and hosts most visiting ballet and opera companies. Prices are reasonable, particularly for matinées. It also has an excellent restaurant. A highly recommended evening out.

Teatro Nelson Rodrigues Av. República do Chile 230, Centro ℡21/2262-8152. This smart and modern large theatre (sometimes advertised as Caixa Cultural) stages mainly contemporary productions, from Tom Stoppard to musicals and Rodrigues' own plays.

Teatro Sesc Ginástico Av. Graça Aranha 187 ℡21/2279-4027, ⊛www.sescrio.com.br. A recently refurbished theatre showing musicals and plays. Look out for performances featuring old samba singers and Carnaval stars, especially in the summer season.

Teatro Sesi Graça Aranha 1, Centro ℡21/2563-4163 An intimate auditorium often staging classics or musicals, sometimes performed by smaller companies including Nós do Morro (see below).

Zona Sul

Casa de Cultura Laura Alvim Av. Vieira Souto 176, Ipanema ℡21/2247-6946. ⊛www .riocenacontemporanea.com.br. Dynamic arts centre by Ipanema beach with a theatre and cinema. Its diverse programme has featured comedy, monologues and offerings by Harold Pinter and Gerald Thomas.

Companhia de Teatro Contemporâneo Rua Conde de Iraja 253, Botafogo ℡21/2537-5204, ⊛www.ciadeteatrocontemporaneo.com.br. A small theatre staging black comedies and

even Oscar Wilde plays. Occasional performances in English.

🏃 **Espaço Sesc Rua Domingos Ferreira 160, Copacabana** ℡21/2547-0156, ⊛www .sescrio.com.br. Copacabana's most interesting and varied programming – from modern-dance productions to social and philosophical plays and *Tropicalia* shows.

🏃 **Nós do Morro Rua Olinto Magalhaes 54, Vidigal, Leblon** ℡21/3874-9411, ⊛www .nosdomorro.com.br. Slick and talented productions from Rio's most successful *favela* community theatre – staged at their rustic home venue and other city theatres.

🏃 **Solar de Botafogo L Rua Gen. Polidoro 180, Botafogo** ℡21/2543-541. A small theatre staging plays for the Zona Sul's socially conscious classes – often adult themed, or historical dramas.

Teatro Cacilda Becker Rua do Catete 338 ℡21/2265-9933. Close to Largo do Machado, this small auditorium features a programme of contemporary dance from local dance schools and occasional community theatre.

Teatro do Leblon Rua Conde do Bernadotte 26, Leblon ℡21/2294-0347, ⊛www.teatrodoleblon .com. This very popular Zona Sul venue shows stand-up comedy, musicals, childrens' shows and new takes on classics.

Teatro Villa Lobos Av. Princess Isabel, Copacabana ℡21/2334-7153. Copacabana's largest theatre with a varied programme of classics, children's plays, dance and samba musicals.

Dance

Despite being the home of **samba**, there is no snobbishness when it comes to dance in Rio de Janeiro. Almost every type of dance is represented including ballet, African, *forró* (Brazilian Northeastern swing), *zouk* (originating from the Caribbean, now a Brazilian form), salsa and break-dancing. The city's finest venue, the Theatro Municipal (see Theatres, above) hosts Rio's own **Ballet do Theatro Municipal** as well as national and international visiting companies, while other top city venues sponsoring major contemporary dance performances include the Centro Cultural Banco do Brasil (CCBB), Teatro Carlos Gomes and Espaço Sesc in Copacabana. Teatro Caçilda Becker offers lower-key dance events (for details on all these venues see theatre lists above). At the beginning of November Rio stages its premier dance event – the Festival Panorama de Dança (see ⊛www.panoramafestival.com). It features both street performance and contemporary dance shows in various venues.

Dance classes

Centro Cultural Carioca Escola de Dança, Rua Sete de Setembro, 237/3° andar, Praça Tiradentes, Centro ℡21/2252-5751. Excellent daytime

courses in samba, *forró*, salsa and Brazilian *zouk* are offered at this atmospheric restaurant and nightspot. Mon–Fri 11am–8pm.

Favela Receptiva Estrada das Canoas 610, São Conrado ℡21/9848-6737,

@ www.favelareceptiva.com. Samba and *forró* classes available from an excellent private teacher – she can also show you where to practise your new moves.

Renata Peçanha Praça Tiradentes, Centro ☏ 21/2221-1011, @ www.renatapecanha.com .br. A reputable downtown dance school teaching jazz, salsa, *zouk*, tango and *forró*.

Film

Brazilians are film fanatics, and the country is one of the world's largest markets, screening titles from the US and Europe, as well as domestic releases (see p.264). Mainstream **cinemas** are easy to find in Rio – American movies are usually released in Brazil before Europe and a variety of cinemas exclusively screen European and local arthouse productions. Films in English will be shown dubbed or with subtitles. Going to the cinema is quite inexpensive (R$10–20). An excellent chain of independent cinemas, Estação (@ www.estacaovirtual .com), shows the latest Brazilian and quality film imports.

In late September and early October Rio also hosts one of Latin America's most important international film festivals, the **Festival do Rio** (@ www .festivaldorio.com.br. see p.221), showing over four hundred international films in cinemas city-wide. A short-film festival of arthouse flicks runs at the same time – pick up a flyer in any cinema.

Centro Cultural Banco do Brasil Rua Primeiro de Março 66, Centro ☏ 21/3808-2040, @ www .bb.com.br/cultura. This major cultural centre has independent film screenings, including classics and occasional documentary festivals on cultural and political themes. Tues–Sun 10am–9pm.

Cine Santa Teresa Rua Paschoal Carlos Magno 136, Largo do Guimarães, Santa Teresa ☏ 21/2507-6841, @ www.cinesanta.com.br. A small community cinema showing local and foreign commercial and arthouse releases.

Espaço Cultural Leblon Rua Conde Bernadote 26, Leblon ☏ 21/2294-0347. A single-screen independent arts cinema within a wider cultural centre.

Espaço de Cinema Rua Voluntários da Pátria 35, Botafogo ☏ 21/2226-1986, @ www .estacaovirtual.com.br. The more arthouse focused of Estação's two Botafogo cinemas, with a programme of mainly French and Spanish-language films.

Estação Botafogo Rua Voluntários da Pátria 88, Botafogo ☏ 21/2226-1988, @ www.estacao virtual.com.br. Arthouse and quality international screenings.

Estação Ipanema Rua Visconde de Pirajá 605, Ipanema ☏ 21/2279-4603, @ www.estacao virtual.com.br. Small cinema showing Brazilian and foreign films.

Estação Laura Alvim Av. Vieira Souto 176, Ipanema ☏ 21/2267-4307,

@ www.estacaovirtual.com.br. Located in the Casa de Cultural Laura Alvim at Ipanema beach, this is a three-screen cinema showing Brazilian and foreign new releases. The stylish on-site bar/café provides an ideal after-beach meeting point.

Instituto Moreira Salles ☏ 21/3284-7400, @ www.ims.com.br. The family behind Unibanco (one member of which, Walter Salles, directed the award-winning *Central Station*) have long been at the forefront of film promotion and this centre has theatres with regular screenings and a film archive.

Odeon Petrobras Praça Floriano 07, Cinelândia ☏ 21/2240-2573, @ www .estacaovirtual.com.br. This restored Art Nouveau cinema offers an excellent programme, a monthly cinema marathon (first Friday of the month from 11pm with three films, food and bar), and *cachaça clube* (see p.45).

Roxy Av. Nossa Senhora de Copacabana 945, ☏ 21/2461-2461, @ severianoribeiro.com.br. An attractive 1930s three-screen cinema showing foreign and local releases.

Unibanco Arteplex Botafogo Praia de Botafogo 316 ☏ 21/2559-8750, @ www .unibancocinemas.com.br. The place in Rio to see quality Brazilian new releases, as well as classic European films.

Gay and lesbian Rio

Amongst the top gay destinations in Latin America, Rio's numerous bars and clubs, lively **gay beaches** and a **samba school** pretty much dedicated to gay theatre ensure you'll not be short of options. While there are some exclusively gay venues (especially for men, though there are also a handful for women), Rio's scene is strikingly integrated, with gay men, lesbians and heterosexuals often sharing the same bars and clubs. There's not much evidence of the very Catholic, conservative Brazil on the streets of night-time Rio, and the city's highly expressive – sometimes brash – traditions are even more obvious at **Carnaval**, where **transvestites** both straight and gay can be seen all over town. The city's high-spirited **Gay Pride** in October offers an even more riotous forum for expression. While there are no Brazilian laws actively against homosexuality, Rio has emerged as one of the most relaxed places in the country in terms of people's attitudes to sexual orientation, something reinforced by the acronym **GLS** (gays, lesbians and sympathizers), which you'll see as often as **GLBT** (gays, lesbians, bisexuals and transsexuals). Overall, Brazil also has a high proportion of bisexuals. The main GLBT organization is **Grupo Arco Íris** (Rua Monte Alegre 167A, Santa Teresa ☎21/2222-7286, Ⓦwww.arco-iris.org.br), which provides advice and support as well as lobbying for gay rights across Brazil.

Gay-friendly accommodation

In Rio there's little accommodation that is gay-unfriendly – especially in Copacabana and Ipanema. Even so, a few hotels and guesthouses attract a mixed crowd or have **gay owners** that can help you get the best out of the city. It's also worth noting that the one or two hostels in Ipanema that specifically attract gays offer poor value for money and don't appear in this guide; at the budget end far better options are found in the Ipanema hostels listed on p.176.

The most obvious choice (though by no means exclusively gay) is the **Ipanema Plaza** on Rua Farme de Amoedo (see p.175). Yards from Ipanema's rainbow beach it offers really good mid- to high-level accommodation as well as a 24-hour bar, Asian restaurant, and both mixed and single sex saunas on the rooftop. The Copacabana seafront option at a similar level is the **Orla Copacabana** (see p.172), while the slightly cheaper **Apa Hotel** (see p.171) at the other end of the *bairro* a few blocks back from the beach is also gay-friendly. In terms of *pousadas*, **O Veleiro** in Botafogo (see p.101) has a wonderfully peaceful location in the hills as well as friendly and helpful gay owners, and the **Cama e Café** B&B network in charming Santa Teresa (see p.168) can match you up with a gay host. For a top-end boutique hotel look no further than the unbeatable **La Suite** in Joá, (see p.177), which has genial décor and gracious gay owners.

At night the gay scene focuses primarily on Lapa, Copacabana and Ipanema, but there are **gay clubs** across the city. For the latest entertainment options, including theatre and nightlife, see the weekly gay **listings** (Fridays) in newspapers *O Globo* and *Jornal do Brasil*. A GLBT **film club** meets monthly at the Odeon in Cinelândia, see Ⓦwww.cineclubelgbt.com.br for details. Rio is not well blessed with up-to-date what's on websites, but Ⓦwww.riogaylife.com and tour operator Ⓦwww.riog.com.br have useful information, including on tours. Details on Rio's sauna scene – which ranges from gay health clubs such as *Studio 64* (Rua Redentor 64, Ipanema) through to those featuring bars, DJs and dark rooms like *Club 117* (Rua Cândido Mendes 117, Glória) – can also be found on these sites.

On the beach

The beach, of course, is central to the *Carioca* way of life, and gay muscle-hunks ("**barbies**") playing volleyball or beach tennis are a distinctive sight. The strip of Ipanema's **beach** between postos 8 and 9 – designated by a large **rainbow flag** is the best-known daytime gay meeting point in Rio. In January and February you'll find thousands of people on this section of beach – and on bar-lined Rua Farme de Amoedo in general.

Copacabana, too, has an area frequented by gay bathers in front of the *Copacabana Palace Hotel*. Together with its daytime bar/café, the *Quiosque Arco-Iris* (Rainbow Kiosk), it's a good spot for sunset, though it tends to be seedier than the equivalent space in Ipanema due to its more mature tourist crowd and young, local male prostitutes.

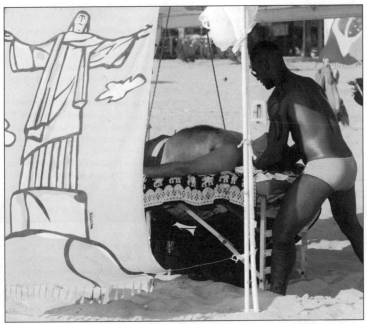

▲ Posto 9, Ipanema

Eating, drinking and nightlife

There are several decent gay and lesbian **clubs** in Rio, with venues in Lapa, Copacabana and the outer zones attracting people from across the social spectrum – including many transvestites – those in Ipanema, Leblon and Gávea are a good deal more affluent. Fridays and Saturdays are the busiest nights, but there are good promotions at other times, too. If you're here in January or February, look no further than samba school Unidos da Tijuca (see Gay Carnaval, opposite) for an excellent night out. GLBT **rave parties** tend to happen at the Marina da Glória (see p.201) or in Barra da Tijuca – look out for flyers or ads in the media (see p.209). Much of Rio's general nightlife is gay-friendly, especially in Lapa and also Botafogo – friendly alternative club *Pista 3* (see p.202) often draws a mixed crowd. Ipanema's **Rua Farme de Amoedo** is the first port of call for exclusively gay bars, but the options below are also known for attracting gays and lesbians.

Eating and drinking

Bofetada Rua Farme de Amoedo 87, Ipanema. Farme's more traditional *botequim* is enormously popular at all hours, with outdoor tables where you can watch street life.

Copa Café Av. Atlântica 3056, Copacabana (see p.187). This bar and upmarket burger restaurant is open late and has a reliably regular GLS clientele.

Felice Caffé Rua Gomes Carneiro 30, Ipanema (see p.188). More than a café, this is open till midnight for food, drinks and ice cream, and draws a mixed crowd.

Miam Miam Rua General Góes Monteiro 34, Botafogo (see p.185). Excellent restaurant and bar attracting a very mixed, arty crowd, with imaginative cocktails.

To Nem Aí Rua Farme de Amoedo 57, Ipanema. Head to this hip bar for post-beach or pre-club drinks as well as great fast food in a friendly environment.

Up Turn Bar Av. Américas 2000, Barra da Tijuca ☎21/3387-7957. Rapidly becoming a trendy gay spot for outdoor food and drink, sometimes with live DJs. Accessed from a supermarket car park.

Nightlife

00 (Zero Zero) Gávea ⊛www.00.com.br (see p.203). Sunday night (from 10pm) here is probably Rio's smartest gay night, with a great music selection, patio and attached fine-dining restaurant.

1140 Rua Capitão Menezes 1140, Praça Seca, Jacarepaguá, Zona Oeste ☎21/3017-1792, ⊛www.boite1140.com.br. This friendly, inclusive GLS club is busiest on Fridays and attracts up to 1200 people. Eclectic ambience and music, including electronic, samba, funk, MPB and live *pagode* over six floors. From 11pm.

Le Boy Rua Raul Pompéia 102, Copacabana ☎21/2513-4993, ⊛www.leboy.com.br. Though suffering since the opening of *The Week*, Le Boy is still popular. It has three dance floors, drag and go-go boy shows, dark room and gay baths. Electronic and pop music. Nightly except Mon, from 11pm.

Cabaré Casanova Rua Mem de Sá 25, Lapa ☎21/2221-6555. Behind a pink facade a short way east from the Arcos, Rio's oldest and most interesting gay bar has been in business since 1929 – in large part due to their infamous drag shows. Lambada, samba and dance music are played as ceiling fans cool down the frenetic dancers. Wed–Sun, from 11pm.

Casa da Lua Rua Barão da Torre 240, Ipanema ☎21/3813-3972. A small lesbian bar/club serving excellent cocktails including *batidas* (made with *cachaça* and fresh fruit juices). Open for lunch/dinner and until 3am.

Cine Ideal Rua da Carioca 62, Praça Tiradentes, Centro ☎21/ 2221-1984, ⊛cineideal.com.br. Huge converted cinema hosting young and wild GLS parties Saturday (and occasional other) nights, from 11pm. The R$35 entrance includes an open bar, with predictably messy results. Large balcony, non-stop house music and occasional drag shows.

La Cueva Rua Miguel Lemos 51, Copacabana ☎21/2267-1364, ⊛www.boatelacueva.com. This classic introduction to Rio's more traditional gay scene has been open since 1964. Popular with older men – and their younger partners. 1960s, 1970s and 1980s music. Tues–Sun, from 10pm.

Dama de Ferro Rua Vinicius de Moraes 288, Ipanema ☎21/2247-2330, ⓦwww.damadeferro .com.br. Trendy spot *Dama de Ferro* is part-smart club, part-art gallery/lounge, almost exclusively playing dance music to a hip male and female crowd. Wed–Sun, from 10pm.

Fosfobox Rua Siquiera Campos, Copacabana ⓦwww.fosfobox.com.br (see p.202). This basement GLS club attracts a gay crowd on certain nights – check the website. From 11pm.

Galeria Café Teixeira de Melo 31, Ipanema ☎21/2523-8250, ⓦwww .galeriacafe.com.br. A tiny yet popular club, especially Thursdays with pop classics on the turntables (from 11pm). Funkily decorated with temporary art exhibitions; Wednesday nights feature alternative theatre performances (from 10pm); Sunday's BAZAR has fashion shows by local designers (11am–8pm).

La Girl Rua Raul Pompéia 102, Copacabana ☎21/2513-4993, ⓦwww.lagirl.com.br. Rio's biggest lesbian club attracts a young crowd and features two dance floors, podium dancers and an eclectic music policy. Partitions with Le Boy are removed late at night on weekends. Nightly except Tues, from 11pm.

Papa G Travessa Almerinda Freitas 42, Madureira ☎21/2450-1253, ⓦwww.papag .com.br. The most famous GLS club in the north of the city is near two big samba schools but a good hour from the Zona Sul. The street outside fills with makeshift bars and a cross-section of the northern GLBT scene on weekend nights, while inside anything-goes – go-go boys/girls, drag shows, house and techno music. From midnight.

Star Club/Buraco da Lacraia Rua André Cavalvanti 58, Lapa ☎21/2242-0446, ⓦwww .buracodalacraia.com. Mainly famous for its nude waiters, the *Star Club* has a dark room and regular drinks promotions – known as a place to go if you're cruising. From 11pm.

The Week Centro ⓦwww.theweek.com .br (see review on p.201). This immensely popular São Paulo club has opened up a branch in Rio, with Saturday here Rio's biggest gay night – house music for a young crowd and a pool on the lower floor. Women pay almost double (R$70) to get in. From midnight.

Pride and Carnaval

Rio's **Gay Pride** event is growing in stature and usually takes place during the second weekend in October. The grand parade through Copacabana draws well over 100,000 people, and there's a "Gay Day" of theatre, film and music in many city locations – check the websites and newspapers listed above for more details.

The **samba school** with the largest GLBT participation is **Unidos da Tijuca** (Av. Francisco Bicalho 47, São Cristovão ☎21/2516-2749, ⓦwww .unidosdatijuca.com.br), whose base *(quadra)* close to Rio's *rodoviária* holds lively samba events from November through February in the run up to Carnaval. **Portela samba school** in Madureira (see p.215) also has larger-than-average gay participation. The **Scala Gay GLS Party**, usually held on the Tuesday of Carnaval (Av. Afrânio de Melo Franco 296, Leblon ☎21/2239-4448, ⓦwww .scalario.com.br), is the most vibrant **gay ball** in Rio, with food, drink, bands and a lively stage show with numerous drag artists. Other grand balls are held at nightclubs *Le Boy* and *La Girl*.

Among Rio's dynamic Carnaval street parties, the legendary **Banda de Ipanema** normally meets twice on the Saturday and Tuesday of Carnaval at Praça General Osório, traditionally drawing drag artists and other costumed partiers, though in recent years it has grown to unmanageable proportions with crowds of hundreds of thousands. A better bet is the smaller, fun **bloco de Carmen Miranda**; look out for schedules in the media, though you'll need to get a decent hat.

Origins

Attitudes – both legal and social – in Rio towards homosexuality have, since colonial times, been complex and contradictory. Under the Portuguese, acts of homosexuality were officially classified as "vile, dirty and dishonest", against the teachings of the Catholic Church and punishable by death. With independence, the Brazilian government sought to distance itself from the Church – a new legal framework was introduced and in 1830 sodomy was **decriminalized**.

By the end of the nineteenth century a rich homosexual subculture had developed in Rio, with **Praça Tiradentes** appropriated by men seeking sex with other men. The praça's central location and accessibility encouraged the development in neighbouring Lapa of new theatres, music halls, cabarets, bars and cafés, as well as boarding houses catering to single men and brothels. Wealthy men would visit Lapa to mingle, beyond the gaze of family, with others of like-minded sexual interests. The **masked balls** of the elite had long given free licence to fancy dress, while Carnaval, enabling people to temporarily free themselves of the constraints of class, race and gender, allowed for cross-dressing, and drag artists became major stars in Bohemian Rio. If you're looking for a tour highlighting Rio's gay history, **Carlos Roquette**, a rather dapper former federal judge turned tour guide, can also help you to explore (☎21/3322-4872, ⓦwww.culturalrio.com.br).

Around Rio

In the state of Rio de Janeiro beyond the city, gay life generally follows a more typical Brazilian pattern of enforced discretion. To escape ridicule or hostility, gay men and women have long flocked to the city of Rio from other parts of the state (and, indeed, Brazil more widely), attracted by social acceptance and a freely expressed gay culture. That said, the beaches and resorts that dot the coast of Rio are popular with gay visitors, with **Búzios** (see p.147), on the Costa do Sol, and **Paraty** (see p.153), on the Costa Verde, being the prime attractions.

Pretty-well all of Búzios's *pousadas*, restaurants, bars and nightclubs are gay-friendly because of the liberal, Bohemian and cosmopolitan nature of the resort. The more luxurious of the *pousadas*, in particular *Pérola Búzios Design* (see p.149), usually have a high proportion of gay visitors. Only the elegant *Our House* (☎22/2623-1913, ⓦwww.ourhouse.com; R$190) at Rua J-II Lote 14, Praia da Ferradura, caters exclusively to gay (largely lesbian) guests. During the daytime the nudist beach **Olho de Boi** is especially popular with gay sun seekers, while at night the bar and disco *Deep* at Rua das Pedras 27, attracts a largely gay crowd.

Entertainment in Paraty is much more low-key. Curiously for such a gay-friendly place (it had one of Brazil's first out-gay mayors), Paraty has no exclusively gay *pousadas* or bars. While gay guests are unlikely to feel uncomfortable at any of Paraty's *pousadas*, a few excellent places owned and managed by gay men are exceptionally hospitable, notably *Vivenda*, *Bambu Bamboo* and *Vila Volta* which is far simpler and more secluded (see p.155).

14

Carnaval

From the Friday before Ash Wednesday to the following Thursday, Rio shuts up shop and throws itself into **Carnaval** – the world's most famous manifestation of unbridled hedonism. In a city riven by poverty, Carnaval represents a moment of freedom and release, when the aspirations of *Cariocas* can be expressed in music and song. This intense energy and the creativity it generates ensure that the celebrations never become stale.

If you thought Carnaval in Rio de Janeiro was just a three-day affair, think again. Its status as the most important celebration on the Brazilian calendar – easily outstripping either Christmas or Easter – entails preparing more or less the whole year in advance, and energetic events take place in Rio's *escolas do samba* (samba schools) from September through to the main event in February or early March. Carnaval is celebrated in all of Brazil's cities, but Rio's party is the most extravagant.

There are many elements to enjoy, most notably the all–night grand *desfiles* (parades) of the **samba schools** at the **Sambódromo** – Rio's purpose-built parade ground – without doubt the greatest theatrical show on Earth. But in the long run up to the main event there are also *bailes* (dances and balls) both at samba schools' *quadras* (home buildings) and at other venues across the city. The other central ingredient is **Carnaval da Rua**, where thousands of revellers enjoy giant organized street parties, which take place all over the city. For more information about any aspect of Carnaval, try Ⓦ www.ipanema.com/carnival or Ⓦ www.rio-carnival.net.

Carnaval dates

Carnaval is a pre-Lenten celebration revolving around Easter, so the dates change each year. Below are the **official dates** of the four main days of festivities from Saturday to Tuesday until 2014 – though celebrations are intense for a week before-hand and continue unabashed until the Sunday after.

2010 February 13–16
2011 March 5–8
2012 February 18–21
2013 February 9–12
2014 March 1–4

A short history of Carnaval in Rio

The influences that have shaped modern Carnaval stretch back through a combination of European and African traditions. Stemming from the Latin *carne vale* meaning "farewell to the flesh", it directly relates to Christian preparations for **Lent**, an indulgence in pleasures of the flesh in advance of forty days of fasting and frugality. Carnaval in Rio can be traced back to a fifteenth-century tradition of Lenten revelry in the Azores, which caught on in Portugal and was exported to Brazil. Celebrations of **music** and **dance** combined with the French tradition of **masquerade balls**, where nobles would dress as their servants or men as women, and the poor as royalty. By the mid-nineteenth century anarchy reigned in Rio's streets for four days and nights, the festivities often so riotous that they were formally abolished in 1843; this edict was nonetheless ignored and removed under popular pressure – to this day street celebrations remain the most accessible and widely enjoyed feature of Carnaval.

The elite's balls (*bailes*) continued throughout the ban, later including grand **masked processions** with carriages decorated in allegorical themes. Rio's masses, who were denied admission to the *bailes*, had their own music, *jongo*, and street celebrations were reinforced through Zé Pereira bands, named after the Portuguese tambor that provided the basic musical beat. Zé Pereira bands morphed into organized groups of *ranchos* (bands of revellers), a structure that today's samba schools are partly a legacy of. They introduced a more disciplined approach: marching to string and wind instruments, wearing costumes and appointing people to coordinate different aspects of the parade, such as flag-bearers and opening presentations called *abre alas*. It was Afro-Brazilian migrants from Bahia, living in the poor areas west of Centro, who were generally credited with the invention of samba at the turn of the century (see p.260). Spiritualist ceremonies in Candomblé and Macumba religious cults comprised trance-inducing syncopated drums, dancing and singing – and led to similar music being composed specifically for Carnaval. The composer Chiquinho Gonzaga wrote *Pelo Telefone*, the first recorded samba piece in 1917.

Costumed street celebration came together with samba music in the 1920s as groups of organizers across Rio's new suburbs sought out greater sophistication and competition with the *sambistas* and *ranchos* of other *bairros*. The first **samba school**, Deixa Falar, was formed in 1928 in the *bairro* of Estácio – close to where samba was born – though it disbanded a few years later. Distant industrial areas Madureira and Oswaldo Cruz also became hotbeds of **bloco** activity in the 1920s, leading to the foundation of what would later be called Portela samba school. It was in fact the sports journal *Mundo Esportivo* that in 1932 first informally judged the parading schools, declaring Estação Primeira Mangueira the winner. The judging format was officially adopted the following year. Today Portela, champions 21 times, hold the record number of titles, though they last won in 1984.

The format has remained virtually unchanged since the early 1930s, except for a 1960s resurgence of street *blocos* or *bandas*; these processions today still eschew style, discipline and prizes and give themselves up to the most traditional element of Carnaval – street revelry. Since 1984, the major parades have taken place in the Sambódromo, a purpose-built street parade ground designed by master architect **Oscar Niemeyer**. Stretching for 1700m and able to accommodate 88,000, it is built on the spot where the very first samba sessions allegedly took place; most *Cariocas* still refer to the Sambódromo parades by the road it was built along, the Sapucaí.

Samba schools and Carnaval rehearsals

Samba schools each represent a different neighbourhood and are divided into three leagues that vie for top ranking following the annual Carnaval parades. The **Grupo Especial** (top league) schools parade in the Sambódromo on the Sunday and Monday nights of Carnaval, the **Grupo de Acesso** (Grupo A) schools on the Saturday night before, and the smaller **Grupo B** schools parade on Tuesday, though with very small crowds attending. Additionally, the **children's parade** takes place on the Friday evening beforehand, and on the Saturday after Carnaval, the **Desfile de Campeõs** gives you another chance to see the six top-ranking schools from the Grupo Especial.

Schools' preparations start in the year preceding Carnaval, when thousands of supporters are mobilized to create complex costumes and floats. A theme is chosen, music written and costumes designed, while the Carnavelesco, the school's director, choreographs the dances. By Christmas, the individual samba songs are recorded and released to record stores. If you're not in town for Carnaval, don't worry; the city's most memorable nights out are at samba schools' rehearsals (*ensaios*) held at their home buildings (*quadras*), often at the edge of *favelas* in the Zona Norte (R$5–30), from August to February/March. These are in effect more like big late-night parties with dancing, drumming and other live music. After New Year, they get packed solid and prices rise; try to go to one on its advertised mid-week night (see below) or on a Sunday afternoon for a **feijoada**, a food-themed event with live music and dance. The schools closest to the Zona Sul – hence attracting a more middle-class and touristy crowd – are Salgueiro, Mangueira and Unidos da Tijuca (the latter a gay favourite), though Vila Isabel, Rocinha and São Clemente are also easily accessible from the hotel districts. Tour companies like Rio Hiking (see p.239) also visit most schools on request. Beija Flor and Portela in particular have great atmospheres and stage some of the classiest performances. Check schools' websites for rehearsal agendas, and if in doubt telephone.

As Carnaval approaches (Dec–Feb/March) there are also timetabled daily technical rehearsals (*ensaios técnicos*) at the Sambódromo itself, where schools practise parading with a small crowd in the stands. They're free to enter and great fun; see the league of samba schools website ⓦ www.liesa .com.br for schedules, and practicalities (below) for transport details.

The following are a selection of schools from across the first two *grupos*, and host events from August to February; check individual websites for details:

Beija-Flor Rua Pracinha Wallace Paes Leme 1025, Nilópolis ⓣ 21/2791-2866, ⓦ www .beija-flor.com.br. Since the late 1990s this school has won the most Carnaval titles – it also has some of the city's most vibrant rehearsals, usually Saturdays or Thursdays.

Império Serrano Av. Ministro Edgard Romero 114, Madureira ⓣ 21/2489-8722, ⓦ www .imperioserrano.com. A large, traditional school with lively rehearsals, but in recent years it has dropped to the second tier.

Mangueira Rua Visconde de Niterói 1072, Mangueira ⓣ 21/2567-4637, ⓦ www .mangueira.com.br. A very popular school with a strong and successful history; Saturday night sessions here resemble more nightclub than samba school, but are excellent fun.

Portela Rua Clara Nunes 81, Madureira ⓣ 21/3390-0471, ⓦ www.gresportela.com.br. One of the oldest schools, with a lively monthly daytime event and regular Wednesday and Friday night sessions.

Rocinha Rua Bertha Lutz 80, São Conrado ⓣ 21/3205-3318, ⓦ www.academicosdarocinha .com.br. The closest school to the Zona Sul beaches, Rocinha has been in the second tier for many years but has good Saturday night rehearsals.

Salgueiro Rua Silva Telles 104, Tijuca ⓣ 21/2238-5564, ⓦ www.salgueiro.com.br. One of the biggest and most successful schools, winning most recently in 2009, they often incorporate circus troupes into their act. Their Saturday and Tuesday night events are among the very best, and the venue is easily accessible.

São Clemente Av. Presidente Vargas 3102, Cidade Nova, Centro ℡21/4104-4866 ⓦwww .saoclemente.com.br. Located close to the Sambódromo, this school has grown quickly and moved regularly between the top two tiers. Rehearsals take place on Tuesdays and Fridays.

Unidos da Tijuca Clube Dos Portuários, Av. Francisco Bicalho 47, São Cristóvão ℡21/2263-9836, ⓦwww.unidosdatijuca.com.br. A

centrally-located old samba school with imaginative presentations; the venue is especially popular with gay men at weekends.

Vila Isabel Av. 28 De Setembro 382, Vila Isabel ℡21/2578-0077, ⓦwww.gresunidosdevila isabel.com.br. Title winners in 2006, this is another very accessible venue, yet receives fewer Zona Sul visitors than Salguiero/ Manguiera for its Saturday rehearsals.

The Sambódromo

The best way to experience the Sambódromo's atmosphere is to parade with a **school**. All those listed above sell costumes, which are needed to take part, though prices for those in the Grupo Especial tend to cost upwards of R$400 – much more if you want a place on a float (*carro alegórico*). You can contact the schools directly or go through the websites listed above, although with the latter you'll pay a commission. You'll need to attend a few practices at either the school's neighbourhood venue (*quadra*) or at the **Cidade do Samba** (see p.67), as well as learn the relevant **anthem** sung repeatedly throughout the parade. Of course, it also helps to learn some decent samba moves – options are listed on p.206.

Some 50,000 people take part in the spectacular **parades** – and schools compete to gain maximum points for their presentations, a mix of song, story, dress, dance and rhythm. Each school must parade for between 60 and 80 minutes, and judges allocate points both on overall performance and enthusiasm, as well as the schools' separate parts, or *alas*, each containing hundreds of

Understanding the parades

Regardless of the theme adopted by an individual samba school, all include certain basic elements within their performances – factors on which they're judged. The **bateria** is the percussion section, which sustains the cadence that drives the school's song and dance. The **samba enredo** is the music, the **enredo** (theme) the accompanying story or lyric. The **harmonia** refers to the degree of synchronicity between the *bateria* and the dance by the thousands of **passistas** (samba dancers). The dancers are conducted by the **pastoras** who lead by example. The **evolução** refers to the quality of the dance, the choreography of which is judged on its spontaneity, the skill of the *pastoras* and the excitement the display generates. **Fantasias** (costumes) too, are judged on their originality. The **carros alegóricos** are the gigantic, richly decorated floats (no more than ten metres high and eight metres wide), which carry some of the **Figuras de Destaque** (prominent figures), who could be anyone from the school's community or even celebrities, while the **Porta Bandeira** (flag bearer), a woman who carries the school's symbol, is judged alongside her **Mestre-Sala**, the dance master who wows the crowds with complicated steps. The **Comissão da Frente**, traditionally a school's board of directors, marches at the head of the procession, a role often filled these days by guest TV stars or sports teams, and they're followed by an **abre alas**, an inventive choreography involving ten to fifteen people that hints at the school's theme and greets the audience. Each procession also includes an **Ala das Baianas** – hundreds of women dressed in round-skirted costumes and African-style headdresses typical of Salvador – in remembrance of the debt owed to the Bahian emigrants who introduced many of Carnaval's traditions.

▲ The Carnaval procession

costumed individuals linked to a part of the school's theme. The winning school gains a trophy, and a higher ranking in citywide league tables leads to a greater financial contribution from the government. Full nudity is not allowed at Carnaval, but many schools have women parading topless and both men and women wear costumes that leave little to the imagination. Samba schools cosset their top **Rainha** (samba queen) – whose elaborate dancing introduces the band and draws it forward – making sure they stay in shape for a gruelling schedule of parades, clubs and other appearances – all arenas in which their school may be judged in public. In the last decade or so, famous models and soap stars have taken up these glamorous roles, although a few schools are doing their best to choose queens from their own community. The Rio media follows the queens' every movement in advance of Carnaval, commenting on their dancing, diet, costumes, schedules – and, of course, love life.

Practicalities

Tickets are available cheaply from the league of samba schools, **LIESA** (☎21/3213-5151, ⓦwww.liesa.com.br), though they usually sell out in December. Closer to the main event, you can buy them from ⓦwww.rio-carnival.net or at varying prices from travel agents in Rio – Elos Exchange Turismo, at Rua Djalma Ulrich 57 in Copacabana (☎21/3507-2102, ✉elos_exchange@hotmail.com) is a reliable agent with competitive prices – but don't be afraid to barter a little with any agent. Prices are 60 percent lower for Saturday night's parade of samba schools in the Grupo de Acesso; it's great fun but doesn't equate to the Grupo Especial parades on Sunday and Monday nights. **Seating options** vary enormously: the cheapest are the **arquibancadas** – high stands with unreserved seating of which the best with a reasonable view is Sétor 3 (from R$220), while sétors 4, 6 and 13 (from R$120) have restricted views and are barely worthwhile. **Frisas** are lower stands with ringside boxes (from R$4000 for groups of six) and waiter service, and **camarotes** are larger, exclusive boxes (from R$25,000 for eight people), with a private bar and often a DJ playing between each school's performance. Sétor 9 (*arquibancadas* and *frisas*) is reserved for foreign visitors (from R$500 per night). The **Sambódromo** is at Rua Marquês do Sapucaí, two of three blocks west of Central do Brasil **metrô** station on Avenida Presidente Vargas. If you're in an odd-numbered stand get off at Central metrô station, which is a ten-minute walk away; if you're in an even-numbered stand, continue to the Praça Onze stop and walk back eastwards for ten minutes to the entrance. Keep cameras hidden and be aware of your surroundings as you walk to and from the *metrô*; there's quite a lot of crime outside of the Sambódromo. Although the *metrô* runs all night through Carnaval, taxis are probably the easiest and safest way to arrive there. Arrive before 8pm for a decent seat in the *arquibancadas*. Sitting through the ten-hour show can be a real test of endurance unless you have a very tough backside – take a cushion or towel to soften the hard seat. *Cerveja*, soft drinks and hot dogs are served in each stand. A camera with a good zoom is essential if you want to take decent pictures.

Carnaval da Rua – blocos and bandas

Rio's street celebrations, known as **blocos** and **bandas**, are a great way to experience Carnaval outside of the Sambódromo – and it's hard not to enjoy yourself when surrounded by thousands of dressed-up and hyped-up party fanatics, with a *caipirinha* or two in hand. Led by small samba groups or schools that don't enter the official parade, these parties happen all over town, though the biggest are the day and evening processions that fill Avenida Rio Branco (go by *metrô* to Largo da Carioca or Cinelândia). Preferably dress up in a *fantasia* (costume) or at least an item of fancy dress (hat, feather boa or wings for example), to enter into the spirit of it all – even many of the most macho Brazilian men indulge in some none-too-serious cross-dressing. All buses and trains operate flat out to carry the hordes all over town; be prepared for crowds and pickpockets (consider keeping cash in hard-to-reach places like your shoe). Starting any time of day, from 8am to midnight, and lasting for between two and four hours, the popular *blocos* gather tens or even hundreds of thousands of followers. They all have a regular starting point, and some have set routes while others wander freely through the neighbourboods.

There are dozens of *blocos* in every *bairro* but the biggest of them all is the **Cordão de Bola Preta**, a historic parade centring on Cinelândia, which draws crowds of up to half a million on Saturday from 10am (most dressed in black and white). It's so big you'll be lucky to see any official *bloco* trucks at all, but there are also stages, and it engulfs half of Centro in street parties – a good place to base yourself is outside the *Bar Luiz* (see p.180) – if the Praça Floriano gets too hectic. The **Banda de Ipanema**, on Saturday and Tuesday afternoons, has also grown uncomfortably large, but it's still the biggest gay parade and often a real spectacle with hundreds of men in drag; it gathers behind Praça General Osório. Aside from these, some of the better smaller *blocos* include **Carmelitas de Santa Teresa**, which gathers at Largo das Neves, normally on Sunday and Wednesday, with an imaginatively-costumed, arty crowd; **Volta Alice** at Rua Alice in Laranjeiras, which attracts a reliably enthusiastic crowd from all surrounding *bairros*; **Bloco do Afroreggae** in Ipanema (and the week after Carnaval in Lapa), with a wider music choice; and the unmissable drum extravaganza of **Monobloco** (various days and times, Avenida Rio Branco and Lapa). Numerous other small and friendly *blocos* meet around Lapa every day during the Carnaval period.

Carnaval balls

Bailes de Carnaval (Carnaval balls) and other events really signal the start of festivities for many people, with warm-up sessions in the weeks preceeding the main event taking place in clubs and hotels. In Lapa, *Fundição Progresso* (see p.198) is a great venue to catch excellent *baterias* (samba schools' percussion groups) and dancers, while *Rio Scenarium, Democráticos* or *Estudantina* (see p.197) also have special events, with the latter two more geared towards practising your dancing. Carnaval balls are a strong tradition in the Zona Sul, starting late and getting progressively more raunchy as the night wears on. A continual samba beat supplied by live bands drives the festivities into the new day. Private clubs along the edge of Lagoa close to Leblon such as *Monte Libano* (☏21/3239-0032) or *ABB* host *bailes*, with groups from samba schools often appearing. At most of the balls elaborate **costumes** are the order of the day, brightening the already hectic proceedings; if you haven't got one – just dress reasonably smartly.

The grand **Magic Ball**, held at the *Copacabana Palace Hotel* (☏21/2545-8790; see p.103), attracts the international elite, as well as the locally rich and famous. For the privilege of joining in, expect to pay well over R$1000, with black tie, mask or luxurious costume obligatory. If you've got yourself a good costume but a little less money, other lavish balls worth checking out include the **Pão de Açúcar** (🌐www.veraodomorro.com.br lists events), a dramatic yet somewhat snobby venue. More raucous and exhibitionist affairs are held at *Rio Scala* at Av. Afrânio de Melo Franco 292, Leblon (☏21/2239-4448, 🌐www.scalario.com.br); their *baile* **Vermelho e Preto** (named after the colours of Rio's favourite football team, Flamengo) on the Friday of Carnaval is perhaps the most important and has developed a reputation as a no-holds-barred affair. Other balls are held each night here, including Tuesday's **Scala Gay** (see p.211). To reserve a table at any (R$300), go to the box office a few days before the event.

If you want to hear something other than samba, there are big Carnaval electronic music parties too, usually held at *Vivo Rio* (see p.197), the docks, at Marina da Glória (see p.201), or the atmospheric hilltop Morro da Urca, by Sugar Loaf mountain. Check the newspaper listings in Friday's *Globo* or *Jornal do Brasil* or the websites listed above for details.

The best option if you're in Rio outside of the Carnaval season – or just like the idea of an organized samba spectacle – is the Thursday night show at the **Cidade do Samba** in Centro (see p.196). While touristy, it's far more elaborate and authentic than Leblon's famous *Plataforma* (see p.200), with artists from major schools performing. You can also visit the Cidade do Samba in the daytime all year round to see the gigantic floats being constructed.

Festivals and events

t sometimes feels like you're in one perpetual festival in Rio de Janeiro, each weekend the streets are filled with thousands of people and many weeks of the year are marked by national or state holidays. *Cariocas* have an indomitable party spirit and need few excuses to spend a whole day dancing and drinking – usually complemented by a *churrasca* barbecue. Rio's residents also love fancy dress and performance; something they'll encourage in visitors, too.

The major event is, of course, **Carnaval**, the world's greatest theatrical spectacle. It is accompanied by riotous behaviour at balls and on the streets (see p.218) – preparations officially begin in August the previous year. Carnaval is followed in size and significance by **Reveillon**, the gigantic New Year's celebration that is centred on massive firework displays on Copacabana beach and engulfs much of the city in parties.

We've listed some of the festivals you may be aware of below, but Rio also offers a host of more unusual events appealing to most tastes – whether film, fashion, literature, sports or history. Experience travelling on trains with samba bands in each carriage carrying you to a frenzied party in a distant suburb, or a *favela* dance group performing a mix of samba and break-dancing to rapturous applause. Music (from choral to electronic and everything in between), dance and socializing are central to most events – creating a feast for the senses that few can resist.

January–February

Dia de São Sebastião Jan 20. One of the biggest annual Masses, where Rio's patron saint is celebrated. Singers and idol-bearers process from the *bairro* of Tijuca to the Nova Catedral Metropolitana, where the largest Mass takes place.

Carnaval dates vary between early Feb and early March, see p.213. Intense preparations culminate in the world's wildest and most famous party.

Rio Music Conference Feb/March ⓦwww.riomusicconference.com.br. If Carnaval has left you tired of samba, this new electronic music festival could be the perfect antidote. Top DJs and imaginative décor at venues across the city – including Marina da Glória.

March–April

Rio Circuit March/April ☎21/2707-6700, ⓦwww.fecierj.org.br. Rio's premier cycling event attracts thousands of spectators who watch cyclists tackle an exhausting circuit of mountains and beaches.

É Tudo Verdade (It's All True) Documentary Film Festival late March–early April, ☎11/3064-7485, ⓦwww.itsalltrue.com.br. Simultaneously held in São Paulo and Rio (venues include CCBB and Unibanco Arteplex, see p.207), the event showcases the best in Brazilian and international documentaries, often with hard-hitting political and cultural themes. **Dia do Índio mid-April ⊤21/2286-8899, ⓦwww .museudoindio.org.br, see p.94.** Held at the Museu do Índio in Botafogo, this artistic celebration of Brazil's indigenous peoples includes exhibitions, talks, food stalls, dance, crafts and children's events such as face painting and dancing.

May–June

Rio Boat Show mid-May ⊤11/2186-1000, ⓦwww.boatshow.com.br. Luxury speedboats and yachts are displayed at Marina da Glória to be shown off – and ideally sold. There's also an attractive regatta and races.
Rio das Ostras Jazz & Blues second week of June ⓦwww.riodasostrasjazzeblues.com. A short drive from Búzios, this annual jazz and blues festival draws thousands to see acts from across Brazil and the US.
Dia dos Namorados Valentine's Day, celebrated on June 12 in Brazil, is fully embraced. You'll find booked-out restaurants and special events for couples and singles in bars and clubs.
Rio Marathon late June ⓦwww.maratonadorio .com.br. Rio's biggest running event follows a flat course starting in Recreio and finishing at Aterro do Flamengo. A shorter half marathon and 6km family event also take place. If you're not up for the run, join the party atmosphere at Aterro do Flamengo and the Zona Sul beaches.
Festas de Junho Bonfires, folkloric dances and clothing from Brazil's Northeast are typical on the feast days of St Anthony (June 13), St John (June 24) and St Peter (June 29), often held in *favelas* in Santa Teresa, and across Zona Norte. The largest celebrations take place at the Feira Nordestina (see p.140).
Fashion Rio early June ⓦwww.fashionrio.com .br. Rio's premier fashion event, held at the Marina da Glória, showcases stylish local and international talent through catwalk shows and stands.

July–August

Parati International Literary Festival (FLIP) usually held in July ⓦwww.flip.org.br. Brazil's largest literary event draws an enthusiastic crowd and diverse international authors and musicians – past attendees have included Eric Hobsbawm, Salman Rushdie and Gilberto Gil (see p.155).
Portas Abertas mid-July ⓦwww.vivasanta.org .br. see p.75. Santa Teresa's resident artists open their studios for a major event showcasing their work. There's also a lively concurrent street party.
Grande Prêmio Brasil first Sun in Aug ⊤21/3534-9000, ⓦwww.jcb.com.br. The annual classic of the Brazilian horseracing calendar takes place at the Jockey Club in Gávea, watched by an enthusiastic crowd of thousands.
Dia de Nossa Senhora da Glória do Outeiro mid-Aug. The most appealing church in the Zona Sul celebrates its namesake Our Lady, with Mass, beautiful decorations lighting up the hilltop and a range of stalls, food and music in the streets of Glória.

September–October

Independence Day Sept 7. This national celebration is marked in Rio with a parade along Av. Presidente Vargas, starting at 8am at the Candelária church and finishing at Campo de Santana where independence was declared. Day-long sports and cultural events and parades are held city-wide.
Gay Pride mid-Oct. Rio's major GLBT event attracts a crowd of hundreds of thousands to its noisy street celebration. It includes queen-laden floats, outrageous costumes and a parade through Copacabana. Club events continue through the night at the Zona Sul's discos (see p.211).
Rio International Film Festival (Festival do Rio) late Sept–early Oct ⓦwww.cima.org.br. A hugely popular two-week event showcasing up to 200 mainstream and independent

films across the city's cinemas, with occasional screenings on Copacabana beach. A short-film festival of arthouse flicks runs concurrently.

Children's Day Oct 12. Brazil celebrates its children with activities in city libraries, parks and schools. There are special performances by and for kids in many of the city's theatres (see p.226).

Tim Music Festival late Oct; ⓦwww.timfestival .com.br. Rio's biggest music festival is held in the Marina da Glória and features local and international popular artists. Recent performers have included Kanye West, the Killers and Gilberto Gil.

November–December

Panorama de Danca early Nov; ⓦwww .panoramafestival.com. Rio's premier dance festival features a range of smaller contemporary dance groups from across the city, alongside foreign guest companies. Performances take place in the city's main theatres (particularly at cultural organization SESC's venues in Centro and Copacabana, see p.206) and on the streets.

Zumbi dos Palmares Nov 20. Masses, dances and other events dedicated to this eponymous semi-mythical escaped slave who battled for black rights, are held in *favelas* and churches, including at Centro's Igreja de Nossa Senhora do Rosário e São Benedito dos Homens Pretos (see p.61).

Festa de Igreja da Nossa Senhora de Penha mid–late Nov. The culmination of a month of festivities and sacrifices in honour of Our Lady takes place at this most famous of Zona Norte churches (see p.143). Pilgrims climb hundreds of steps up to the church,

on their knees if capable, swiftly following the pain with a long and emotional Mass.

National Day of Samba 2 Dec. This official celebration of samba is a highlight of the city's calendar. Packed trains loaded with samba musicians and partiers leave Central do Brasil train station every thirty minutes between 7 and 9pm for an unmissable night of festivities in the samba hotspot of Oswaldo Cruz. Check newspapers for details.

Christmas The day itself is a family affair in Rio, but the lighting of the giant Christmas tree placed in the middle of Lagoa during the first weekend of December is an enjoyable communal event; crowds gather for food, drink and music.

Reveillon and Festa de Iemanjá Dec 31. Rio's second biggest festival draws up to two million people to Copacabana beach for the ultimate in New Year's celebrations, which includes offerings to the Goddess of the Sea (see box below).

Reveillon and the Festa de Iemanjá

Rio's gigantic **New Year's Eve celebrations**, attracting millions of people from across Brazil and overseas, are undoubtedly one of the highlights of the city's calendar. While huge club events take place near Lagoa (such as at Jóquei Clube) or on the beach at Barra da Tijuca, the main location for the party is Copacabana beach. Top musicians perform on a large temporary stage and the impressive fireworks display (launched from barges off the coast) at midnight lasts nearly an hour.

The night is also the **Festa de Iemanjá** (*Yemanja*), a mother-goddess, who in *Umbanda* ritual (linked to the Afro-Brazilian faiths Candomblé and Macumba) merges with St Anne, the Catholic patron saint of the sea. Almost everyone in Copacabana is dressed head to toe in white. The colour white is an offering to *Iemanjá* to ensure good luck for the forthcoming year. In a twist of significance within popular culture, those wearing white are also supposed to wear different-coloured underwear to signify their wishes: red for passion, pink for love, yellow for financial success, green for youthfulness and black to be seduced by the unknown. More serious adherents to the faith place white flowers, paper requests, candles or white rice flour on tiny boats and send them out to the goddess in the hours preceding midnight; if you want to see this, get to Copacabana at sundown or take a trip out to the beaches at Barra and Recreio.

16

Kids' Rio

Rio is a very young and **child-friendly** city; despite its rightful claim to be one of the world's top party spots, it's also a great choice for families with many attractions and special events for children. The family in Brazil is seen as the centre of life, and children are usually included in whatever the adults are getting up to. While most cultural activities in the city welcome children, parents should check the age indication of any events beforehand – and telephone if in doubt. For some music and theatre performances, an under-16 or 18 age limit applies, and teenagers are occasionally refused entry to venues if alcohol is being served. For commercial concerts in the city's large venues, **age restrictions** are also quite common. There are no special health concerns for children in and around Rio.

In terms of **accommodation**, almost all options are child-friendly with the exception of a few boutique hotels and *pousadas* which don't accept kids under the age of 13 or 15 – check in advance. Many hotels allow young children to stay for free or have reasonably-priced babysitting services. Children are also welcome in all except the very smartest of **restaurants**, and the local tendency to eat leisurely and late applies as much to the younger generation as adults. It's certainly not uncommon to see kids' birthday parties finishing as late as midnight – perhaps good preparation for the vibrant city nightlife to come in later years.

If you're prepared to get a little off-the-beaten track – both within the Zona Sul and in Zona Oeste – there are some truly excellent kids' **activities** in Rio. Some of the best of the city's options for kids are listed here for more information including lists of **crèches** and **medical services**, see ⓦwww .kidsinrio.com.br. In terms of **transport**, if you don't have your own rented vehicle, negotiating daytime sights can be quite exhausting with or without children. It's possible to use bus services (listed on p.25) with kids, but you'll be best off avoiding rush hour times (8–10am and 4–7pm) when buses can be uncomfortably packed. A better bet is to take a taxi, which is relatively inexpensive. For tours and adventure attractions listed here, hotel pickups may well be possible; check in advance.

Indoor activities

Rio is blessed with an array of museums and centres offering well-designed, interactive displays which are ideal for a rainy day. One of the best is the **Fundação Planetaário** in Gávea (see p.117), which has childrens' sessions of space-related painting and design, as well as a solar observation room and a film on the planets and stars (6 years and over; afternoons twice weekly Mon–Sat; check in advance for exact times). Also on a scientific theme, the

Centro Oi Futuro in Flamengo (see p.87) has an excellent and highly interactive museum on communications and technology.

Children of all ages will love the 🎨 Museu do Indio in Botafogo (see p.94), whose artefacts, walk-through displays and hands-on painting and tattooing sessions provide an inspiring and educational experience. The **Museu do Folclore Edison Carneiro** (see p.86), located in Flamengo, will appeal to older children in a similar – though less interactive – way, with darkened rooms full of crafts, designs and folkloric characters from Brazil's interior. Even better for curious older children, however, is Zona Oeste's **Museu Casa do Pontal** (see p.134), where thousands of folkloric figures – some life-sized – are inventively displayed, including a five-metre-long moving imitation Carnaval parade.

Some of Rio's more traditional museums also make a creative effort at engaging young people; the **Museu Nacional** in São Cristovão (see p.138) has life-sized models of dinosaurs and fascinating artefacts relating to indigenous peoples and ancient civilizations, including Egyptian mummies, and the **Museu Naval** in Centro (see p.52) is good for older children, with displays of model boats through the centuries, cannon balls and push-button panels illustrating naval battles.

Outdoor activities

In a city of beaches, mountains, forests and lakes, there are enough outdoor trips and sports to keep even the shortest attention span occupied – including **boat trips**, **kayaking**, **climbing**, **surfing**, and **adventure playgrounds**. The most child-friendly **beaches** are at Leblon (postos 11–12) and to a lesser extent Arpoador (posto 7), though the latter gets especially crowded at weekends.

Parks and adventure playgrounds

Rio de Janeiro's **parks** range from landscaped gardens to the mighty **Tijuca forest** and from the **ecological parks** of the Zona Oeste to **adventure playgrounds**.

One of the most child-friendly parks is **Lagoa** (see p.112), which has a surrounding walkway and pedal boats for hire at its southeastern corner close to Copacabana and Ipanema. On the hillside nearby, **Parque da Catacumba** (ⓦwww.lagoa aventuras.com.br; Tues–Sun, 8am–6pm; R$25–50) has a zip line, canopy walkway and offers indoor and outdor climbing for kids; hotel pickups are available.

Cachoeiras (waterfalls) and pools can be found at **Jardim Botânico** and **Parque Lage** (see p.115) – especially appealing due to their rainforest location within the Zona Sul (the latter also has a small playground; remember to apply insect repellent on or near waterfalls as there is a low risk of dengue fever from mosquitoes). **Parque do Catete** (p.86) and **Parque Eduardo Guinle** (see p.90) are both attractive and central parks with play areas (the latter also has tricycles available for hire); **Bairro Peixoto** in Copacabana (p.104) also has a good playground for younger children.

Rio's more adventurous options include the amazing **Parque da Tijuca** which has a variety of hiking possibilities and waterfalls (see p.123), and the **Floresta Aventura** – located between São Conrado and Barra (open daily; R$35 for one course, R$50 for two; over 6's only; book in advance; ☎21/3390-5613, ⓦwww.florestaventura .com) – which offers two different hour-long obstacle courses including zip lines, tunnels, and walkways mounted in the tree tops. Rio's one and only water park, **Rio Water Planet,** makes a great day out (10am–6pm; R$25–60; Estrada dos Bandei-rantes, Vargem Grande, ☎21/2428-9000, ⓦwww.riowaterplanet.com;); and the large and beautiful park **Quinta da Boa Vista**, also home to **Rio Zoo** (close to Centro at São Cristovão), has a lake and playground to entertain children (see p.138).

▲ A young shopper at the Feira Nordestina

Leblon beach offers amenities for children at the **Baixo Bebe** (Ⓦwww
.baixobebeleblon.com.br), a beach play area for small children, and **beach
volleyball** classes at any number of schools (postos 10-12), who tend to offer
lessons at around 10am. If your children are interested in **football**, most
evenings from 5pm close to posto 3 in Copacabana, a five-a-side beach soccer
school run by former professionals Juninho and Robertinho has practice
matches for teenagers, though they'll need to be reasonably nifty with the ball
– arrange with the organizers if you want to take part.

At all beaches be aware of waves and a strong undertow, most are not perfect
for **swimming**; Arpoador alone is a little more sheltered. Another alternative is
to head out to Rio's best and most beautiful beach, **Grumari** (see p.134), west
of Recreio and a good hour's drive from the Zona Sul. The far end of the beach
is calmer and more sheltered, with swimming possible at the mouth of the river.
Rio's numerous parks offer a variety of activities (see opposite).

If you're looking for a more cultural experience, older children will enjoy the
sights, sounds and smells of the giant market **Feira Nordestina** at São
Cristovão (see p.140). Its stalls sell bric-a-brac, foods, crafts and clothing, and
there's live music to add to the lively atmopshere.

Boat trips The Espaço Cultural da Marinha in
Centro (see p.56) offers trips on mock-
historic boats around the islands in
Guanabara Bay that are very popular for
local school trips. The centre also has a
docked submarine where kids can indulge
their underwater fantasies. The Cagarras
islands just off the Zona Sul coast also
make an enjoyable trip from either Urca or
the Marina da Glória, with quiet (tiny)
beaches ideal for a *churrasca* before
returning home. Contact operator Rafael
Tavares (☎21/7858-3768 Ⓔrafael
.oliveiratavares@gmail.com) or speedboat
operator Macuco Adventure (☎21/2205-
0390, Ⓦwww.macucorio.com.br).

Bowling A very popular 20-lane centre is
located at Barra Shopping (☎21/2431-
9566, Ⓦwww.barrabowling.com.br;
noon–late).

Capoeira Classes for young children (aged
3 upwards) are offered at Brincadeira de
Capoeira (Rua Piratininga, Gávea,
☎21/2279-6298).

Ice skating Available from 2pm daily at mall Shopping Barra Garden (☎21/3151-3354, ⓦwww.patinacaonogelo.com.br).

Kayaking, hiking and climbing Day, half-day, and tailor-made family itineraries are offered by Rio Hiking (see p.239), including around Guanabara Bay, the Parque da Tijuca and further afield.

Surfing and kitesurfing Barra and Recreio are the best places for lessons: K08 (☎21/2494-4869 ⓦwww.k08.com.br;)

offers surfing lessons for ages 5 upwards and kitesurfing for teens upwards; located close to posto 3 in Barra, in front of Av. do Pepê 900. Lessons for older children are also offered at Praia do Pepino in Recreio, see ⓦwww.riosurfnstay.com for details. In the Zona Sul, visit the various surf shops inside mall Galaria River (Rua Francisco Otaviano 67, Arpoador) for details of lessons closer to the city centre.

Kids' Carnaval

Children often get involved in **Carnaval** at a young age (from 4 or 5) in Rio: the official **Junior Parade** is held at the Sambódromo on the Friday evening before the main event – and is free to watch – check with RioTur for details (☎21/2271-7000, ⓦwww.riodejaneiro-turismo.com.br). Taking part is an amazing experience for children who like dressing-up and dancing, though you will need to link up with a samba school at least two weeks in advance of the main event to get a costume and practise parading (see p.215).

A lower-key option for dressing-up in a self-made costume and dancing is at a children's street **bloco** in the lead up to Carnaval; these draw big crowds of kids in face paint and fancy dress, following a float along the street. These events can happen anywhere, but there are always *blocos* in Ipanema and Copacabana – check with RioTur. The Saara market (see p.62) is the perfect place to buy clothing and sequins to create your own outfit. If Carnaval all gets a bit too much, huge kids' parties are held at the Hard Rock Café in Barra (Shopping Cittá América, Av. das Américas 700, ⓦwww.hardrock.com), with football and games.

If you're not in town during the main event, children will enjoy a trip to the **Cidade do Samba** (☎21/2213-2503; see p.67), where you can see giant Carnaval characters and floats under construction throughout the year. Guided tours and workshops where you can learn to play samba instruments are also occasionally put on; call in advance for a schedule.

Theatre

Lots of *Carioca* kids get involved in theatre – especially the under-10s – and there are numerous **children's shows** held on weekends at Teatro de Leblon or in Gávea. The "Infantil" page in newspaper *Globo*'s "Segundo Caderno" supplement has all the latest goings-on, and website ⓦwww.brincandoporaqui.com.br is an excellent **what's on** guide for kids' theatre and circus. As mime and slapstick are typical, language is rarely a problem. The Centro Cultural Banco do Brasil (see p.56) also has a programme for children featuring drama alongside other activities, it's usually held on Saturday or Sunday afternoons – these events are geared more to Portuguese speakers, however.

Shopping

As a sophisticated, modern city, it's hardly surprising that Rio offers a wealth of **shopping** possibilities. Whether you're in search of a pair of **Havaianas** or an unusual piece of modernist furniture, you'll find something to remind you of your visit. There are **souvenir shops** geared to tourists (most of which specialize in inexpensive semi-precious stones, mounted piranha fish and T-shirts) throughout the city, and on the beaches **hawkers** offer inexpensive, sometimes very attractive, *kangas* (beach wraps). For more sophisticated purchases visit one of Rio's vast shopping **malls**, **craft markets** or upscale **Zona Sul boutiques,** where *Cariocas* enjoy shopping. If you want to avoid mainstream souvenirs, traditional ceramics, prints and other Brazilian crafts can be found, alongside interesting modern designer pieces. Thanks to the dynamic local music scene, **CDs** that may be impossible to find outside of Brazil are great purchases, and Rio's relatively few, but excellent, **bookshops**, are good places to browse. **Food and drink** also make distinctive purchases, whether it be top-quality *cachaça*, an unusual wine from the south of the country, or locally produced tropical fruit jams and preserves.

Rio is second to none when it comes to **beachwear**, while the choice of casual clothes is sometimes impressive too. Bear in mind, though, that in terms of most areas of fashion, Rio displays the effects of globalization as explicitly as in London or New York , and prices for most items of clothing here are considerably higher, while quality is usually lower.

When it comes to **payment**, credit cards are widely accepted although some shops may give you a discount for using cash. As **ATMs** are almost always close to hand, for smaller purchases you'd be wise to pay with **cash** as your card's issuer is likely to apply a fixed charge for its use abroad. Some tourist-oriented shops accept dollars but be cautious about the rate of exchange that's being offered. As everything related to **electronics**, cameras and computers – even digital photo cards and memory sticks – are extremely expensive in Brazil, be sure to bring anything that you may need with you.

Beauty products and fragrances

Lying amongst the toned, waxed, bronzed and beautiful bodies soaking up the sun of Ipanema beach, you may well ask yourself how such beauty is attainable. Agreed, Brazilians just look good anyway, but it's not effortless. They spend hours at gyms and **beauty parlours** (*salões de beleza*) each week and, perhaps unsurprisingly, the beauty industry is the fastest-growing sector of the Brazilian economy. *Beleza* is a Brazilian national pastime – and Rio's Zona Sul is the centre of it. What's more, trimming, waxing, pedicures and the like aren't seen

SHOPPING | Beauty products and fragrances

ly for women. Every Brazilian woman has their favourite *salão*
visit for treatments ranging from a *depilação de virilha* (bikini wax)
(manicure or pedicure), but many men regularly visit *salões* too.
ny in every *bairro*, though quality and cost vary.

Pello Menos Ⓦ www.pellomenos.com.br. A very reliable, mid-range option, with salons across the Zona Sul and short waiting-times. There are branches at Rua Visconde de Pirajá 318 in Ipanema and Rua Siqueira Campos 50 in Copacabana, and an exclusively male *salão*, Poko Pello, on the 13th floor of Rua Siqueira Campos 53.

Werner Coiffeur Rua Barata Ribeiro 764, Copacabana, Rua Dias Ferreira 228, Leblon; Ⓦ www.wernercoiffeur.com.br. If you want higher-level treatment and service, try Werner Coiffeur. Most of its *salões* stay open untill 7 or 8pm Mon–Sat.

Stores

O Boticario Ⓦ www.oboticario.com.br. Although this massively successful chain has positioned itself as Brazil's answer to the Body Shop, the perfumes, soaps, lotions, shampoos and other products are overly scented and rarely authentically Brazilian. That said, the prices are quite modest and

you may find something appealing. There are dozens of branches in Rio, including at most malls.

Chammada da Amazônia Shopping Rio Sul, Botafogo Ⓦ www.chammadaamazonia.com.br. Eco-friendly lotions and fragrances made with fruits, herbs, essential oils and seeds sourced from remote communities in the Amazon region. Attractively packaged, the products' colours and smells are fantastic.

Espaço Kurä Le Monde Office, Avenida das Americas 3500, Barra da Tijuca ☎ 21/32825133. Seek out this exciting range of natural soaps and essential oils by Karina Araújo, Rio's most talented aromatherapist, either at her own store in Barra or at homeopathic pharmacies such as Caminhoá, Rua Visconde de Caravelas 1, Botafogo.

Ms Divine Rua Visconde de Itaboraí 6, Centro. Located in one of the most charming of the narrow roads and alleys behind the Arcos de Teles, this wonderful perfumery sells its own range of scents, soaps, shower gels and lotions, all of which are locally produced from natural ingredients.

Books and magazines

Although Rio has some excellent bookshops, for a city of its size and significance, since the reading public has traditionally been small and books are considered to be expensive, there are relatively few. The quality of book production is generally high though, and beautifully illustrated coffee-table books on Brazilian art, nature and history make good souvenirs. Text in such books is quite often in English, as well as Portuguese.

Baratos da Ribeira Rua Barata Ribeiro 354, Copacabana Ⓦ www.baratosdaribeiro.com.br. A well-organised secondhand book store with an interesting selection of academic and mainstream titles on the tightly packed shelves. In addition, there's a varied collection of old records including hard-to-find Brazilian labels. Mon–Sat 9am–8pm, Sun 11am–4pm.

Letras e Expressões Rua Visconde de Pirajá 276, Ipanema Ⓦ www.letraseexpressoes.com.br. Though fairly small, Letras has a good choice of art and other coffee-table books, and Brazilian and foreign magazines and newspapers. Mon–Fri 8am–midnight, Sat 8am–2pm.

Livraria Argumento Rua Dias Ferreira 417, Leblon and other branches Ⓦ www.livraria argumento.com.br. A gathering point of writers and intellectuals since the military dictatorship, this bookshop is an important literary institution where you're likely to stumble on a book launch most evenings. Apart from a varied selection of titles, there's also a pleasant café serving light meals and cakes. Mon–Sat 9am–midnight, 10am–midnight.

Livraria da Travessa Rua Visconde de Pirajá 572, Ipanema and other branches Ⓦ www.travessa.com.br. One of the best bookshops in Brazil, it sells a fine range of art and coffee-table books on Brazilian subjects as well as English-language novels and travel guides. They also have a fairly

small, but carefully selected range including many by Brazilian artists excellent café. Mon–Sat 9am–m/ 11am–midnight.

Clothing and accessories

In keeping with Rio's relaxed, beach-oriented atmosphere, **fashion** – even at the designer end of the spectrum – is very much oriented towards the **informal** and is rather conventional. Styles are generally derivative of those in Europe and the US, with the exception of very distinctive **beachwear**, which can be found in stores selling casual clothes as well as in dedicated shops. You'll find very good selections of **clothes** and **accessories** shops in Rio's malls (see p.235) where pretty-well all the big-name brands (and many smaller ones) are represented. Alternatively, head for Ipanema's Rua Visconde de Pirajá which has branches of many of the same stores as those found in the likes of Rio Sul and Shopping Leblon, while on the side roads you'll come across independent boutiques selling more unusual items. There are also plenty of cheaper clothes shops in Copacabana and Centro, but the styles are typically functional.

Accessories and shoes

Amazon Life Rua Visconde de Pirajá, 2nd floor, Ipanema Ⓦ www.amazonlife .com.br. Amazon Life sells rugged-looking, yet stylish, bags – including tote bags, courier bags and handbags – made with natural rubber from the Amazon rainforest, jute, untreated cotton and other natural products.

Constança Basto Shopping Leblon, Leblon Ⓦ www.constancabasto.com.br. Constança's admirers consider her the Manolo Blahnik of Brazil, and she produces similarly elegant, high-quality and expensive shoes. More casual (and slightly less costly) footwear is sold in the designer's Peach stores located in the São Conrado Fashion Mall, Shopping da Gávea and Rio Sul.

Gilson Martins Rua Visconde de Pirajá 462, Ipanema and other branches Ⓦ www.gilsonmartins.com.br. Brightly coloured bags and funky accessories, often featuring deliberately kitsch-looking iconic imagery (Sugar Loaf mountain, Christ the Redeemer and a *bonde* all feature) are the hallmark of this *Carioca* designer. Fairly expensive, though highly distinctive.

Mr. Cat Rua Visconde de Pirajá 414, Ipanema and other branches Ⓦ www.mrcat.com.br. Attractive, reasonable quality and not hugely expensive shoes are hard to find in Rio, but the Mr. Cat range offers pleasing, though fairly traditional, footwear for men and

women as well as selling handbags and belts with a similarly classic look. There are over 30 branches across Rio, including in most of the *shoppings*.

New Order Rio Sul Shopping and other branches Ⓦ www.neworder.com.br. A wonderful range of stylish, yet fun, canvas beach bags and tote-bags, handbags, women's sun hats and sandals.

▲ Havaianas

Ousadiario Rua Farme de Amoedo 76, Ipanema. ⓦwww.ousadiario.com.br. Although Havaiana sandals are easily found in Rio, surprisingly few stores stock the complete range. You'll find cheaper Havaianas elsewehere, but at Ousadiario you'll be able to select from all available colours and styles.

Soulier Rua Vinícius de Moraes 121, Ipanema and other branches. Handbags, women's belts and sandals with designs that convey a look of Rio: vibrant and both effortlessly casual and discreetly elegant.

Beachwear

Blue Man Fórum de Ipanema, Rua Visconde de Pirajá 351, Ipanema and other branches ⓦwww.blueman.com.br. Stylish swimwear with beautiful prints for men and women – *tangas* (string bikinis) and skimpy one-pieces for women and *sungas* for men.

Bum Bum Fórum de Ipanema, Rua Visconde de Pirajá 351, Ipanema and other branches ⓦwww.bumbum.com.br. Established in 1979, Bum Bum was the world's first specialist bikini store, its designers best known for having created the much-copied *fio dental* (dental floss) style. If you want to cover yourself up a bit, check out the *saídas de praia* (ultra lightweight long-sleeved beach shirts) and *kangas* (beach wraps).

Lenny Fórum de Ipanema, Rua Visconde de Pirajá 351, Ipanema and other branches ⓦwww.lenny.com.br. Lenny Niemeyer's chic range of women's swimwear has attracted considerable international attention, her approach being to cover just a tiny bit more skin than is typical locally! Lenny also produces a fine collection of bags, purses and other women's accessories.

Salinas Shopping Rio Sul, Botafogo and other branches. One of Rio's most admired bikini labels, it's amazing that such tiny items can be so stylish – beautiful cuts and lovely, high-quality fabrics.

Casual

Eclectic Leblon Shopping and other branches ⓦwww.eclectic.com.br. A chain of good-quality, but not too expensive, women's clothes that are stylish and youthful.

Hering Rua Visconde do Pirajá 401, Ipanema and other branches ⓦwww.hering.com.br. If you simply need a new T-shirt or shorts, you can do far worse than looking in a branch of Hering – a Brazilian institution for inexpensive and hard-wearing clothes for adult and kids, dating back decades.

Lojinha do Rio Shopping Rio Sul ⓦwww.lojinhadorio.com.br. Playful clothes and accessories featuring Rio imagery including T-shirts with silhouettes of the landscape, Carmen Miranda-inspired bags and racy underwear.

Osklen Rua Maria Quitéria 85, Ipanema ⓦwww.osklen.com. Originating in Búzios, Osklen makes chic designer sports and casual men's and women's wear. Expensive, but the quality of the fabrics match the originality of their very Brazilian designs.

Richards Rua Maria Quiteria 95, Ipanema and other branches ⓦwww.richards.com.br. Despite the name, Richards is an authentic, hugely successful *Carioca* brand of comfortable, smart men's and women's clothes. Although expensive, the quality cotton, linen and other fabrics wear extremely well – not always the case with Brazilian clothing.

Taco Jeans Shopping Rio Sul and other branches ⓦwww.taco.com. Brazil's immensely popular answer to Gap, featuring brightly-coloured, unsophisticated designs but hard-wearing and reasonably-priced clothes.

Track & Field Shopping Rio Sul, Botafogo and other branches ⓦwww.tf.com.br. A sporty, surfer look dominates here with a good choice of Bermudas, rather larger bikinis than typical for Rio, and light, loose-fitting dresses.

Children

I'm not a Baby Rua Visconde de Pirajá 414, Ipanema ⓦwww.imnotababy.com.br. This Rio brand is great for colourful T-shirts and dresses with amusing images and slogans aimed at babies (or, rather, their parents) and the under-8s.

Joana João Rua Visconde de Pirajá 525, Ipanema and other branches ⓦwww.joanajoao.com.br. Comfortable, hard-wearing and reasonably-priced Brazilian-made casual and smart clothes for kids under the age of 11.

Mercado Infantil Rua Visconde de Pirajá 287 and other branches ⓦwww.mercadoinfantil.com.br. Sports and beach wear for fashion-conscious *Carioca* kids.

Designer

Clube Chocolate São Conrado Fashion Mall ⓦwww.clubechocolate.com.br. This Rio outpost of an incredibly expensive São Paulo fashion emporium is largely devoted to major European names, interspersed with varied, though always classy, collections of guest Brazilian designers. Clothes, jewellery and, strangely, houseware are all sold here. There's also a very pleasant and, considering the surroundings, almost reasonably priced, French restaurant.

Contemporâneo Rua Visconde de Pirajá 437, Ipanema. This large boutique showcases the collections of some two dozen Brazilian fashion designers, both established and up-and-coming, and it sells nice handbags, jewellery and other accessories too. There's also an excellent small restaurant and bar here, perfect for light, contemporary Brazilian nibbles.

Dona Coisa Rua Lopes Quintas 153, Jardim Botânico ⓦ www.donacoisa.com.br. Although there is considerable stylistic variety amongst the sixty or so established and up-and-coming Brazilian designers who display here, with their very attractive womenswear – and sometimes childrenswear – the general tone is classical rather than avant-garde.

Favela Hype Galeria River, Rua Francisco Otaviano 67, Arpoador ⓦ www.favelahype.com.br. Established in Bohemian Santa Teresa in 2001, there's a clear hippy-chic imprint to Favela Hype's clothes, all made in small workshops in outlying parts of Rio that promote good labour practices.

Isabela Capeto Rua Dias Ferreira 45, Leblon ⓦ www.isabelacapeto.com.br. This Italian-trained designer is one of Rio's foremost fashion designers, her output ranging from casual-chic to haute couture. The collection – for women, children and young teens – is displayed in a lovely, airy boutique alongside the work of local artists who are invited to produce creations inspired by Isabela's designs.

Jewellery

Antonio Bernardo Rua Garcia d'Ávila 121, Ipanema and other branches ⓦ www.antoniobernardo.com.br. Imaginative, contemporary design, skilled craftwork and high-quality materials are the hallmarks of this sophisticated jewellers.

Parceria Carioca Rua Jardim Botânico 728, Jardim Botânico ⓦ www.parceriacarioca.com.br. Fun-looking, incredibly distinctive bracelets – made with leather straps and colourful glass beads or semi-precious stones, are the real attraction here, but brooches and T-shirts

Beachwear: where Rio leads the world

Given the importance of **beach culture** and the distinctive bathing suits you'll encounter on the city's beaches, it's hardly surprising that Brazil ranks first in the world for the sale of **beachwear**. Rio's beach-orientation and natural sense of the exotic make it the best place in the country to buy swimwear.

Compared with other clothing items, design possibilities for bathing suits are limited, the focus being on vibrant colours, patterns and fabrics. But what makes Brazilian swimwear unique is the the cut and fit. Men tend to wear **sungas** (speedo-style briefs) or cover up with surfer-style shorts, although extremely stylish one-pieces are certainly sold; women often wear the tiniest of bikinis, though you can ask for **a sunkini**, a variation of *sungas* for women, if you want to purchase a rather bigger two-piece. Each November Rio now hosts a high-profile fashion week, **Claro Rio Summer** (ⓦ www.clarioriosummer.com.br), entirely devoted to swimwear. Taking place against some unbelievably glamorous backdrops and featuring world-famous Brazilian supermodels, it showcases the collections of the country's top brands and designers to an international audience.

If you are set on buying, you'll find the full range of swimwear – from items designed for sports swimming, such as those found at the always trendy Osklen (see p.230), to elegant evening cover-ups designed by Lenny Niemeyer (see p.230) – in the boutiques in the city's *shoppings* and along Ipanema's fashionable Avenida Visconde de Pirajá and its equally fashionable side roads. Although there's a tendency towards the stylish when it comes to swimwear, fashion isn't that prescriptive – indeed women's stores typically encourage buyers to mix and match tops and bottoms. Tempted or not, you won't be able to say that they'll take too much luggage space.

with amusing, rather kitsch, motifs are also sold. Most of the items are produced by artisans working with community organizations and rural cooperatives.

H. Stern Rua Visconde de Pirajá 490, Ipanema and other branches ⓦwww.hstern.com.br. Rio is the global headquarters of this internationally renowned jeweller and while you won't pick up a bargain, you can be absolutely confident that the precious and semi-precious gems are genuine and that the attractive gold settings are totally secure. Even if you have no intention of buying, stop by at the excellent museum of gemology (see p.108).

Maria Oiticica Rua Elvira Machado 118, Botafogo with a branch in the Shopping Leblon ⓦwww.mariaoiticica.com.br. This range of beautiful, Brazilian-looking, and affordable costume jewellery has been created using material from native trees, such as seeds and bark, leather and Amazonian fibres.

O Banquete Rua Visconde de Pirajá 611, Ipanema. Unique rings, necklaces and bracelets, with a very contemporary look and produced by artists working with a range of materials including ceramic and glass, as well as silver, gold and semi-precious stones, are sold here.

Marzio Fiorini Rua Visconde de Pirajà 611, Ipanema. This well-known local designer's diverse range of rubber jewellery can be extremely simple or complex, but items are always stunning.

Crafts and design

Rio has some excellent **handicraft shops**, but the items on sale are usually from distant parts of Brazil. Apart from the places listed here, there are several markets (see p.233) with craft sections, the best option is the **Feira Nordestina** which showcases crafts from Northeastern Brazil (see p.140). Alternatively, look out for modern pieces – Brazilian designers have made a strong impact on the world of furniture and you can view their creations in their natural environment.

Modern

Atelier Ricardo Fasanello Rua do Paraíso 42, Santa Teresa. Ricardo Fasanello's elegant, yet functional, chairs and tables have become icons of Museu de Arte Moderna's 1960s and 1970s Brazilian design. Although the designer died in 1992, his creations are still produced in his former workshop.

Daqui do Brasil Av. Ataulfo de Paiva 1174, Leblon ⓦwww.daquidobrasil.com. A wonderful showcase for new Brazilian designers with items ranging from furniture and household utensils to jewellery and clothes at all prices.

Elementos da Terra Rua Constante Ramos 61, Copacabana ⓦwww.elementosdaterra.com.br. Fusing traditional and modern design elements and using natural fibres and reclaimed wood, the handcrafted pieces in this home décor store are truly distinctive.

No Meio do Caminho Av. General San Martín 1247, Leblon. Beautiful (though expensive) ceramics, woodwork, paintings and other contemporary decorative – and sometimes practical – items by talented Brazilian artists and designers.

Novo Desenho MAM – Museu de Arte Moderna, Av. Infante Dom Henrique 85, Centro ⓦwww.novodesenho.com. A fine range of mainly household items – including jewellery, stools, vases and woven hangings – produced by talented new Brazilian designers are sold at this museum shop with prices ranging significantly.

Traditional

Brasil & Cia Rua Maria Qutéria 27, Ipanema ⓦwww.brasilecia.com.br. A range of carefully chosen ceramic, paper, textile and other crafts sourced from throughout the country. The shop will ship purchases abroad.

Casa de Artesanato do Estado do Rio Rua Real Grandeza 293, Botafogo. Crafts from around the state of Rio, but the quality is unlikely to impress. Even so, look for occasional interesting items of basketry and embroidery.

Do Século Passado Rua do Lavradio 106, Lapa. Oil paintings, furniture, glasswear and every other conceivable thing pack this impressive nineteenth-century townhouse. While here, stop by the similarly intriguing Arquitetura e

Decoração at no. 34. And Alfonso Nunes Antiquario at no. 60.

Loja Artíndia Museu do Índio, Rua das Palmeiras 55, Botafogo Ⓦ www .museudoindio.gov.br. Housed in the grounds of the supurb Museu do Indio (see p.94), this is by far the best place in the city for Amerindian crafts. There's an excellent selection of wooden carvings, bows and arrows, basketry, necklaces, feather items and ceramics with the tribes and places of origin all clearly identified. The prices are very fair.

Pé de Boi Rua Ipiranga 55, Laranjeiras Ⓦ www.pedeboi.com.br. Beautiful textiles, wooden carvings, ceramics and other crafts, sourced from artisans throughout Brazil, in particular the states of Amazonas, Minas Gerais and Pernambuco. The gallery also features exhibitions by guest artists.

O Sol Rua Corcovado 213, Jardim Botânico Ⓦ www.artesanato-sol.com.br. A non-profit outlet selling Brazilian folk art such as basketware, textiles, ceramics and wood carvings.

Raiz Forte Produtos da Terra Av. Ataulfo de Paiva 1160, Leblon. Specializing in crafts and popular art, including distinctive lithographs and simple ceramic figurines from the northeastern state of Pernambuco.

La Vereda Rua Almirante Alexandrino 428, Largo dos Guimarães, Santa Teresa. One of the best handicraft shops in Rio, with a varied collection from all over the country (including work by local artists).

⑰

Food and drink

Exotic food items or *cachaça* make excellent purchases and you won't do much better than wandering the aisles of a local supermarket: particularly good ones are the branches of Zona Sul at Rua Visconden de Pirajá nos. 25, 118, 504 and 577 in Ipanema, at Av. N.S. de Copacabana nos. 595, 936, 1200, 1369 or at Rua Dias Ferreira 290 in Leblon.

Confeitaria Colombo Rua Gonçalves Dias 32, Centro Ⓦ www.confeitariacolombo.com.br. The Belle Époque origins of this iconic tearoom are apparent in the wonderful designs of the packaging of the small, but high quality, range of jams and biscuits that are sold here.

Garcia & Rodrigues Av. Ataúlfo de Paiva 1251, Leblon Ⓦ www.garciaerodrigues.com.br. While their delicious cakes and salads will need to be consumed in Rio, there are plenty of easily transportable items available at this gourmet food store. The jams and preserves are delicious: of the many tropical varieties, *jabuticaba* (a deep-purple berry with a taste resembling a lychee) must count as the most distinctively Brazilian of fruit.

Lidador Rua da Assembléia 65, Centro and other branches Ⓦ www.lidador.com .br. Rio's foremost gourmet food and liquor store since 1924, this is *the* place to visit for alcoholic drinks of all varieties. Although most of what's sold here is imported, there's a good stock of *cachaças* and Brazilian wines that you rarely see in Rio – the white wines of Villa Francioni are outstanding.

Mundo Verde Ⓦ www.mundoverde.com.br. With some fifty branches spread across Rio, and dozens more elsewhere in Brazil, this is by far the largest chain of health food stores in Latin America. The individual branches are all quite small, but have varied stocks of nuts, dried fruit, sweet and savoury biscuits as well as beauty products made with natural ingredients.

Markets

Whether you're seeking local handicrafts, antiques or food, Rio's **markets** are well worth a visit for their lively atmospheres and a chance to mingle with locals. **Ferias livres** – outdoor produce markets – circulate Rio throughout the week, typically selling exotic fruit and vegetables, as well as cheese, preserves and *doces* (puddings or sweets). In the Zona Sul, market days are Monday at Rua Henrique Dumont in Ipanema, Tuesday at Praça General Osório in Ipanema, Wednesday at Rua María Eugênia in Humaitá, Thursday at Rua Ronald de Carvalho in Leblon and Rua Conde Lages in Glória, and Fridays at N.S. da Paz, Ipanema, and Praça Santos Dumont in Gávea. Apart from these general produce markets, on Saturdays, rather more gourmet fare is to be found at the market at Rua Frei Leandro in Jardim Botânico and **organic produce** at Rua do Russell in Glória.

Crafts, antiques and accessories

With a keen eye and a bit of luck you may be able to find original, and reasonably priced, souvenirs at one of Rio's atmospheric craft or antique markets.

Babilônia Feira Hype Av. Das Americas 1510, Barra da Tijuca Ⓦ www.babiloniahype.com.br. A good place to search out talented new clothes and jewellery designers. While there's plenty of uninteresting stuff to pass over, you shouldn't have much problem finding some distinctive items sold at fair prices. Generally the first weekend of the month, 2–10pm.

Feira do Rio Antigo Rua do Lavradio, Lapa. As well as stalls selling antiques and bric-a-brac, including vintage clothes and old records, street entertainers and bands play samba and *choro* throughout the day. First Sat of the month, 10am–6pm.

Feira Hippie de Ipanema Praça General Osório, Ipanema Ⓦ www.feirahippie.hpg.ig.com.br. First held in 1968, it has probably been years since a hippy was last seen at the market. Now very touristy, with cheap jewellery, leather and embroidered items predominating. Sun 7am–7pm.

Feira Nordestina Campo de Cristóvão Ⓦ www .feiradesaocristocao.org.br. Nearly 700 stalls selling food, drink and handicrafts typical of the Brazilian Northeast. Weekend evenings are the best time to visit when live music is performed and *forró* is danced. Tues–Thurs 10am–4pm & Fri 10am–10pm Sun non-stop.

Saara Rua da Alfândega and around, Centro. There are well over 1200 commercial establishments in the eleven streets that make up Saara, most of which display their wares on stalls on the pavement in front of their typically small shop fronts. The area is always packed with shoppers – you can find just about anything here, from a cheap travel holdall to a reproduction football shirt, to sequin-adorned fabrics and fake feathers needed to create a unique Carnaval costume. Mon–Fri 9am–6pm, Sat 9am–2pm.

Music and CDs

Whether it's a recording of the work of the Brazilian folk-inspired, classical composer Heitor Villa-Lobos, a bossa nova compilation, or something by a rising samba-funk star, few visitors to Rio will return home without having purchased at least one CD. The quality of Brazilian recordings is invariably good and the range and amazing vitality of the local music is phenomenal (see p.259). Prices of CDs compare favourably with those in either Europe or North America, while the choice is naturally far superior. If you're not sure what's specifically available within the genre that appeals most to you, you'll find sales assistants in music stores are usually delighted to offer recommendations, and it's perfectly acceptable to listen before you buy. As well as the places listed below there are vast numbers of small stores throughout the city selling CDs, and the Livraria da Travessa (see p.228) and Baratos da Ribeiro (see p.228) are also good for browsing. If your musical interest lies in performance, the place to go is Rua da Carioca in Centro where half a dozen music shops sell sheet music, guitars, mandolins, accordians and Brazilian percussion instruments.

Bossa Nova e Companhia Rua Duvivier 37, Copacabana Ⓦ www.bossanovaecompanhia.com .br. Despite the name, the shop isn't completely dedicated to bossa nova, it also stocks CDs, score music and books on other Brazilian musical genres, especially samba and *choro*.

Modern Sound Rua Barata Ribeiro 502 (near the corner of Rua Santa Clara), Copacabana Ⓦ www.modernsound.com.br. The largest music store in Rio with a vast array of well-ordered CDs by both Brazilian and foreign artists. In the early evening jazz recitals are often held.

Saraiva Megastore Rua do Ouvidor 98, Centro and other branches Ⓦ www.livrariasaraiva.com. The best of the Brazilian music/bookstore chains with a solid, essentially unimaginative, stock of CDs by Brazilian and other performers.

Toca de Vinicius Rua Vinicius de Moraes 129, Ipanema Ⓦ www.tocadovinicius.com.br. The name says it all: a temple devoted to bossa nova, in particular renowned poet and composer Vinicius de Moraes. Apart from bossa nova recordings, song books and music scores, the shop sells a limited range of recordings by contemporary artists influenced by the style.

Top Sound Av. N.S, de Copacabana 1103, Copacabana. A vast stock of secondhand and hard-to-find CDs as well as old vinyl LPs which will appeal to true enthusiasts of Brazilian music.

Tracks Praça Santos Dumont 140, Gávea. A great range of Brazilian sounds are found here, both on CD and vinyl. The staff are extremely friendly and always available to share their knowledge.

Shopping malls

Vast, purpose-built **shopping malls** – or *shoppings*, as they are called in Brazil – have mushroomed in Rio during the last few decades. As with malls the world over, apart from their chain stores and one-off boutiques – they boast food courts, restaurants, multiplex cinemas, banks and ATMs. As you wander through the air-conditioned floors, utterly insulated from the realities of the city around you, it's all too easy to find the hours – and your cash – slipping away.

Barra Shopping Av. das Américas 4666, Barra da Tijuca Ⓦ www.barrashopping.com.br. With some 600 stores, this is Brazil's – and Latin America's – largest mall, fittingly situated in Rio's most Florida-like outer suburb. All major – and many minor – brands can be found here, with stores to suit most tastes and budgets. Apart from the usual food courts and cinemas, it has a large indoor amusement park and a bowling ally. Mon–Sat 10am–10pm, Sun 1–9pm.

Rio Sul Shopping Rua Lauro Müller 116, Botafogo; Ⓦ www.riosul.com.br. Located at the end of the Pasmado Tunnel that links the *bairro* with Copacabana, this is the best known of Rio's large shopping malls and, with over 400 units representing most Brazilian (and many foreign) brands, one of the most varied choice of shops. A free tourist bus links Rio Sul with Zona Sul hotels and the Cardeal Arcoverde *metrô* station. Mon–Sat 10am–10pm, Sun 3–9pm.

São Conrado Fashion Mall Estrada da Gávea 899, São Conrado Ⓦ www.scfashionmall.com.br. This mall's approximately 150 stores feature exclusively high-end Brazilian and international designer brands, mainly clothes and household items. The food court is excellent and boasts a range of high-quality restaurants. Mon–Sat 10am–10pm, Sun 3–9pm.

Shopping Cassino Atlântico Av. Atlântica 4240, Copacabana Ⓦ www.shoppingcassinoatlantico.com.br. Located alongside the Sofitel Hotel, a short stroll from Ipanema, most of the 180 or so shops specialize in antiques, jewellery or art. Prices are high but browsing can be fun, especially on Saturdays when an antique market (10am–7pm) takes over the mall. Mon–Sat 9am–9pm, Sun 2–8pm.

Shopping da Gávea Rua Marquês de São Vicente, Gávea Ⓦ www.shoppingdagavea.com.br. While not nearly as big as its rivals, this upmarket mall is especially good for decorative and household items and jewellery. Mon–Sat 10am–10pm, Sun 3–9pm.

Shopping Leblon Av. Afrânio de Melo Franco 290, at the intersection of Av. Ataulfo de Paiva, Leblon Ⓦ www.shoppingleblon.com.br. Located in the heart of one of Rio's most exclusive *bairros*, the look and feel of this *shopping* is more like a luxury hotel than a conventional mall, with comfortable armchairs, plush ultra-modern washrooms and discreet, yet plentiful, security guards. The overwhelmingly upmarket boutiques represent both Brazilian and foreign brands. Mon–Sat 10am–10pm, Sun 3–9pm.

18

Sports and activities

A dramatic city of beaches, mountains and forest, Rio is the perfect location for **adventure and water sports** – activities such as hang-gliding, hiking and climbing. **Swimming** at the beaches is the most obvious of pursuits to enjoy (advice is given on p.99) and the waves also make Rio a popular **surfing** and **kitesurfing** centre. Almost all *Cariocas* enjoy one beach sport or another, and Brazil leads the world at **volleyball**. Native martial arts **capoeira** and Brazilian **Jiu-Jitsu** are practised at gyms and centres across the city – pursuits which generate massive enthusiasm and commitment from a population known for its toned and muscular bodies.

If watching sport is more your thing, Rio de Janeiro's major obsession is **football** (soccer), with phenomenally passionate and atmospheric games played almost year-round – our in-depth guide to the stadiums, teams and championships means you won't miss a thing. Another popular spectator sport is **horse racing**, the Jockey Club in Gávea (see p.116) – located in a beautiful lake- and mountain-side setting – is the city's major course.

Participation and adventure sports

Rio is an exceptionally active place, with **gyms** on every corner and most hotels offering weight-training, fitness classes, **yoga**, and very often Rio-born martial art Brazilian **Jiu-Jitsu**. On the beaches **volleyball** and **futevôlei** occupy restless bodies, and a lively surf scene takes advantage of forty kilometers of Atlantic waves. **Capoeira** has a long history here; first brought to the city by early migrants from Bahia in the Northeast, it now draws visitors from schools in Europe and North America. **Hang-gliding** is also a very popular pursuit in Rio, many visitors are tempted by the stunning beach and mountain setting to try it for the first time. Innumerable forests and cliffs within the city create excellent opportunities for **climbing** and **hiking**, but if you're seeking a slightly less adrenaline-charged pursuit, golfers enjoy extraordinary views from the city's courses.

Beach volleyball and futevôlei

Beach volleyball is the second most popular sport in Brazil (after football), and inland areas even import sand to practise on. With miles of beaches, however, Rio has hundreds of courts throughout Copacabana, Ipanema, Leblon, São Conrado and Barra da Tijuca. Informal "schools" (teachers who rent out courts to give lessons) are based between postos 10–12 in Ipanema-Leblon (arrange on the beach the day before) and most classes start at around 10am. If you want to see the professionals in action then stop by between 5 and 8pm at the same location.

You'll also see people practising **futevôlei** (foot-volleyball) on and off the volleyball courts. This sport started in the 1960s when football was banned on Copacabana beach – footballers, including professionals like Almir, started playing on the volleyball courts then near to Rua Bolivar instead. It's a two-a-side game played by both men and women, using feet, head and chest. For more information, see Ⓦwww .futevolei.com.br.

Brazilian Jiu-Jitsu

Adapted from the Japanese Judo style which arrived in Brazil in the early twentieth-century, **Jiu-Jitsu** became famous when its founders, various members of a Rio family, the Gracies, challenged and consistently beat competitors from every other martial art at international fighting championships. Rio has now developed a Jiu-Jitsu tourism industry, and since it seems likely that this grappling and ground-fighting technique will follow Judo in becoming an Olympic sport, an increase in worldwide practitioners keen to train in the sport's spiritual home seems probable. There's a plethora of teachers around the city, the best value classes are at smaller city gyms whose prices aren't marked up by the Gracie name – nonetheless, Gracie Barra has the greatest international standing. Courses at higher-level gyms generally offer 25-hours of tuition per week and can arrange accommodation as part of a package, though you'll always get a better rate showing up on spec (around R$100 per week).

Alliance Jiu-Jitsu Humaitá ☎21/9428-4395, Ⓦwww.alliancehumaita.com.br.

Centro de Treinamento em Artes Marciais Strauch Av. Nossa Senhora de Copacabana 1063, Copacabana ☎21/2247-3862, Ⓦwww .jiujitsustrauch.com.br.

Gracie Barra Academia ByFit, Av. Com. Júlio de Moura 300, Barra da Tijuca ☎21/3153-3694, Ⓦwww.graciebarra.com.br.

Capoeira

Originating from eighteenth and nineteenth century African slaves in Bahia in Brazil's Northeast, but also developed in Rio, **capoeira** mixes martial art avoidance moves with dance and music. Its origins are slightly unclear, with no consensus on whether it hailed directly from Africa (particularly Angola) and then arrived in Brazil, or whether it was an African-originating style of fighting disguised as a dance by Brazilian slaves banned from practising any form of violence. In Rio, similarities can certainly be drawn between a *roda da capoeira* and *roda do samba* – both are dances performed in the round, surrounded by musicians including *pandeiro*-players (Brazilian tambourine), though *capoeira* also uses the *berimbau*, a one-stringed instrument. Masses of international practitioners now arrive in Brazil to perfect their technique. There are numerous classes in all *bairros* of Rio, and rates vary (under R$20 per session): see Ⓦwww .portalcapoeira.com or contact the relevant school for details.

Casa Rosa Rua Alice 550, Laranjeiras ☎21/2557-2562, Ⓦwww.casarosa.com.br.

Centro de Capoeira Angola Rua do Catete 164, Catete ☎21/2558-8015 or 9954-3659, Ⓦccarj .magaweb.com.br.

▲ *Capoeira* on the beach

Nestor Capoeira Galpão das Artes Urbanas, Rua Padre Leonel Franca, Gávea ☏21/2232-4902, ⓦwww.nestorcapoeira.net.

Golf

Golf has become popular in Brazil amongst the wealthier sections of the population, and there are several very attractive courses in the city and state of Rio. Greens are as well-kept as the best courses in Europe or North America, but it is the stunning landscape that makes a round of golf a special experience here.

Búzios Golf Club and Resort Estrada Bento Ribeiro Dantas KM 9, Praia Rasa, Búzios ☏22/2629-1338, ⓦwww.buziosgolf.com.br. This 18-hole links course is located outside the resort of Búzios (see p.147), to the northeast of Rio. Although built in 1995, the landscaping remains spartan. The course is considered one of Brazil's most difficult, due to the abundance of water hazards and bunkers and, especially, the high winds that sweep across the greens. Open to non-members, R$165 daily.

Gávea Golf and Country Club Estrada da Gávea 800, São Conrado ☏21/3322-5975, ⓦwww .gaveagolf.com.br. Founded by British electric company workers in 1921, this is the oldest and most exclusive golf club in Rio. In the midst of the city yet surrounded by tropical forest, the setting is marvellous while the 18-hole course is absolutely immaculately maintained. Normally an invitation from a member is a requirement to play, or contact the club for a list of Rio hotels which have convenience agreements. R$280 Tues–Fri, R$400 weekends.

Japeri Golfe Clube Estrada Vereador Francisco da Costa Filho, Engenheiro Pedreira ☏21/8107-1188, ⓦwww.japerigolfe.com.br. Established by the Gávea Golf and Country Club as an out-reach project to bring golf to the masses (local inhabitants are charged a remakable R$5 for the 18 holes), this club is located 50min south of the city. Although the quality of the greens of this public course cannot really be compared to other courses in the state, the greens are nevertheless well-kept, there are some attractive water features and the surrounding area is being successfully reforested. Visitors pay R$50 daily.

Petrópolis Country Club Av. Country Club, Nogueira ☏24/2221-2534, ⓔgolfpetr @compuland.com.br. A half-hour drive from Petrópolis (see p.158), this beautiful 9-hole, each with two tee bases, course is one of the oldest in Brazil, established in 1939. Given the hilly terrain, mature foliage and the speed of the greens, the course is challenging but immensely enjoyable. The course is open to non-members: R$80 weekdays and R$160 weekends.

Hang-gliding

One of the most memorable activities in Rio is **hang-gliding**. Tandem flights take off from the Pedra Bonita ramp at the southern edge of the Parque Nacional da Tijuca (see p.122), 520m above the beach at São Conrado. Depending on conditions, flights last between ten and thirty minutes, gliding alongside the mountains and over the forest and ocean before landing on the beach at São Conrado. It's a spectacular setting, and memories are preserved on both camera and digital film using equipment strapped to the wing (at no extra cost).

Make sure you go with an expert pilot as there are some companies in operation who have limited experience and may take off in imperfect conditions. The following two operators both speak fluent English and have thousands of flights logged over twenty years:

Just Fly (☏21/2268-0565 or 9985-7540, ⓦwww.justfly.com.br) and **Go Up Brasil** (☏21/9177-9234, ⓦwww.goup.com.br) both offer flights (daily; 10am–3pm; R$240) when weather permits. Hotel pick-up and drop-off are included and flights are cancelled if pilots have the slightest doubt about safety, visibility or strong winds. Make reservations by phone (discounts may be offered if you mention the Rough Guide). By leaving arrangements to your hotel you may end up with a less reliable operator.

Hiking, climbing, cycling and kayaking

There are numerous opportunities for **hiking** in Rio, most notably in the beautiful Parque Nacional da Tijuca, near the Zona Sul (see p.122), which also offers opportunities for **rapelling** down waterfalls. If you'd like to do a shorter hike closer to your accommodation, the Parque da Catacumba (see p.114), Morro do Leme (see p.102), and Morro da Urca (see p.171) all offer thirty- to sixty-minute trails with superb vistas of Lagoa, Copacabana and Guanabara Bay respectively. The trail up mountain Pedra da Gávea is rewarded with the best view you can find in the city, though with short climbing stretches it's also the hardest in Rio. More difficult **climbs** are to be found in the Tijuca forest and most obviously the perilous ascent of the Morro da Urca which attracts the fearless and experienced. **Cycling** is great fun too – particularly along the beaches, Parque do Flamengo and in the Parque da Tijuca; Paulo at Just Fly (see opposite) rents mountain bikes and will drop you off at a location of your choice. **Kayakers** can take to the ocean in Guanabara Bay; river kayaking is only possible in wider Rio state.

Crux EcoAventura ☎ 21/3322-8765 or 21/9392-9203, ✺ www.cruxecoaventura.com.br. A

climbing, rapelling and waterfall-cascading specialist, owner-operator Marcelo will help you get the best out of the Parque da Tijuca or locations further afield. Crux also offers the full range of guided hikes in and out of town — to locations like Pedra da Gávea, Morro da Urca or Tijuca Peak, and ocean kayaking. From R$70.

Rio Hiking ☎ 21/2552-9204 or 21/9721-0594, ✺ www.riohiking.com.br. Founded in 1999 by Denise and Gabriel Werneck, this experienced eco-tour operator has a range of excellent adventure-oriented trips both in and out of the city, including Pedra da Gávea, Grumari beach and Serra dos Orgãos. They also offer occasional three-day walking trips to Ilha Grande (see p.150) and Itatiaia National Park. Other possibilties include cycling trips, climbing, rapelling, ocean kayaking and river rafting. From US$70.

Horseriding

Greater Rio has some fantastic opportunities for riding with its combination of mountains, forest and inland water. The best area for **horseriding** is Vargem Grande, inland from Recreio in the Zona Oeste. **Haras Pégasus** (Estrada dos ndeirantes 24845 ☎21/2428-1228, ✈www.haraspegasus.com.br) is an extensive equestrian complex offering lessons jumping, and trails, including combined river and mountain trips. **Rio Hiking** (see above) also offers horseriding trips in the Serra dos Orgãos near Petrópolis.

Surfing and kitesurfing

Rio has a lively **surfing** and **kite-surfing** scene, mainly based around the Praia do Pepe (posto 2) in Barra da Tijuca. There's even an area of beach set aside for kite schools here, with plentiful beginners and advanced surfers. If you're looking for surf lessons or board rental within the Zona Sul, your first port of call should be the small shopping mall Galaria River at Rua Francisco Otaviano 67, Arpoador (Ipanema), which is filled with surf shops – you can also rent boogie boards here. To get out to Barra and the beaches beyond, take the excellent **Surf Bus** service (☎21/2539-7555 or 21/8702-2837,

Ⓦwww.surfbus.com.br), which departs Largo do Machado at 7am, 10am, 1pm and 4pm, passes along the Copacabana-Ipanema beach front and goes all the way out to Prainha (see p.134) – buses are timetabled to return ninety minutes later. On-board facilities include a TV with surf clips, drinks and space for all boards and equipment.

K08 In front of Av. do Pepê 900, close to posto 3, Barra da Tijuca ☎21/2494-4869, Ⓦwww.k08 .com.br. Experienced and reliable surf/kite school offering surf lessons for all ages and kitesurfing for teens upwards.

O'Surfe Almirante Heleno Nunes 203, Recreio ☎21/2490-6412, Ⓦwww.lelot.com.br/osurfe .htm An excellent combined surfing and board shaping (manufacturing) school run by professionals, which engages poor communities in the sport through its Projeto Surf Social. Classes offered for all ages at Praia da Macumba.

Rio Surf and Stay Rua Raimundo Veras 1140, Recreio ☎21/3418-1133, Ⓦwww.riosurfnstay .com. A hostel and surf school offering excellent beginners and advanced lessons for most ages, open to non-residents and close to several different beaches.

Football

Seeing a game of *futebol* (soccer) is one of the highlights of a visit to Rio. Great silken banners wave across the packed *arquibancadas* (stands), shrouded by the smoke from fireworks, while support for each team is proclaimed by the insistent rhythm of massed samba drums. It's enough to get the heart racing before the game even starts; when it does, the pace, energy and tricks of the players will keep you entertained whether you're a football lover or not. **Futebol** has played a central role in the story of modern Brazil, bringing together classes and races behind national and local team colours (see p.256), and Rio's **Maracanã stadium** is the sport's high temple – the best place to see an international match or local derby between any of the four main teams: Botafogo, Flamengo, Fluminense or Vasco. The Maracanã is due to host group matches and the final of the 2014 World Cup and will be closed for refurbishment from Jan 2010 until well into 2012 – matches during this period will be played at Engenhão, the startlingly modern stadium built for 2007's Pan American Games and Botafogo's home ground (see p.142), and São Januário, Vasco's stadium in São Cristóvão (see p.141). The latter is also a great bet for seeing a match at any time, in a more intimate (25,000 capacity) location than the Maracanã. For all local match and team details, see Ⓦwww.globoesporte.com and *Globo* and *Jornal do Brasil* newspapers; Ⓦwww.sambafoot.com has news and fixture lists in English.

▲ Spectators at the Maracanã

If you are interested in a football **tour** independent guide Robert Shaw (℡21/9874-8962 or 21/2275-8811, @brazsoc@hotmail.com) offers fun and insightful trips to see the best games at most Rio stadiums (from R$100 per person including transport and ticket). He also provides you with a paper outlining the significance of the match, details of key players and the latest gossip. His tailor-made day-tours can take in a number of different clubs (including impressive trophy rooms and on request Ronaldo's first club, São Cristóvão) and the Maracanã's **Museu do Futebol** (see p.141); matches can even be arranged against local teams.

Seeing a match

The largest football stadium in the world, Rio's **Maracanã** looks like a futuristic colosseum, its upper stand rising almost vertically from the playing surface. For big games aim to arrive at the stadium at least an hour before kick-off and buy your *ingresso* (ticket) at any of the **ticket offices** set in the perimeter wall (see p.141 for directions and transport). Depending on the game, seats in the *gerais* (lower terracing) cost R$15–30, the *arquibancadas* (all-seated upper terracing) about $20–40 – after purchasing your ticket go to the entrance and pass your card through a machine at the turnstile. The areas of the stadium are colour-coded according to areas for home and away supporters (ask stewards for directions to the side you want), and there's also a white section popular with families and more passive fans of both teams. Tickets are also available in advance from the clubs themselves (see p.243); Flamengo, Fluminense

Football taunts and chants: essential Portuguese

Enter into Rio's passionate football-spectating spirit by learning a few key chants:

Flamengo fans sing a song which includes the line "*sempre te amarei*" (I'll always love you) which opposing fans turn into "*sempre te na Maré*" (you'll always be in Maré) – Maré is one of Rio's most notorious *favela* slums. If Flamengo is losing and their fans are quieter than usual then opposing supporters shout "*silencio na favela!*" (silence in the *favela*!) Even fierce Flamengo rivals Vasco – who draw large sections of their support from poor communities – chant this to the opposition in an ironic show of superiority.

Botafogo fans often break into renditions of famous *sambista* Beth Carvalho's song with the lyrics "*Vou festejar. O seu sofrer…Pode chora!*" (I'll celebrate your suffering… You can cry!) They also love to sing their main club tune, but with astonishing factionalism fans disagree about the line stating the year the club was first champions – some sing the melody 1907, others 1910.

Fluminense are relentlessly humiliated for having been the only *Carioca* team to be relegated to the Third Division; responding they take to whistling the tune of Colonel Bogey from *The Bridge over the River Kwai* – instead of Alec Guinness or William Holden you find Young Flu (their largest supporter's group) humming it with occasional yelps of "*Nense!*"

Fans of all teams chant "*Sai de chão, sai de chão!*" (leave the floor!) to get their fans bouncing up and down in the *arquibancadas* (stands).

A match/game – *o jogo*

Friendly match – *o amistoso*

To support (a team) – *torcer para* (*um time* "*ti-me*")

Coach/manager – *técnico*

Referee – *juiz*

Whistle – *apito*

Linesman – *juiz de linha*

A forward – *o atacante*

A midfielder – *o meio campista*

Offside – *fora de jogo*

Kick – *pontape*

Free kick – *tiro livre*

Back heel – *Chilena*

Half-time – *intervalo*

A draw – *impate*

The score – *o placar*

and Botafogo sell tickets for each other's games. The Maracanã's ticket booths get quite frantic before big games and if you're not there early enough you may get stranded outside, as the attendants often leave their positions as soon as the starting whistle blows. Watch your belongings in the dense crowds and avoid the huge *torcidas organizados* (organized supporters' groups) unless you're ready for frenzied shouting and jumping – you'll easily see where they're stood. *Carioca* supporters are passionate to say the least, often near hysterical, but their love for the game is infectious.

Football championships and teams

Due to Brazil's crazily congested system of leagues and cups, football is played all year round with just a few weeks break at Christmas time, so you needn't fear missing a good match. The state championship – in Rio's case the **Campeonato Carioca** – (Jan-May) which includes all professional clubs, with two separate rounds of qualifying groups, semi-finals and finals, and a grand final for the two winners, is perhaps the most animated and exciting competition for supporters, when they get to see a series of regular derbies against their fiercest local rivals. The national league – the **Campeonato Brasileiro** – (May–Nov/Dec, depending on World Cup or Copa America breaks in June) only began in the 1970s when travel across Brazil's vast distances became easier. Now a standard tri-league format, there is little travelling support and a strong home advantage. Further games are played in the national knock-out cup competition – the **Copa do Brasil** – fought out between April and July and featuring the 64 sides that contested their previous year's state championship final. In a highly original format, larger teams must play smaller sides (most often in poorer states) away from home and must win by a margin of two goals or more to go through – something that inevitably leads to frequent upsets with the likes of huge clubs Vasco and Botafogo having never won the cup. Finally, winners of national league and cup are admitted to the South America-wide **Copa Libertadores** (May–Nov), which very often includes a Rio side. Offering a chance to see top-level teams from across the continent, these few matches ensure a packed Maracanã.

Botafogo (⊛ www.botafogonocoracao.com.br, see p.96) plays its matches at home ground Engenhão or at the Maracanã for local derbies. 'Fogo's supporters, *Botafoguenses*, had most to cheer about from the 1950s–1970s with skilled players like Didi, Garrincha, Nilton Santos and Gérson ensuring a local winning streak and providing the backbone of the 1958 and 1962 winning Brazil World Cup

squads. Founded in 1904, the club sold its stadium, which became the Rio Plaza shopping mall, in Botafogo in 1977 – the club's practice ground is still there, relegated to the rooftop.

Flamengo (⊛ www.flamengo.com.br, see p.109) has a small home ground at Gávea but plays all its matches at the Maracanã. Supported by *Flamenguistas*, their top players were Dida in the 1950s, and more recently Zico and Júnior who helped the club to their 1981 Copa Libertadores triumph – to date they've earned five league and 31 state titles. Called Mengão by its fans, the club claims to have the largest body of supporters of any club worldwide (40 million). The *Clube de Regatas do Flamengo* formed in 1895 as a rowing outfit; football was added in 1911 after a defection from Fluminense.

Fluminense (⊛ www.fluminense.com.br, see p.91) is Rio's first football club, founded in 1902 and traditionally associated with the city's wealthy classes. 'Nense boasts Brazil's oldest stadium (3000 capacity), but plays all home matches at the Maracanã. 1950s players Machado and Castilho are legendary idols for fans, called Tricolores, though they have the record on state titles (at 30) and success at the *Copa do Brasil* in 2007. Former manager Renê Simões has twice jumped between Fluminense and Jamaican, whom he took to the 1998 World Cup.

Vasco de Gama (⊛ www.crvascodagama.com, see p.141) is the only Rio club to have its own large stadium, São Januário, though local derbies are still played at the Maracanã. Its supporters, *Vascaínos*, have cheered a list of international stars through the decades: Ademir in the 1950s, Roberto Dinamite in the 1970s, Romário in the 1980s and Edmundo in the 1990s – earning them four national league titles and the Copa Libertadores in 1998. Rio's original Portuguese team, in 1923 they started a tradition of giving players a pig for a win. In 2008 Vasco were relegated to Série B for the first time in their 110-year history, to the delight of Flamengo and Fluminense, their main rivals.

Smaller (but equally historic) Rio teams known for their production lines of young talent are Madureira (see p.143), Bangu (⊛ www.bangu.net) and América (⊛ www .america-rj.com.br); all have small home grounds in Rio's suburbs.

Futsal and beach soccer

Futsal and **beach soccer** are football-based games that were invented in Brazil; there are now national and even international championships for both – Brazil unsurprisingly dominates.

Futsal is a fast, indoor, five-a-side game with three periods of twelve minutes each. Started in the 1950s, there has been a professional Brazilian *futsal* league since 1996, which no doubt is partly responsible for Brazil's consistent production of top young players. For details of competitions and venues, see Ⓦwww.brazilfutsal.com and Ⓦwww.lifserj.com.br. Playing in a match or practising is generally limited to talented youngsters, and will involve contacting supporting clubs – if there's a competition on when you're in town spectating is certainly possible.

Beach soccer was popularized in 1993 by big Flamengo stars Júnior and Zico on Copacabana beach, and quickly developed into a large-scale FIFA sport with an annual World Cup – often contested at its home in July. For more details see Ⓦwww.cbbsbrasil.com.br; most games are played on Copacabana beach, close to posto 4; schools practise here too.

Contexts

Contexts

History

By the time of the arrival of the first Europeans in what is now Rio there were several rival indigenous **Tupi Indian** groups, whose ancestors had arrived some six thousand years ago – the **Tupinambás** (or Tamoios) and the **Teminós** who had a strong presence around the bay, the **Goitacases** to the north in the region of present-day Campos, and the **Guaianás** to the south in the area of present-day Paraty. Very little is known about their way of life and culture apart from being hunter-gatherers and fishers. The arrival of the Europeans was, in common with indigenous peoples in most other parts of the Americas, a catastrophe. Within little more than a century few indigenous traces remained in the area, the people and their cultures wiped out as a result of illness, disappointed alliances and enslavement. Today, only around Paraty are there still indigenous communities, surviving on small and isolated patches of land and selling trinkets to tourists.

Early settlement

On April 23, 1500, the Portuguese navigator and explorer **Pedro Álvares Cabral** landed in southern Bahia, his ship having been blown off course on its way to India. When word of this accidental "discovery" reached Lisbon, King Manuel I sent another fleet to investigate, this time led by the Florentine explorer Amerigo Vespucci. On New Year's Day 1502 a ship under the command of **Gaspar de Lemos** sailed into Guanabara Bay, the crew being the first Europeans to see the magnificent body of water: the area was named Rio de Janeiro ("January River") because the bay was mistakenly thought to be the mouth of a river.

For the first decades of the sixteenth century the Portuguese paid scant attention to Brazil, being far too occupied with Africa and the development of the valuable East Indies spice trade. Along the coast a few lumber and military encampments were established, but no attempts made at permanent settlement. The only product that attracted interest was **brazilwood** (*pau-brasil*), a hardwood found in the **Mata Atlântica** (see p.124) – the forest that covered the immediate hinterland of most of Brazil's Atlantic coast. Of great commercial value in Europe, brazilwood was a source of red dye used in the production of luxury textiles and for making bows for string instruments.

In 1555, six hundred French Huguenots, convicts and soldiers landed on a small, barren island near the entrance to Guanabara Bay, to establish the colony of **France Antarctique**. Under the leadership of **Nicolas Durand de Villegaignon**, an ambitious entrepreneur, the driving forces of the colony were notions of religious freedom and securing a share of the brazilwood trade. Villegaignon's strict rule soon resulted in discontent, and many colonists fled to the mainland. With his colony fast haemorrhaging and with the remaining colonists living in fear of being attacked by the Portuguese, Villegaignon called for reinforcements from Europe. A party of Calvinists from Geneva was sent out, but their presence worsened morale, causing fierce theological disputes. With the disruption that the new arrivals were causing, in 1559 Villegaignon abandoned France Antarctique and returned to France.

Not realizing that France Antarctique was on the verge of self-implosion, the Portuguese feared the colony would be a base for French raids on the shipping lands to India or that they would expand southwards. In 1560,

Mem de Sá, the governor of Portuguese Brazil, led a naval force to attack the French island fortress, forcing the colonists to flee to the mainland. Lacking the personnel to maintain a presence in Guanabara Bay, the Portuguese soon withdrew, leaving it to Estácio de Sá, Mem de Sá's nephew, to dislodge the French in 1565, establishing a base at the foot of Sugar Loaf mountain. Portuguese reinforcements were called and, after a series of grisly skirmishes, the French were finally defeated in a battle on Praia do Flamengo, though with the loss of Estácio de Sá, killed by an Indian's arrow. Determined to retain control of Guanabara Bay, on March 1 the city of **São Sebastião do Rio de Janeiro** was established. It was from this germ that the city and state of Rio de Janeiro emerged.

Portuguese colonial rule

To populate and protect Rio from future invasions, Portugal not only defined the newly created city as one of the two administrative centres of Portuguese Brazil (the other was Salvador), but also created several *feitorias* (strongholds) along the coast, including Angra dos Reis, Paraty, Cabo Frio and Macaé. The economy of this backwater of empire, however, grew only slowly. With brazilwood soon exhausted, the area around Cabo Frio turned to the exploitation of **sea salt**, the vast salt flats remaining to these days. **Sugar cane** was introduced but even the largest estates (to the north of the city, around Campos) were never as productive as those in Northeast Brazil. Even so, by the end of the seventeenth century sugar was Rio de Janeiro's most important export. In addition to sugar, **cachaça** from Rio was exported, an important item Africans traded for slaves who, together with Indians, laboured in the cane fields.

Reflecting the lack of dynamism of the economy around it, Rio grew only slowly. It was a typical colonial settlement: unplanned, with irregular streets in medieval Portuguese style, with the most important buildings being forts, stockades and churches. Even so, by 1660 – just a century after its foundation – Rio was Brazil's third-most-important settlement, though with less than four thousand people it was hardly a major metropolis.

In 1697 **gold** was discovered in Minas Gerais, to the northwest of Rio, hundreds of kilometres inland, heralding a gold rush that would last for most of the following century. To facilitate taxation and to combat smuggling, the Portuguese authorities decreed that all the gold should be exported through the port of Rio. Initially the main trail linking the mines with the coast terminated at Paraty (see p.157), from where gold was shipped to Rio for export to Lisbon. This wealth made Rio an attractive target for French and Dutch **privateers** who plundered ships carrying gold bound for Rio or being transferred to Lisbon. The most serious attack was in 1711 when a French force numbering six thousand captured Rio, prompting the city's entire population to flee and forcing the Portuguese to pay a huge bounty of gold, sugar and cattle.

With the colony's wealth increasingly concentrated in this central area of Brazil, the city's population steadily rose with immigrants arriving from Portugal, slaves from Africa and migrants from the north. In 1763, Rio de Janeiro, its population now exceeding fifty thousand, replaced Salvador as the administrative capital of Brazil. A consequence of the population growth was the initiation of important public works. In particular, the Aqueduto da Carioca was built between 1751 and 1753, a structure so solid that it remains in use, albeit now as an overpass for the tram to Santa Teresa.

The transition to independence

In 1807, **Napoleon** invaded Portugal, placing Lisbon under siege. In a remarkable evacuation of the city, **King João VI** and his entire court and civil service, numbering as many as fifteen thousand people, fled to Brazil under the protective escort of a British fleet. After a brief stop in Salvador, the exhausted royal family arrived in Rio in 1808, becoming the first European monarch to set foot in the New World.

While the king and his immediate retinue moved into the Paço Imperial, the governor's palace, there were no available structures to accommodate the thousands of people who had arrived with him. As a consequence many of the existing inhabitants of Rio were simply evicted from their homes, the city's population having increased by twenty percent in the course of a few weeks.

Rejecting the provincialism of colonial Rio, Dom João immediately began overseeing massive changes to Rio's **social and cultural life**. Within two years of his arrival, new schools, colleges, theatres, libraries and gardens were created, and the **first newspaper** was established – Brazil, until this point, had been deliberately left without even a printing press, the fear being that the availability of news would foment unrest. Even more dramatic were the economic changes to Rio that suddenly became the centre of the Portuguese empire. For the first time Brazil's ports were opened to direct foreign trade (effectively meaning trade with Britain, the royal family's ally and protector), the Banco do Brasil was established and the freedom to manufacture goods in Brazil was allowed. Having already replaced Salvador as the capital of Brazil, Rio in effect now replaced Lisbon as the capital of the Kingdom of Portugal.

While Dom João's colonial subjects did their best to ingratiate themselves to their sovereign he, in return, distributed titles, creating a new local nobility. Dom João took to life in the tropics but faced with a rebellion in Portugal, he was unable to delay his return any longer. In 1821 he returned, leaving his son **Dom Pedro** behind in Rio to serve as prince regent and governor. With the king back in Lisbon, Portugal sought to reclaim direct control of Brazil. In 1822 Brazil declared **independence**, with Dom Pedro I proclaimed Emperor of Brazil. Preoccupied with problems at home, the Portuguese made only half-hearted efforts to suppress the rebellion, making Brazil unique in South America for achieving a relatively peaceful transition to independence.

Rio, capital of the Empire of Brazil

Independence was remarkably easily achieved, but Dom Pedro proved to be an ineffective ruler. He was becoming both increasingly autocratic and estranged from his subjects, scandalizing his court by the openness with which he displayed his mistresses and the children he fathered. In 1831 he abdicated in favour of his five-year-old son and namesake Pedro. The misrule of Pedro I, and the power vacuum following his abdication, resulted in years of political turmoil, provincial rebellions and conflict with Argentina, with stability only restored when **Dom Pedro II** was crowned as emperor in 1840.

Rio's fortunes, however, fared well, benefiting from the province's substantial budget as the centre of the new Empire and the profitability of a new product:

Slavery and African Rio

During the eighteenth and much of the nineteenth centuries, fear dominated the lives of Rio's white elite. There was both the constant threat – and occasional reality – of pirate invasions from the sea, and a perceived threat from **slaves** who had fled the plantations in the interior and were hiding out in the forests surrounding the city, either as individuals or in *quilombos*, communities of runaways. The urban black population – the labourers and domestic slaves who formed most of the workforce – were also feared, with regular rumours of mass insurrection circulating. With the violent revolution that occurred in Haiti in 1792 and the declaration of the republic in 1804 by former slaves there, Rio's white population was reduced to a state of absolute terror. Although organized **rebellions** did not occur in Rio as they did in other parts of Brazil, slaves sometimes responded to the oppressive conditions that they suffered by lashing out against the lower levels of white society amongst whom they lived.

Despite this, the white elite was slow to halt the import of enslaved Africans, let alone abolish slavery in Brazil. With the rise of Rio's coffee-based economy in the early nineteenth century, **plantation owners** tried to import as many slaves as possible, both to labour in the fields and in the city. Although Dom Pedro agreed to end the slave trade in 1831 in exchange for the recognition by Britain of Brazilian independence, the law was completely ignored. By the 1840s, the enslaved population of the city of Rio numbered 80,000 or almost forty percent of the inhabitants, while if freed slaves were taken into account, the figure increased to almost half the population, the largest concentration of African and African descended people in the Americas. Only in 1850 did the Atlantic slave trade effectively end. In 1871 the **"law of the free womb"** granted freedom to children born of slaves, while in 1885 slaves over the age of 60 were freed. Finally, on May 13, 1888, the **golden law** abolished slavery, with Brazil the last country in the western hemisphere to do so.

Following abolition, former slaves flocked to the city. The ethnic balance of Rio, however, gradually altered with the arrival of Portuguese immigrants – part of the government's policy of **"whitening"** the Brazilian population – and of migrants from other parts of the country. But the importance of the African influence on Rio remained strong. **Afro-Brazilians** probably form a majority of Rio's population (though who is "white" and who is "black" is a thorny issue in Brazil), and Africa's cultural impact is immense, if more subtle than in some other parts of Brazil such as Salvador. For example, **dance and music** – in particular samba's rhythmic drumming – displays a clear African lineage. **Umbanda** and **Candomblé** – syncretic **religions** that blend Catholicism with African religions and spiritism – are powerful influences, attracting almost as many white as black followers.

coffee. By 1860, vast areas of the southwest of the province, in particular the hills of the Paraíba Valley, had been stripped of their dense Atlantic forest to be planted with coffee bushes. The crop was responsible for more than half of Brazil's export income, and as Rio produced over seventy percent of Brazilian coffee, the province was the economic heart of the country.

Dom Pedro II could hardly have been more different from his father: he was highly cultured, enlightened and permitted limited democracy. And with the enormous income from coffee, financiers from Britain and elsewhere were eager to invest in the city, helping to create a modern infrastructure that included railways and trams, port facilities, gas streetlights, a sewage system and a telegraph system. This rapid **modernization** led to the creation of a middle class which increasingly rejected the monarchy. The final blow came when landowners, angry that the emperor had not prevented the final **abolition of slavery** in 1888, withdrew their support from the monarchy. In 1889 Dom Pedro II suddenly abdicated and slipped away with his family into exile in France, where he died two years later.

The Republic and political turmoil

The wealthy landowners who seized political power in the peaceful 1889 revolution effectively controlled the selection of Brazilian presidents. Already in decline due to soil erosion, Rio's vital coffee crop could not withstand the end of slavery. Many plantation owners went bankrupt, though others successfully adapted their land holdings to cattle ranching. With this sudden and dramatic economic decline, the state of Rio de Janeiro lost political dominance of the country, while São Paulo and Minas Gerais – their own economies expanding thanks to wealth from the expansion of coffee and industrial development – became the most powerful Brazilian states, with their politicians alternating in the presidency.

In 1930 **Getúlio Vargas**, from Brazil's southernmost state of Rio Grande do Sul, seized power in a collision of junior officers and the urban working class, who were appalled at the vast sums spent to protect coffee producers in Minas Gerais and São Paulo when the export markets collapsed as a consequence of the **Great Depression**. For over two decades, Vargas dominated Brazilian life, declaring himself dictator in 1937 and imprisoning opponents from across the political spectrum. Vargas called his regime the **Estado Novo** (the New State), modelled on the fascist dictatorships of Portugal and Italy. Rio received an economic boost, as Vargas's nationalist economic policies led to the development of steel mills, oil refineries and naval facilities in the state.

With the outbreak of **World War II**, Vargas tried to maintain Brazilian neutrality, but in 1942 he succumbed to United States pressure and declared war on the Axis powers. A military force of 25,000 men were sent to fight in the Italian campaign but, in 1945, after the units returned to Brazil, Vargas was forced to resign the presidency in the face of the arguments from the military that it was impossible to tolerate a dictatorship at home, having just been fighting a war in the name of democracy. Elections were held, with the army general **Eurico Dutra** emerging as the victor. Vargas, however, had not given up on power, standing for election in 1950 and securing an easy victory. The next four years were marked by political and economic turmoil, with Vargas now being accused of being a communist, of political murder and corruption. The military high command again demanded his resignation, whereupon an emotional and disillusioned Vargas withdrew to his bedroom in Rio's Palácio de Catete and shot himself.

Expansion and urban development

Although Rio de Janeiro had surrendered its economic and political dominance of Brazil, under the republic Rio continued to prosper as the capital. Boosted by European immigration (overwhelmingly Portuguese) and internal migration (including emancipated slaves and former coffee plantation workers), the city's **population** had grown steadily during the nineteenth century, rising from 100,000 in 1850 to over 500,000 in 1889, when Brazil became a republic. The population continued to rise, reaching over one million by 1920, two million by the mid-1940s and exceeding three million in 1960 when, for the first time, São Paulo had become Brazil's largest city.

A consequence of the rise in Rio's population was its **physical expansion**, leading the city to be redrawn and reshaped. Until the beginning of the twentieth century, the inhabitants were still concentrated in the neighbourhood now known as Centro. The wealthy, though, had long left the area, moving south to spacious mansions in Botafogo. In 1892 and 1904 **tunnels** were built under the mountains between Botafogo and Copacabana, shifting the city's centre of gravity further south and west.

Architecturally, too, Rio was also changing. Already under the Empire there was a move away from Portuguese styles as the city reinvented itself as a tropical Paris. Although plans were laid as early as 1871 and formal parks and public buildings started to emerge, the real work was the creation, at the beginning of the twentieth century, of **Avenida Rio Branco**, a grand boulevard cutting north–south across the old centre of the city. Along here ornate, Neoclassical public buildings were built including the Museo Nacional de Belas Artes (1908), the Theatro Municipal (1909) and the Biblioteca Nacional (1910). The 1930s witnessed yet further change to the basic layout of the city centre with the creation of the **Avenida Presidente Vargas** – a megalomaniac project several kilometres in length and eighty metres wide, that necessitated the demolition of hundreds of old houses and several colonial-era churches and the erasing of the Afro-Brazilian community of Praça Onze, for generations considered the very soul of samba and Carnaval.

Massive **landfill projects** were also undertaken, to ease the strain on a city restricted by its mountainous geography as well as to let the governments of the day boast that they were exemplars of modern development in which the airplane and motorcar would play centre stage. The first was created in 1936, just alongside Centro, to be **Aeroporto Santos Dumont**, while in the 1950s the **Aterro do Flamengo** was created and in the 1960s Copacabana beach was expanded.

Modernist Rio

During the 25 years preceding World War I, Rio recreated its own version of the Belle Époque, with the literary and artistic elite largely copying French styles, leaving little space for artistic innovation. Following the war more varied influences crossed the Atlantic, in part because of major new artistic developments in Europe, but also because of vibrant creative forms emerging in Brazilian art, music and architecture.

Since the 1930s, Brazilian **Modernism** has taken centre stage in almost all areas of the arts, a clear rejection of (European) classical forms. The architect **Oscar Niemeyer** – born in 1907 and still taking commissions aged over 100 – has been one of the key figures cementing Modernism as the default style for buildings and inspiring generations of architects. Comparatively little of Niemeyer's prolific output is actually located in Rio de Janeiro, although one of his most eye-catching creations – the **Museu de Arte Contemporânea** (see p.146) – is located across the bay in Niterói. But there's certainly no lack of important Modernist buildings in Rio and wandering through the city can sometimes feel like stepping into an issue of *Wallpaper** magazine. Classic examples of *Carioca* Modernist buildings include the graceful former home of the Moreira Salles banking family (see p.118) designed by **Olavo Redig de Campos** (1906–84) and completed in 1951, and the low, horizontal concrete **Museu de Arte Moderna** (see p.47), opened in 1954 and designed by **Affonso Reidy** (1909–64). From the same generation is the now iconic wave-like mosaic pavement running alongside Copacabana's Avenida Atlântica (1970 – see p.100), a perfect example of Modernist form and function created by the internationally renowned landscape architect and naturalist **Roberto Burle Marx** (1909–94).

The transfer of the capital

The idea of transferring the capital from Rio to a more central part of the country had first been floated in 1827, while in 1891 an article calling for this to happen was inserted into the constitution. When **Juscelino Kubitschek** became president in 1956, it was partially on the strength of an electoral campaign that promised to build a new capital. On April 21, 1960 the capital was transferred to **Brasília**. Between 1960 and 1975 the city and western hinterland of Rio became the state of **Guanabara**, only merging with the state of Rio de Janeiro in 1975.

The transfer of all federal institutions to Brasília, combined with São Paulo having firmly established itself as Brazil's industrial powerhouse and most populous city, made Rio look as if it was heading further into economic and political irrelevance. With state finances dwindling, the infrastructure entered a prolonged period of decay. It would be decades before the city's fortunes appeared to revive.

The military dictatorship

In 1961 Kubitschek was succeeded as president by **Jânio Quadros**, a populist politician from São Paulo who is best remembered in Rio for banning women from wearing bikinis on the beach. More importantly, however, was his act of establishing relations with the Soviet Union at the height of the Cold War – a decision that led to a series of events culminating in a military coup in 1964 and a dictatorship that would endure for 21 years. Having lost the support of a crucial coalition partner in Congress, Quadros resigned just six months after taking office, expecting that there would be a popular outcry calling for his return to the presidency. This failed to happen and instead his vice-president, **João Goulart**, was sworn in as president. Feared by the right (and by Washington) as a closet communist, Goulart threw his support behind the country's trade unions and the Peasant Leagues, a movement demanding land reform. On March 31, 1964, troops from Minas Gerais moved towards Rio to mount a military coup. The commanders there refused to oppose them and Goulart fled into exile.

Although the coup was bloodless, the army soon acted with levels of ferocity towards opponents that was uncharacteristic of previous experiences of military governments. Protests during the dictatorship's first years (in Rio most notably in 1968 when some 100,000 marched upon the Palácio Tiradentes) led to a tightening of the military's grip on power. The final straw came in 1968 when **Márcio Moreira Alves**, a young politician from Rio, made a speech in the Chamber of Deputies in Brasília, calling on Brazilian women to refuse to sleep with military officers. Feeling humiliated by a civilian, the government closed the Chamber of Deputies and Brazil entered the darkest period of the dictatorship, with five years of the total **suppression** of trade unions, routine torture, strict censorship and the exile of thousands of opponents. Several years of spectacular rates of growth, followed by deteriorating economic conditions, led in the late 1970s to increased opposition to the military. The metalworkers' strike – led by **Lula**, Brazil's future president – in 1977 in the industrial heartlands of São Paulo resulted in greater confidence of trade unions. The mass campaign for elections in 1983–84 resulted in rallies throughout the country, including a turnout of a million people on April 10, 1984 outside Rio's Igreja da Candelária. The military was forced to concede power and elections were held in January 1985, the victor being the mineiro politician **Tancredo Neves**.

Democracy

The night before his inauguration as president, Tancredo was rushed to hospital with a stomach tumour, and he died six weeks later, without assuming office. His deputy, **José Sarney**, assumed office, presiding over five years of endemic corruption, hyperinflation and economic meltdown. **Fernando Collor de Melo** won the elections that followed and was inaugurated in 1990. Collor became a hate figure amongst Brazil's growing middle class for freezing bank accounts as part of his hopelessly failed attempts to control inflation. Two years into his term of office, evidence emerged of Collor being directly involved in massive skimming from the government's coffers, and he was impeached in September 1992. Again, a deputy became an accidental president, with **Itamar Franco** being widely considered a buffoon. There was one saving grace to his administration: his finance minister, **Fernando Henrique Cardoso**, who introduced a new currency (the real) and succeeded in taming inflation. Widely respected, even by political opponents, Cardoso's skills in stabilizing the economy enabled him to be elected president twice, in office from 1995 to 2003. Despite these achievements, economic growth was sluggish during his presidency, hugely problematic for a country with a high rate of population growth. Corruption, social inequality and regional imbalances continued to characterize Brazil. The presidential elections of 2002 resulted in a remarkable break from the past: the victory of **Luiz Inácio Lula da Silva** and his Workers' Party, the PT. Lula was inaugurated in 2003 and, now in his second term, will remain in office until the end of 2010. Despite the once impeccably clean PT having been mired in corruption scandals, the continuance of ramshackle social security, education and health systems and urban violence, Lula somehow consistently maintains approval ratings of well over 70 percent, thanks to a strong economy benefiting the country's middle class and cash transfers claimed by eleven million poor families.

Rio's present – and future

After years of decline in Rio's economic, political and even cultural status, the city's fortunes are looking up. Most dramatically there's the benefit from the apparently huge **oil deposits** offshore in the Santos Basin: the **Tupi field**, discovered in November 2007, could be the world's largest-ever deep-water oilfield discovery. These oil discoveries have been followed by others that are similarly impressive, but their development will pose significant geological challenges that will be difficult to finance unless petroleum prices rise steeply. Earlier, smaller, oil discoveries, from which the state of Rio benefits through tax receipts, have swelled the city's coffers, producing, for the first time in decades, a real buzz of seemingly unstoppable energy and enabling long-awaited urban redevelopment and social projects to finally be financed.

Despite positive signs and hopes for the future, it is also easy to see what is wrong with Rio de Janeiro. **Violence** is a real and present danger for the city's inhabitants, much of it drug-related, with gangs controlling vast swaths of the city. The poorly trained, poorly paid and corrupt police are more part of the problem than the solution: although Brazil's murder rate has been falling, in Rio killings by police have risen dramatically, from three hundred in 1998 to nine hundred in 2008. Although there have been some successes at relieving

Favelas

Since the emergence of Rio's first *favela* on the slopes of the **Morro da Providência** (see p.66) in 1897, established by former soldiers returning from the Canudos war, these informal settlements have been a major feature of the urban landscape. Although *favelas* are certainly not specific to Rio, there are few cities in Brazil where they are such a dominant presence. Rio's *favelas* sprawl across much of the **Zona Norte** and are clearly visible alongside the highways leading into the city, while they exist cheek-by-jowl with the exclusive *bairros* of the **Zona Sul**.

With the collapse of the state's coffee-based economy, Rio attracted a steady flow of **migrants** from the former plantations in search of work. Lacking the means to rent, let alone purchase, a home, these new arrivals would typically "invade" unused land, generally on unused publicly-owned property on steep hillsides, narrow areas alongside roads and other similarly undesirable locations. Communities formed as the migrants were joined by their extended families and others from their former homes. With the industrialization policies of Getúlio Vargas's government in the 1940s, migrants flocked to the city in search of greater opportunities from more distant parts of Brazil, in particular the poverty-stricken Northeast, and with little in the way of available housing, new – and often larger – *favelas* were created, their populations also swelled by the ranks of poor locals. This pattern continued with many of the present-day *favelas* on the Zona Sul hillsides having developed in the 1960s and 1970s to provide conveniently located housing for construction and service workers. Today an estimated one in five of Rio's population live in a *favela*.

For more privileged residents of Rio, *favelas* have long been seen as a problem – as well as an eyesore – rather than as a practical solution to the lack of affordable housing. With the government traditionally exerting minimal control over *favelas*, they have been seen as dens of vice and police no-go areas. Since the 1950s, schemes to **eradicate favelas** have been attempted, forcibly relocating their inhabitants to government housing projects. The best known of these – thanks to Fernando Meirelles' internationally successful 2002 film – is the **Cidade de Deus** (City of God), created in 1960 in the Zona Oeste. Isolated from places of employment, with little in the way of community cohesion and infrastructure hardly better than a *favela*, the Cidade de Deus rapidly descended into a lawless slum where local gangs hold sway.

Eliminating *favelas* is no longer on the political agenda, but issues concerning their conditions, lawlessness and spread remain. As shows of force by Rio's incompetent and notoriously corrupt police to dislodge drug lords have done little but create local resentment, the authorities have opted for other controlling tactics. The **Favela-Bairro** project has, since 2003, gone some way to integrate *favelas* into the city by providing basic health and sanitation, schools, community centres and transportation links; improving the quality of life of residents. Far more controversial have been the measures taken since 2009 to build **walls** around forty *favelas*, in particular around the Zona Sul. While Rio's authorities claim that this is being done both to protect forests from enroachment and the *favelas* from landslides and floods, critics argue that this move is essentially to appease the city's wealthy residents who want to be physically separated from their poor neighbours.

poverty, divisions between rich and poor remain alarming, with much of the city's population living in appalling conditions. Educational prospects are poor, while the condition of public health care is strikingly bad, as witnessed by the authorities' inability to cope with annual outbreaks of dengue fever.

Football

With five World Cups to their name, **futebol** (football or soccer) has become quintessentially Brazilian, and Rio's **Maracanã stadium** the sport's spiritual home. No other facet of Rio life unites – and divides – *Cariocas* to the same extent: everyone has an affiliation to one of the city's big four teams – Flamengo, Vasco, Botafogo or Fluminense – regardless of their liking for the game itself. Over more than a hundred years different races and classes have found in football enough common ground to confront injustice and wear the flamboyant yellow national shirt with pride.

Some history

In some ways the progress of football mirrors Brazil's own development. The sport began in Rio in the final years of the nineteenth century when Oscar Cox, the 17-year-old son of a British diplomat, began playing with friends at his father's expatriate club, Rio Cricket, in Flamengo. The club split soon after, one branch moving to Niterói where it remains today (see ⓦwww.riocricket.com.br), and another eventually ending up in Leblon. Cox organized the first official match between the two rival sides in 1901 in Niterói – though it was the formation of dedicated football club **Fluminense** in 1902 that sparked a real interest in the game beyond just the expat minority.

Alex Bellos, in his remarkable book *Futebol, the Brazilian Way of Life* (see p.269), traces the roots of the Brazilian game through two tiers of development. At one level, the game was an elite and exclusive pastime which provided the Zona Sul classes with a connection to their European origins, while at the second level, interest in the game generated rapidly among the poor and, especially, recently liberated slaves. In 1904 the distant Rio suburb of Bangu started a football team made up of mainly black players working in the *bairro*'s textile factory, though Fluminense quickly moved to ban blacks from entering the annual **Campeonato Carioca**, the Rio championship which began in 1906. It took until the 1920s for a big shake up, by which time the game had already become massively popular; clubs **Botafogo** and **América** fielded teams in 1904, new club **Flamengo** after a split from Fluminense in 1911, and historic Zona Norte club Madureira in 1914. The most radical development was within Rio's close-knit Portuguese community, however. Named after explorer Vasco de Gama, a powerful team comprising blacks, whites and *mulattos* won the 1923 state championship, something so controversial that the club was excluded from the league for the next six years – but the football skill exhibited had set a precedent. Undeterred by being cast out of the official fold, Vasco's supporters clubbed together and built their own São Januario stadium (see p.145) in 1927, which today remains Rio's most historic sports arena – and arguably its most atmospheric, too. On completion Vasco declared themselves professional, and other clubs had to follow suit – not least because rivals in São Paulo were developing apace. Fluminense were forced to reconsider their position after deciding to field a *mulatto* who had tried to whiten his face with rice powder. To this day throwing white rice powder in the stadium is a hallmark of dedicated Fluminense fans. By 1930 **Vasco** and other excluded clubs were welcomed back into the league, and, now unified, *futebol Brasileira* began its ascent to global dominance.

Just as football provided a way for poor communities to unite and develop in the early days, today the sport continues to play a powerful role – promoting education and preventing poor young people from sliding into the open arms of drugs gangs.

Bola Pra Frente (T21/3018-5858, Wwww.bolaprafrente.org.br) Started by **Jorginho**, a national player in the 1990s, this successful social project is located where he grew up in Guadalupe, one of the Zona Norte's toughest neighbourhoods. The programme offers a thousand 5–17-year-olds an education complementary to state schooling, with additional academic classes, as well as sports training. Football is a reward for good behaviour, and the methodology used on the pitch to promote both individual drive and teamwork is transferred to the classroom. A red card for bad behaviour, for example, results in the ultimate punishment – no football that week. Bola Pra Frente has many success stories, with former pupils in good company positions and higher education, but the most remarkable statistic is that 99 percent of participants go on to finish school and stay out of crime, compared to 49 percent of the same age group outside the project. It has also won high-profile corporate sponsorships (including HSBC and Nike), with some companies encouraging teenagers with presentations on the world of business and internships. Despite insecurity and violence in the area, the project draws great community respect. If you are interested in volunteering or coaching, contact the organization direct, or journalist and football guide Rob Shaw at Ebrazsoc@hotmail.com.

Centro Unica das Favelas (CUFA; Wwww.cufa.org.br) operates a youth project in Cidade de Deus in partnership with former Brazil star Ronaldo and Brazilian rapper MV Bill, running programmes in art, theatre and football. **Gold Eletra** (Wwww .goldeletra.org.br) was founded in Caju by footballers Raí and Leonardo, with the aim of instilling self-support for youths to transform their own realities. Both organizations offer volunteer and coaching opportunities.

Brazilian football came into its own in the 1940s when players like Flamengo's **Zizinho** dazzled crowds with their tricks. Foreign commentators remarked on this new style, where individual skill and dribbling technique seemed to be winning over more organized European-style passing formations. Bellos notes how some critics saw this as evidence of the Brazilian "*malandro*" – a master of trickery and deceit – using the ball to get one over on his colonial master, turning an elite game to his advantage through shrewdness and agility. However it happened, football had crossed the boundaries of race and slavery, and – like Carnaval – offered a level playing field where people of Portuguese, African, Amerindian or other European origins could unite behind something perceived as wholeheartedly Brazilian.

Incredibly, the Maracanã stadium was built in just two years in preparation for the 1950 World Cup, employing a workforce from all over the country. As the biggest football stadium in the world, holding at that time an astonishing 10 percent of Rio de Janeiro's total population, the construction was a clear statement of intent. When Brazil lost the final to Uruguay in front of 200,000 silenced fans, Rio remained in shock for years. But the national team made amends by winning the 1958 and 1962 World Cups, a period when (aside from Pele) it was dominated by three great Botafogo stars – Didi, Nilton Santos and Garrincha, all of whom have since made FIFA's all-time world-starting eleven. **Garrincha** in particular is seen as a football genius, born with dribbling skills that just couldn't be marked. When he played with **Pele**, Brazil never lost a game. Television footage shows the glorious '58 team being paraded through a packed Rio de Janeiro, something that was repeated after a Garrincha-inspired World Cup victory four years later.

The game today

These days, Flamengo has taken over as Brazil's most popular team with around forty million fans – something due as much to their 1980s triumphs led by star-player **Zico** as to open support by Brazil's largest TV network, *Globo*. While the best young talent is now usually whisked off to Europe before becoming established locally, Brazil has developed a whole industry in producing it, most notably through football-based five-a-side games like **Futsal** and **Beach Soccer**.

Football in Brazil – and in Rio especially – plays a different role in society than elsewhere. Brazilians will often talk about the aesthetics of a game – the beauty and the theatricality of the fans, for example. The prettiness of the **"Fla-Flu"** (Flamengo-Fluminense) classic fixture with its beautiful colours, streamers and flags, for example, is now one of the game's main draws. Supporters' groups for the same team compete with each other for the best flags, samba music and fancy dress to demonstrate their passion. Coming to prominence, like Carnaval, in the first few decades of the twentieth century has resulted in undoubted parallels being drawn between the two.

Football continues to offer a means of escape and hope for those in poverty, with thousands of success stories. Perhaps the most famous is of **Ronaldo**, who was picked from poor insignificance at minor club São Cristovão in Rio's Zona Norte and went on to play for Real Madrid and win the title of world player of the year. Analogies are often drawn between what the world sees of Brazil in a World Cup final, and the kind of football they imagine kids playing on the streets or beaches of Rio – where barefoot boys dance their way around opponents and gain kudos from the tricks employed. It's a stereotype, no doubt, but one which few Brazilians would dispute. Rio's Maracanã maintains Brazil's position as leader in world football, and as the **2014 World Cup** final to be held there approaches, expectations will run very high for Brazil not just to be there, but to win.

Music

You're rarely far from **music** in Rio de Janeiro. From the city's samba dancehalls and bossa nova bars to *favela* funks and trendy nightclubs, it seems to pulsate with a rhythm all of its own. Pretty much every Brazilian dances, and in Rio you'll find few people who can't manage a little samba or to tap out a rhythm on the *pandeiro*, the classic Brazilian tambourine.

Throughout the twentieth century, the city became the ultimate location for fusions of different musical genres. Brazil began to embrace its melting pot of European, African and Amerindian influences, giving birth to an extremely open musical culture where styles were absorbed, combined, and new forms reinvented. As Brazil's cultural capital, artists flocked to Rio to practise and perform in front of a reliably wealthy crowd of locals and tourists. Ever-present in the city, Americans and Europeans have also carried their music to the airwaves: jazz, rock, pop, hip-hop and electronic sounds have found open ears among local musicians and DJs, always keen to recreate them with their own Brazilian stamp.

The foundations

The origins of Brazilian music lie in the mixing of Portuguese and African elements in the nineteenth century. An Angolan folkloric dance called the **lundu** fused with Portuguese guitar and song, and its raunchy undertones became popular among the middle class. Cape Verdean **batuque**, too, was brought to Brazil, its 6/8 time signature seen to be a major influence on rhythms to come later. But by 1870 the popular sound in Rio was **maxixe**, a rapid two-step tango style originating from Mozambiquean slaves. With Rio and Bahia in the Northeast the central hubs of Brazil, they offered the ideal forums for performance and practice, with numerous religious and other traditional festivals of which Carnaval became the most famous.

Rio composer **Heitor Villa-Lobos** was also instrumental in bringing together forms and developing a European-influenced classical style in Brazil in the early twentieth century. He played traditional Brazilian music on the street, drawing on all of Rio's ethnic influences, before undergoing classical training. He later wrote numerous operas, symphonies and quartet works, including a Brazilian interpretation of Bach and 1920s *choro* transcribed as pieces for the classical guitar.

Choro

Choro (often called *chorinho*) emerged from Rio's musical melee in the nineteenth century, with European classical influences joining Afro-Brazilian styles. It found its feet in the centre of Rio musical life from 1910 to 1940 through artists like Ernesto Nazareth and Pixinguinha, and later regained popularity in the late 1970s when sambista Paulinho da Viola released his seminal album *Memórias Chorando*. Predominantly instrumental, it is semi-improvised on guitar, *cavaquinho* (a tiny high-pitched guitar like a ukulele) and flute, most often joined by percussion on drums or *pandeiro*. It's a highly rhythmic yet graceful sound, sharply contrasting with bold, expressive modern samba. Still popular today, you can regularly hear *chorinho* in Lapa and at street performances and special events across the city.

Samba

It was **samba**, however, that appeared from the musical experiments of the nineteenth century to the greatest public acclaim. Directly related to the emergence of Carnaval (see p.214), the genre also has clear origins in Afro-Brazilian religious forms like Candomblé, which was practised by migrants from Bahia in the port areas of the city, its accompanying drums and singing containing the call-and-response structure of *batuque*. As Carnaval developed, **samba de enredo** (themed samba) became the genre's defining form, where massed bands of hundreds or thousands of drummers answer a couple of lead vocalists. Still the form you'll hear in the Sambódromo or at Carnaval *blocos* today, the sound is an overwhelming cacophony of noise and intense rhythm; the more you hear of it the more hypnotized you become.

By the 1950s **samba–canção** became the popular form as the genre found its way into wider Rio society. Led by a single singer with a small group of musicians comprising guitar, *cavaquinho*, floor drum, *pandeiro* and other percussion, its theme is usually love – singers like Elza Soares (wife of former top footballer Garrincha), Beth Carvalho, Monarco, Alcione and above all the husky atmospheric tones of Dona Ivone Lara all made their marks on the genre in its heyday. Though this older generation of artists doesn't perform as much as they used to, you can still catch all of them around Rio at different times of the year (see p.197). Younger samba stars have also grown up alongside Lapa's resurgence – distinctive singers like Teresa Cristina and Thais Villela grew out of Lapa's Comuna do Semente music sessions (p.69), and now perform across higher-level venues.

Sambas with less celebrated singers, performed commonly in the street or at lower-key venues, are often called **rodas de samba** (samba in the round), where musicians sit and play in a circle, just as *capoeira* is practised. In Rio you'll also see **samba de mesa** advertised, indicating that musicians and much of the audience will sit around tables, always with healthy portions of food and drink as an accompaniment. **Samba de gafieira** refers to the jazz-charged form from the pre-bossa days, designed to get couples twirling on the dance floor. In the 1980s a form of samba emerged called **pagode**, concentrating on love songs and slower rhythms that are easier to dance to in a couple. Zeca Pagodinho has been the major proponent of this form alongside other singers like Beth Carvalho.

Forró

The term **forró** (pronounced "fawhaw") originates from the English "for all", a reference to the dances financed by English engineering companies for their manual labour forces, as opposed to the balls organized for the elite. As drought and poverty forced *nordestinos* to migrate south in the 1940s and 1950s in search of employment in Brazil's large urban centres, so the culture followed – in recent years *forró* has gained a following across the class divide and can often be heard in *gafieiras* and even in glitzy Zona Sul discos. Characterized as a very close couples' dance, it projects the parched interior of the Northeast through its use of accordion, and while older songs spoke of the trials of life and lack of food, these days songs tends to be light-hearted and there have even been covers of famous international pop songs, by artists such as Britney Spears and Madonna, in *forró* style. You can hear *forró* at *Asa Branca* or *Democráticos* in Lapa, or at the **Feira Nordestina** (see p.200).

Radio, new beats and Brazilian pop

As **radio** and a corresponding **record industry** developed in the 1930s, new opportunities arose for Brazilian artists, and the sounds of North America and Europe arrived to keen ears. **Carmen Miranda** was, of course, the most famous *Carioca* singer of all, a product of Lapa's artistic scene in the 1920s whose powerful voice was immortalized (see p.90) when she starred in a number of Hollywood movies. The domination of the singer/songwriter was a new development in Rio – a city used to reworkings of traditional *choros* and sambas – but with the influence of first jazz and later pop and rock on the Brazilian sound, bossa nova, Tropicália and MPB (*Música Popular Brasileira*) followed.

Bossa nova

With the growth of the new Zona Sul middle class in the 1950s, the perfect space and atmosphere emerged for a new, sophisticated genre. The influence of American jazz enchanted guitarist **João Gilberto** and Ipanema-based composer/musicians **Tom Jobim** and **Vinicius de Moraes**, the creators of **bossa nova** ("new beat"). Bossa essentially slowed samba down, adding smooth lyrics, jazz guitar and double bass – the first bossa nova album released in 1958, *Canção do Amor Demais*, was written by Jobim-Moraes and featured Gilberto on guitar and famous singer and actress **Elizete Cardoso** on vocals, a deeply relaxing and instantly popular combination.

Bossa attracted worldwide attention through the music of American saxophonist **Stan Getz** in the early 1960s, and collaboration between Jobim, Gilberto, Getz and Gilberto's wife, **Astrud Gilberto**, resulted in two internationally best-selling albums. Moraes and Jobim also wrote *A Garota de Ipanema* ("**The Girl from Ipanema**"), easily the most well-known Brazilian song worldwide, a dreamy ode to the 1960s Ipanema good life (see p.108).

While bossa nova only achieved a brief reign as genre of choice, other major proponents like Sergio Mendes and Marcos Valle have had long bossa careers, their longevity due to further fusion with jazz, funk, and in the latter's case, rock music and electronics. Mendes's album *Brasil '66* is now considered among the best bossa nova works; he went on to collaborate with Stevie Wonder and recently, the Black Eyed Peas.

Tropicália

Between the 1930s and 1960s Brazil had only known dictatorship, but with unchecked nationalism and extensive censorship of lyrics, a musical rebellion was inevitable. Coinciding with the major demonstrations of the mid to late 1960s, **Tropicália** (also called *Tropicalismo*) emerged, a cultural movement that drew on outside influences like the Beatles and psychedelic rock as much as it did traditional Brazilian sounds.

Tropicália left aside the intimacy of samba and bossa nova, opening up politics as a subject of discussion. **Caetano Veloso** and **Gilberto Gil** – both from Bahia – were the primary exponents. The former's *Alegria, Alegria* and *Cotidiano* are two famous tracks from the period, often dropping into different time signatures and keys. Veloso and Gil were exiled from Brazil at the end of the decade along with many other performers, but both have gone on to have glitteringly successful and innovative careers. Gil collaborated with Pink Floyd andYes before returning to Brazil in 1972 and producing 36 albums to date; he is also credited as the man who introduced reggae to Brazil after covering a Bob Marley song in 1980. He became Minister of Culture under the government of Lula between 2003 and 2008.

MPB

Música Popular Brasileira – always known as just **MPB** – also emerged in the 1960s climate of musical experimentation (though it was never as radical as Tropicália), and it survives today in various forms. **Chico Buarque** was the main 1960s artist to develop the new sound, contrasting *choro* and samba with slow ballads and new imported influences to create a light and rhythmic popular take on the other musical movements of the time. His songs effortlessly move between soothing ballad and something approaching an espionage thriller soundtrack – his 1971 hit *Construcão* demonstrates a skilled voice punctuated by muted trumpets and big-band percussion.

A multitude of artists drove MPB forward through the 1970s, but **Milton Nascimento** is recognized as one of the greatest singers, documenting the experiences of black Brazil with immense vocals. **Jorge Ben Jor** is one of Rio's most famous artists, his much-covered 1963 hit *Mas Que Nada* propelled him to fame, becoming the most played song outside of Brazil – though the 1969 *Charles, Anjo 45* was his most popular song at home. His style is described as samba-rock, and while at times he overlapped with the tropicalistas, his music spans a range of genres. Other major singers of the 1970s were **Elis Regina** and **Gal Costa**, who crossed bossa and MPB, while **Ney Matogrosso** remains popular to this day with his form of expressive, theatrical rock. The 1980s and 1990s saw artists like **Barão Vermelho** and **Chico Science** experimenting with forms, and **Marisa Monte** has been a seminal vocalist who ties modern MPB with popular older sambas.

In the new millennium, the most famous and talented Rio singer to emerge is **Seu Jorge**, who grew up in a *favela* in the Belford Roxo district, rising to fame as an actor with parts in *City of God* and *The Life Aquatic* before becoming a critically acclaimed singer/songwriter with three albums to his name. Jorge's music draws on Jorge Ben Jor and Gilberto Gil in its popular fusion of samba and MPB, though he is also clearly influenced by hip-hop and reggae. A new female MPB voice to look out for is **Vanessa da Mata** – she has a gentle voice that combines soothing song with a distinctly Brazilian rhythm.

Modern sounds

The influx of electronic equipment and drum machines in the 1980s and 1990s had a profound effect on music in Rio, as it did everywhere. American hip-hop arrived, following soul and funk the previous decade, picked up on by a multi-racial and rapidly increasing *favela* population. **Funk carioca** emerged in this youthful space to become the single most popular genre among Rio youth today, though samba-based *pagode* is also still in vogue, having progressed into a form of romantic popular music which draws on rap and electronic sounds.

Funk Carioca

In the 1980s record imports carried the bass-heavy Miami hip-hop sound to Rio, characterized by rapid drum-machine bass beats and sometimes angry, often sexually explicit, lyrics. In the sprawling urban ghettos, where tensions are generally relieved by partying hard; local MCs overlaid lyrics and samples on the imported Miami bass to create **funk carioca** – "funk" as that was the previous genre of American records to be imported – and also known as *baile funk* as it comes from the *favela bailles* (dances). The new sound struck a chord with young people, the ideal type of music to rebel against what wealthy Rio was doing with MPB down near the beaches, embracing booty-shaking bass beats and raw, lewd lyrics. Like early hip-hop in the States and dancehall reggae in the Caribbean, *funk carioca* is certainly not designed to be liked by anyone in authority. A sub-genre, *funk proibido* or *funk realidade*, specifically raps about government corruption and how *favela* law is the only system they need to subscribe to.

Like samba before it, funk was born in the slums to widespread suspicion from the middle classes, but as time goes on, both rhythmic genres proved irresistible. Funk has found its way into the clubs and is gaining ground overseas, too – and it's a very common sound on the streets of Rio. Most larger *favelas* have a hall or club in which they hold dances – some are safer than others to go to – a good bet is usually the two-thousand-capacity *Castelo das Pedras* in Zona Oeste (see p.203). **Sany Pitbull** is currently the most popular club DJ on the circuit, known to mix up his sets with all kinds of live sounds. Funk hasn't escaped **scandal**, however – numerous violent incidents have occurred at *favela bailles* as most are controlled by rival drugs gangs – and there have been many reports of underage sexual exploitation. There's no denying that funk takes pride in its loose lyrics and dancing, and many people point to the danger presented by rapidly rising rates of HIV – but as with similar debates elsewhere, funk's protagonists argue that violence and sex were there long before the music.

Home-grown hip-hop and electronica

Outside of funk, Brazilian **hip-hop** and **electronica** have become hugely popular forms. Rapper **MV Bill** from Cidade de Deus was the first to draw real attention to Brazilian hip-hop in the late 1990s, and more recently Rocinha-based **Gabriel o Pensador** ("Gabriel the Thinker") has become the best known, with an intelligent and poetic style enthused with jazz. Similarly, groups **Afro-Reggae** and **Rappa** combine reggae, hip-hop, rock and Brazilian rhythms, both having become two of Rio's top musical outputs.

Rio's **dance music/electronica** scene is also considered groundbreaking, with DJs mixing up five decades-worth of contemporary Brazilian music with foreign house and drum'n'bass sounds, sometimes chopping and changing between an assortment of genres from hip-hop to funk to electronica and more traditional Brazilian musics. Even old-time bossa/samba singer Marcos Valle has albums, such as 1999's *Nova Bossa Nova*, incorporating electronica. The diaspora, too, is producing innovative music which eventually filters back home – London's Rio-born DJ **Amon Tobim** has been busy creating new electronic sounds, using drum and bass, hip-hop and Brazilian music, for ten years.

Film

Whether they are home-grown or foreign productions, portrayals of Rio on **film** often veer towards either escapism or gritty realism. Rio has a long tradition of starring as an exotic escape in foreign films, starting with Thornton Freeland's 1933 extravaganza *Flying Down to Rio* (see p.100). In more recent times, Rio's extraordinary backdrop continues to attract film-makers, although the steamy stereotypes have hardly been shaken off with films such as *Blame It on Rio* (1984) and *The Girl from Rio* (2001).

Naturally, the Rio portrayed by Brazilian film-makers is much more varied, with realism rather than escapism the more dominant style. Since the innovative 1956 film *Rio 40 Graus*, inhabitants of *favelas* have been the subjects and stars of films set in Rio, though other topics and genres have inspired film-makers, including historical dramas, musicals and documentaries, making Rio, second only to São Paulo, as Brazil's film capital.

The selection of post-1945 films reviewed here is primarily based on whether they have clear Rio content. Many are excellent films regardless of their location, though some rather significant ones are likely to make you cringe in terms of the plot, dialogue or cinematic quality. All can be tracked down on DVD with English subtitles or dialogue.

Brazilian films

Central do Brasil *Central Station*, Walter Salles, 1998. A deeply moving story of a joyless, cynical former schoolteacher (Fernanda Montenegro) who earns a living writing letters for illiterate people at Rio's Central Station. Following a chance and tragic encounter, he crosses paths with a young boy. The story charts the bond that develops as they flee Rio to search for the boy's father.

Cidade de Deus *City of God*, Fernando Meirelles, 2002. A hard-hitting coming-of-age film following the life of a young man in a crime-infested Rio housing project from the late 1960s to early 1980s. There are scenes of utter inhumanity that are hard to watch, but the fine storytelling turns what could be an unremittingly grim film into one that's totally compelling.

Como Era Gostoso o Meu Francês *How Tasty Was My Little Frenchman*, Nelson Pereira dos Santos, 1971. Set in 1594 Guanabara Bay, with dialogue largely in French and in the indigenous language of Tupi, the story is that of a French army deserter who is captured by a tribe of cannibals – who decide to eat him. In part a black comedy, the film explores Brazil's colonial origins as well as the nature of modernity.

Madame Satã Karim Ainouz, 2002. A wonderful, immensely atmospheric portrait of the Lapa underworld during its 1930s and 1940s Bohemian heyday, as told through the story of João Francisco dos Santos – popularly known as Madame Satã – drag artiste, bandit, convict and father to seven adopted children.

Ônibus 174 *Bus 174*, José Padilha, 2002. In 2000, a cocaine-addicted street kid called Sandro do Nascimento hijacked a bus in Rio's Jardim Botânico neighbourhood and held eleven women hostage. As the police failed to cordon off the area, the entire siege was shown live on Brazilian TV, including the horrifying conclusion. The focus on Nascimento's short and unremittingly grim life and the poverty, crime and fear that afflicts much of Rio make this a gripping documentary.

Orfeu Negro *Black Orpheus*, Marcel Camus, 1959. This internationally acclaimed Franco-Brazilian co-production recasts the Orpheus and Eurydice myth, setting it against Carnaval in Rio's *favelas*. The cinematography is impressive, while the original bossa nova musical score of Tom Jobim and Luís Bonfá sets the pace.

Os Desafinados *Out of Tune*, Walter Lima Jr., 2008. The story of a fictional struggling bossa nova band in Rio and New York, set in the 1960s and 1970s. With a great score, this is mainly one for bossa nova fans, but the film also succeeds in evoking the atmosphere of the time and place.

O Outro Lado da Rua *The Other Side of the Street*, Marcos Bernstein, 2004. Regina (Fernanda Montenegro), a lonely busybody who snoops on her neighbours in Copacabana, passing on information to the police, believes that she has witnessed a murder in the building opposite. In contrast to Hitchcock's *Rear Window*, the film focuses less on the possible crime, but more on the relationship between the witness and alleged murderer.

O Que É Isso, Companheiro? *Four Days in September*, Bruno Barreto, 1997. Based on the true story of the kidnapping of Charles Elbrick, the United States ambassador to Brazil, by a group of radical students in Rio in 1969. It's both a gripping, though slow-paced, political thriller and a meditation on whether armed resistance to the military dictatorship was in fact counterproductive.

Rio 40 Graus *Rio 40 Degrees*, Nelson Pereira dos Santos, 1956. This neo-realist film deals with ordinary events one Sunday, ranging from the efforts of boys from a *favela* selling peanuts to tourists, to a woman worried about telling her boyfriend that she's pregnant, to a football star reaching the end of his career. With multiple characters and parallel stories, it still remains utterly riveting.

Rio Zona Norte Nelson Pereira dos Santos, 1957. Grande Otelo – one of Brazil's most renowned black actors – leads the cast as an illiterate samba composer who dreams of having one of his compositions sung by real-life samba star Ângela Maria. Filmed on location in the *favelas* of Rio's Zona Norte, this tale of the exploitative music business is based on the experiences of the great samba composer Zé Kéti (who wrote the songs for the film).

Tropa de Elite *The Elite Squad*, José Padilha, 2007. A box-office sensation in Brazil, this film about Rio's paramilitary elite squad tells the story of a 1997 operation to clean up one of the most violent *favelas*, in time for a visit from the Pope. Profoundly depressing, the elite squad revels in tactics as brutal as those of the gangs they're intent on defeating.

O Xangô de Baker Street *A Samba for Sherlock*, 2001. Set in 1886, Holmes and Watson arrive in Rio to investigate a series of grisly murders of women that have shocked the city and left the local police mystified. Once in Brazil, the normally straight-laced Holmes and his powers of deduction are laid to waste in the face of the steamy climate and exotic women, while his investigation bungles its way towards a conclusion.

Films by non-Brazilians

Blame It on Rio Stanley Donen, 1984. Two best friends holiday in Rio only to find that one falls for the other's teenage daughter. A cringe-inducing plot but at least it was filmed on location in Rio – although the cameras rarely ventured off Copacabana beach. One that the star, Michael Caine, probably prefers to forget.

The Girl from Rio Christopher Monger, 2001. Through a twist of fate, Raymond (Hugh Laurie), a mild-mannered bank clerk whose true passion is samba, robs his bank and then flees to Rio in search of the beautiful Orlinda, a samba dancer with whom he is besotted. Hugh Laurie fans are likely to enjoy this, but others will groan at the British and Brazilian stereotypes that litter the film. Still, there are good location shots of Santa Teresa, *favelas* and Copacabana.

The Incredible Hulk Louis Leterrier, 2008. For reasons not entirely clear, Dr Bruce Banner lives in Rio's huge Rocinha *favela*, working in a soda factory while attempting to find a cure for the condition that turns him into the Hulk. Filming of this great-looking movie included Santa Teresa, Rocinha, Lapa and Tijuca locations, although the greater part of the story is set not in Rio but in the US and Canada.

Notorious Alfred Hitchcock, 1946. Cary Grant and Ingrid Bergman star in this espionage thriller in which the American daughter of a convicted Nazi spy is recruited to infiltrate a group of Germans who have relocated to Brazil after World War II. The movie was largely filmed in Hollywood using rear projection, where actors are filmed on a studio set while location footage is shown on a screen behind them.

Road to Rio Norman Z. McLeod, 1947. Bing Crosby, Bob Hope and Dorothy Lamour lead a cast in this musical comedy about two musicians who stow away on a ship bound for Rio and rescue a Spanish beauty about to be forcibly married. The Hollywood interpretation of Rio is a mix of the modernity of Copacabana, the exoticism of Sugar Loaf and a pan-Latin feel of Carmen Miranda.

Books

T here is not a vast range of **books** in English specifically on Rio. That said, because for much of Brazil's history Rio has been the political and cultural heart of the country, there are some important books that either directly or indirectly relate to the city. Easily available titles are given here, together with a selection of others that a good bookshop or library will have in stock or will be able to order.

The term "o/p" denotes that a book is currently out of print, but these are easily tracked down from second-hand bookstores – Abe Books (ⓦwww .abebooks.co.uk or www.abebooks.com) is a good place to start.

Architecture

Lauro Cavalcanti *When Brazil Was Modern: Guide to Architecture, 1928–1960.* This valuable guide to Brazil's unique contribution to modernist architecture discusses the work of over thirty architects, with sections on specific sites such as the Ministry of Health and Education building in Rio. Compact, but well illustrated, the book makes a perfect travel companion for modernist junkies.

Deutsches Architektur Museum (ed) *Oscar Niemeyer: A Legend of Modernism.* This sumptuously produced book is a concise survey of Niemeyer's work from his first commissions in Rio in the early 1930s to Niterói's Museu de Arte Contemporânia of the late 1990s. Included are essays by architectural

critics which help illuminate Niemeyer's architectural legacy.

Annika Gunnarsson and Paulo Venancio Filho *Time & Place: Rio de Janeiro 1956–1964.* During the 1950s and early 1960s, cultural change in Rio manifested itself with bossa nova, *cinema nova* and neo-concretism. This well-illustrated, scholarly but very readable book links these cultural developments with modernist movements that went before.

Marta Iris Montero *Burle Marx: The Lyrical Landscape.* A beautifully illustrated book celebrating the life and work of one of the twentieth century's foremost landscape architects, who designed many of Brazil's prominent parks, gardens and other urban spaces.

Cooking

Yara Castro Roberts and Richard Roberts *The Brazilian Table.* In this beautifully illustrated book, the authors successfully link food with Brazil's diverse cultures. The

state of Rio de Janeiro is well covered – not least because the authors live in Paraty, where Yara hosts guests at the Academy of Cooking and Other Pleasures (see p.157).

Fiction and literary studies

Works by Brazilian authors

Machado de Assis *Posthumous Memoirs of Brás Cubas.* The most important work by Brazil's finest novelist. Told by one of the most remarkable characters in fiction, this is a hilarious tale of absurd schemes to cure the world of melancholy and half-hearted political ambitions unleashed from beyond the grave.

Luiz Afredo Garcia-Roza *The Silence of the Rain.* Inspector Espinosa is the unorthodox detective who solves a complex web of crime – murder, robbery and fraud – against the backdrop of the sometimes seedy, sometimes exotic, setting of Copacabana. The first of a fine police thriller series.

K. David Jackson (ed) *Oxford Anthology of the Brazilian Short Story.* A tremendous collection of short stories from Brazilian authors from the late nineteenth century to the present. Included are ten stories by the author Machado de Assis but there are also works by other Rio authors including Nélida Piñon and Lima Barreto.

Paulo Lins *City of God.* The author, who went on to become a photo-journalist, was brought up in Rio's Cidade de Deus housing project and uses his knowledge of drug trafficking and gang warfare as the basis of this remarkable novel, the book behind the internationally acclaimed film.

Patrícia Melo *Inferno.* A thriller set in a *favela* in Rio, this is a powerful story of an 11-year-old boy who becomes a local gang leader. Though his story's often grim, the central character is a complex figure in terms of his relationships with other gang members and his family.

Robert Giroux and Lloyd Schwartz (eds) *Elizabeth Bishop: Poems, Prose and Letters, 1927–1979.* One of America's foremost twentieth-century poets, Bishop spent much of her adult life in Brazil, living in Rio, Petrópolis and Ouro Preto from 1951 to 1969. This selection from her poems, letters, diaries and other writing includes much concerning her years in Brazil.

Carmen L. Oliveira *Rare and Commonplace Flowers: The Story of Elizabeth Bishop and Lota de Machado Soares.* A gripping and often moving account of the seventeen-year long relationship, in Rio and elsewhere, between prize-winning American poet Elizabeth Bishop and Brazilian designer and architect Lota Soares. As recognition for Bishop grew, she returned to the United States where, just a few days after joining her, Soares committed suicide.

Jean-Christophe Rufin *Brazil Red.* The winner of France's prestigious Goncourt literary award, this action-packed historical novel is set against the ill-fated French settlement of Rio de Janeiro in the sixteenth century and France's attempts to conquer Brazil.

Flora and fauna

Clive Byers *A Photographic Guide to Birds of Southern Brazil.* An attractive, easy-to-carry guide describing 252 types of birds, including those you might spot in the city and state of Rio.

Warren Dean *With Brandaxe and Firestorm.* Compelling and essential reading for anyone wanting to understand how the Mata Atlântica, the coastal rainforest that once covered the state of Rio, was almost completely destroyed from colonial times to the twentieth century.

History

Rosana Barbosa *Immigration and Xenophobia: Portuguese Immigrants in Early 19th Century Rio de Janeiro.* Although Portuguese immigrants were vitally important to Rio's economic and cultural development, the subject has been strangely overlooked by scholars. This important study looks at the role they played in Rio at a time when either enslaved or free Africans still formed the mainstay of the local workforce, and attitudes to them shortly after independence.

Mary C. Karasch *Slave Life in Rio de Janeiro 1808–1850* (o/p). A clear, authoritative, encyclopedic-breadth examination of slavery that became the standard work on a population that shaped the cultural fabric of the city.

Eduardo Silva *Prince of the People: The Life and Times of a Brazilian Free Man of Colour* (o/p). Was Dom Obá II d'Africa a genuine prince, or an unbalanced son of slaves with delusions? Whatever the truth, Dom Obá was revered by the poor around him, and his story sheds light on the final decades of slavery and the life of slaves and people of colour in Rio.

Thomas E. Skidmore *Brazil: Five Centuries of Change.* A very readable general history of Brazil, from the first European contact to the present day.

The author, a renowned US "Brazilianist", made important contributions to the discussion of racial ideology and the analysis of twentieth-century Brazilian political development, and this book is an excellent synthesis of his work and that of other Brazilian and foreign scholars.

Stanley Stein *Vassouras: A Brazilian Coffee County, 1850–1900.* Re-edition of a 1940s classic that improves with age. Superficially a straightforward reconstruction of the rise and fall of the coffee-plantation system in a town in the interior of Rio, beneath that is a devastating indictment of slavery, based on archive work and, uniquely, on the memories of the last generation to have been born as slaves. It includes a fascinating selection of photos.

Patrick Wilcken *Empire Adrift: The Portuguese Court in Rio de Janeiro 1808–1821.* In 1807 the Portuguese royal family, accompanied by ten thousand aristocrats, servants, government officials and priests, fled Lisbon in advance of Napoleon's invading army, which was sweeping across the Iberian Peninsula. In this wonderfully lively account, the author brings to life the incredible atmosphere in Lisbon and Rio during this key episode in Brazilian history.

Music and football

Alex Bellos *Futebol: The Brazilian Way of Life.* Long-overdue, literate and engaging analysis of Brazilian football, covering its early history to the present day and its compulsive mix of world-class players and equally world-class levels of corruption. Written by a journalist with an eye for original stories such as homesick Brazilians playing in the Faroe Islands, tactics for transvestites, and much more.

Ruy Castro *Bossa Nova – The Story of the Brazilian Music That Seduced the World.* A welcome translation of an excellent book by a Brazilian journalist and biographer. This is basically an oral history of bossa nova, packed with incidental detail on Rio nightlife and city culture of the 1950s and early 1960s. A very good read.

Darién J. Davis *White Face, Black Mask: Africaneity and the Early Social History of Popular Music in Brazil.* This is an innovative study of how class, gender and race intertwined in the development of popular music in Brazil – in particular in Rio – between the 1920s and 1950s.

Chris McGowan and Ricardo Pessanha *The Brazilian Sound: Samba, Bossa Nova and the Popular Music of Brazil.* An easy-to-flick-through and well-written manual on modern Brazilian music and musicians. With a new edition published in 2009, this is good to carry with you if you're planning on doing some serious music buying. There's also a useful bibliography and a good discography.

Society

Ruy Castro *Rio de Janeiro.* Ruy Castro, a respected Brazilian journalist, offers a historical and cultural overview of Rio and, far more importantly, captures his fellow *Cariocas'* soul. Leaving aside Castro's sometimes irritating generalizations, this book is an alluring entry into Rio life.

Herbert Daniel and Richard Parker *Sexuality, Politics and AIDS in Brazil* (Falmer Press, US). Excellent, clearly written history of AIDS in Brazil, covering the way the epidemic has developed in relation to popular culture at one end, and government policy at the other.

Robert Gay *Lucia: Testimonies of a Brazilian Drug Dealer's Woman.* This is a true account of the life of one young woman in a Rio *favela*, a portrait of a person negotiating and surviving the conflicting pressures of gangs, drugs, family and church. Highly readable and a perfect companion to *City of God* (see p.268).

Richard Parker *Bodies, Pleasures and Passions.* An analysis of the erotic in Brazilian history and popular culture, written by an American anthropologist resident in Brazil. Tremendous subject matter and some fascinating insights into sexual behaviour, combining insider and outsider perspectives.

Daphne Patai *Brazilian Women Speak: Contemporary Life Stories.* Oral testimony forms the core of this very readable work that lets ordinary women from the Northeast and Rio speak for themselves to describe the struggles, constraints and hopes of their lives.

Thomas E. Skidmore *Black into White: Race and Nationality in Brazilian Thought.* First published in 1974, this 1993 edition has a new preface to bring the book more up to date. A landmark in the intellectual history of Brazilian racial ideology, examining scientific racism and the Brazilian intellectual elite's supposed belief in assimilation and the ideal of "whitening" the population by encouraging European immigration.

Jewel Woods and Karen Hunter *Don't Blame It on Rio: The Real Deal Behind Why Men Go to Brazil for Sex.* A thoughtful, at times provocative, examination of sex tourism in Rio that focuses on black American men.

Language

Language

Portuguese

L earning some **Portuguese** before you go to Rio is an extremely good idea. Although many well-educated Brazilians speak English, and it's now the main second language taught in schools, this hasn't filtered through to the vast majority of the population. If you know Spanish you're halfway there: there are obvious similarities in the grammar and vocabulary, so you should be able to make yourself understood if you speak slowly, and reading won't present you with huge problems. However, Portuguese pronunciation is utterly different and much less straightforward than Spanish, so unless you take the trouble to learn a bit about it you won't have a clue what Brazilians are talking about.

Brazilian Portuguese is a colourful, sensual language full of wonderfully rude and exotic vowel sounds, swooping intonation and hilarious idiomatic expressions. You'll also find that Brazilians will greatly appreciate even your most rudimentary efforts, and every small improvement in your Portuguese will make your stay in Rio ten times more enjoyable.

People who have learned their Portuguese in **Portugal** or in **Lusophone Africa** won't have any real problems with the language in Brazil, but there are some quite big differences. There are many variations in vocabulary, and Brazilians take more liberties with the language, but the most notable differences are in pronunciation: Brazilian Portuguese is spoken more slowly and clearly; the neutral vowels so characteristic of European Portuguese tend to be sounded in full; in much of Brazil outside Rio the slushy "sh" sound doesn't exist; and the "de" and "te" endings of words like *cidade* and *diferente* are palatalized so they end up sounding like "sidadgee" and "djiferentchee".

The best **dictionary** currently available is the *Collins Portuguese Dictionary*. There is a pocket edition, but you might consider taking the fuller, larger version, which concentrates on the way the language is spoken today and gives plenty of specifically Brazilian vocabulary.

Pronunciation

Non-nasal vowels

a shouldn't present you with too many problems. It's usually somewhere between the "a" sound of "bat" and that of "father".

e has three possible pronunciations. When it occurs at the beginning or in the middle of a word, it will usually sound either a bit like the "e" in "bet" – eg *ferro* (iron) and *miséria* (poverty) – or like the "ay" in "hay" – eg *mesa* (table) and *pêlo* (hair). However, the difference can be quite subtle and it's not something you should worry about too much at the start.

The third pronunciation is radically different from the other two: at the end of a word, "e" sounds like "y" in "happy", eg *fome* ("fommy", hunger) and *se* (if), which actually sounds like the Spanish "si".

i is straightforward. It's always an "ee" sound like the "i" in "police", eg *isto* (this).

o is another letter with three possible pronunciations. At the beginning or in the middle of a word, it normally sounds either the way it does in "dog" – eg *loja* (shop) and *pó* (powder) – or the way it does in "go"– eg *homem* (man) and *pôquer* (poker). At the end of a word "o" sounds like the "oo" in "boot", so *obrigado* (thank you) is pronounced "obri-GA-doo". And the definite article "o" as in *o homem* (the man) is pronounced "oo".

u is always pronounced like "oo" in "boot", eg *cruz* (cross).

There are also a variety of vowel combinations or diphthongs that sound pretty much the way you would expect them to. They are: **ai** (pronounced like "i" in "ride"); **au** (pronounced as in "shout"); **ei** (pronounced as in "hay"); and **oi** (pronounced as in "boy"). The only one that has an unexpected pronunciation is ou, which sounds like "o" in "rose".

Nasal vowels

The fun really starts when you get into the nasal vowel sounds. Generally speaking, each "normal" vowel has its nasal equivalent. The trick in pronouncing these is to be completely uninhibited. To take one example, the word *pão* (bread). First of all, just say "pow" to yourself. Then say it again, but this time half close your mouth and shove the vowel really hard through your nose. Try it again, even more vigorously. It should sound something like "powng", but much more nasal and without really sounding the final "g".

There are two main ways in which Portuguese indicates a nasal vowel. One is through the use of the **tilde**, as in pão. The other is the use of the letters **m** or **n** after the vowel. As a general rule, whenever you see a vowel followed by "m" or "n" and then another consonant, the vowel will be nasal – eg *gente*. The same thing applies when the vowel is followed by "m" at the end of a word, eg *tem, bom* – in these cases, the "m" is not pronounced, it just nasalizes the vowel.

Below are some of the main nasal vowels and examples of words that use them. However, it must be emphasized that the phonetic versions of the nasal sounds we've given are only approximate.

- **-ã and -am or -an followed by a consonant** indicate nasal "a" – eg *maçã* (apple), *campo* (field), samba.
- **-ão or -am at the end of a word** indicate the "owng" sound, as explained above in *pão*. Other examples are in *estação* (station), *mão* (hand), *falam* ("FA-lowng"; they talk).
- **-em or -en followed by a consonant** indicate a nasalized "e" sound – eg *tempo* (weather), *entre* (between), *gente* (people).
- **-em or -ens at the end of a word** indicate an "eyng" sound – eg *tem* ("teyng"; you have or there is), *viagens* ("vee-A-zheyngs"; journeys).
- **-im or -in at the end of a word** or followed by a consonant are simply a nasal "ee"

sound, so *capim* (grass) sounds a bit like "ka-PEENG".
- **-om or -on at the end of a word** or followed by a consonant indicate nasal "o". An obvious example is *bom* (good), which sounds pretty similar to "bon" in French.
- **-um or -un at the end of a word** or followed by a consonant indicate nasal "u"– eg *um* (one).
- **-ãe** sounds a bit like "eyeing" said quickly and explosively – eg *mãe* (mother).
- **-õe** sounds like "oing". Most words ending in "-ão" make their plural like this, with an "s" (which is pronounced) at the end – eg *estação* (station) becomes *estações* (stations).

Consonants

Brazilian **consonants** are more straightforward than the vowels, but there are a few little oddities you'll need to learn. We've only listed the consonants where they differ from their English counterparts.

c is generally pronounced hard, as in "cat" (eg *campo*). However, when followed by "i" or "e", it's pronounced softly, as in "ceiling" (eg *cidade*, city). It's also pronounced softly whenever it's written with a cedilla (eg *estação*).

ch is pronounced like English "sh", so *chá* (tea) is said "sha".

d is generally pronounced as in English. However, in most parts of Brazil it's palatalized to sound like "dj"whenever it comes before an "i" or final "e". So *difícil* (difficult) is pronounced "djee-FEE-siw", and the ubiquitous preposition *de* (of) sounds like "djee".

g is generally pronounced hard as in English "god" (eg *gosto*, I like). But before "e" or "i" it's pronounced like the "s" in English "vision" or "measure" – eg *geral* (general) and *gíria* (slang).

h is always silent (eg *hora*, hour).

j is pronounced like the "s" in English "vision" or "measure"– eg *jogo* (game) and *janeiro* (January).

l is usually pronounced as in English. But at the end of a word, it takes on a peculiar, almost Cockney pronunciation, becoming a bit like a "w". So Brasil is pronounced "bra-ZEEW". When followed by "h", it's pronounced "ly" as in "million"; so *ilha* (island) comes out as "EE-lya".

n is normally pronounced as in English, but when it's followed by "h" it becomes "ny". So *sonho* (dream) sounds like "SON-yoo".

q always comes before "u" and is pronounced either "k" or, more usually, "kw". So *cinquenta* (fifty) is pronounced "sin-KWEN-ta", but *quero* (I want) is pronounced "KE-roo".

r is usually as in English. However, at the beginning of a word it's pronounced like an English "h". So "Rio" is actually pronounced "HEE-oo", and *rádio* (radio) is pronounced "HA-djee-oo".

rr is always pronounced like an English "h". So *ferro* is pronounced "FE-hoo".

s is normally pronounced like an English "s", and in São Paulo and the South this never changes. But in Rio and many places to the North, "s" sounds like English "sh" when it comes before a consonant and at the end of a word (*estação*, "esh-ta-SOWNG").

t is normally pronounced as in English but, like "d", it changes before "i" and final "e". So *sorte* (luck) is pronounced "SOR-chee", and the great hero of Brazilian history, Tiradentes, is pronounced "chee-ra-DEN-chees".

x is pronounced like an English "sh" at the beginning of a word, and elsewhere like an English "x" or "z". So *xadrez* (chess) is pronounced "sha-DREYZ", while *exército* (army) is pronounced "e-ZER-si-too".

Stress

Any word that has an accent of any kind, including a tilde, is stressed on that syllable, so *miséria* (poverty) is pronounced "mi-ZE-ree-a". If there is no accent, the following rules generally apply (the syllables to be stressed are in capitals):

• Words that end with the vowels a, e and o are stressed on the penultimate syllable. So *entre* (between) sounds like "EN-tree", and *compro* (I buy) "KOM-proo". This also applies when these vowels are followed by -m, -s or -ns: *falam* (they speak) is stressed "FA-lowng".

• Words that end with the vowels i and u are stressed on the final syllable: *abacaxi* (pineapple) is pronounced "a-ba-ka-ZEE". This also applies when i and u are followed by -m, -s or -ns, so *capim* (grass) is pronounced "ka-PEENG".

• Words ending in consonants are usually stressed on the final syllable, eg *rapaz* (boy or man), stressed "ha-PAZ".

Some useful examples:

Rio de Janeiro HEE-oo djee zha-NEY-roo

Belo Horizonte BE-loo o-ri-ZON-chee

Rio Grande do Sul HEE-oo GRAN-djee doo Soow

Recife he-SEE-fee

rodoviária ho-do-vee-A-ree-a

onde (where) ON-djee

não entendo (I don't understand) now en-TEN-djee

sim (yes) SEENG (but hardly sound the final "g")

ruim (bad) hoo-WEENG (again hardly sound the "g")

vinte (twenty) VEEN-chee

correio (post office) co-HAY-oo

Brazilian Portuguese words and phrases

Basic expressions

yes, no	sim, não	big, small	grande, pequeno
please	por favor	a little, a lot/very	um pouco, muito
thank you	obrigado (men)/ obrigada (women)	more, less	mais, menos
		with, without	com, sem
where, when	onde, quando	another	outro/a
what, how much	que, quanto	today, tomorrow	hoje, amanhã
who	quem	yesterday	ontem
this, that	este, esse	but	mas (pronounced like "mice")
now, later	agora, mais tarde		
open, closed	aberto/a, fechado/a	and	e (pronounced like "ee" in "seek")
entrance, exit	entrada, saída		
pull, push	puxe, empurre	also	também
with, without	com, sem	something, nothing	alguma coisa, nada
for	para	sometimes	ás vezes
good, bad	bom/boa, ruim		

Useful phrases and colloquial expressions

What's the Portuguese for this?	Como se diz em português?	I want to see a doctor	Quero ver um medico
Excuse me (getting attention)	Com licença	What's the matter?	Qual é o problema?
		There is (is there?)	Há…(?)
Excuse me (sorry)	Me desculpa	I want, I'd like…	Quero…
Do you have the time?	Você tem as horas?	I can…	Posso…
		I can't…	Não posso…
Everything's fine	Tudo bem	I don't know	Não sei
OK	Tá bom	It's hot	Está quente
How much is it?	Quanto que é?	It's cold	Está frio
Do you take credit cards?	Aceita cartão de credito?	It's great	Está legal
		I've had it up to here	Estou de saco cheio
I'm hungry	Estou com fome	There's no way	Não tem jeito
I'm thirsty	Estou com sede	Crazy	Louco/a, maluco/a
I feel ill	Me sinto mal	Tired	Cansado/a

Greetings and responses

Hello, goodbye	Oi, tchau (like the Italian "ciao")	Nice to meet you	Um prazer
		Congratulations	Parabéns
Good morning	Bom dia	Cheers	Saúde
Good afternoon/night	Boa tarde/boa noite	Sir	Senhor
Sorry	Desculpa/perdão	Madam/Ms/Mrs	Senhora
How are you?	Como vai?	Do you speak English?	Você fala inglês?
Fine	Bem		

I don't understand	Não entendo	I am American	Sou dos Estados Unidos
I don't speak Portuguese	Não falo português	I am British	Sou britânico/a
What did you say?	O que você disse?	I am Canadian	Sou canadense
My name is…	Meu nome é…	I am Irish	Sou irlandês/a
What's your name?	Como se chama?/ qual é o seu nome?		

Asking directions, getting around

Where is…?	Onde fica…?	How do I get from downtown to Ipanema?	Como eu chego em Ipanema do Centro?
the bus station	a rodoviária		
the bus stop	a parada de ônibus	Is this the bus to Copacabana?	É esse o ônibus para Copacabana?
the nearest hotel	o hotel mais próximo		
the toilet	o banheiro/sanitário	Do you go to…?	Você vai para…?
left, right, straight on	esquerda, direita, direto	I'd like a (return) ticket to…	Quero uma pasagem (ida e volta) para…
Go straight on	Vai direto e	What time does it leave/arrive?	Que horas sai/chega?
and turn left	dobra à esquerda		
Where does the bus to…leave?	De onde sai o ônibus para…?	far, near	longe, perto
		slowly, quickly	devagar, rápido

Accommodation

Do you have a room?	Você tem um apartamento?	It's fine, how much is it?	Está bom, quanto é?
with two beds/ double bed	com duas camas/ cama de casal	Do you have anything cheaper?	Tem algo mais barato?
with a view	com uma vista	Is there a hotel/ campsite nearby?	Tem um hotel/camping por aqui?
It's for one person/ two people	É para uma pessoa/ duas pessoas		

Numbers

1	um, uma	15	quinze
2	dois, duas	16	dezesseis
3	três	17	dezessete
4	quatro	18	dezoito
5	cinco	19	dezenove
6	seis	20	vinte
7	sete	21	vinte e um
8	oito	30	trinta
9	nove	40	quarenta
10	dez	50	cinquenta
11	onze	60	sesenta
12	doze	70	setenta
13	treze	80	oitenta
14	quatorze	90	noventa

100	cem	1000	mil
200	duzentos	2000	dois mil
300	trezentos	5000	cinco mil
500	quinhentos	million	milhão

Days and months

Monday	segunda-feira (or segunda)	March	março
		April	abril
Tuesday	terça-feira (or terça)	May	maio
Wednesday	quarta-feira (or quarta)	June	junho
Thursday	quinta-feira (or quinta)	July	julho
Friday	sexta-feira (or sexta)	August	agosto
Saturday	sábado	September	setembro
Sunday	domingo	October	outubro
January	janeiro	November	novembro
February	fevereiro	December	dezembro

A Brazilian menu reader

Basics

açúcar	sugar	garrafa	bottle
alho e óleo	garlic and olive oil sauce	jantar	dinner, to have dinner
almoço	lunch	legumes/verduras	vegetables
arroz	rice	manteiga	butter
azeite	olive oil	mariscos	seafood
café de manhã	breakfast	molho	sauce
cardápio	menu	ovos	eggs
carne	meat	pão	bread
colher	spoon	peixe	fish
conta/nota	bill/receipt	pimenta	pepper
copo	glass	prato	plate
entrada	hors d'oeuvre	queijo	cheese
executivo	set menu	sal	salt
faca	knife	sobremesa	dessert
farinha	dried manioc flour	sopa/caldo	soup
garçom	waiter	sorvete	ice cream
garfo	fork	taxa de serviço	service charge

Cooking terms

assado	roasted	mal passado/	rare/well done
bem gelado	well chilled	bem passado	(meat)
churrasco	barbecue	médio	medium-grilled
cozido	boiled, steamed	milanesa	breaded
cozinhar	to cook	na chapa/na brasa	charcoal-grilled
grelhado	grilled		

Petiscos and salgadinhos (bar snacks)

acarajé	deep fried black bean croquette	kibe	deep fried minced beef croquette
aipim/mandioca frito	deep fried cassava/ yucca	pastel de camarão	deep fried pastries with shrimp stuffing
bolinho de bacalhau	deep fried codfish and potato croquette	pastel de palmito	deep fried pastries with hear of palm stuffing
coxinha de galinha	deep fried chicken croquette		

Seafood (*frutos* do *mar*)

agulha	needle fish	pescada	seafood stew, or hake
atum	tuna	polvo	octopus
camarão	prawn, shrimp	siri	small crab
caranguejo	large crab	sururu	a type of mussel
lagosta	lobster	vatapá	Bahian shrimp dish, cooked with palm oil, skinned tomato and coconut milk, served with fresh coriander and hot peppers
lula	squid		
mariscos	shellfish		
moqueca	seafood stewed in palm oil and coconut sauce		
ostra	oyster		

Meat and poultry (*carne e aves*)

bife	steak	frango	chicken
bife a cavalo	steak with egg and *farinha* (manioc flour)	leitão	suckling pig
		lingüiça	sausage
cabrito	kid	pato	duck
carne de porco	pork	peru	turkey
carne do sol	sun-dried beef	peito	breast
carneiro	lamb	perna	leg
costela	ribs	picadinha	stew
costeleta	chop	salsicha	hot dog
feijoada	black bean, pork and sausage stew	vitela	veal

Fruit (*frutas*)

abacate	avocado	goiaba	guava
abacaxi	pineapple	laranja	orange
ameixa	plum, prune	limão	lime
caju	cashew fruit	maçã	apple
carambola	star fruit	mamão	papaya
cerejas	cherries	manga	mango
côco	coconut	maracujá	passion fruit
fruta do conde	custard/sugar apple (also **ata**)	melancia	watermelon
		melão	melon

| morango | strawberry | pêssego | peach |
| pera | pear | uvas | grapes |

Vegetables and spices (*legumes e temperos*)

alface	lettuce	dendê	palm nut oil
alho	garlic	ervilhas	peas
arroz e feijão	rice and beans	espinafre	spinach
azeitonas	olives	mandioca	manioc/cassava/yucca
batatas	potatoes	milho	corn
canela	cinnamon	palmito	heart of palm
cebola	onion	pepinho	cucumber
cenoura	carrot	repolho	cabbage
coentro	coriander/cilantro	tomate	tomato
cravo	clove		

Drinks

água mineral	mineral water	caipirovska	vodka, lime and sugar cocktail
com gás/sem gás	sparkling/still		
batida	fresh fruit juice with *cachaça*	cerveja	bottled beer
		chopp	draught beer
cachaça	sugar-cane rum	pinga	*cachaça*
café com leite	coffee with hot milk	suco	fruit juice
cafézinho	small black coffee	vinho	wine
caipirinha	*cachaça*, lime and sugar cocktail	vitamina	fruit juice made with milk

A glossary of Brazilian terms and acronyms

alfândega customs

artesanato handicrafts

azulejo decorative glazed tiling

baile funk modern Afro-Brazilian electronic music

bairro neighbourhood within town or city

barraca beach bar

batucada literally, a drumming session – music-making in general, especially impromptu

bloco large Carnaval group or street party

bosque wood

bunda/s buttock/s, bum

bossa nova literally "new trend"; a jazz form that evolved from samba

Candomblé Afro-Brazilian religion

capoeira Afro-Brazilian martial art/dance form

Carioca someone or something from Rio de Janeiro

choro traditional musical style, largely instrumental

confusão throng of people, confusion

correio postal service/post office

correio electrónico email

dono literally "owner", also means drug lord

danceteria nightspot where the emphasis is on dancing

engenho sugar mill or plantation

Estado Novo the period of dictatorship under Getúlio Vargas, from the mid-1930s to 1945

EUA USA

favela (also morro, comunidade) shantytown, slum (also meaning hill, community)

fazenda country estate/plantation

ferroviária train station

forró dance and type of music from the Northeast

gringo/a foreigner, Westerner (not derogatory)

Ibama Government dept. running national parks and nature reserves

Iemanjá goddess of the sea in Candomblé

igreja church

jeitinho bribe or small offering to smooth the way

kanga a sarong or bikini cover-up

largo small square

litoral coast, coastal zone

louro/a fair-haired/blonde – Westerners in general

maconha marijuana

Macumba African-Brazilian religion, usually thought of as more authentically "African" than Candomblé

marginal petty thief, outlaw

Mata Atlântica Atlantic forest – the native jungle that once covered most of Rio de Janeiro

mercado market

mineiro person or thing from Minas Gerais

mirante viewing point

moço/a person (especially used for a waiter when wanting attention)

mosteiro monastery

movimentado lively, where the action is

MPB Música Popular Brasileira, common shorthand for Brazilian popular music

Nordeste (Nordestino/a) Northeastern Brazil (person from)

Nova República The New Republic – the period since the return of democracy in 1985

Paulista person or thing from São Paulo state

pousada an inn/guesthouse

praça square

praia beach

prefeitura town hall, and by extension city governments in general

quebrado out of order

quilombo community of escaped slaves or their descendants

rodovia highway

rodoviária intercity bus station

senzala slave quarters

serra mountains

sesmaria royal Portuguese land grant to early settlers

Umbanda Afro-Brazilian religion common in the urban South and Southeast

visto visa

Slang

Much *gíria* (slang) is common across the whole of Brazil, though some differences exist between Rio and, say, São Paulo or the Northeast, as well as between Rio's extraordinary mix of social classes – *favela* and *baile funk gíria*, for example, is quite different to what you'll hear among the Zona Sul's middle class. You'll find, too, that there's a whole (often hilarious) vocabulary relating to relationships and sex – terms that just don't exist in English and when banded about between friends aren't considered derogatory.

alemão: (*favela* slang) enemy, outsider

auê, bagunça: mess, chaotic situation (especially a *festa* or party)

bacana, legal gente boa, beleza: great, excellent – used for things and people

bagulho: (multiple meanings) ugly woman; marijuana; something inferior/worthless

barangueiro/a: a person that only dates ugly people

bate papo: have a conversation

bicheiros: (street) gamblers or game organizers

boiola, bicho, biba: gay man

cabeçada: full pace

cara, malek, rapaz: man (used as in "yeah man", or "that man"); *pô cara* "shit, man" (contraction of *porra cara*)

cara de pau: person without shame

caraca, por caramba! wow, gosh!

corno/a: person whose partner is unfaithful

desse uma cerva gelada: give me a cold beer

fala sério: speak the truth (used like "really?" or "you lie!")

galera: group of people (eg on beach "*Oi galera!*" – hi people!)

já é: of course (literally "already is" – a confirmation to do something). Eg question: "*partiu na praia sabado?*" (in slang: "let's go to the beach Saturday?") Reply "*ja é!*"

mermão: (contraction of *meu irmão*) my brother; man

noitada: night out, a dance (elsewhere in Brazil "*balada*")

partiu: (corruption of past participle of verb *partir*) let's go (eg to the beach, to Buzios)

pegador: person (especially man) who stays, dances with or kisses many people the same night

perna de pau: bad football/game player (literally "dick legs")

Qual a parada? What's going on?

roda presa: bad driver

sapatão: lesbian

tomar um caldo: get knocked over/swept away by a wave

171 (um sete um), trambiqueiro/a: an untrustworthy person, con artist, fraudster (171 is the Brazilian law relating to fraud)

valeu: thanks, respect

zoar, sacanear: to enjoy yourself

Visit us online
www.roughguides.com
Information on over 25,000 destinations around the world

- **Read** Rough Guides' trusted travel info
- **Access** exclusive articles from Rough Guides authors
- **Update** yourself on new books, maps, CDs and other products
- **Enter** our competitions and win travel prizes
- **Share** ideas, journals, photos & travel advice with other users
- **Earn** points every time you contribute to the Rough Guide
  community and get rewards

Small print and
Index

A Rough Guide to Rough Guides

Published in 1982, the first Rough Guide – to Greece – was a student scheme
that became a publishing phenomenon. Mark Ellingham, a recent graduate in
English from Bristol University, had been travelling in Greece the previous summer
and couldn't find the right guidebook. With a small group of friends he wrote his
own guide, combining a highly contemporary, journalistic style with a thoroughly
practical approach to travellers' needs.

The immediate success of the book spawned a series that rapidly covered dozens
of destinations. And, in addition to impecunious backpackers, Rough Guides
soon acquired a much broader and older readership that relished the guides' wit
and inquisitiveness as much as their enthusiastic, critical approach and value-for-
money ethos.

These days, Rough Guides include recommendations from shoestring to luxury
and cover more than 200 destinations around the globe, including almost every
country in the Americas and Europe, more than half of Africa and most of Asia and
Australasia. Our ever-growing team of authors and photographers is spread all
over the world, particularly in Europe, the US and Australia.

In the early 1990s, Rough Guides branched out of travel, with the publication of
Rough Guides to World Music, Classical Music and the Internet. All three have
become benchmark titles in their fields, spearheading the publication of a wide
range of books under the Rough Guide name.

Including the travel series, Rough Guides now number more than 350 titles,
covering: phrasebooks, waterproof maps, music guides from Opera to Heavy
Metal, reference works as diverse as Conspiracy Theories and Shakespeare, and
popular culture books from iPods to Poker. Rough Guides also produce a series of
more than 120 World Music CDs in partnership with World Music Network.

Visit www.roughguides.com to see our latest publications.

Rough Guide travel images are available for commercial licensing at
www.roughguidespictures.com

SMALL PRINT

Rough Guide credits

Text editor: Lucy Cowie
Layout: Anita Singh
Cartography: Katie Lloyd-Jones, Maxine Repath
Picture editor: Nicole Newman
Production: Rebecca Short
Proofreader: Wendy Smith
Cover design: Chlöe Roberts
Photographer: Roger d'Olivere Mapp
Editorial: Ruth Blackmore, Andy Turner, Keith Drew, Edward Aves, Alice Park, Lucy White, Jo Kirby, James Smart, Natasha Foges, Róisín Cameron, Emma Traynor, Emma Gibbs, Kathryn Lane, Christina Valhouli, Monica Woods, Mani Ramaswamy, Harry Wilson, Helen Ochyra, Amanda Howard, Lara Kavanagh, Alison Roberts, Joe Staines, Peter Buckley, Matthew Milton, Tracy Hopkins, Ruth Tidball; **Delhi** Madhavi Singh, Karen D'Souza, Lubna Shaheen
Design & Pictures: **London** Scott Stickland, Dan May, Diana Jarvis, Mark Thomas, Chlöe Roberts, Sarah Cummins, Emily Taylor; **Delhi** Umesh Aggarwal, Ajay Verma, Jessica Subramanian, Ankur Guha, Pradeep Thapliyal, Sachin Tanwar, Nikhil Agarwal, Sachin Gupta
Production: Vicky Baldwin

Cartography: **London** Ed Wright; **Delhi** Rajesh Chhibber, Ashutosh Bharti, Rajesh Mishra, Animesh Pathak, Jasbir Sandhu, Karobi Gogoi, Alakananda Bhattacharya, Swati Handoo, Deshpal Dabas
Online: London George Atwell, Faye Hellon, Jeanette Angell, Fergus Day, Justine Bright, Clare Bryson, Aine Fearon, Adrian Low, Ezgi Celebi, Amber Bloomfield; Delhi Amit Verma, Rahul Kumar, Narender Kumar, Ravi Yadav, Debojit Borah, Rakesh Kumar, Ganesh Sharma, Shisir Basumatari
Marketing & Publicity: **London** Liz Statham, Niki Hanmer, Louise Maher, Jess Carter, Vanessa Godden, Vivienne Watton, Anna Paynton, Rachel Sprackett, Libby Jellie, Laura Vipond, Vanessa McDonald; **New York** Katy Ball, Judi Powers, Nancy Lambert; **Delhi** Ragini Govind
Manager India: Punita Singh
Reference Director: Andrew Lockett
Operations Manager: Helen Phillips
PA to Publishing Director: Nicola Henderson
Publishing Director: Martin Dunford
Commercial Manager: Gino Magnotta
Managing Director: John Duhigg

Publishing information

This first edition published November 2009 by
Rough Guides Ltd,
80 Strand, London WC2R 0RL
14 Local Shopping Centre, Panchsheel Park, New Delhi 110017, India
Distributed by the Penguin Group
Penguin Books Ltd,
80 Strand, London WC2R 0RL
Penguin Group (USA)
375 Hudson Street, NY 10014, USA
Penguin Group (Australia)
250 Camberwell Road, Camberwell, Victoria 3124, Australia
Penguin Group (Canada)
195 Harry Walker Parkway N, Newmarket, ON, L3Y 7B3 Canada
Penguin Group (NZ)
67 Apollo Drive, Mairangi Bay, Auckland 1310, New Zealand
Cover concept by Peter Dyer.

Typeset in Bembo and Helvetica to an original design by Henry Iles.
Printed in Singapore
© Robert Coates and Oliver Marshall 2009
Maps © Rough Guides
No part of this book may be reproduced in any form without permission from the publisher except for the quotation of brief passages in reviews.
296pp includes index
A catalogue record for this book is available from the British Library
ISBN: 978-1-84836-190-4
The publishers and authors have done their best to ensure the accuracy and currency of all the information in **The Rough Guide to Rio de Janeiro**, however, they can accept no responsibility for any loss, injury, or inconvenience sustained by any traveller as a result of information or advice contained in the guide.

1   3   5   7   9   8   6   4   2

Help us update

We've gone to a lot of effort to ensure that the first edition of **The Rough Guide to Rio de Janeiro** is accurate and up-to-date. However, things change – places get "discovered", opening hours are notoriously fickle, restaurants and rooms raise prices or lower standards. If you feel we've got it wrong or left something out, we'd like to know, and if you can remember the address, the price, the hours, the phone number, so much the better.

Please send your comments with the subject line "**Rough Guide Rio de Janeiro Update**" to ⊛mail@roughguides.com. We'll credit all contributions and send a copy of the next edition (or any other Rough Guide if you prefer) for the very best emails.

Have your questions answered and tell others about your trip at ⊛community.roughguides.com

Acknowledgements

Robert Coates: Numerous people gave their time and knowledge to help me get the best out of Rio. Patrícia Pacheco deserves special mention for her passion for samba, her love, and timely insights into the *Carioca* soul. Phelipe Coutinho and Rob Shaw also went above and beyond in regularly sharing their enthusiasm for history and football, and Lapa and Copacabana respectively. Marcelo Armstrong ably assisted with useful contacts and timely favela insights, while Denise and Gabriel Werneck provided a great welcome and some memorable trips. Marjon van Royen, Shawn Blore, Marcelo (Santa), Nanko (IBISS), Paulo Celani, the Bressane family, and Marcelo (Crux) variously offered beds, excellent trips, nights out and information. Thanks also go to Antonio (Vila Cruz), Aline (Semente), Chico Santos, Servula (Sobrenatural), Eneida (Vila Canoas), Ronald (Niteroi), Aarti (posto 9) Waghela, Erika Robb, Marlies and Rafael, Bindu Mathur, Carolina Massad, Doug Gray, Tim Cowman, Nasher (Saquarema), Matthew Goodwin, and John Stewart – who all contributed in small yet fundamental ways. My gratitude goes to Riotur, especially Armando Martins and Patricia Alqueres, and to staff at the Rio Convention & Visitors Bureau. Finally, thanks to my co-author Oliver Marshall and editor Lucy Cowie for all their hard work, patience and excellent contributions.

Oliver Marshall wishes to thank Rough Guides editor Lucy Cowie for her painstaking work on the book. In Rio, thanks are owed to Karin Hanta, Darién J. Davis, Leslie Bethell, Eduardo Silva, Graça Salgado and Isaur; in Paraty Ben Berry and Yara and Richard Roberts; Alicia and Kevan Prior in Búzios; and Jo Marcos and Virginio Mello in Petrópolis.

SMALL PRINT

Photo credits

All photos © Rough Guides except the following:

Title page
Ipanema beach © Ethel Davis/Photolibrary

Things not to miss
06 Carnaval © Alex Robinson/Rough Guides
07 Paraty © Rieger Bertrand/Photolibrary
15 Carnaval *blocos*, Ipanema © David Noble/
Alamy
16 Ipanema beach © Jtb Photo/Photolibrary
18 Palácio Imperial, Petrópolis © Cassio
Vasconcellos/Getty Images
20 Ilha Grande © Tim Whitby/Alamy

Black and whites
p.153 Paraty © Photolibrary
p.160 Catedral São Pedro Alcântara, Petrópolis
© Cassio Vasconcellos/Getty Images
p.217 Carnaval © Alex Robinson/Rough Guides
p.237 *Capoeira* © Stuart Freedman/Corbis

ROUGH
GUIDES

SMALL PRINT

Index

Map entries are in colour.

INDEX

INDEX

Map symbols

maps are listed in the full index using coloured text

▬▬▬ Motorway	𝕏 Waterfall
═══ Main road	ⓘ Tourist office
── Minor road	⊠ Post office
- - - - Tunnel	★ Bus stop
ⅢⅢⅢ Steps	✈ Airport
▬▬▬ Pedestrianized street	🅿 Parking
- - - - - Footpath	⊞ Hospital
— — Ferry route	⊙ Statue/monument
━━◆━━ Railway	▣ Restaurant
—Ⓜ— Metrô	⬆ Beach marker post (posto)
·········· Tram (bonde)	⚲ Chapel
──── Waterway	⊞ Church
◆ Point of interest	▬ Building
∴ Ruins	⬭ Stadium
▲ Mountain peak	Cemetery
⚱ Fountain/gardens	Park
⬇ Viewpoint	Beach
♦ Museum	Marsh
⚑ Golf course	

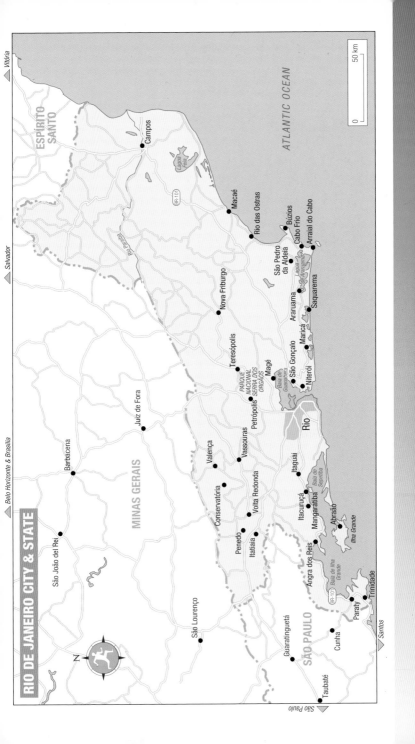

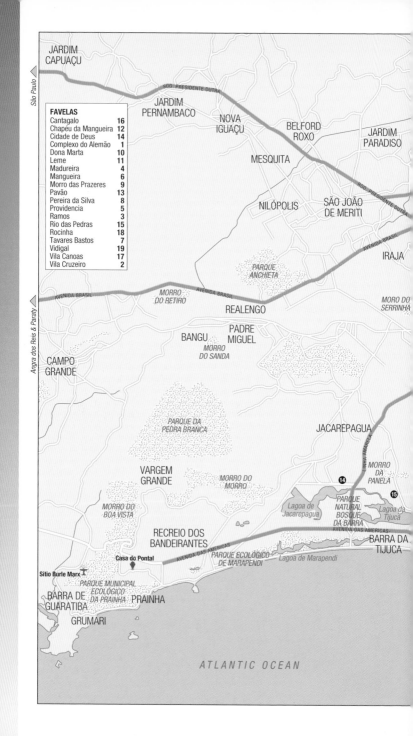

JARDIM
CAPUAÇU

São Paulo

Angra dos Reis & Paraty

ROD. PRESIDENTE DUTRA

JARDIM
PERNAMBACO

NOVA
IGUAÇU

BELFORD
ROXO

JARDIM
PARADISO

MESQUITA

NILÓPOLIS

SÃO JOÃO
DE MERITI

ROD. PRESIDENTE DUTRA

AVENIDA BRASIL

IRAJA

FAVELAS

Cantagalo	16
Chapéu da Mangueira	12
Cidade de Deus	14
Complexo do Alemão	1
Dona Marta	10
Leme	11
Madureira	4
Mangueira	6
Morro das Prazeres	9
Pavão	13
Pereira da Silva	8
Providencia	5
Ramos	3
Rio das Pedras	15
Rocinha	18
Tavares Bastos	7
Vidigal	19
Vila Canoas	17
Vila Cruzeiro	2

PARQUE
ANCHIETA

MORRO DO
SERRINHA

AVENIDA BRASIL

MORRO
DO RETIRO

AVENIDA BRASIL

REALENGO

CAMPO
GRANDE

BANGU

PADRE
MIGUEL

MORRO
DO SANDA

PARQUE DA
PEDRA BRANCA

JACAREPAGUA

VARGEM
GRANDE

MORRO DO
MORRO

MORRO
DA
PANELA

LINHA AMARELA

⓮

⓯

MORRO DO
BOA VISTA

Lagoa de
Jacarepagua

PARQUE
NATURAL
BOSQUE
DA BARRA

Lagoa da
Tijuca

AVENIDA DAS AMERICAS

BARRA DA
TIJUCA

RECREIO DOS
BANDEIRANTES

AVENIDA DAS AMERICAS

PARQUE ECOLÓGICO
DE MARAPENDI

Lagoa de Marapendi

Casa do Pontal

Sitio Burle Marx

PARQUE MUNICIPAL
ECOLÓGICO
DA PRAINHA

PRAINHA

BARRA DE
GUARATIBA

GRUMARI

ATLANTIC OCEAN

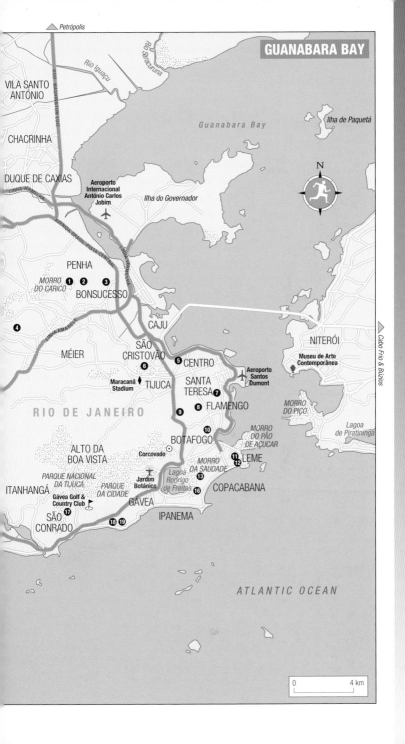

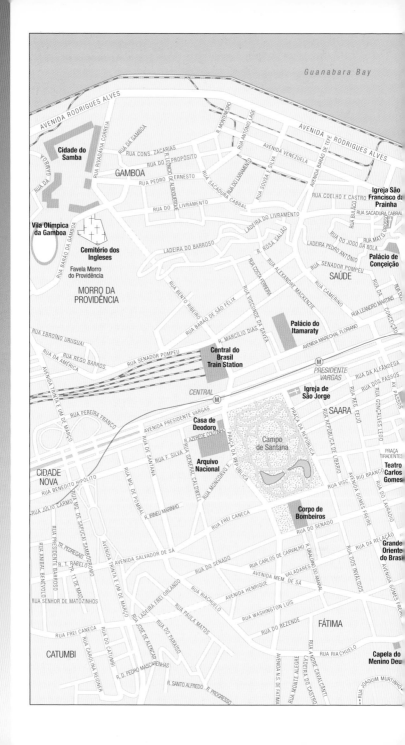

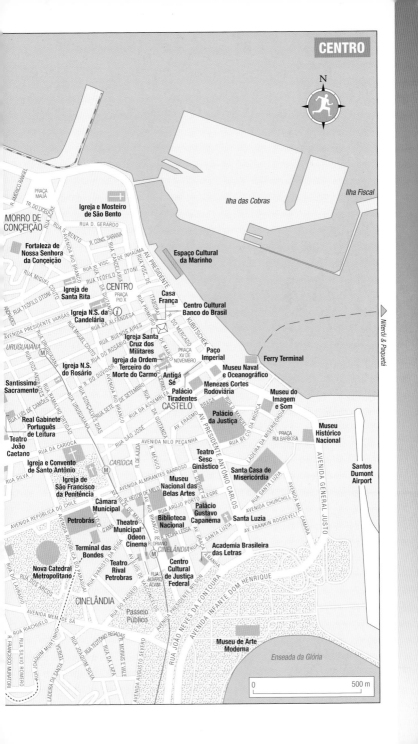

CENTRO

N

Ilha Fiscal

Ilha das Cobras

PRAÇA
MAUÁ

TR. DO LICEUCE

R. AMÉRICO RANGEL

RUA SÃO BENTO

Igreja e Mosteiro
de São Bento

MORRO DE
CONCEIÇÃO

RUA D. GERARDO

R. CONS. SARAIVA

Espaço Cultural
da Marinho

RUA VISC. CANDELÁRIA

RUA TEÓFILO OTONI

RUA VISC. DE INHAÚMA

RUA S. BENTO

AVENIDA RIO BRANCO

Fortaleza de
Nossa Senhora
da Conceição

RUA MIGUEL

RUA TEÓFILO OTONI COUTO

RUA MIGUEL COUTO

ANDRADAS

Igreja de
Santa Rita

CENTRO

PRAÇA
PIO X

Casa
França

AV. PRESIDENTE VARGAS

RUA PRIMEIRO DE MARÇO

AV. PRESIDENTE ANTÔNIO CARLOS

Centro Cultural
Banco do Brasil

AVENIDA PRESIDENTE VARGAS

Igreja N.S. da
Candelária

RUA DA ALFÂNDEGA

Igreja Santa
Cruz dos
Militares

RUA BUENOS AIRES

PRAÇA
XV DE
NOVEMBRO

AV. KUBITSCHEK

Paço
Imperial

Ferry Terminal

Niterói & Paquetá

URUGUAIANA

Igreja N.S.
do Rosário

RUA DO OUVIDOR

Igreja da Ordem
Terceiro do
Morte do Carmo

Antigá
Sé

Museu Naval
e Oceanográfico

Santíssimo
Sacramento

RUA RAMALHO ORTIGÃO

RUA URUGUAIANA

RUA GONÇALVES DIAS

Palácio
Tiradentes

CASTELO

Menezes Cortes
Rodoviária

Museu do
Imagem
e Som

RUA LUÍS DE CAMÕES

RUA DA ASSEMBLÉIA

Palácio
da Justiça

RUA DO MERCADO

Real Gabinete
Português
de Leitura

RUA DA QUITANDA

AV. ERASMO BRAGA

RUA BECO DA MISÉRIA

PRAÇA
RUI BARBOSA

Museu
Histórico
Nacional

Teatro
João
Caetano

RUA DA CARIOCA

RUA SÃO JOSÉ

AVENIDA NILO PEÇANHA

Teatro
Sesc
Ginâstico

LADEIRA DA MISERICÓRDIA

AVENIDA GENERAL JUSTO

Igreja e Convento
de Santo Antônio

CARIOCA

R. MÉXICO

RUA SILVA

Igreja de
São Francisco
da Penitência

AVENIDA ALMIRANTES BARROSO

Museu
Nacional das
Belas Artes

Santa Casa de
Misericórdia

RUA SANTA LUZIA

Santos
Dumont
Airport

AVENIDA REPÚBLICA DO CHILE

RUA HEITOR DE MELO

RUA DEBRET

RUA ARÚJO PORTO ALEGRE

AVENIDA CHURCHILL

Câmara
Municipal

Palácio
Gustavo
Capanema

Santa Luzia

AVENIDA MAL CÂMARA

Petrobrás

AVENIDA REPÚBLICA DO PARAGUAI

Theatro
Municipal

Biblioteca
Nacional

AV. FRANKIN ROOSEVELT

Odeon
Cinema

FLORIANO

PR.P. PEDRA LESSA

Academia Brasileira
das Letras

RUA DO LAVRADIO

RUA EVARISTO DA VEIGA

GAMA

Terminal das
Bondes

CINELÂNDIA

Teatro
Rival
Petrobras

R. ÁLVARO
ALVIM

Centro
Cultural
de Justiça
Federal

RUA ARANHA

AVENIDA INFANTE DOM HENRIQUE

Nova Catedral
Metropolitana

RUA DO PASSEIO

RUA LUÍS DE VASCONCELOS

CINELÂNDIA

AVENIDA MEM DE SÁ

RUA DO LAVRADIO

RUA RIACHUELO

Passeio
Público

AVENIDA AUGUSTO SEVERO

AVENIDA JOÃO NEVES DA FONTOURA

AVENIDA INFANTE DOM HENRIQUE

R. FRANCISCO MURATORI

R. SILVIO ROMERO

RUA JOAQUIM MURTINHO

LADEIRA DE SANTA TERESA

RUA TEOTÔNIO REGADAS

RUA MORAIS E VALE

RUA DA LAPA

Museu de Arte
Moderna

Enseada da Glória

0   500 m

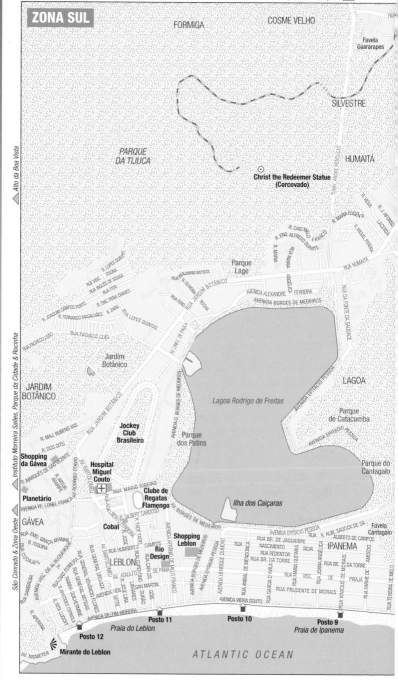

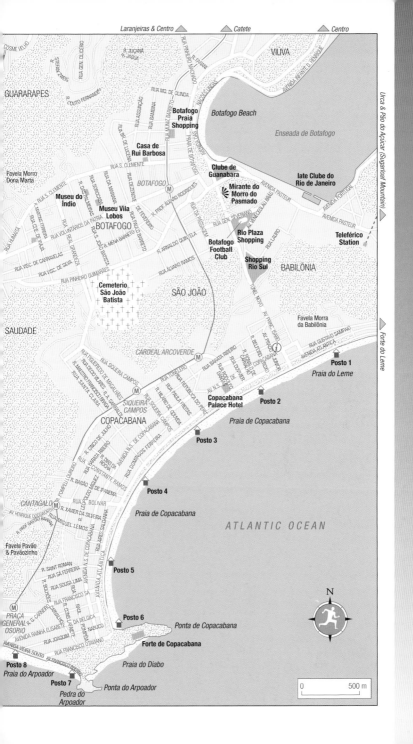

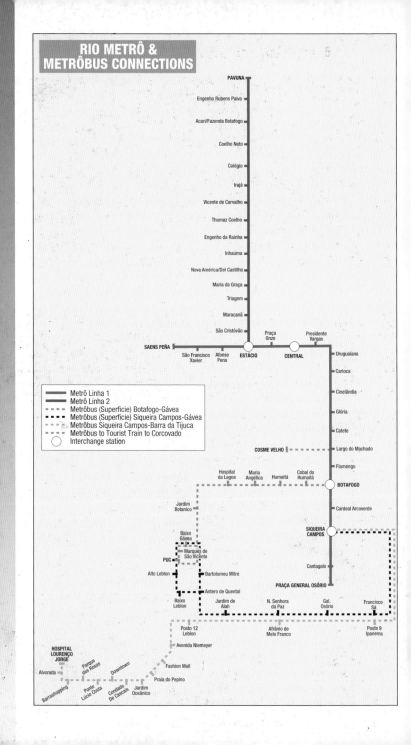